THE ANNUAL OF THE AMERICAN
SCHOOLS OF ORIENTAL RESEARCH

VOL. XXXIX

EDITED FOR THE TRUSTEES BY
JAMES L. SWAUGER

THE EXCAVATION OF BETHEL
(1934–1960)

William F. Albright, Director 1934

James L. Kelso, Director 1954, 1957, 1960

(Joint Expedition of the Pittsburgh Theological Seminary and the American School of Oriental Research in Jerusalem)

JAMES L. KELSO

With chapters by

William F. Albright
Lawrence A. Sinclair
Paul W. Lapp
James L. Swauger

PUBLISHED BY THE

AMERICAN SCHOOLS OF ORIENTAL RESEARCH

CAMBRIDGE

WITH THE AID OF THE
JANE DOWS NIES PUBLICATION FUND
1968

*Made and printed in Great Britain by
William Clowes and Sons, Limited
London and Beccles*

To the memory of

MELVIN GROVE KYLE
Teacher, Colleague, and Friend

PREFACE

This volume brings the publication of the results of the four campaigns of the excavations at Bethel to a close, with the exception of the coins, which will appear separately. We wish to thank all the collaborators and officials who made the excavations possible. They will be mentioned in detail in the text.

In 1927 a sounding was made at Beitîn, but the major Bethel dig was done in 1934 with Prof. Wm. F. Albright as archaeological director. The basic pattern of most of the city's history was uncovered in that campaign. The plates of that date were all prepared for publication by Albright and the first chapter of this volume written by him. He later requested James L. Kelso to prepare the final text of the 1934 campaign at the same time that he was writing up the 1954, 1957, and 1960 campaigns which Kelso had directed.

Prof. Albright later went over most of the detailed study of the pottery of the 1934 campaign which appears in Chapters XI and XII. Dr. Lawrence A. Sinclair wrote the chapter on the sixth century pottery and Dr. Paul W. Lapp the chapter on Late Hellenistic and Early Roman pottery. Profs. Howard Jamieson and Robert Coughenour aided in the other pottery studies.

Prof. Albright assisted in the solution of numerous difficult problems of interpretation covering all the campaigns. Dr. James L. Swauger, associate director of the Carnegie Museum in Pittsburgh, Pa., very graciously reviewed this volume. He had earlier prepared the chapter on flints found above the ancient Canaanite high place. Prof. Kelso, however, is alone responsible for any errors that may be found in the text.

Since all these campaigns were joint ventures of the American School of Oriental Research in Jerusalem and the Pittsburgh Theological Seminary, Prof. Kelso wishes to express his appreciation to the officials of both institutions for their financial and scholarly help in the excavations. He is also indebted to the American Philosophical Society which made him a grant of $865.50, from the Penrose Fund, No. 2693 (1959). This enabled him to prepare the final drawings and do the research work necessary to the completion of this book.

This publication begins with a résumé of all the data relative to the identification of Bethel and a study of the major geographic features of the site. This chapter was written by Prof. Wm. F. Albright. Chapter II is a brief description of the four major campaigns: 1934, 1954, 1957, 1960. Chapter III deals with the fortifications of Bethel. These were so important that a special chapter covering a whole city's history is devoted to them.

Next comes detailed studies of each of the archaeological periods represented on the site. These are Chalcolithic, Early Bronze, Middle Bronze, Late Bronze, Iron I, Iron II, Persian, Hellenistic, Roman, and Byzantine. These chapters (IV–IX) are primarily a study of the architectural remains: fortifications, houses, cult areas, and any other features appearing on the published plans. Chapter X on Bethel's history will be the most interesting to the non-specialist. The archaeological conclusions arrived at in the earlier chapters are here summarized and related to all known literary sources of the periods studied. The Bible is the major source book. Here Bethel is actually mentioned more often than any city with the exception of Jerusalem.

Since the expedition directors were very interested in ceramics, the pottery of each archaeological period is studied in great detail in Chapters XI–XV, relating this pottery to the major studies made by Wm. F. Albright at Tell Beit Mirsim and those of Baramki and Kelso made at New Testament Jericho. Pottery from other excavations which throw special light on Bethel's ceramic forms are also treated. Two of these chapters are written by specialists in their fields, Dr. Lawrence A. Sinclair and Dr. Paul W. Lapp. Chapter XVI is a study of the artifacts other than pottery and Chapter XVII, written by Dr. James L. Swauger, is a study of flints from the early Canaanite high place and the Middle Bronze I temple above it.

The book has 120 plates showing photographs of all phases of excavation work on the site, plans of the excavated areas, photos, and drawings of the pottery and sherds as well as many of the other objects found in the excavations such as beads, scarabs, figurines, weapons, tools, etc. This large number of plates with their wealth of individual items and cross reference data to them in the text was made possible by the generous grant from the American Philosophical Society referred to above.

THE AUTHOR.

TABLE OF CONTENTS

List of Plates		ix
List of Abbreviations		xiii
CHAPTER I.	The Site of Bethel and its Identification, Wm. F. Albright	1
CHAPTER II.	The Kyle Memorial Excavations at Bethel	4
CHAPTER III.	The Fortifications of Bethel	10
CHAPTER IV.	Bethel in the Chalcolithic, Early Bronze, and Middle Bronze Ages	20
CHAPTER V.	Bethel in the Late Bronze Age	28
CHAPTER VI.	Bethel in Iron I	32
CHAPTER VII.	Bethel in Iron II	36
CHAPTER VIII.	Bethel in the Persian and Hellenistic Periods	38
CHAPTER IX.	Bethel in the Roman and Byzantine Periods	41
CHAPTER X.	The History of Bethel	45
CHAPTER XI.	Bethel Pottery in the Chalcolithic, Early, Middle, and Late Bronze Ages	54
CHAPTER XII.	Bethel Pottery in Iron I and Iron II	63
CHAPTER XIII.	Bethel Pottery of the Sixth Century B.C., Lawrence A. Sinclair	70
CHAPTER XIV.	Bethel Pottery of the Late Hellenistic and Early Roman Periods, Paul W. Lapp	77
CHAPTER XV.	Bethel Roman and Byzantine Pottery from the Mosque Area, 1954	81
CHAPTER XVI.	Bethel Artifacts other than Pottery	82
CHAPTER XVII.	Bethel Flints from Early Canaanite High Place and Middle Bronze I Temple above it, James L. Swauger	93
Catalogue of Pottery Plates		96
Catalogue of Artifacts other than Pottery		113

LIST OF PLATES

1934 Campaign

1. Plan of excavated areas.
2. Middle Bronze I & II.
3. Late Bronze, phases 1 & 2.
4. Iron I, phases 1 & 2.
5. Iron I, phases 3 & 4.
6. Iron II.
7. Persian and Hellenistic, phase 1.
8. Hellenistic, phases 2 & 3.
9. Roman and Byzantine.
10. Sections through areas I & II.
11. Area III, Middle Bronze—Byzantine.
12a. View of Beitîn village from the east.
   b. Iron II dye vat in a field east of area I.
13a. Interior face of MB II B west city wall with Iron I silo in foreground. See plate 11 (earlier phase), 207A.
   b. Interior face of MB II B west city wall showing Iron I repairs, where stones stand on edge (to the left).
14a. Wall of LB II phase 1 destroyed by earthquake and left as it fell.
   b. Over a meter of ashes in destruction of LB II city (area II), shown between the wavy black lines.
15a. LB II walls of thin flat stones characteristic of that period. Under them with larger well-shaped stones are MB II walls. Note a drain in upper left.
   b. General view of area II. Higher walls are Iron I. Note pillar construction at extreme left. Lower walls are LB over MB II. Dark areas are bedrock or virgin soil.
16a. General view of area II. LB II walls in foreground. Iron I and Iron II in background.
   b. LB II, area II. Stone pavements in left center. Stone table near the center of right edge. Walls in background are Iron I, Iron II, and Hellenistic.
17. Superimposed LB II flag stone pavements in L 165.
18a. Excellent LB II dressed stone drain in L 169.
   b. Blocked doorway in north wall of L 161, phase 2 of LB II.
19a. Ḥúwar floor (upper right) above two stone drains crossing one another in X pattern.
   b. Double stone drain under ḥúwar floor in L 160.
20a. LB II stone pavement, phase 1, and house walls L 52.
   b. To the right is an Iron II tower with quoin construction cutting through earlier levels and resting on bedrock. To the left is an excellent LB II house wall and doorsill. (Upper course of outer face missing.)
21a. Iron I, area I, general view looking west. Pier constructions of large irregular-shaped stones at the left are 3rd phase of Iron I.
   b. Enlargement of lower left corner of 21 a. Lowest wall is LB II, phase 1. Other walls are Iron I, phase 1.
22a. Large massive walls in center belong to a patrician house in LB II. Meter stick is above doorway leading from central courtyard to L 56 (Plate 3, area I). Iron I, phase 3, pier construction is seen above LB II house wall.
   b. Shows various types of piers used in Iron I walls. At upper left note pier technique used for a door jamb. The normal Palestine walls in photo are Iron I, phases 1 and 2.
23a. General view of area I looking northeast with typical variety of Iron I house walls.
   b. Best type of Iron I wall, L 146.
24a. Clearing away phase 1 of Iron I before digging up LB II level.
   b. LB II burning at bottom of photo. Phase 1 of Iron I burning at top of meter stick. Phase 2 burning near center of right edge.
25a. All four phases of Iron I are represented in this photo, see 1, 2, 3, 4. Walls of tallest house in background were begun in Iron I and remained in use until the destruction of the city in sixth century B.C.
   b. Various types of Iron I construction, including collapsed wall, are phases 1 and 2.
26a. Wall to the left with quoin construction is Iron II laid on three courses of LB II. This LB II masonry continues in the center. Wall to the right is Iron I.
   b. Two LB II walls abut on one another just left of the meter stick. L 165 with pavement was used in phases 1 and 2. L 171 is probably phase 2. Upper walls above L 165 are Iron II.
27a. Iron II walls in area II looking north.
   b. Iron II south wall of L 145. Wall behind meter stick is ninth century B.C. The wall above that was still used in sixth century B.C.
28a. Broken store jars and pottery loom weights found *in situ* in Iron II house L 129.
   b. Area I looking south. These structures made with stones taken from the old city wall may be sheep folds from the Persian period.
29a. Area II looking southeast. Hellenistic walls (all three phases). A perfectly preserved coin of Alexander the Great was found under the drain in the foreground.
   b. Area II looking north. Hellenistic walls are phases 2 and 3.
30. Late Chalcolithic sherds.
31. Middle Bronze I sherds.
32. Middle Bronze II sherds and vessels.
33. Middle Bronze II sherds.
34. Middle Bronze II sherds.
35. Late Bronze painted sherds, phase 1.
36. Late Bronze painted sherds.
37a. Late Bronze sherds of imported ware.
   b. Late Bronze sherds.
38a. Base-ring sherds.
   b. Philistine sherds.
39. Iron I painted sherds.
40. Iron I sherds.
41. Iron II sherds.
42. Hathor sistrum handle.
43. Astarte seal cylinder.
44a. Scarabs, scaraboid, seal, and weight.

b	Jar handle, human head.	86a	Iron I and II cross sections C–D.
45	Miscellaneous objects, bone, pottery, and stone.	b	Iron I and II plans. (Most Iron II houses follow Iron I plans.)
46	Miscellaneous objects, beads, and metals.	87a	Iron I and II cross sections A–B.
47a	Coins, obverses, and reverses.	b	Mosque area plan.
b	Rhodian jar handles and ostracon.	88a	Digging through floor of an Iron I house immediately above Late Bronze olive oil factory.
48	Middle Bronze I pottery.	b	Iron I wall built upon a Late Bronze foundation course, which is laid upon a wide Middle Bronze II wall.
49	Middle Bronze II pottery.	c	Socle of a wide Middle Bronze II wall.
50	Middle Bronze II pottery.	89a	Section of south wall of 304, 307, 308, 310, Iron I, phase 2 through Iron II.
51	Middle Bronze II pottery.	b	Canaanite *maṣṣebah* used as doorjamb in Iron I. Doorway to the right was blocked up late in Iron II.
52	Middle Bronze II (Nos. 1–5, 7) and Late Bronze, phase 1 (Nos. 6, 8–23) pottery.	c	Late Bronze olive oil factory below Iron I walls. Upper walls and doorway are Iron II.
53	Late Bronze, phase 2 (Nos. 1–15); phase uncertain (Nos. 16–30) pottery.	d	Late Bronze olive oil factory.
54	Late Bronze, phase 2 (Nos. 1–14); phase uncertain (Nos. 16–17) pottery.	90a	Roman cistern mosque area. Shadow at top of photo is cast by part of the vault still intact.
55	Late Bronze (Nos. 1–5, 7–8) and Iron I (Nos. 6, 9–19) pottery.	b	Pavement of Byzantine building, mosque area.
56	Iron I pottery.	c	Roman cistern below; Byzantine walls above, mosque area.
57	Iron I pottery.	d	Architectural units from Byzantine church and lower half of Roman millstone.
58	Iron I pottery.		
59	Iron I pottery.		
60	Iron I pottery.		
61	Iron I pottery.		
62	Iron II pottery.		
63	Iron II pottery.		

1957 Campaign

91a	Middle Bronze II plans, phase 1. North city wall and house walls.
b	Middle Bronze II plans, phase 2. Patrician house with grain silos.
92a	Late Bronze plans.
b	Iron I and II plans. (Most Iron II house walls follow Iron I plans.)
93a	North city wall, exterior view.
b	Hellenistic and Roman houses built across north city wall.
c	Cross section A–B of glacis of north city wall.
94a	West wall of city in Abu Tabar area.
b	*Maḍâfeh* area.
95a	Foundations of south gate of Roman city (lower drawing).
b	Northeast city gate of Byzantine city.
96a	Outer face of north city wall; see also *BASOR*, No. 151, Fig. 2.
b	Revetment of Byzantine city wall forming rear wall of Arab house.
97a	Middle Bronze II room (with meter stick) abutting on north city wall (to the right.)
b	Inside view of north city wall with opposite house wall of the above room abutting on north city wall.
98a	Exterior of west city wall (upper courses only). See Plate 94a.
b	Courtyard of Middle Bronze II patrician house (403, 404, 405, 406) in foreground with 411 beyond the courtyard. See Plate 91b.
99a	Doorway of an Iron I house with the right jamb made from a Late Bronze doorsill and the left one made from a stone taken from the Middle Bronze II city wall.
b	Tower patch on west wall of city in Abu Tabar area probably blocking former city gate, see lower drawing in Plate 94a.
100a	West wall of courtyard of a Middle Bronze II patrician

64	Sixth century B.C. pottery.
65	Iron II pottery.
66	Sixth century B.C. pottery.
67	Sixth century B.C. pottery.
68	Hellenistic pottery, phase 1.
69	Hellenistic pottery, phase 1 (1–9), phase 2 (10–23).
70	Hellenistic and Early Roman pottery.
71	Hellenistic and Early Roman pottery.
72a	Hellenistic and Early Roman pottery.
b	Stamped jar handles, Middle Bronze II—Iron II.

* * * *

73	Late Bronze (No. 1) and Iron I (Nos. 2–15) pottery, 1954.
74	Iron I (No. 4), Iron II (Nos. 1–3, 5, 8), Roman (No. 6) and Byzantine (No. 7) pottery, 1954.
75	Roman and Byzantine pottery, 1954.
76	Roman and Byzantine pottery, 1954.
77	Middle Bronze II (Nos. 1–7) and Late Bronze (Nos. 8–12) pottery, 1957.
78	Iron I (Nos. 6–12), Iron II (Nos. 4, 13), and sixth century B.C. (Nos. 1–3, 5) pottery, 1957.
79	Iron II (Nos. 1–5) pottery, 1957; Byzantine limestone architectural units (Nos. 7–12), 1954 and (No. 6), 1957; Roman millstone (No. 13), 1954.
80	Sixth century B.C. pottery, 1957.
81	Chalcolithic (No. 1), Middle Bronze II (Nos. 2–6, 8) and Iron II (No. 7) pottery, 1960.
82	Middle Bronze II (Nos. 1–2, 4) and Late Bronze (Nos. 3, 5–8) pottery, 1960.
83	Iron I (Nos. 3–8) and Iron II (Nos. 1–2) pottery, 1960.
84	Iron II pottery, 1960.

1954 Campaign

85a	Middle Bronze II plans.
b	Late Bronze plans. Olive oil factory in L 305.

x

house; upper center portion is a poor Late Bronze repair.
  b Two types of Iron I walls and a pavement.

1960 Campaign
101 Plan and elevation of Middle Bronze II gateway complex and Canaanite high place. The latter is shown in the right half of the long east–west passageway. The northwest city gate, with the three steps outside it, is at the east end of the passageway. Steps also lead up from the west end of the passageway toward the south. Then the gateway turns east. The ḥaram area lies north of the city gate.
102a West city wall where it abuts on the northwest city gate.
  b West city wall running through a peasant's house.
103a Roman room (A) south of the northwest city gate.
  b Pit 5, southeast of the northwest city gate.
  c South city wall area, plans and elevations. For detailed description see §70ff.
104a Expedition staff: (standing left to right) Messrs. Abu Dayeh, Brownlee, Kelso, Jackson, R. Jones, Coughenour, McClellan, T. Taylor, (sitting left to right) Messrs. M. Taylor, Land-owner, Olsen, J. Jones, Mehl, Mrs. Wolfe, Bayyuk, Wolfe. For other members not in photo see §31.
  b Northwest corner of U-shaped city gateway complex, looking almost due east early in the excavation. The gate itself is to the right and behind the meter stick. The ḥaram area was discovered under the debris to the left.
105a Steps leading southward from the west end of the north corridor of the northwest city gateway. A portion of the ḥûwar platform is visible behind the steps.
  b Steps outside the same city gateway leading up to the gate proper.
  c Middle Bronze II gateway, looking east from the passageway after the floor had been excavated. The east wall of the MB I temple with its blocked doorway lies immediately below the gateway.
106a Northwest city gate above; temple walls immediately below. Ḥuwar floor of gateway in foreground.
  b Section of high place rock ledge with south wall of temple and some paving stones of temple floor above the ledge.
107a Doorway into ḥaram area. Top of meter stick leans against stones forming Byzantine grave.
  b East wall of northwest city gateway. In foreground is debris left by Byzantines who plundered the Middle Bronze II city wall for stone to build their new city wall.
  c Dark areas are blood spots on the limestone at the east end of high place.
  d Bin of high place with temple walls above it.
108a Temple above the high place; south wall of temple below (with meter stick) and south wall of city gate above. The latter is laid directly on the former.
  b High place ledge and north walls of temple and city gate. West end of the floor of the gate's north corridor is beyond the ledge.
109a Southwest corner of an MB II temple in pit 5.
  b South jamb of northwest city gate (reconstruction).
110a West wall of city where it abuts on northwest city gate. Meter stick leans against the gateway complex.
  b Interior face of west city wall (near northwest gate) with Middle Bronze II house wall abutting on it.
111a Exterior face of west city wall showing junction of two units of that wall on slightly different alignments.
  b Exterior face of the west wall north of junction. Foundation courses in foreground.
112a At the top of photo is an Iron I wall. Below it a large triangular stone marks the preserved top of the Middle Bronze II B city wall. The main south wall is at the right. The one with the meter stick is the inner side of a south city gate or the outer side of a tower. The wall in foreground is Roman.
  b Roman and Byzantine house walls above city's south wall. Roman city gate was under the house to the left and in front of it. Byzantine reservoir in background.
113 Middle Bronze I sherds with some earlier sherds from Canaanite high place area under the gateway complex.
114 1954 artifacts.
115 1957 artifacts.
116 1960 artifacts.
117 Iron I store-jars. Left to right, Nos. 2271, 1151, 2272. The center jar is from the 1954 campaign, the others from 1957.
118 Ninth century B.C. South Arabian stamp seal from Bethel. Bottom photo compares Bethel script with that from the Tübingen squeeze A 727.
119a Ceramic pieces: Hathor pillar to left; handle with a serpent motif; serpent motif at bottom of store-jar and bull's leg to the right.
  b Hyksos seal impression on jar handle.
  c Scarabs 7 and 63 (Nos. 3007 and 3063). Plate 119 is from 1960 work.
120 Plan of excavated areas 1934 through 1960.
  A 1934 area I, plate 1.
  B 1934 area II, plate 1.
  C 1934 area III, plate 1.
  D 1934 area IV, plate 1.
  E 1954 area of old 1934 campsite, plates 85 & 86.
    1954 mosque area, south of Beitîn, does not appear on this chart, plate 87.
  F 1957 north wall of Bethel with house walls north and south of it, plates 91, 92, 93.
  G 1957 Abu Tabor area with west wall of Bethel, plate 94.
  H 1957 Maḍâfeh area, plate 94.
  I 1957 test pit locating east wall of Bethel.
  J 1957 south gate of Roman town does not appear on this plan, plate 95.
  K 1957 Bethel's Byzantine gateway, plate 95.
  L 1960 Bethel's northwest gate area, plate 101.
  M 1960 west wall of Bethel where it joins northwest gate, plate 102.
  N 1960 west wall and farmer's house, plate 102.
  O 1960 Room A in east garden, plate 103.
  P 1960 pit 5 in east garden, plate 103.
    1960 south wall of Bethel does not appear on this plan, plate 103.
  Q 1960 main street of Byzantine Bethel.
    Areas not specified were test pits which yielded no valuable data.

* * * *

Fig. 1 Conoid seal of agate, sixth to fifth century, B.C.
Fig. 2 Combing patterns on MB II pottery.

LIST OF ABBREVIATIONS

AASOR	*The Annual of the American Schools of Oriental Research.*
Ain Shems I	Grant, *Ain Shems Excavations, I*, 1931.
Ain Shems IV	Grant and Wright, *Ain Shems Excavations, IV, Pottery*, 1938.
BASOR	*Bulletin of the American Schools of Oriental Research.*
Beth Shemesh	Grant, *Beth Shemesh*, 1929.
Beth-zur	Sellers, *The Citadel of Beth-zur*, 1933.
Bib. Arch.	*The Biblical Archaeologist.*
et-Tell	Marquet-Krause, *Les Fouilles de ʿAy (et-Tell)*, 1949.
Gerar	Petrie, *Gerar*, 1928.
Gezer III	Macalister, *The Excavation of Gezer, III*, 1912.
Hazor I	Yadin *et al*, *Hazor, I*, 1958.
Hazor II	Yadin *et al*, *Hazor II*, 1960.
JBL	*Journal of Biblical Literature.*
Jericho, K. & B.	Kelso and Baramki, *Excavations at New Testament Jericho and Khirbet en-Nitla*, 1955.
Jericho I	Kenyon, *Excavations at Jericho, I*, 1960.
Jericho, S. & W.	Selin and Watzinger, *Jericho*, 1913.
Lachish II	Tufnell, Inge and Harding, *Lachish II: The Fosse Temple*, 1940.
Lachish III	Tufnell, Murray and Diringer, *Lachish III: The Iron Age*, 1953.
Lachish IV	Tufnell, *Lachish IV: The Bronze Age*, 1958.
Meg T	Guy and Engberg, *Megiddo Tombs*, 1938.
Meg I	Lamon and Shipton, *Megiddo I: Seasons of 1925-34*, 1939.
Meg II	Loud, *Megiddo II: Seasons of 1935-39*, 1948.
Naṣbeh I	McCowan *et al*, *Tell en-Naṣbeh, I: Archaeological and Historical Results*, 1947.
Naṣbeh II	Wampler *Tell en-Naṣbeh, II: The Pottery*, 1947.
PEFA VI	*Palestine Exploration Fund Annual, No. VI*, Harding, 1953.
PJB	*Palästinajahrbuch.*
QDAP	*Quarterly of the Department of Antiquities in Palestine.*
Samaria	Crowfoot and Kenyan, *Samaria-Sebaste III: The Objects from Samaria*, 1957.
Taʿannek	Sellin, *Tell Taʿannek*.
TBM I	Albright, *The Excavation of Tell Beit Mirsim, I*, Annual XII, 1932.
TBM I A	Albright, *The Excavation of Tell Beit Mirsim, I A: Bronze Age Pottery of the Fourth Campaign*, Annual XIII, 1933.
TBM II	Albright, *The Excavation of Tell Beit Mirsim, II: The Bronze Age*, Annual XVII, 1938.
TBM III	Albright, *The Excavation of Tell Beit Mirsim, III: The Iron Age*, Annual XXI-XXII, 1943.
Tirzah, R.B.	*Revue Biblique.*
ZAW	*Zeitschrift für die Alttestamentliche Wissenschaft.*
ZDPV	*Zeitschrift des Deutschen Palästina-Vereins.*

CHRONOLOGY OF BETHEL

A Chalcolithic open-air sanctuary at least as early as	*c.* 3500 B.C.
First extended occupation of site in Late Chalcolithic	*c.* 3200 B.C.
Site abandoned during most of Early Bronze	
Second occupation toward end of Early Bronze	*c.* 2400 B.C.–*c.* 2200 B.C.
Site abandoned during nomadic invasions	*c.* 22nd–20th cent. B.C.
Continuous occupation begins MB I	*c.* 19th cent. B.C.
MB II A	*c.* 18th cent. B.C.
MB II B marked the building of the fortifications which were used through most of the town's history	*c.* 1650 B.C.
New west wall built late in MB II C	
Town destroyed by Egyptians	*c.* 1550 B.C.
Site unoccupied through LB I	15th–14th cent. B.C.
Town rebuilt quickly in LB II (phase 1)	14th cent. B.C.
Phase 2	13th cent. B.C.
Town destroyed by Israelites but quickly reoccupied	*c.* 1240–1235 B.C.
Iron I, phase 1 (TBM " B_1 ")	late 13th and early 12th cent. B.C.
Iron I, phase 2 (TBM " B_1 ")	12th cent. B.C.
Iron I, phase 3 (TBM " B_1 " with some " B_2 ")	early half of 11th cent. B.C.
Iron I, phase 4a (TBM " B_2 and B_3 ")	late 11th and early 10th cent. B.C.
Iron I, phase 4b (TBM " B_3 ")	late 10th cent. B.C.
Iron II occupation was continuous except for a brief period following the fall of Samaria. Bethel was not destroyed when Jerusalem fell in 587 B.C.	*c.* 900–587 B.C.
Sixth century phase	587 to late 6th cent.
Site unoccupied	*c.* 5th cent. B.C.
Late Persian and Early Hellenistic	*c.* 4th cent. B.C. to 165 B.*c.*
Late Hellenistic (Maccabaean)	165–63 B.C.
Early Roman (to town's capture by Vespasian)	63 B.C.–A.D. 69
Late Roman	A.D. 69–A.D. 323.
Byzantine	A.D. 323 to Islamic invasion.

CHAPTER I

The Site of Bethel and its Identification

William F. Albright

1. The site of Biblical Bethel (Pl. 12a), mentioned more frequently in the Old Testament than any other town except Jerusalem, was well known in the Byzantine Age, especially since it was still occupied in part by a village, with churches and monasteries. In the Middle Ages, however, it was completely forgotten by the Latin clergy, though it is possible that the Greek Orthodox preserved a faint recollection of its location.[1] In the early nineteenth century there seems to have been a vague idea in Greek and Protestant circles that there was a ruin named *Beitîl* (the common pronunciation of literary Arabic *Baitîl*, Bethel) in the region between Rāmallāh and eṭ-Ṭaiyibeh, the leading Christian villages north of Jerusalem.[2] But no scholar made the obvious identification of Beitîl with Khirbet Beitîn, an hour's walk northeast of el-Bîreh, until it fell into the lap of the great American Biblical topographer, Edward Robinson, along with many other sound identifications, in May, 1838.[3] He examined the extensive ruins of the ancient city, then entirely unoccupied, and noted that the phonetic relation of *Beitîn* to *Beitîl* is entirely normal in Arabic.[4]

2. Since the publication of Robinson's results in 1841 no competent topographer has hesitated for a moment to accept the identification as essentially correct, though some have thought of the possibility that the Israelite town might have stood on some site within a radius of a mile or so from modern Beitîn. Thus A. Alt called attention to the fact that no Israelite or older remains, not even pottery, were to be detected on the surface of the site, and that the site does not look superficially like that of a Canaanite or Israelite fortified city.[5] The site was settled by families from Burqah in the late forties of the last century,[6] and the village grew rapidly until it numbered several hundred inhabitants.[7] This was accompanied by the usual process of destroying ancient buildings and covering up older remains, so that the prospects of archaeological work there were far from encouraging, and the site was usually dismissed as quite impracticable. Meanwhile the population increased steadily from a few score to 446 in the census of 1922 and 566 in that of 1931. A curious detail, that women outnumbered men by no less than forty in the first census, is to be explained by the fact that scores of men from Beitîn settled more or less permanently in America. In 1959 the population of Bethel according to their water ration was 983. In addition to this number, there were about 200 persons who were immigrants in various countries of North and South America. Several of our workmen spent years as Syrian peddlers in the United States.

3. In 1915 a pupil of Dalman, G. Sternberg, published a detailed study of Bethel, its surface remains and its identification.[8] This paper gives an excellent foundation for treatment of these points, and will save us a good deal of space in the present monograph. Sternberg was unable to use the surface potsherds for chronological purposes, and so escaped the difficulties which Alt and the writer encountered when they failed to find surface traces of early occupation.

4. There was practically no more investigation of Bethel and its history until November, 1927, when W. F. Albright undertook to make soundings there, in collaboration with the late Harold M. Wiener, who furnished the money for the

---

[1] Cf. Edward Robinson, *Biblical Researches in Palestine* (London, 1841), Vol. II, p. 449, n. 4, and p. 450, above.

[2] See Robinson, *loc. cit.*, and John Wilson, *The Lands of the Bible* (Edinburgh, 1847), Vol. II, p. 288, on the visit to the ruins made in 1836 by Nicolayson and Elliott.

[3] *Op. cit.*, Vol. II, pp. 125–30.

[4] See Kampffmeyer, *ZDPV*, XV (1892), 32, 2; note the following clear cases where the final *ēl* ("God") of Hebrew proper names has become *în* in vernacular Arabic; *Yisrāʾēl > Isrāʾîn*, *Yizreʿēl > Zerʿîn*, *Yišmāʿēl > Ismāʿîn*, *Gabrīʾēl Jibrāʾîl > Jibrîn* (cf. also *Rūbîl* and *Rūbîn* for Heb. *Reʾûbēn*). This change is analogical rather than phonetic in the strict sense.

[5] See his remarks, *PJB*, 1927, 20; 1928, 31.

[6] See Sternberg, *ZDPV*, XXXVIII (1915), 5. Lutfiyya, *Baytîn a Jordanian Village*, pp. 35–37.

[7] Guérin's estimate, repeated later by others, that the population of the village was about 400, was certainly greatly exaggerated; Sternberg's estimate of 250 before World War I is reasonable.

[8] *ZDPV*, XXXVIII (1915), 1–40.

purpose.[9] They were so fortunate as to strike a spot just inside the western city wall of the ancient town, west of the building known as ʿIllîyet esh-Sheikh, which became our workroom in 1934. Here they dug down over 6 m. to bedrock, exposing the inside face of the old city wall. The stratigraphic sequence and the chronology of occupation and masonry which they then established were entirely confirmed by our campaign in 1934.[10] In this sounding the antiquity of the site and the correctness of its identification with Canaanite and Israelite Bethel were definitely proved. They estimated that "fully a hectare and a half, or nearly four acres, of the site of ancient Bethel was free from buildings and thus available for the excavator." After this initial success, it was only a question of time until more extensive excavation would be undertaken in so promising a site.

5. The site of ancient Bethel consists of a comparatively low spur jutting out from the main ridge to the north, on which rise the curiously eroded piles of rock known to the natives as el-qalʿât.[11] At the southern foot of this spur there is a fine spring, which fed a large reservoir in the Byzantine period. Within half a mile of the site are two or three other springs, so that the ancient town was very well supplied with water, except, of course, during cycles of drought, like the drought of 1923–24. The spur on which Bethel was located is separated from the higher ridge to the east by the Wâd eṭ-Ṭahûneh, and from the next ridge on the west by a much narrower and shallower valley. The latter is now actually a little higher than the bedrock just inside the western city wall, a fact which is caused by the gradual filling of the valley-bed with earth and stones washed down from the higher ground on both sides. The change in the level of the eastern valley is equally great, but not relatively so striking. These changes in terrain give the present site an appearance of physical insecurity which hardly existed thirty-five hundred years ago. It is, however, true that the town was not so well protected by nature as many other fortresses in the hill-country of Palestine, so that it became necessary to construct a particularly massive city wall, just as at Shechem (Balâṭah), which was even less defended by nature. From this northern end of the town, the terrain sloped down gradually toward the south, where the modern village stands, leaving the northern half of the spur more or less unoccupied by houses.

6. On the next ridge to the northeast stands a tumulus, named today Rujm Abū ʿAmmâr, which is covered with Hellenistic sherds from about the second century B.C. and has remains of masonry, suggesting that it was a watch-tower of the Maccabaean Age. Southeast of Beitîn, north of the road to Deir Diwân, is the ruined fortress called Burj Beitîn, belonging probably to the Mamlûk period, but apparently built of Crusader remains. In and among the ruins are fragments belonging to a Byzantine church of about the sixth century, which A. M. Schneider has shown to belong to the sanctuary of Abraham, where the latter was supposed to have pitched his tent, "between Bethel and Ai, east of Bethel."[12] Almost due south of Burj Beitîn, about half a kilometer across the valley, lies Khirbet el-Maqâṭir, with remains of an important Byzantine church, perhaps of the fourth century, and probably marking the traditional site of the stone on which Jacob pillowed his head.[13] Three kilometers east-southeast of Beitîn lies the great ruin of et-Tell, Hebrew Ai, belonging almost entirely to the third millennium; see also Chapter X.

7. South of Bethel, in the valley from which the modern village rises up the slopes of the ridge on which stood the ancient town, there is a large Byzantine reservoir (see above), fed by the copious stream of ʿAin el-Baḥr, which ran dry during the years of the 1923–24 drought. In the Wâd eṭ-Ṭahûneh, which runs southward east of the reservoir, are numerous rock-cut tombs, mostly of the Hellenistic-Roman period. Other tombs, mainly of the same age, are found farther to the south-

---

[9] *BASOR*, No. 29 (February, 1928), 9–11. On Wiener and his tragic death less than two years later see *BASOR*, No. 35, 22 f.

[10] Much of the material assigned in 1927 to the Late Bronze proved later to be Middle Bronze II, i.e., to belong to the sixteenth rather than the fifteenth century, as we first thought. When this correction was first made, we concluded erroneously that Bethel might have been unoccupied during Late Bronze proper; see *ZAW*, 1929, 11.

[11] These natural formations have been connected by many scholars with the story of Jacob's pillow, which is conceivable, but it is going too far to call them "a natural cromlech," as not infrequently done.

[12] See *ZDPV*, 1934, 187 ff. The sherds strewn over the site are in no case older than the Byzantine period; cf. *BASOR*, No. 29, p. 9.

[13] Cf. Schneider, *ZDPV*, 1934, 189 f.

west of Beitîn, near the road which formerly connected it with el-Bîreh and which was once part of the Roman road from Bethel to Jerusalem. Here are also three springs, which in good times supply a considerable additional flow of water for Bethel and the vicinity.

8. The district in which Beitîn is located is poor in grain fields but rich in valleys and terraced slopes suitable for the cultivation of orchards and vineyards. Enough grain could be grown, however, to take care of the needs of several hundred persons in good years. Around Bethel lie extensive tracts which must have been covered with forest in the Bronze Age, and which were partly forested even in the Iron Age. Wild animals must have been abundant and several passages in the Bible refer to the presence of bears and lions around Bethel (I Kings 13:24 ff., II Kings 2:23 f., 17:25–26).

9. Bethel is situated in the southern part of the high hill-country called Mount Ephraim by the Israelites. The highest point in the ancient site was about 900 m. above sea level, a height which ensured cool and invigorating weather, even in summer.[14] Bethel was thus situated about 100 m. above Jerusalem. Owing to its height and position on the eastern edge of the watershed ridge, the yearly rainfall is heavier than in Jerusalem.

10. As already indicated above, there can be no doubt about the correctness of the identification of Beitîn with Biblical Bethel. Quite aside from the strong evidence furnished by toponymy and a nearly continuous tradition, is the fact that the statements of patristic authors agree exactly with it. Eusebius gives its location three times: once (*Onomasticon*, ed. Klostermann, p. 40:20 ff.) as 12 miles from Jerusalem, on the right of the road to Neapolis; a second time (*ibid.*, p. 4:28 f.) as on the left of the same road, going south from Neapolis to Aelia, instead of northward from Aelia; a third time (*ibid.*, p. 120:8 ff.), connection with the identification of Luz, also as on the left side of the road from Neapolis to Aelia. At nearly the same time (early fourth century A.D.) the *Itinerarium Burdigalense* gives the situation of Bethel as 28 miles from Neapolis, to the left of the Jerusalem road.[15] Since the modern road from Neapolis (Nâblus) to Jerusalem is 67 km. in length, and the ancient Roman road was at least 5 km. shorter, or not over 41 Roman miles in length, there is obviously a nearly perfect agreement between our sources and the actual topography. Beitîn lies opposite a point some 11 Roman miles north of Jerusalem. All other references to Bethel, Biblical and post-Biblical, agree well with the identification, which is regarded by all topographers of competence as one of the corner-stones of ancient Palestinian topography.

11. As will be seen in Chapter X, the results of our archaeological examination of the site are in the fullest agreement with the documentary data. The town was a flourishing Canaanite settlement. occupied more or less continuously through the Patriarchal and post-Patriarchal (Middle and Late Bronze) Ages, at the close of which it was destroyed. It was an important town during Iron I (period of the Judges and United Monarchy), and was almost continuously occupied through Iron II and down to the late sixth century. It was occupied in the Persian period, in accordance with Ezra, and Nehemiah. The vicissitudes of the site in the Hellenistic, Roman, and Byzantine Ages agree remarkably well with the literary sources.

---

[14] The Survey of Western Palestine gives the elevation of Beitîn as 2890 feet, but it is not clear what point was taken. The Cadastral Survey of the Palestine Government fixed the height of its nearest station, a kilometer to the east-north-east, at 913 m.

[15] See Geyer, *Itinera Hierosolymitana*, p. 20.

CHAPTER II

THE KYLE MEMORIAL EXCAVATIONS AT BETHEL

12. The death of Dr. Melvin Grove Kyle in May, 1933,[1] ended a series of joint undertakings of the American School of Oriental Research in Jerusalem and the Xenia (afterwards Pittsburgh-Xenia) Theological Seminary, which began in 1924 with an expedition to Moab,[2] and continued thereafter with campaigns every second year at Tell Beit Mirsim 1926-32.[3] Dr. Kyle was patron of these undertakings, for which he supplied more than half the funds, and was present during nearly all of the fieldwork, acting as president of the staff while Dr. Albright was director of the expedition. Shortly after Dr. Kyle's death his student and colleague, Dr. James L. Kelso of Pittsburgh-Xenia, who had been assistant director of the work at Tell Beit Mirsim, renewed the collaboration with the American Schools which had begun so auspiciously, and proposed Bethel as a suitable site for an excavation in 1934.[4] While we did not then intend to stop work at Tell Beit Mirsim, we felt that it would be easier to secure funds for a new site under the unfavorable economic conditions then prevailing in America. In honor of Dr. Kyle we called our undertaking " The Kyle Memorial Excavation at Bethel." Half the cost of the fieldwork was raised by Kelso, while the Schools contributed the second half and paid for nearly all the cost of working up the materials after the close of the campaign. In return for his share in organizing and sustaining the expedition, Kelso received all the excavator's share of the " finds " for the museum of the Pittsburgh-Xenia Theological Seminary. The first campaign ran from July 6 to September 15, 1934.

Just 20 years after the first Bethel campaign the American Schools of Oriental Research and the Pittsburgh-Xenia Theological Seminary began their second campaign at Bethel with a summer's dig from May 26 to July 20, 1954. The purpose behind this expedition was twofold: (1) to make a check dig near the 1934 work to see whether any new pottery or other historical data could be discovered; and (2) to search anew for the site of Jeroboam's temple. The third Bethel campaign of the American Schools of Oriental Research and the Pittsburgh-Xenia Theological Seminary began July 11 and concluded August 30, 1957. There were two major objectives: (1) to study the town's defenses; and (2) to locate Jeroboam's temple. The fourth Bethel campaign of the American Schools of Oriental Research and the Pittsburgh Theological Seminary began May 26 and concluded July 19, 1960, although various holidays cut the actual work time to 42 days. A major purpose of this campaign, as of all earlier ones, was to locate Jeroboam's temple, but again no clues to it were discovered although we searched diligently for them. We also planned to continue the study of the NE gate and to excavate a section of the E wall of the town. This was impossible, however, because a newly paved street had been laid above both of them since our last campaign. We then turned our attention to the NW corner of the site where an enormous rock pile hinted that some important building must be beneath it. Our work here produced some of the most important finds of all four campaigns and made a fitting conclusion to our work at ancient Bethel.

1934 Campaign

13. Albright directed the expedition; Kelso was assistant director and president of the staff.[5] There were nine other members of the staff: Drs. O. R. Sellers and Immanuel Ben Dor, Messrs. John Bright, M. M. Levine, James B. Pritchard, Pierre M. Purves, Joshua Starr, Lester E. Williams, and George Ernest Wright. Among guest members of the staff we may mention particularly Dr. Hans Steckeweh (field director of the German excavation at Shechem, who spent several weeks with us for the purpose of acquainting himself with Palestinian pottery), Dr. Aage Schmidt, Pro-

---

[1] *BASOR*, No. 51, pp. 5–7.
[2] *BASOR*, No. 14, pp. 1–12.
[3] *BASOR*, No. 23, pp. 2–14; No. 31, pp. 1–11; No. 39, pp. 1–10; No. 47, pp. 3–17.
[4] *BASOR*, No. 29, pp. 9–11.

[5] *BASOR*, No. 55, pp. 23–25; No. 56, pp. 1–15.

fessors G. R. Berry and C. F. Sitterly, and Mr. Theodore Canaan. Dr. W. F. Stinespring spent time with us on various occasions in order to help with the photography. Odeh Jirius of Jifnah, who had had several years of experience as foreman under H. Kjaer, W. F. Albright, and others, was chief foreman, assisted by ʿAbd-el-Ḥâfiẓ, the principal landowner and our consistent friend during the entire undertaking.

14. We endeavored to give ample opportunity for rotation of staff-work and encouraged the younger men to become acquainted with all the more important phases of the work. Sellers devoted most of his attention to the workroom, which he supervised, took charge of the coins, and organized the drawing of pottery. His experience in previous excavations was of great value to us here. Ben Dor spent most of his time on the excavation itself and assisted with the recording. Mr. Levine, a graduate in architecture from the Carnegie Institute of Technology in Pittsburgh, did the surveying and planning, with help from one of the other members of the staff and checked most of the drawings of pottery. Mr. Williams undertook the photography after the first few weeks, producing uniformly good photographs. The other men divided their time more or less equally among supervising small gangs of laborers, sorting and drawing pottery, assisting the surveyor, and helping in numerous other ways. Messrs. Wright and Bright also took charge of the expedition car, which made a trip to Jerusalem once a day.

With so competent a staff we were able to control and analyze our material day by day as we dug, and to double check these conclusions as soon as each set of plans and levels had been completed. There were three major areas under excavation, and thus abundant and excellent data for cross reference were always at hand.

15. On July 2 we began negotiations with the landowners, completing them on July 4. We confined our work to the NW section of Bethel since the other areas were covered with houses (Pl. 12a). The irregular double lines on the map of the excavation site represent peasant boundary walls (Pl. 1).[6] Beyond these walls to the N, E, and S ran a narrow street. The W boundary wall was built on a terrace and separated the fields on the terrace from the lower ones in the valley. Since much of the area dug was a fig orchard,[7] the owners had to be compensated for ten trees cut down and for fruit ruined by the dust of the excavation. Furthermore, since the orchard was owned by several different persons, one of whom did not wish us to excavate his property, we were forced to dig smaller areas than at Tell Beit Mirsim.[8]

16. On July 6 the tents and most of the equipment were taken to the site and the following day camp was set up and organized. On the 9th, the first test pit was dug to a depth of 3 m. over an area 2.5 × 5 m. The sherds were checked at half meter intervals, and the pottery was found to be predominantly Hellenistic, Iron II, and Iron I with some Roman and Byzantine ware and a few Middle Bronze sherds. This sampling showed the area to be highly productive, so the following day the test pit was expanded to a full-scale excavation area, which ultimately covered 300 sq. m. It is called Area I in the excavation reports (Pl. 1). Remains of a Hellenistic building appeared that day, and the area continued to be productive down to bedrock. No Islamic remains of any kind were found, but Byzantine and Roman walls appeared as the area was enlarged.[9] On the 12th the *maḍâfeh*, or guest house, was converted into the expedition workroom where all work on the records was conducted and the pottery drawn to scale. This spacious room was delightfully cool and was an ideal place in which to study the finds. The initial test dig employed only about 20 laborers but the number was quickly increased until we had a maximum of 75 men, women, and boys.

17. On July 16 the workers were shifted southward to Area II so the surveyors could work over Area I in detail. Area II (Pl. 1) at its greatest expansion covered about 253 sq. m. Both areas were at times unproductive but the over-all findings in each were very rewarding. On July 25 work was begun in Area III (Pl. 1) at the SW corner of the fig orchard near the site of the 1927 sounding. This area covered about 156 sq. m. Here a section of the inside face of the Middle Bronze wall of the town was uncovered, along

---

[6] Some new boundary walls were erected shortly before the 1954 campaign, but they did not modify any features in the 1934 plans.

[7] When we returned to the site in 1954, we found that most of the fig orchard had been cut down and new fruit trees were bearing crops of apples, apricots, plums, peaches, etc.

[8] *BASOR*, No. 56, top of p. 3.

[9] The Byzantine occupation at Bethel also reached to the E and S of the *tell* proper.

with some Hellenistic house walls and a few Byzantine graves. On September 10 a small plot E of Area II and across the street from it was tested to see whether there was any trace of an E wall of the town (Pl. 1). Only house walls were uncovered and those only down to Iron I, phase 2. The site was filled in the following week; we named it Area IV.[10] Meanwhile on August 13 some workmen had been moved to the Byzantine gateway at the NE corner of Beitîn to see whether the Byzantine wall was built upon an earlier Iron Age wall. A test trench, however, showed that the Byzantine wall had been constructed hastily in an emergency. No walls of any kind were found under it, although we dug to virgin soil. Work around the gateway was abandoned two days later.

18. On September 4 we began to fill in Area I. On September 10 work began on filling in Area II, a task involving moving about 1000 cu. m. of debris. In all fill-in work the average workman moved about 3 cu. m. of stone and earth per day. We broke camp the afternoon of the 15th and returned to Jerusalem, where Ben Dor and Levine continued work on the Bethel material, working up plans, drawings, etc., under Albright's supervision. The total surface area worked in 1934 was 800 sq. m. and the area excavated down to bedrock was roughly about 200 sq. m.[11]; over much of the remainder of the area virgin soil had been reached before bedrock.

19. All loci in Area I were given numbers from 1 upward; loci in Area II from 100 on and loci in Area III were numbered 200 and upward. The preliminary report of the 1934 expedition was printed in *BASOR*, No. 56 (December, 1934), pp. 1–15.

1954 Campaign

20. Kelso directed the expedition, with the assistance of Professor James Muilenburg of Union Theological Seminary, annual director of the Jerusalem School, Professor Charles Fritsch of Princeton Theological Seminary, and Rev. David Sherwin, a graduate of Pittsburgh-Xenia Theological Seminary. Mr. Emil Abu Dayeh was liaison man with the Bethel people and foreman of the excavations with Mr. Maaz Abdo as assistant. The surveyor was Mr. Soubhi Muhtadi, the *formatore* Mr. Mahfouz Nassar and the photographer Mr. Hanna Safieh. They had all worked with us at Jericho and were skillful at their respective tasks. Mr. G. Lankester Harding, director of the Jordan Department of Antiquities, was most helpful in every way, as was also his assistant Mr. Awni Dajani of the Jerusalem office. Mr. Joseph Saʿad of the Palestine Archaeological Museum assisted us by arranging for the blueprinting of our plans.

21. Père R. de Vaux and Father Sylvester Saller were highly valued consultants. They not only visited the dig on various occasions but also studied the pottery *in toto* again when it was brought to the Jerusalem School. Dr. Carl Kraeling's assistance in planning the dig and inspecting it was greatly appreciated. Weekly summaries on the progress of the work were sent to Albright via air mail and he replied at once with his interpretation of the data. Upon our return to America he went over all the excavation records with great care and examined collections of sherds dealing with points of special interest.

22. On May 22 all the official papers for the excavation were signed. The Department of Antiquities' representative was Mr. Awni Dajani, the community official was the *mukhtâr*, Mohammed Abdullah Daher[12] and the landowner was Abd el-Majeed Mohammed. Workmen were signed up on May 25, the men to be paid 20 piasters a day and the boys 15. When we arrived with our equipment the following morning, however, the workmen insisted on 25 piasters a day. We compromised on 21 and the men went to work happy. They were good congenial workers and there was no further labor trouble. We began with about 25 laborers but used twice that number most of the season. The plot of ground where we began work was the old camp site of the former

---

[10] This work had been initiated in mid-August but quickly abandoned for more important findings elsewhere.

[11] There is a misprint in *BASOR*, No. 56, p. 3, which reads "20 sq. m." instead of 200. This error was corrected in No. 57, p. 27.

[12] In the intervening 20 years there had been a political shift in the village and a new *mukhtâr* had taken office. Relatives of the former *mukhtâr*, however, were employed on the dig. (The two families are inter-married.) Beitîn is still America-conscious, with her men going to the U.S. and Mexico. A son of the former *mukhtâr* had gone to Mexico and married there. He is now living with his Mexican wife in the former *maḍâfeh*. His son in turn is going to Mexico. A son of the present *mukhtâr* studied oil geology in the U.S. Although only 20 years had elapsed since the former dig, very few of the men who had worked for us in the earlier campaign were still alive.

dig. A new stone boundary wall, however, now separated it from old Area I. We measured off 8 × 8 m. just W of this new boundary wall and began digging. The 8 × 8 m. area was divided into four units: $\begin{cases} \text{NW} & \text{NE} \\ \text{SW} & \text{SE} \end{cases}$ The general policy was to dig a NE level first, then in turn a SE, a SW, and a NW level on a descending spiral. Thus check levels were constantly available. The final productive area took on the general form of the letter " T." Before the work was finished, the surface area had been expanded to approximately 110 sq. m. (Pls. 85a–87a).

23. When work began at the old 1934 camp site, we failed to find building installations of any kind in the Byzantine, Roman, Hellenistic, or Persian levels. When we asked the owners about the mysterious absence of these installations, they informed us that they had already dug up this area to secure stone for the erection of the new boundary wall between this old camp site and Area I of the former dig. The detailed findings in each of the succeeding levels will be given at the close of the treatment of the parallel levels in the 1934 campaign. The over-all picture of the two campaigns is very similar wherever parallel levels had been preserved. The four Iron I levels were the most useful of all the levels dug here in 1954. We also tested the SE corner of the camp site to see whether we might recover any Roman, Hellenistic, and Persian levels there. Sherds of these periods were found but the walls were of little value until we got down to Iron II. Trees interfered with our work, and since no new material appeared, we abandoned this experimental area of about 20 sq. m.

24. On June 15 we began work on a major area just E of the village mosque (Pl. 87b). Since the mosque was built directly over a Byzantine church and since holy places have a tendency to remain more or less fixed, we dug here to see whether Jeroboam's temple might be near by. We found no clue to the old temple. Although the site is only a short distance from the city's strongest springs, we were surprised to find the area full of Roman cisterns. Just N of these were Byzantine constructions, perhaps a monastery. Test pits showed sherds going back to the second occupation period on the *tell* itself, i.e., the end of Early Bronze. The work in this mosque area is treated in detail in §165 ff. The area dug was approximately 80 sq. m.

25. On June 29 one of the landowners in the valley E of Beitîn asked us to excavate a new tomb he had just found. We did not have time to do anything except to check the pottery just inside the door which consisted of first century A.D. store-jars (Pl. 74:6) together with a lamp of the same date or perhaps slightly later. The hillside at this point was thick with sherds of excellent Iron I pottery mixed with a little Iron II and a few Byzantine sherds. We dug an exploratory trench here to see whether we might find any building installations. None appeared, so the pottery must have been thrown out of Iron Age tombs which were then reused in Roman and Byzantine times. A second tomb near by was also reported to us; its pottery was Byzantine. On July 20 we closed work at Beitîn and paid the owners to fill in their fields. Week by week all the pottery was taken to the School in Jerusalem after its initial study on the site. In Jerusalem all this pottery was assembled and restudied. The loci numbers used in the 1954 campaign begin at 300. The expedition's preliminary report was published in *BASOR*, No. 137 (February, 1955), pp. 5–10.

1957 Campaign

26. Kelso of the Pittsburgh-Xenia Theological Seminary again served as director of the expedition and Professor T. M. Taylor of the same school was assistant director. Another professor of that institution, Howard M. Jamieson and two of the seminary students, Messrs. John W. Irwin and John W. Stewart, as well as Rev. Glen Harris of Birmingham, Michigan, were members of the staff. The Arab staff members were practically the same as in 1954. Mr. Emil Abu Dayeh was liaison man with the Bethel people and foreman of the excavations, the surveyor was Mr. Soubhi Muhtadi, the *formatore* was Mr. Mahfouz Nassar, and the photographer was Mr. Hanna Safieh. About 45 Beitîn men were employed. The *mukhtâr* of Beitîn, Mohammed Abdullah Daher, was again very cooperative and even allowed us to dig up a section of a street which ran above the N wall of the ancient town.

27. The Antiquities Department of the Hashemite Kingdom of Jordan under Said Bey Dura was helpful. The assistant director, Dr. Awni Dajani, was most gracious and later joined us in carrying out some test digs in the Jericho area where each had been excavating previously. Père R. de Vaux

was, as always, a most gracious and stimulating consultant both at Beitîn and in Jerusalem, where the pottery was again studied. Professor G. E. Wright compared the Bethel pottery with that of his Shechem dig. Dr. and Mrs. Paul Lapp, who were members of his staff, were especially interested in our Hellenistic pottery.

28. Seven areas of the site were tested in searching for the town's defenses, but only four of them were productive. In addition small sections of the town walls were found incorporated into two of the houses of Beitîn. These finds will be treated in detail in the following chapters. Jeroboam's temple still eluded search. Just at the close of the dig, half of an inscribed South Arabian clay stamp of the ninth century B.C. was found in the debris outside the W wall of the town. It must have been the property of the leader of an incense caravan from South Arabia.

29. Since some scholars have suggested that the temple was outside the town, several of the staff and workmen looked carefully for Iron II sherds at Burj Beitîn, on the hill E of Bethel, but none was found.[13] This fortress incorporated a sixth century church erected on the supposed site of Abraham's altar. Most of the sherds were Byzantine, although a few belonged to the transition from EB to MB. We also investigated Khirbet el-Maqâṭir, the site of a fourth (?) century church, but spent less time here, as the site had been plundered to furnish stone for erecting the mosque at el-Bîreh. Not far from the latter ruin but closer to the western edge of the ridge we found what may well have been an altar bearing two cup marks. It was 2.5 m. long; one end was 1 m. wide and the other end 2 m. It was 1.3 m. high. There were numerous flints at the base; some were microlithic. A little to the S was a plundered EB grave. All this shows that the hill was a camp site before Abraham's day.

30. Small housing areas were studied at the N edge of the town both inside and outside the northern MB II B town wall (Pls. 91a–93b). The houses outside the city were Hellenistic and Roman. Those houses adjacent to the town wall but inside the town were MB II of several phases. One was a patrician house. The LB construction that followed it was the poorest of that level found in any campaign. The Iron I level was thin and lacked the fine subdivisions found in former years. The expedition finished work August 30 and the various landowners were paid to fill in their own properties. The total areas excavated were approximately 268 sq. m. The pottery was restudied at the School in Jerusalem. Albright was kept in touch with the work by weekly air mail letters and he later checked over the excavation records carefully and examined its collection of sherds. The loci numbers used in the 1957 campaign begin at 400. The expedition's preliminary report, including a detailed study of the inscribed South Arabian clay stamp by G. W. Van Beek and A. Jamme, was published in the *BASOR*, No. 151 (October, 1958), pp. 3–16. See also No. 163, pp. 15–18.

1960 Campaign

31. Kelso was again the director and his assistant was Taylor, both of Pittsburgh Theological Seminary.[14] The Arab staff members were the same as those of the 1954 and 1957 campaigns. One purpose of this season's work was to train professors and students in archaeological techniques. The following were with us: Professor and Mrs. Edward D. Grohman of Pittsburgh Seminary, Professor and Mrs. Rolland E. Wolfe of Western Reserve University, Professor Wm. H. Brownlee of Claremont Graduate School, Professors J. A. Callaway and E. J. Vardaman of Louisville Southern Baptist Theological Seminary, and Professor Wayne H. Christy of Westminster College. Pittsburgh Seminary graduates and students were: Robert A. Coughenour, Wm C. Cook, Wm. N. Jackson, Michael Kuhtik, John E. Mehl, Chas. M. Olsen, Robert E. Palisin and James A. Snow. College students on the dig were Robert and Jeffery Jones, Valjeane M. Olenn, and Majid Bayyuk; also present were Commander Harvey H. McClellan, U.S.N., and Mrs. C. E. Davis, R.N. (Pl. 104a).

32. The Jordanian Director of Antiquities, Dr. Awni Dajani, was most cooperative in every way. He secured for us the best publicity we have ever had with both Arab and American newspapers. He also arranged an audience for our staff, along with those of other expeditions, to meet King

---

[13] A sounding at Burj Beitîn by Dr. Aage Schmidt yielded pottery of the Byzantine and Islamic periods only. *BASOR*, No. 29, p. 9.

[14] The Pittsburgh-Xenia Theological Seminary and the Western Theological Seminary were merged in 1959 and became the Pittsburgh Theological Seminary.

Hussein in his palace at Amman. Drs. Marvin H. Pope and Oleg Grabar, directors of the American School were helpful in every way, as was Dr. Paul W. Lapp, interim director. Père R. de Vaux was a gracious and stimulating consultant both at Beitîn and in Jerusalem, where the pottery was again studied.

33. In searching for Jeroboam's temple we took another look at the enormous rock pile at the NW corner of Beitîn. Since a few massive stones at the bottom of the pile seemed to be *in situ* we began work here. We failed again to locate Jeroboam's temple but our finds at this point were among the most valuable of any campaign on the site. Here we found a unique " U "-shaped gateway of MB II B (Pl. 101) which is described in detail in Chapter III. Immediately below it was an MB I building which we are tentatively identifying as a temple and below that the bare mountain-top high place of Bethel. There was a large paved area just to the N which may be another sacred enclosure. Here an intrusive Byzantine burial was found.

34. The S wall of the gateway complex was actually the N wall of the town; and the NW corner of the town wall was the SW corner of the gateway building. We traced the outer face of the city's W wall southward for 11.5 m. where we found a new unit of the wall on a slightly different alignment (Pl. 102a). Then we checked the W wall again a little S of where we had found the early South Arabian seal in 1957. Here the outer face of the wall ran through the basement of a modern Arab house and we exposed the inner face in the adjacent yard (Pl. 102b). In both instances house walls abutted on the town wall and MB II B pottery was present. The wall is thus the same date as the N wall and the construction is identical —excellent semi-dressed stone on the faces and well-interlocked stones in the center. The thickness of the N and W walls is virtually the same, *c.* 3.5 m.

35. We also located a section of the town's S wall just N of the Roman gate located in 1957 (Pl. 103c). On a narrow terrace above the spring we sank a test pit 6.1 m. deep and uncovered the outer face of the S wall and the E face of a town gate or tower bonded into it and at right angles with the main wall. This was also an MB II B wall similar to the ones found on the N and W sides of the town. This wall continued in use through LB but was destroyed in the beginning of Iron I. A crude Iron I wall laid in a deep bed of ashes and brick was built directly over the 4 m. stub of the MB II B wall. Above this level we found sections of Iron II, Hellenistic, Roman, and Byzantine walls. For all details on the town's walls and gates, see Chapter III.

36. Only small house areas were dug. They were in test pits sunk to locate the town's main defenses. One corner of a large MB II B building constructed of beautiful semi-dressed stone was exposed; its masonry is as fine as that found anywhere in Palestine. Cultic pottery suggests the building may be a temple but we did not have time to excavate the whole building.

37. Since most of the campaign was devoted to a study of the town's fortifications, comparatively few objects were found. The pottery was again restudied in Jerusalem. Albright was informed by air mail of all findings as the excavation proceeded, and he later checked over all records and samples of pottery sherds. The expedition's preliminary report was published in the *BASOR*, No. 164 (December, 1961), pp. 5–19. The loci numbers used in the 1960 campaign begin at 500. Pl. 120 gives the relative position of all the areas excavated from 1934 to 1960 except for those at the S edge of Beitîn, namely the mosque area, the S MB II wall, and the S Roman gate.

CHAPTER III

The Fortifications of Bethel

38. Bethel was difficult to defend for there were no favorable geographic features such as a high isolated ridge or spur, steep cliffs or deep valleys, §5. Indeed, since these features are strikingly absent, many scholars questioned the identification of Bethel with Beitîn; and it was not until 1927, when Albright's test dig located a massive town wall, that the identification became positive.

39. Bethel, however, was blessed with water, lots of water! Immediately below the site there were two copious springs within a long stone's throw of one another, and several lesser fountains were nearby. So much water so close to the top of the central ridge, which carried the main N and S road of Palestine, naturally demanded a city. A copious water supply near the top of the mountains was too rare to neglect. Furthermore, major E and W valleys on either side of the site carried an important road from Jericho and the Jordan valley via the vale of Aijalon and other westward routes to the Mediterranean. Indeed, the eastern valley served as the boundary between Benjamin and Ephraim, and it was up this road that Joshua's invasion entered the highlands.

40. Late in Chalcolithic times (*c.* 3200 B.C.) a village sprang up just S of the earlier open-air sacrificial high place dedicated to the god El. No signs of fortifications were found. There were no further signs of occupation until late in EB *c.* 2400–*c.* 2200 B.C. The former village area was again occupied and also a new site near the largest of the springs. The areas excavated were too small to warrant any conclusions except those of occupation. Et-Tell (Ai) just E of Bethel had been destroyed a little earlier in EB, and Bethel then replaced Ai as the major city of that district.

Major installations calling for defense by a town wall appeared in MB I, *c.* the nineteenth century B.C. This MB I town must have been defended for it had substantial buildings including the temple erected over the old open-air sanctuary §§96 ff. But no town walls uncovered to date can be assigned to MB I. There are a few massive stones wedged against the foundations of the MB II B temple (?) inside the NW corner of the town that may have come from such a wall. Most of the stones of an MB I wall would naturally have been reused in building the town's great MB II B wall.

41. Some MB II A sherds have been found near the N and the S walls of the MB II B town, but no house walls of this period have been uncovered at the N section of the site. The MB II A area to the S is still unexcavated although sherds of that period were found mixed with MB II B debris.

42. Bethel became a major Palestinian town very early in MB II B. Although the excavations of 1934 and 1954 failed to find the town's N wall the evidence both years suggested that the wall must lie beneath the northernmost streets of the village. In 1957 we dug in the field just N of that street and found that the N wall of the town did lie under that street (Pls. 91a; 93; 96a; 97a, b).

This early MB II B wall (*c.* 1650 B.C.) was exceptionally well built (Pl. 96a; see also *BASOR*, No. 151, Fig. 2). Not only were the large semi-dressed stones of the exterior face accurately fitted together and wedged with small stones, but the face of the wall also had a slight batter—20 cm. in 2.8 m. of the eight courses. The largest stone in the wall was 1.4 m. in length, and a fair percentage of the stones measured 75 cm. or more in length. A quadrangular stone found in the foundation course averaged 1.5 m. on a side. The limestone around Beitîn can be worked easily; it fractures along a fairly even plane. Two quarries are now furnishing excellent building stone for Jerusalem and Amman. This N wall was 3.38 m. wide and its course was traced for 20.5 m. (Pl. 93a).[1]

43. A 5 m. stretch just W of this section of the wall was either the outer face of a tower or a jog in the wall; it projected a little better than 1 m. beyond the line of the wall. It consisted of two foundation courses with only one course of three medium-sized stones of the wall proper *in situ*. Even the foundation courses disappeared beyond this point, and only bedrock was left. Sherds of Byzantine water jars from the ancient robber

---

[1] This N wall runs only approximately E and W, cf. plan.

trench showed that the old wall had been the source of supply for stones used in the hastily built Byzantine city wall, §§175, 214. Similar Byzantine quarrying was also found on the exterior face of the town's W wall studied in 1934, 1957, and 1960. Fortunately, a Roman house built across the old N wall preserved the E section which we have been describing. Apparently this house was still in use in Byzantine times, for it was immediately E and W of it that the Byzantines removed the ancient wall.

The foundation course of the N wall of the town was of heavy stones and wider than the wall above it. It had been laid directly on bedrock. Above it the wall proper was preserved to an average of eight courses. The maximum height preserved was 3.1 m., of which 30 cm. was the foundation course and 2.8 m. the height of the wall still standing.

44. A farmer's massive stone boundary wall (not shown on plans) lay just S of the street, so only a small section of the inside of the town wall was uncovered (Pl. 97a, b). The interior face of the wall, like the exterior, was well constructed although fewer stones over 75 cm. in length had been employed than on the exterior face. It had been laid directly on bedrock without a foundation. Five or six courses of wall remained, the number depending on the contour of the bedrock. The core of the wall consisted of large stones; some were semi-dressed, others were rough, water-worn, and odd-shaped but all skillfully fitted into place, with only a minimum of small stones needed to fill in the interstices. The wall was built as a solid structure, not as two faces with a rough fill between them. Fortunately there was a house wall abutting on the inside face of the town wall, (Pl. 97a) and its pottery dates this N wall of Beitîn c. 1650 B.C. (On the plans the hatched stones on top of the city wall have no relationship to the MB wall but are probably part of a modern boundary wall.)

45. In front of the wall was a heavy glacis (Pl. 93c) with marly clay predominating near the wall and with stone predominating after c. 4.5 m. out from the face of the wall. The glacis was laid on virgin soil. The clay fill near the wall contained a few EB and MB I sherds near the top and early MB II near the foundation. Some of the earlier sherds were water-worn and must have come from elsewhere on the site. A test trench dug through the glacis at right angles to the wall showed the marly clay fill for approximately the first 4.5 m. Then came about 1.5 m. of small stones, which seems to have been the foundation of an earlier stone face of the glacis. Beyond it was more marly clay and then a second mass of stone over twice as wide as the first. The outside face of this second mass of stone measured c. 10.5 m. from the face of the wall at the lowest point reached in digging. Five sherds, each from a different MB II B vase, were found at this point. The outside face of the second mass of stone was at one point preserved for c. 1.5 m. on an angle suggesting a point of convergence between the outer face of the town wall and the projected outer face of the glacis c. 6 m. above the foundation of the former. The original top of the town wall was naturally several meters higher.

46. The remains of the outer edge of the glacis were confused by an E–W Hellenistic house wall and silo, and further complicated by the rapid fall of the terrain (Pl. 93b). In the glacis fill at the base of the wall there was carbonized material extending downward from the top of the foundation course 5–8 cm. There was a second small pocket of similar material at one point 60 cm. from the bottom of the fill. A major burning 8–10 cm. thick appeared about 1 m. below the preserved top of the wall and continued N to the first rock mass. This layer of burning may reflect the destruction of the earlier glacis before the restoration of the wall with a thicker glacis probably in MB II C, since there are MB II B sherds in the fill. At 1.5 m. N of the town wall and about 75 cm. under the surface of the ground a Roman house wall appeared and continued for 10 m. along the W edge of the test trench. Just E of this long wall was a 6 m. section of an earlier Hellenistic house, §174.

47. This MB II B town wall continued to be Bethel's N defense until the town was destroyed in the late sixth century B.C., §150. In 1934 in the E section of Area I we found a massive quoin construction suggesting a tower, with some relatively heavy walls S of it (Pl. 20b). The tower was erected in the eighth century (to judge from the homogeneous pottery) and rebuilt later. This roughly built tower was founded on bedrock and built across an LB threshold of phase 1, destroying the N jamb. Both tower and wall to the S show clear traces of reconstruction. For the use of quoin construction in houses see Pl. 26a. There is a possibility that in 1954 another tower may

have been located in 306 and 311. Much of this area contained nothing but dirt and small stone chips such as would have been used in wedging large stones into place. The Byzantines had probably robbed the tower at this place. These repairs on the wall were eighth and seventh centuries. When the Jewish exiles returned to the site, their first constructions were built of the large stones which had been scattered about when the city wall was destroyed. At some later time, however, the old town wall was repaired and remained in use until Roman times.

48. This repaired wall had a gate near the NE corner of the town. To study it we had to tunnel under the street and had only one day in which to do it. Since the work on the gate was unfinished it does not appear on the plans. Furthermore, the area was a fill consisting chiefly of small stones which kept constantly sliding into our dig. The wall had collapsed toward the gateway until only the lowest course was intact. This course consisted of three well-dressed stones and the large corner one was shaped like an inverted "L." The Byzantine gate nearby had stones of the same shape to hold the wooden gates in position and to protect the pivot edges. The outer stone had been subjected to fire and crumbled under pressure. There were paving stones in the gateway, and in places they were two deep showing that the pavement had been relaid. These paving stones were of entirely different shape from the foundation stones of the town wall proper. The level of the lowest pavement slab is 6.845, a level only 20 cm. above bedrock inside the town wall W in 410. Because of the rock slides in our tunneling and the brief time we were allowed to close off the street, we could only examine the W jamb of the gate. Although we worked toward the E against time, we were unable to locate the E jamb before we had to fill in the pit. Returning to the W jamb, above the lowest course of three well-aligned dressed stones were remains of two courses, each consisting of one undressed stone which had obviously been pushed far out of place by the collapsing city wall behind them. (The uppermost actually slipped from its place after being cleared of earth before the surveyor had time to include it in his plans.)

49. The date of the destruction of the gate is uncertain, for the few sherds found permit a date anywhere from Pompey to Vespasian. After the collapse of the upper part of the wall a Roman house was built across the wall W of the gate (Pl. 93b). Only its foundation remained. This house must have been in use down to Byzantine times, for the Byzantines removed the stones of the city wall on either side of this house but left the house and the wall beneath it intact. A few Hellenistic sherds were found between the stones of the town wall just W of the gate, but one can only conjecture whether they had any relationship to a destruction by Bacchides or whether they were part of the later rock fill.

50. The area immediately S of the gate was occupied by a peasant's massive boundary walls, but just beyond them was the wall of a very poorly built Roman house (Pl. 92b, hatched wall N of 406). Its W end was on an earth fill and its E end on a stone fill; this latter may be part of the stone fill found outside the town gate. Immediately S of this Roman wall but at a lower level was an Iron I wall—a continuation of the S wall of 402. S of it and E of 404 and 405 was a large fill, 406. The surface area of this dump was 3.5 m. by c. 2.25 m. although the fill itself was larger for it extended both E and S beyond our excavations. No walls were found in situ except a small stub of a wall of LB at the E edge of the dig. The level of the ground surface of the fill was 10.55, but more than 2 m. below it a Herodian lamp and a Maccabaean coin were found. At 7.7, however, the fill ended and a N–S wall appeared along the E edge of the dig, and a grain pit just W of the wall at 7.535 was built against it in the courtyard of an MB II C patrician house. Carbonized material was taken from the bottom of the grain pit and 20 cm. of ashes covered the top of the pit.

51. This fill area S of the gate was completely unlike any of the room areas which had been worked by the Beitîn peasants in their search for stones. Furthermore, the striations made in dumping this fill showed plainly. Along the E edge the debris had been dumped from N to S; on the S side it had been thrown in from W to E. This ancient dump area extended from the surface of the ground to the ashes above the courtyard of the patrician house of MB II C. All this area with the exception of the stub of an LB wall must have been unoccupied by houses from MB times on. The open area to the N, however, had been cut off later by an Iron I wall.

Since the material at the top of the fill was chiefly Iron II and that at the bottom was Maccabaean and Herodian, the date of the fill seems to be Roman and perhaps contemporaneous with the destruction and abandonment of the NE gate. The fill at the gate, however, differed from that of the fill S of the gate. The former was predominantly of small stones but the fill S of the gate consisted of normal debris. Since we dug the fill early in the campaign, the finding of the gateway was not unexpected. We had assumed that the fill area was a street leading to a town gate. Unfortunately time prevented us from connecting the two areas.

52. The first work scheduled for the 1960 dig was the completion of the excavation at the town's NE gate, but on our return we found that during our absence the street above the gate had been paved, and so we were forced to abandon this project.

We then turned our attention to the NW area of the site to get the NW corner of the MB II B town wall, but this area was covered by a high massive rock pile,[2] whose removal slowed our work greatly. We uncovered, however, not only the NW corner of the wall but also a gateway at that point (Pl. 101). Because of the unique nature of this U-shaped gateway in Palestinian archaeology, it was described in great detail in the *BASOR*, No. 164 (December, 1961) pp. 6–11. The following is only a modest expansion of that report.

53. The NW gate (*c.* 1650 B.C.) is a rhomboid whose N wall is 14.6 m., the E wall 9.7 m., and the W wall 9.2 m. This building actually had no S wall of its own, but abutted directly upon the outer face of the N wall of the town and thus used the town wall to complete the building complex. The S dimension along the town wall was approximately 15.3 m. The N and W walls (Pl. 104b) were approximately 1.5 m. wide; the E wall, which contained the gateway proper, was irregular in width (narrowing to the S), but approximately 1.75 m. The NE corner of the building was standing *c.* 5 m. above bedrock.[3] The largest stones used in the building were over 1 m. long.

Three stone steps led up to the gateway proper, which was 2.5 m. wide (Pl. 105b). These stairs with a total height of *c.* 70 cm. were doubtless replacements for they still show sharp corners and only a fair polish from use. The original stones of the threshold are, on the other hand, highly polished from long service. The first and third risers were *c.* 20 cm. high; the middle one varied from 25 to 30 cm. The lower treads were 35 to 40 cm. deep and the top one 45 to 50 cm. The N jamb of the gate was still standing *c.* 2 m. high; the S jamb was slightly lower. The latter showed a reconstruction done in semi-dressed stone and was better workmanship than the N jamb (Pls. 105c; 109b). There was no sign of burning here; perhaps earthquake action destroyed the old jamb. The corridor leading W from the gateway was approximately 3.5 m. in width and the N side of the corridor, which was the longer, measured 11,35 m. (Pl. 106a).

54. Most of the floor area was *ḥuwar c.* 10 to 15 cm. thick with the *ḥuwar* of the floor in places continuing upward as a thin plaster on the walls. There were nine flagstones *in situ* near the W end of the corridor and another about the center of it.[4] These suggested that originally the whole area was paved with stone. This original stone pavement theory was later verified for under the *ḥuwar* at one point was a sterile earth layer about the same thickness, then a double layer of stones well fitted together. These lay on a 30 cm. bed of small stones and earth. At another point beneath the *ḥuwar*, there was *c.* 25 cm. of red earth and ash and below that *c.* 60 cm. of interlocked rocks. A heavy layer of fallen *ḥuwar* at the W end of the corridor shows that this room had been roofed over or that there had been a second story.

55. The S wall of the corridor which was 1.7 m. wide, continued 8.45 m. westward where it ceased and was replaced for the remainder of the distance to the W wall of the building (3.35 m.) by a stairway consisting of four steps (Pl. 105a). These four steps lead up from the stone pavement of the corridor to a *ḥuwar* platform 86 cm. above it—an average height of 21.5 cm. to each riser. Because of the angle of the W wall of the gateway, each ascending step increased slightly in length. The top one was 3.85 m. The stairway was in very poor condition but the four steps can be seen in the plan as follows: The first step is represented

---

[2] The rock pile above the NW town gate doubtless came from the clearing of the land for farming by the first Arab settlers who came here in the 1840s. The sherds in this rock pile were Iron I (rare), Iron II, Hellenistic, Roman, and especially Byzantine. This landmark goes by the name of Tell el-Kufru which to the natives has the meaning of mound of covering over, or atonement, or of desecration.

[3] This figure represents work done after the elevation drawing was made.

[4] This latter does not appear on the plan.

by 54 and 47; 54 is the original height of that step; 47 has sunk to corridor level by usage. In the second step 55 rises above 54; 56 and 46 have the same relationship as the lower step 47. 64 is the only stone of the third step still in original position; 57, 58, 59, 65, are all foundations for the third step. 63 is the fourth step. 45 is the *ḥúwar* platform to which the stairs led. In most places the resurfaced platform covered the top step.

56. Two steps with 30 cm. treads (62 and 61), then appeared at the E end of this platform where they apparently led to a second corridor similar and parallel to the N corridor but shorter. Its *ḥúwar* floor showed up at a point where this corridor ended against the E wall of the building. Because of the great height of the rock pile over the corridor it was impossible to confirm this circumstantial evidence. The corridor must ultimately have made a right angle turn to the S somewhere near the E wall of the building and there pierced the N wall of the town proper. Inside the town wall there is some evidence pointing toward a palace-temple complex, see §§113 f. The U-shaped gateway had no guard room.

57. There was no definite sign of reconstruction except at the S jamb of the gateway where seven courses of excellent semi-dressed stone marked a rebuilding (Pls. 105c; 109b). They contrast sharply with the cruder stones of the N jamb. The S end of the E wall where it must have originally abutted on the N wall of the town, ended in a rough jagged pattern (Pl. 107b). Some of its stone as well as that of the N wall of the town against which it abutted, had been robbed to build the city's defenses in Byzantine times.[5] We tried to reach the foundation course of both walls but it was impossible because of dangerous rock slides. No heavy timbers were available for shoring. The N wall of the gateway building leaned to the N, but we could not tell whether this was due to earthquake action or to irregular pressure from the temple wall directly beneath it which served as its foundation courses. Although the N unit of the gateway pier did not lean as much as the rest of the N wall, the largest stones of the pier showed pressure cracks.

58. The problem of the missing S wall of the building was not solved until we had cut down a large expensive apple tree. Under it we found the lowest courses of the NW corner of the town wall. The SW corner of the gateway complex was abutting directly upon the town's N wall just 80 cm. short of the NW corner of the town wall (Pls. 102a; 110a). The 80 cm. may have been a buttress or glacis. The stones of the five courses of the W wall of the gateway complex preserved here were not laid in the normal pattern of corner construction but simply abutted directly on the town's N wall of the city. The only object found in the building with the exception of sherds was a beautiful bone handle for a spindle whorl. All sherds found in the gateway complex were MB II, B and C.

59. We date the construction of the gateway about the same time as the town wall and its destruction about the middle of the sixteenth century B.C., probably by the Egyptians after their capture of Jericho, for the main road W out of Jericho in those days ran through Bethel. (Joshua also used this same route.) The building was burned as shown by ashes in the gateway and outside the building. After its destruction, loose rocks were heaped over the entire structure. These rocks averaged *c*. 30 cm. in size and seldom exceeded 50 cm. There were some small stones and stone chips. The rocks not only covered the structure but formed a talus slope around it. Some of this rock fill still showed that it had been put in from the E and the N. Some grey earth was found, colored by ashes of the burning. The fill was more complex outside the gate and there may have been a revetment there. A modern paved road prevented a more detailed study of this feature. The only sherds found were MB II, B and C; no LB sherds were present although there was an occasional MB I sherd. The absence of LB sherds here is significant in dating the destruction, as these sherds are plentiful inside the town wall just to the S. This type of desecration is most unusual in Palestine. Only the lowest courses of the N wall near the NW corner of the town were *in situ* but they were similar to the section of the N wall excavated in 1957.

60. The town's W wall, which lies just to the S of this U-shaped city gate, presented several complications in interpretation (Pls. 102a; 110; 111). We were unable to solve all these problems because we did not have time to remove the massive rock pile above the extreme N section of the wall. Owing to the danger of rock slides, only the W face of the N unit could be uncovered and

---

[5] See sections on Byzantine history, §§77 ff.

that only to the average width of a single stone. This section was 11.5 m. long. Toward its S end a wide foundation course appeared, but the true face of the wall was shown by the courses above these foundation stones (Pl.111b).

61. At this point we picked up a new unit of the W wall coming up from the S, and here we could get the wall's complete width (Pl. 102a). It was a typical Bethel MB II B wall (3.5 m. wide) with semi-dressed stone on both faces and well-interlocked stones between. There was nothing like a loose fill between the dressed faces. Some water-eroded or sponge stone was used in the core, but occasionally it was semi-dressed and used on the face. The wall's maximum height (four or five courses) was only 1.75 m. The two units on the W wall were not in a direct line but approached one another from slightly different angles (Pl. 111a). One can only conjecture how the two units of the W wall were joined. Did the face of the N unit originally continue S alongside the S unit until they blended? Do the respective units represent two different periods of construction? Stone #31 complicates the problem for it continues the fine face of the S unit N on still a third angle. Only the future removal of the massive rock pile over the N unit can untangle this puzzle. At one point the N unit was four courses high; often it was only one course or so high. A revetment had been placed against the wall as shown by the nature of the fill against the wall and *ḥúwar* lines appear in the fill. Most prominent is a band some 30 cm. thick consisting of a major *ḥúwar* stripe 13–16 cm. thick with a thin one 3–6 cm. both above and below it. The normal chocolate-colored fill appeared between the stripes. Some of the lower fill was almost virgin soil with only a few rocks and those seldom over 10 cm. thick. The MB II B date of the wall is confirmed by the preservation of a house wall abutting on the E face of the S unit.[6] Including foundation, it was *c*. 75 cm. high and was a normal house wall (Pl. 110b). Then came a reconstruction marked by traces of a pavement and above it seven thin courses (1.1 m.) of very poor MB II work. The wall extended 140 cm. to the E, i.e. to the edge of the test pit. Sherds of MB II B storage jars were found here. The shaded area on the plan of the S unit represents Byzantine terrace walls. This work was done in 1960.

---

[6] This wall is not shown on the plan.

62. After we had completed work on the N wall in 1957, we asked the oldest men of the village if in their youth they had remembered seeing any walls like this. We were shown what appeared to be such a wall, built into the basement or animal quarters of a house on the W edge of the village and some distance down the hill from the W wall which had been discovered in 1927. Since the hill appeared to level off to the S, we turned our attention to the N. In this steep hillside there was only one small area that could be dug safely, and even it required caution because of the massive boundary walls perched above. In such terrain (Abu Tabar area) we were fortunate to get about 8 m. of the exterior face of an MB II B city wall (Pls. 94a; 98a; 99b). The 3.5 m. of height averaged six to eight courses. The longest stone was 1.25 m. The interior face could be reached only by tunneling and then only in the corner of one room inside the wall.

63. The oldest section of this wall was about 1 m. of well-laid lower courses at the N end. S of that point the wall consisted of a tower built against this older wall at a point where it had been breached (Pl. 99b). It is strange, however, that the repair did not also cover the breached area just N of it. The breached area not covered by the tower had been carelessly plugged. Although the stones were placed cross-wise in the wall, they were not interlocked, nor were smaller stones inserted into the wide spaces between the large stones. The patch was not dovetailed into the breach; only one stone of the tower overlapped the old wall and that by less than 20 cm. Not only was the tower masonry inferior to that of the N wall, but this repair was actually laid on fallen rock! The core of the repaired wall was very inferior to the core of the N wall. The corner of the tower, however, was excellent workmanship. The tower projected *c*. 1 m. beyond the earlier wall.

64. The tower was reinforced by a glacis, which was quite different from the glacis of the N wall, described above. The core of the fill against the W wall was of small loose stones, and there seemed to be a facing only of clay. Sherds found in the glacis were MB I and MB II, together with four unexpected sherds of Khirbet Kerak ware (EB III A) and one Neolithic sherd.

There was a guard room (412) in this MB II tower (Pl. 94a) which occupied 2.5 m. of the 5.75 m. width of the wall. There was a 10–20 cm.

thick burning at the bottom of its third course. The only way we could reach a house behind the wall was by tunneling through, where we fortunately located the corner of a room with a *ḥuwar* floor (413) and on it was a large store-jar with combed decoration, dated to MB II C. Since a wall of this room was bonded into the tower, the reconstruction cannot be later than MB II C. The floor level of this room, however, was only 40 cm. below the top of the tower so the original wall must be considerably earlier and may well be contemporary with the N and W walls already excavated.

65. This W wall of the town continued in use during LB times, for LB pottery was found in the guard room of the tower.[7] Several sherds of cooking pot rims of MB I ware were also found there, but they must have been washed down the hill into the room after the wall's destruction rather than being contemporary with the building of the tower room. After LB the history of the wall at this point is lost. The exact dating of this section of the town's W wall is uncertain but apparently it is MB II B in the earliest phase, with the repair dating in MB II C.

There was a large stone vat *c*. 1 m. in exterior diameter and 75 cm. in interior diameter, which rested half on the wall and half on adjacent soil (Pls. 94a; 98a). This accounted for the crack in the vat. There was a second vat of the same interior dimension but with 1.75 m. exterior diameter; it was made of several stones (Pls. 94a; 98a). These vats were built side by side. The Beitîn workmen suggested that they were wine or olive presses. There was no clue as to who did this work. The hillside around and above the vats consisted of debris (Iron I to Byzantine) washed down from above. No house walls were related to them. There were also some indications of burning above the city wall.

66. In 1960 we again asked to work in the yard of the Arab house where in 1957 we found the outer face of the W wall running through the basement. This time the owners gladly cooperated and we uncovered the inner face of the wall (Pl. 102b). It was approximately 3.5 m. wide with semi-dressed stones on the faces and with well-interlocked stones within. It was still standing 2.8 m. high. At the bottom of this city wall and on bedrock, a 65 cm. house wall five courses high appeared abutting on it. MB II B storage jars were on the floor. In the debris alongside the wall we had already found a Hellenistic lamp and cooking pot along with sherds from Iron II, Iron I, LB, and MB II. So this section of the W wall remained in use at least as late as Hellenistic times.

67. The first section of the W wall of the town had been discovered in 1927 and excavated in Area III in 1934, Pl. 11. It was an MB II C wall and therefore later than the W walls found in 1957 and 1960. In 1927 a test pit had been sunk to see whether Beitîn was correctly identified with Bethel.[8] Fortunately the test pit came down directly inside an old town wall, which was still standing *c*. 4 m. high. Unfortunately, however, no floor levels were found abutting on this wall or near it, and the wall had to be dated from sherds in the debris nearby, which favored an LB date. The 1934 campaign demonstrated that the wall was erected earlier, i.e. in the MB II C period. The inner face of the wall was then cleared for *c*. 15 m. (Pl. 13a, b). A trench dug along the outer side showed that the outer face had here been quarried away in Byzantine times. The town wall was formed of large, roughly squared blocks of stone 60–80 cm. in length. The workmanship was excellent and superior to everything else of its age and type previously excavated in Palestine. The closest parallel is the MB wall of Beth-zur, which was attributed to the very end of the period. This MB wall continued in use after the town's fall to the Israelites.

68. This MB wall seems to have been unmodified in LB. Early in Iron I, however, it was breached by the Israelites but repaired at once. The old MB stones were set on edge instead of being laid flat, as the art of fortification demanded (Pl. 13b). The succeeding history of the wall is as follows. Three silos were built against the town wall, all of which went down to bedrock (Pl. 13). The silo in 207 A (Pl. 13b) showed Persian pottery in the upper part and Iron I in the lower. Fourteen baskets consisting almost exclusively of sherds from Iron I store-jars with collared rims were taken from this site.[9] The silo in the angle of the city wall was roughly square in shape, utilizing the town wall for two of the sides. It was 2 m. deep, resting on bedrock, and the filling

---

[7] This was 1.2 m. below the top of the wall.

[8] *BASOR*, No. 29, pp. 9–11.

[9] There were also a few MB II and possibly some LB sherds.

consisted of black earth, stone, and potsherds of Iron I. At the bottom, however, there was a thin layer of light grey powder, hardened in places to lumps and containing carbonized grain. The third silo was roughly oval in shape and built against the town wall at a lower level than the last one, owing to the rapid slope of the terrain. It was 2.3 m. deep and the pottery was Hellenistic and Byzantine, except for three sherds of Iron I and Iron II at the very bottom. The roof of the silo was a continuation of the walls, which converged into the shape of a vault. These silos plus a roomful of store-jars testify that the old Canaanite town wall was also used by the Israelites and that the wall was well provisioned for a siege. Near the silos was a large beautifully worked wafer-like circular stone used as a cover. It must have been reused because its excellent workmanship is too good for Iron I.

69. Just S of the "square" silo, in the jog of the city wall, was a pavement of flat stone slabs resting upon debris. The pavement was about 50 cm. below the top of the town wall. Some of the E half of the pavement was covered with a layer of ashes and there were traces of carbonized wood. Fragments of goat bones were scattered about, brown from burning, some with particles of charred wood adhering. At the edge of the pavement was a large Iron I store-jar with collared rim, sunk about 40 cm. below the surface of the pavement; there were a few bones inside the jar. Someone had been cooking goat stew just as the city was stormed. All units of the W wall uncovered to date were on a slightly different alignment.

70. In 1960 we found the S wall of the MB II B town (Pl. 103c) looking S, W, and N. We dug a bench on the hillside above the spring just N of the Deir Diwân road (Pl. 112b), which spring furnishes Beitîn with its best drinking water although its flow is much less than that of the great spring, ʿAin el-Baḥr, across the road near the mosque. Just under the surface we found the foundation course of an irregularly aligned Byzantine wall 1.4 to 1.65 m. wide with a drain along the E side (Pls. 103c, phase A; 112b). This was originally c. 30 cm. wide but had been pressed out of shape by pressure of stones above it. There was also the stub of an excellent Roman wall 1.25 m. wide, phase B. The latter was still standing with four courses (70–80 cm.) of well-bonded semi-dressed stone ending in a door jamb. Below both walls and on a different line from either was a 1.25 m. Hellenistic wall, a part of which had been destroyed in the building of the Roman wall. The stones were c. 45 cm. high and had been laid on edge, well fitted together. Below it was a ḥuwar floor and then about 1 m. of debris, the lower half of which was sundried brick with some rock.

71. At the W edge of the pit less than 1 m. below ground level, the top of an Iron I house wall of crude construction appeared (Pl. 103c, looking W). It was a jumble of large and small stones arranged haphazardly but it still stood 1–1.5 m. high. A similar Iron I wall was on the S side of the pit. Below it was 1.75 m. of ash and brick, see plan. There is a possibility that the E wall of this Iron I room may be represented in a few stones aligned on the E side of the pit. The W wall was laid directly upon the ruins of an earlier massive MB II B town wall (Pls. 103c, looking W, 112a) and in the ashes of a heavy burning, mingled with burnt brick debris, which in some places was c. 1 m. thick. At the NW corner of the pit was a small section of Iron II wall above the Iron I wall. At a depth of 2.125 m. below ground level about half the area of the pit was covered with a flagstone pavement apparently laid late in LB and on it were c. 8 cm. of ashes. Immediately below it a good amount of LB painted pottery appeared.

72. An MB II B town wall appeared 1.8 m. below the surface in the W part of the pit and it continued to a point 6.1 m.[10] below the surface. The large triangular stone is the highest one *in situ* (Pls. 103c, looking W; 112a). The wall was of excellent MB II B masonry of very heavy stone construction similar to that found in the town's N and W walls. Some of the larger stones in the S and W faces of the wall (Pl. 103, phase C) were 90 × 50 cm., 60 × 75 cm., and 95 × 55 cm. The W wall in the pit formed a right angle with the town's S wall and was bonded into it. It was the wall of a tower or a gateway. The latter seems the more likely to judge from the large quantity of pottery removed from both the LB and the MB levels as well as the prominent LB pavement in the angle at 2.125 m., and a second pavement at 3.5 m. with a possible third floor at c. 5 m. below the surface.[11] The town wall had lost some of its outer facing,

---

[10] We went deeper than the point shown on the plan.

[11] Because of lack of time we were unable to locate the E wall of this suggested gateway.

but tunneling proved that the wall continued on to the E (not shown on drawing), giving its excavated lengths as 3.95 cm. Because of the steep hillside above us, we could not get the thickness of the town wall although we tunneled into the hill until we got a width of 2.5 m. Doubtless the wall here was the same in thickness as the N and W town walls (*c.* 3.5 m.).

73. At the corner where the two walls met and were bonded together, we went down to the lowest courses in the wall. We found them laid on large irregular stones which were probably a foundation course. Because of the cramped quarters at the bottom of the pit, it was impossible to go deeper without enlarging the whole test area but the approaching close of the campaign made this impossible. We did, however, find some MB II A pottery here. After removing dangerous fallen rock on the S face of the pit, we were able to trace the W or gateway (?) face of this MB wall to where it ended in an S-shaped bulge *c.* 3 m. from the town wall proper, indicating that the wall is broken beyond this point. Some stones were missing and some have toppled outward under pressure. This MB II B wall was reused by the LB population, but it was destroyed by Joshua. No casemate walls have yet been found anywhere at Beitîn.

74. The defenses of the MB II B town have now been uncovered at the NE and the NW gates and what appears to be part of the S gate. Two sections of the N wall and one of the S wall were excavated. Four units of the W wall of the MB II B town with the guard room of a W gate were exposed. We also found one unit of an MB II C wall on the W side of the city. The E wall probably lies beneath the N–S section of a newly paved street in the village, as suggested by test pits on either side of the road. We had planned to excavate the road in the 1960 campaign but because of the new pavement we had to abandon this project.

75. After Bethel was captured *c.* 1550 B.C., it lay abandoned until *c.* 1400 B.C. when the MB II walls were repaired and the town quickly became prosperous. The NW gate was never rebuilt. The town was captured by Joshua *c.* 1240–1235 B.C. The section of the S wall which we excavated was destroyed by the Israelites, and part of an Iron I house had been erected over this MB II B wall. The Israelites breached the W wall at one place, as already described, §68, but they repaired and reused it. These were the only sections of the town's walls excavated which showed any sign of change at the conquest. The next new major information on the walls was at the N where an upper section of it was destroyed at the town's capture about the middle of the sixth century B.C. By the time of Alexander the Great, the town was again prominent and fortified on the line of the old MB II B walls. At least as early as the Roman period the NE town gate was destroyed.

76. In 1957 test pits were sunk to find the S wall of the town at points where the older inhabitants reported having seen massive walls in their youth. The test pits brought to light only large buildings of Roman or Byzantine date. No trace of an ancient town wall was located. Just S of the spring near the S wall of the MB II B city, we uncovered the foundations of a large Roman tower (Pl. 95a). Four of the stones were over 1 m. in length. These foundations also extended under a new house which had just been erected immediately S of our test dig. This was doubtless the location of the S gate of the Roman period, for the sherds found here were predominantly Roman with only a little Hellenistic and Byzantine ware. Owing to the large modern paved area around the spring and the nearby Arab houses, we were unable to excavate further.

77. We found no major changes in Bethel's defenses from the Hyksos period onward until Byzantine times, when there was a radical shift. The Byzantines built their city gate a little E of the MB II B gate at the NE corner of Bethel (Pl. 95b). Three courses of both jambs of the gateway (*c.* 2 m.) show very plainly (Pl. 95b) and there were two courses of foundation beneath the pavement. The upper socket in which the gate turned and the deep square hole into which the bolt slid were still intact. Just inside the gate and on the W side there was a guard room. The wide threshold and one jamb were still in position.[12] The stone work between the jambs and the vault above is recent peasant reconstruction. The original gateway was approximately 4.4 m. wide on the outside of the gate and 3.3 m. wide on the inside. The street leading S from it was about 6.4 m. wide. For details see Pl. 120. The gate and the adjacent

---

[12] The socket hole for the original wide door was still in good condition. In a later period a much smaller door had been used and that door swung in the opposite direction, as shown by the new socket.

part of the street are the property of Abdullah Badran.

78. In 1934 this Byzantine gate area was tested to see whether the Byzantine wall was built on earlier Iron Age walls. No earlier constructions of any kind were found under the gate and at 1.25 m. we were down to virgin soil. There were a few MB II sherds immediately above the latter. Everything about this gateway demonstrated emergency construction. It may have been built as a quick defense against one of the tragic Samaritan revolts which devastated central Palestine in A.D. 484 or A.D. 529. This period of Samaritan history is well worth studying; a good résumé is found in J. A. Montgomery's work *The Samaritans*.[13] The old MB II B wall was the source of supply from which this hastily built Byzantine city wall was erected.

79. From this Byzantine gateway a wide street led S through the city, and modern Arab houses have been built along it, utilizing the ruins of the old house walls which lined both sides of the street. This is one of the best preserved Byzantine streets in Palestine. Most of the street is used by the present inhabitants for courtyards and sheep-folds. Only a narrow passageway is now left for pedestrians. It is such present-day reconstruction as this that enables one to see exactly how these ancient cities were rebuilt down through the centuries. The 1957 expedition surveyed this gateway and as much as possible of the street leading S from it which is still above ground, i.e., about 100 m., stopping only when modern houses blocked the street and heavy debris stopped work (Pl. 120).

80. A short stretch of the revetment of the E city wall in Byzantine times was found incorporated into the rear wall of a house owned by Safieh Id (Pl. 96b). The angle of the revetment is approximately 70 degrees and eight visible courses of stone extend for 2.88 m.

81. Although Bethel was no citadel of nature's making she was an integral part of the nation's defense system. She was located on the main N–S road where the most important E–W road in southern Palestine crossed. This made her an ideal supply depot especially for a Transjordanian campaign via Jericho. Later in the days of the Divided Kingdom, she was the extreme southern fortress of Israel. From Assyrian days on, she lost her military value. At the restoration she was the extreme northern city of the returning colonists. She figured in the Maccabaean campaign and was refortified by Bacchides. Rujm Abū ʿAmmâr on the ridge E of Beitîn is part of that work, §6. It was the last town captured by Vespasian before he left Palestine to become emperor of Rome. The final military episode that is recorded in Bethel's ruins is the Byzantine city wall just mentioned. No clue was found relative to the Islamic conquest.

---

[13] pp. 98–124, esp. 110 ff. and 114 ff.

CHAPTER IV

BETHEL IN THE CHALCOLITHIC, EARLY BRONZE, AND MIDDLE BRONZE AGES

82. In 1934 we dug to bedrock in about one-quarter of the area excavated.[1] Two baskets of Late Chalcolithic sherds were recovered from pockets of the virgin red earth.[2] These sherds were identified as Early Bronze in the preliminary report (*BASOR*). But later study proved them to be Late Chalcolithic similar to the sherds found at Tulûl Abû el-ʿAlâyiq near Old Testament Jericho, the next city SE of Bethel (*AASOR*, Vols. XXXII–XXXIII, Pls. 21–37). Although no building remains were found, these sherds came from nearly every locus, thus dating the site's earliest extended occupation to Late Chalcolithic *c*. 3200 B.C.

83. During the 1960 campaign when we dug through the floor of the town's NW gate, we learned that the walls of that gateway complex had been erected directly on those of a temple, and that this building, in turn, was built immediately upon a Canaanite mountain-top high place (Pls. 101; 105c; 106, 107c, d; 108). This high place was found when we excavated to bedrock directly inside the threshold of the town's gate (Pl. 107c). When this bedrock was being washed in preparation for photography, we saw that some of it was normal white limestone, some of it was stained red, and part of the rock surface was powdered as if it had been subjected to a very hot fire.

84. Bedrock was very irregular at this point, and the stains were concentrated on the higher ridges or ran down over the faces of the crevices in the rock. When the rock was wetted and then permitted to dry, the stains showed as light pink splotches. This led Taylor, who was in charge of the work at this point, to believe these dark spots splattered about over the cleared area were blood. Majid Bayyuk, a medical student from the American University of Beirut, who was on our staff, secured the chemicals to run the American Federal Bureau of Investigation (F.B.I.) test for blood. Acetic acid in benzidine activated by the addition of hydrogen peroxide to intensify color, and applied to the stains turned them blue or green and proved they were old blood. All the stained areas gave this reaction, but none was obtained from test areas of the white limestone. We next sank a test pit at the extreme W end of the gate corridor and another outside the NW corner of the gateway building in the large ḥúwar courtyard. Stains on the bedrock in both pits were tested and proved to be blood. The widest E–W bedrock area tested was *c*. 13 m.

85. Much of the bedrock was milk-white and powdery. Pieces broken from it felt much like soapstone. A number of spherical-shaped stones (10–20 cm.) found nearby had a similar texture. This suggested to us that a sacrificial fire had been built on part of the area. We felt sure we had found the old bare mountain top that the Canaanites had used as an open air sacrificial shrine to their god El. To increase the area of the high place open for study, we next cleared everything below the floor level of the entire E half of the N corridor of the gateway complex to bedrock.

86. The irregular surface of the mountain top rises quickly perpendicularly to a ledge whose nearly level surface slopes only gently to the SE (Pl. 106b). A test pit sunk at the W end of the corridor showed the ledge to be of approximately the same level there. We found some ashes above it and toward the W end of the cleared section, but otherwise the ledge gave no evidence of burning. Dark stained areas concentrated toward the center and W portion of the ledge gave positive blood reaction to the F.B.I. test while the smaller normal white areas of the rock gave negative reactions. The F.B.I. test identifies a stain as blood but does not differentiate between animal and human blood. We could not run the complicated test used to differentiate them. We therefore submitted bone fragments found in the debris above the rock's surface to the surgeons at the Lutheran Hospital on the Mount of Olives. They reported that none of the bones were human. Although Jordan had had a tragic three years'

---

[1] The figure 20 sq. m. in *BASOR*, No. 56, p. 3, is a printer's error. It should read 200 sq. m., see correction in *BASOR*, No. 57, p. 27.

[2] For the significant difference between red and black earth see *AASOR*, Vol. XVII, §17.

drought prior to 1960, the clay below the *ḥúwar* floor was very moist. This wet clay doubtless has been a factor in the preservation of the blood stains through the centuries.

87. Under the deep foundations of the floor of the gate corridor, in some areas 85 cm. thick, flints and sherds were found everywhere in great quantity. A variety of forms of flints were found, some of them of types used in butchering or scraping of skins. About 60% of the Chalcolithic sherds found in the extreme E end of the fill near the burned surface of the rock were from cooking pots. There were some EB sherds, but more were MB I representing a wider variety of forms. There were no MB II sherds. In a hollow immediately above bedrock and directly below the center of the E doorway of the MB I temple was a jar identified by Père de Vaux as Chalcolithic, (Pl. 81:1). Broken by pressure from the fill above, it contained two small animal bones, one the eye ridges of a skull, the other probably a femur fragment. Although the jar's position might lead to the speculation that it was a foundation sacrifice for the temple built above the high place, the jar is approximately 1500 years earlier than the temple and comes from the time of the original mountain-top shrine. Because the jar is dated at least as early as 3500 B.C., it establishes the earliest firmly dated human use of the Bethel high place as 3500 B.C. although the site was doubtless used much earlier.

88. The only actual installation in connection with this earliest place of sacrifice was a shallow elliptical pit or bin, 55 cm. long and 15 cm. deep (Pl. 107d). It was on a thin layer of debris just above bedrock and *c.* 50 cm. E of the ledge. It was made by standing thin slabs of limestone on edge in the ground. They averaged *c.* 1 cm. thick and 15 cm. in height. The thickest was 2 cm. and the highest 20 cm. There were a few stone slabs on the bottom of the bin, the longest being 22 cm. There were also some pieces of charcoal, the largest 2–5 cm. Some yellow ochre was nearby. The N wall of the temple was built directly over the N half of this bin.

89. This bare mountain-top was the ancient high place (Pl. 106b) where the Canaanites worshipped El, the chief god of the old Canaanite pantheon; and the city became one of his major shrines as witnessed by its name, Beth-el. The antiquity of the site and worship is shown by the continuing use of the name El whereas most Palestinian shrines preferred to honor the new god Baal. Although we did not discover Jeroboam's temple, we did find its ancestral high place. The area excavated at Bethel is too small for exact comparisons with the Jebusite high place at Jerusalem above which Solomon erected his temple, but the ledge at Bethel reminds one of that " rock " in Jerusalem. Although Jeroboam did not build a temple directly on the original Bethel site, the MB I population did, laying their pavement on the ledge itself and aligning their door directly to the E, see §§85–90, 96 ff. Furthermore there was what we believe to be a large *ḥúwar* paved *ḥaram* area just N of the gateway complex of the MB II B city (Pl. 107a), see §111. In the debris of various shaped rocks in a field NW of our work was a large stone that may have served as a *maṣṣebah* or sacred pillar.

90. About all that can be said at present of the history of Bethel in the Chalcolithic period is that the NW corner of the site was occupied by a large, well used open air sanctuary which can be dated at least as early as 3500 B.C. To the S of that high place and extending along what later became the W wall of the town, there was a settled occupation *c.* 3200 B.C. The village showed no signs of fortification nor could house walls be traced. This masonry was doubtless all used later in constructing the W wall of the MB II town. All the sherds found belonged to the category of " kitchen ware " and one can conjecture that the new settlers were poor.

91. The ridge E of Bethel was sacred soil, for in 1934 a *maṣṣebah* stood in a roughly squared socket at the nearest point on the ridgeline from the town. Unfortunately the farmers cleared the land of rocks for cultivation before the installation could be studied. On the same ridge S of the Deir Diwân road and near the W edge of the ridge, was an excellent table-shaped stone altar with cup marks. The rock was 2.5 m. long and 1 m. wide at one end and 2 m. at the other. The surface was semi-flat. One cup mark was very shallow, the other deeper. Many flints were strewn about at its base. Some were microlithic. L. Vestri reports another altar on this ridge, *Bibbia e Oriente* 7, 1965/1, pp. 27–31. Abraham's altar was somewhere on this long N–S ridge, which has a clear view of the Mt. of Olives. A few sherds belonging to the transition from EB to MB I were found at Burj Beitîn, the Byzantine identification of Abraham's altar, §29.

Early Bronze (EB)

92. During the 1954 campaign no EB floors or walls were discovered, but sherds of late EB, similar to the TBM " J " level, were found in the lowest debris at the old camp site in 305, 308, and 310. Similar sherds were found in test pits in the mosque area close to the springs. Some similar sherds had been washed down from the tell above, and their edges had been abraded in the process. The only new information added by the 1957 campaign was based on the finding of sherds still earlier than those found in 1954. One Neolithic sherd and four Khirbet Kerak sherds (EB III A) were found in the glacis of the W wall of the city. Sherds similar to those of the 1954 campaign were found in the glacis of the N wall as well as the W wall. During the 1960 campaign late EB sherds were also found in the fill of the MB I temple, and in the lowest debris in the NW corner of the town. No building remains were uncovered in any campaign.

The EB age at Bethel (c. 2400 B.C. to c. 2200 B.C.) may be summarized as follows. After the Chalcolithic period the site was abandoned. We could find no clue for the town's disappearance. Four Khirbet Kerak sherds were the only signs of life here until the very close of early EB. The town suddenly came to life showing occupation around the great spring in the mosque area and also in the NW section of Beitîn adjacent to the old high place. No building remains were found. Stones from these walls were doubtless used to construct the massive MB II fortifications in the same general area.

Middle Bronze I (MB I)

93. The EB occupation had ended c. 2200 B.C. and the site was unoccupied until c. the nineteenth century, when the first major urban installations still intact were found (Pl. 2). This marks the MB I town. Pottery found in the 1934 campaign was no longer in the red earth but in the black occupation soil. This MB I pottery was succinctly described in the preliminary report[3] as follows: " This ware is nearly all thin and free from grits, red-baked or creamy grey in color, with a creamy grey slip. It is decorated with vestigial folded ledge-handles and with elaborate bands of incised design, including horizontal bands, wavy bands, and rows of dots or dashes. This class of ware is identical with that from TBM level H, the Copper Age at Tell el-ʿAjjûl, the extensive parallel remains from Tell ed-Duweir, and Watzinger's *Spätkanaanitisch* at Jericho. It may be observed that the closest relations of our Bethel ware seem to be with Jericho and Tell el-ʿAjjûl, while the TBM pottery is more or less identical with that at Tell ed-Duweir. There can no longer be any question that this category of pottery continued in use over two centuries, roughly from the 21st to the end of the 19th century."

94. In the S part of Area I of the 1934 campaign sections of two parallel walls were found, see hatched lines on plan, Pl. 2a. Their fragmentary nature makes it uncertain whether they outlined a long chamber or were parts of different buildings. Their width (c. 80 cm.) shows substantial wall building. Furthermore, parts of these walls were incorporated into later constructions. In Area II no walls could be attributed to this phase; nor were any walls found in the 1954 or 1957 campaigns.

95. In the 1954 campaign only a few characteristic MB I sherds were found at the old camp site and in the test trenches of the mosque area. They were more numerous in the 1957 campaign, especially in the revetments. For a detailed study of this pottery see §§215 ff., and for other artifacts of MB I see Chapter XVI.

96. In 1960 we had better success with the MB I level. Immediately above the bedrock high place was an MB I building which we are identifying as a temple, Pls. 105c; 106; 108. Apparently the building was identical in size (11.35 × 3.5 m.) with the N corridor of the town's NW gateway for the lowest walls of the E half of the gateway, the only part excavated to bedrock, are laid directly upon the stubs of the temple wall, Pl. 108. A test pit sunk at the W end of the corridor showed the same fill with flints and MB I sherds as at the E end.

97. Both the N and S walls of the new structure (Pl. 108) were battered as can be seen on Pl. 101a, although the E wall with its door facing almost due E was perpendicular (Pls. 105c; 106a). The latter wall had a foundation course similar to the S wall. The striking difference between the E wall

---

[3] Cf. *BASOR*, No. 56, p. 4, and also *TBM*, §§20 and 23. See also G. E. Wright in *BASOR*, No. 71 (1938), pp. 27–34. Numerous sites with this pottery have been found by Nelson Glueck E of the Jordan and in the Negeb. Quantities of pottery have been excavated at Khirbet Kerak (Beth-yerah) at the SW end of the Sea of Galilee. The classical stratigraphic locus for caliciform pottery is now at Hamath where eight phases covering some four meters of depth, reflect an occupation c. 2100–1850 B.C.; see *BASOR*, No. 155, p. 32.

and the adjacent N and S walls makes us wonder if it is not the result of a repair of the E wall. The blocked doorway in the E wall was *c*. 1 m. wide and was well centered—1.1 m. to the N and 1.15 m. to the S (Pls. 105c; 106a). The course below the blocking formed the doorsill and established the floor level.

The N wall was still standing 2.25 m. above bedrock at the E end but only *c*. 1.5 m. above the ledge of bedrock which is farther W. The lowest course in the S wall was roughly squared stones rising to *c*. 30–45 cm. above the ledge and forming a foundation course, wide to the W but narrow to the E. Isolated flagstones (28, 24, etc.) doubtless belonged to this paved floor. Since the building is directly above the blood-stained and calcined high place, and since the flagstones at the W end of the excavation were virtually on bedrock, it seems natural to identify this building as a temple, especially in the light of the many cooking pot sherds and butchering flints found in the fill of this building. (The same kinds of flints and sherds were found both above and below the temple floor.) The far end of the room where the altar and cult objects should be found, has not as yet been excavated.

98. We found no exact clue to the date of the erection of the temple except that the town began at the very end of EB and reached quick prosperity in MB I, a prosperity leading us to believe the likely date for the temple's erection is early in MB I. The chief evidence for the date of its abandonment was the flints and sherds which were mostly MB I. No MB II sherds were found in the fill. Since the walls of the town's NW gate complex were laid directly on the temple walls except at the outer edge of the N jamb, where they were laid on debris, there must not have been a great lapse of time between the abandonment of the temple and the building of the gateway, §§52 ff. The temple may have been destroyed by fire since a scattering of ashes was found at two points. Perhaps an earthquake toppled it and the new builders used the stubs of the walls as foundations for the new NW gate.

The temple may have had a longer life than the town proper, for the temple seems to have remained in use longer than the adjacent house walls of the N area of the town. If so, the temple may have lived through the initial phase of MB II A, which is not true for the N area of Beitîn.

99. The MB I town is dated *c*. nineteenth century B.C. The temple described above certainly gives evidence of the town's importance. The few house walls that have been preserved belonged to substantial buildings and the change of soil from red earth to black shows that there was a much heavier population. The site was doubtless fortified although no defenses have yet been discovered *in situ*. This is not unexpected for the MB II builders would likely have used the stone of any former wall and the line of the town's two walls was probably somewhat similar at the N end of the site. The section of an MB II B building near the town wall was laid in the debris of MB I rocks similar to those used in the MB II B city wall.

Middle Bronze II A   (MB II A)

100. The N section of Bethel where we have been excavating houses has only a small amount of pottery corresponding to MB II A. No building installations were found unless, as suggested above, the temple continued in use during the first part of MB II A. Test pits sunk in the S, or built-up area of the town, might present a different story. MB II A sherds were being found in larger numbers at the base of the S wall of the MB II B town and we seemed to be reaching an MB II A level at the time we had to close the 1960 campaign and before we could excavate below that wall.

Middle Bronze II B and C   (MB II B and C)

101. In MB II B Bethel *c*. 1700–1650 reached the status of a fullgrown town. In contrast to the structures of preceding periods, MB II B Bethel had more strong, good buildings and excellent defenses, §§42 ff. The 1934 campaign provided clues to the town's importance in MB II B. Later excavations proved that the walls of the MB II B town were so strong they remained her major defense through most of the rest of Bethel's history.

102. More masonry and pottery were found in the MB II level uncovered in 1934 than in its MB I predecessor (Pl. 2). Two phases of MB II were proved by pottery differences, but no such distinction could be seen in the building remains in Area I. The earlier ceramic phase corresponded to the E level at TBM and is characterized by pottery covered with a highly burnished slip. The later phase must be put rather later than

TBM D on typological grounds. Its closest analogy is the latest MB occupation at Jericho, which may be dated about 1550 B.C.

103. The houses excavated tell the following story. At the extreme S edge of Area I the wall S of sub 56[4] belonged to MB II. This was shown not only by the large stones, which were quite different from the thin flat ones used in the LB constructions above it (Pls. 15a; 16a), but also by the greater width of the MB wall, 1.25 m. This contrast was especially clear where the narrower LB construction reused an MB wall.[5] The LB wall between 56 and 58 began at the S by reusing an MB II wall, whose big stones had been bonded into the S MB II wall, but the LB wall quickly changed to typically small flat stones of the first phase. In the S wall of 56 the same was true but it was difficult to show it on the plans; the S wall of 56 became less and less MB as it ran W, and more and more Iron I in construction, until the MB II wall disappeared completely just E of the LB partition wall separating 56 and 56W. Further W the wall was entirely rebuilt in Iron I and ran over an LB pavement. In sub 58S there was an MB II pavement with a raised ledge or border of stones on the N. This pavement fitted tightly against the edge of the MB wall. N of sub 63 we found a wall of heavy construction, 1 m. wide with a jagged stump of wall projecting from it at right angles at the NE, where it was broken away by the later N–S LB I wall. The short wall separating sub 51 and sub 52 was also MB II, and reused in LB. All house walls found in 1934 that were 1 m. or more in thickness, were either MB II or continuations of MB II, whereas the 70–80 cm. walls related to them were LB; the 1957 campaign, however, showed thinner MB walls in a poorer area. In sub 63 there was an MB II fireplace and floor level with MB II sherds below and MB plus LB sherds above. The rise of terrain here was so considerable that there must have been either steps or a ramp in it, but we found no clear trace of either in the excavated area.

104. In Area II all MB walls found were attributed to phase 2. The N and E walls of 161 and the W wall of 170 were reused in LB. The doorway between 173 and sub 170 had an MB and two LB phases.[6] Some LB pavement in 163 was laid above the N wall of MB 175 and 176. The new wall, number 173 in Pl. 17b, served as a socle with a flat surface on which a mud-brick wall had been erected. For cross sections of Areas I & II, see Pl. 10.

105. In the 1954 campaign (Pl. 85a), MB II was again represented by a stone socle (Pl. 88c) typical of those built to carry a brick wall (307–308).[7] The width of most of the wall was 107 cm. but in places it varied from 103 to 109 cm. This roughly approximated the width of the solid stone walls found in the MB phase of the 1934 campaign. A trench had been dug for the socle, and after the large stones had been laid in place, small stones were wedged in at the edges of the trench. Brick from the wall was in the debris above and beside the foundation. The use of brick in large buildings in the mountainous interior of Palestine was characteristic of the Hyksos period, and the pottery checked with that dating. It was predominantly MB II C rather than MB II B. There was a heavy burning above this socle, telling the story of the destruction of this building and marking the end of MB II. The only MB II floor levels are in 303 and 304; the former room had a *ḥúwar* floor and the latter a stone pavement. MB II sherds were found at these points, and in 305, 306, 309, and 310. The best MB pottery was found in 310. In 307 and 308 there was evidence of a fierce burning containing bricks and the remains of a collapsed roof under this 107 cm. wall. In the debris there was a broken toggle pin as well as MB II B sherds. Similar sherds were found between this level and bedrock.

106. Although there were some indications in the 1934 campaign that the latest MB town had been destroyed by fire, they were not impressive enough to justify a definite conclusion. In the 1954 campaign we did not find enough floor levels to settle this question. The 107 cm. wall was, however, destroyed by a fierce fire. There was a section of stone pavement still intact in 305 that probably dates from MB II B, since it was *c*. 50 cm.

---

[4] The prefix sub signifies that the locus is MB; the absence of sub in a corresponding locus number signifies LB.

[5] Some MB walls were reused or modified through two LB phases and on into Iron I.

[6] In the LB phase these same rooms are renumbered 165 and 170.

[7] Megiddo has similar constructions at this same time, although at Megiddo they also appeared in earlier levels. *Meg II*, Text, p. 97.

below the other building remains of MB II. A few EB sherds (hand-molded and combed) were found here and below it but no typical MB I sherds were discovered.

107. The best MB II installations were found during the 1957 campaign and they enabled us to work out the history of this phase of the town's occupation better than in the earlier campaigns, Pl. 91a, b. (Bench mark is 10.00 m.). MB II B pottery similar to the F. ware at TBM was found with the first phase of construction, Pl. 91a. These MB II house walls were built on or near bedrock and were contemporary with the erection of the town's N wall. (The surface of the bedrock was irregular.) There was an isolated wall in 406 at the E edge of the excavation, but the other walls were bonded together and formed one large house. One wall of 410 abutted on the town wall. It was six courses high and 70 cm. wide while two other walls nearby were 50 cm., Pl. 97a. There was a stone pavement laid on a *ḥúwar* bed in 410. This first major phase of construction was completely destroyed by fire at the 7.9 m. level. There had been an earlier partial burning in MB II B at 7.5 m.

108. The succeeding phase of construction (Pls. 91b, 98b) was MB II C. The pottery associated with it corresponded to D ware at TBM. It was built on a new plan, and the only earlier MB wall carried through into this phase was the isolated one at the extreme E edge of the excavations, which was used only in the first phase of MB II C. The new construction was excellent MB masonry. To be appreciated this masonry must be seen in photographs rather than in the plans, which are often complicated by LB repairs (Pl. 100a).

There were two phases in MB II C, separated by a very thick layer of ashes which at one place was 30–40 cm. deep. Only minor changes were introduced into the construction of the second phase. The dominant feature of both phases was a patrician house built around a courtyard (403–406) *c.* 8.6 m. × 4.25 m. in extent. There were two grain pits in the courtyard at pavement level, and a third grain pit in the pavement of 408, which was only *c.* 16 cm. higher. The courtyard (403–406) had been repaved. The remnants of a very solid pavement on its S side are 45 cm. higher than the earlier and thinner pavement along the N wall. There were two pavements in 408. The one on the plans is *c.* 40 cm. above the lower one which apparently belongs to the earlier courtyard pavement. This lower pavement continues under the S wall of LB 408. The pavement in 411 goes with the earlier courtyard.

109. The N wall of the courtyard was 1.4 m. wide and the S wall was approximately the same. In phase 2 the N wall was modified so that it was only about half as thick. Against it on the S side two piers stood on the projecting ledge left by the wider earlier wall. We do not know their use. Only the W section of the S wall of the courtyard was preserved. It ended in an excellent door jamb on the E but the other jamb was missing. Opposite, in the next phase, was an isolated pier. The W wall of the court was approximately 75 cm. wide with a doorway at each end (Pl. 100a). In the lower left corner of Pl. 98b, this wall is shown in the process of being excavated. Six courses were preserved, with one of the original doorsills which was a single stone. The central section of the upper two courses had been replaced by a very inferior LB repair. The W walls of 407 and 411 were also of excellent masonry and of about the thickness of the wall just mentioned. No walls separated 410 and 411 in the first phase. In the second, a wall between the rooms was extended N to abut on the town wall. This wall, including repairs, was preserved for about ten courses. Because of the cost of removing and replacing the heavy boundary walls along the N street of Beitîn, we excavated only this small area along the inner face of the town wall. Room 409 was not dug below the LB level.

110. The E wall of the courtyard marked the E boundary of the excavations. Grain pit No. 1 was built directly against it; it was bell-shaped with a maximum width of 1.5 m. and a height of 2 m. It was well preserved and contained charred material. The last of these successive MB houses was also burned, unlike the corresponding levels excavated in 1934 and 1954.

111. In the 1960 campaign, just N of the U-shaped gateway and abutting on it, we found the E and S walls of a large MB II B structure which we are tentatively calling a *ḥaram* area something like the Dome of the Rock esplanade at Jerusalem (Pls. 101; 107a; 120 upper left corner). Its E wall (3.5 m. long) was on the same alignment as that of the NW town gate. The wall was irregular in thickness but was approximately 1.25 m. wide. The doorway (later filled in) was 1 m. wide on the outside but wider inside. The S

jamb was nine[8] courses high. Just W of the door was some stone paving although most of the floor in the area was *ḥúwar*. We believe there is a blocked doorway at the N edge of the excavation. We were unable to locate the corresponding W wall of this large area although we went some distance beyond the W wall of the adjacent gate complex. At that point we found a second thin *ḥúwar* pavement 25 cm. above the former. We found no cross walls. The whole area was a single unit. We did not locate the N wall, although we dug a narrow test trench (Pl. 120, upper left hand corner) *c.* 6 m. N from the NW corner of the gateway complex so the area covered by this building was at least 28 × 5 m. We conjecture sections of fallen *ḥúwar* found upon the floor are accounted for by collapse of the roof of a colonnade built against the N wall of the gateway complex. The large size of this area suggests that it may have been an open courtyard used for worship after the abandonment of the temple which lies underneath the gateway just to the S. A test area still farther to the NW yielded what may have been a *maṣṣebah* or stone pillar located in a great mass of discarded rocks of all sizes. This courtyard was dated by its MB II B and C sherds to the same period as the adjacent NW gate, and the courtyard floor was on the same level as the bottom of the lowest step that leads up to the gate.

112. The lower section of the blocked doorway in the E wall of this courtyard area was a normal blocking but the upper section was a Byzantine grave 2.1 m. long (Pl. 101b).[9] Three well-dressed rectangular stones formed each side of the grave which was oriented E and W. It was covered by five thin irregular slabs with small stones which filled the cracks.

The contents were unusual. Dr. T. Canaan identified one skeleton as that of a man *c.* 40 years of age, taller than usual for that time and well built. The teeth were in excellent condition. The bones gave no clue to reason of death. There was also the lower half of the skeleton of a man *c.* 21 years old, and what was apparently his lower jaw, plus another lower jaw of a still younger person. In digging this grave through the talus slope of the rock fill over the city gate, the Byzantine diggers had been troubled by rock slides and the grave was at the bottom of a wide funnel-shaped hole. The funnel-shaped area, however, was not refilled with the rocks removed from it but with earth which contained MB II sherds which sifted into the grave through the cracks between the irregular stone coverings. There was a sort of rock pavement a little above the grave apparently to discourage hyenas and jackals. The doorway leading E out of this large *ḥúwar* courtyard went into another *ḥúwar*-paved area but the wall of this new room was thin—only a single stone wide. This room could not be traced more than three stones when it disappeared under a paved street of modern Beitîn.

113. When we first began looking for the W wall near the NW gate, three test pits were sunk. One pit came down directly over the corner of one of the finest masonry structures yet excavated from early Palestine, see NE room in Pl. 103b. It was made of fine semi-dressed limestone and the section uncovered looks much like the corner of an expensive city church today (Pl. 109a). It had very heavy foundations and a drain at floor level.[10] The S wall still stands 3.7 m. high, without counting the three foundation courses (1.12 m.) which were laid in debris containing MB I sherds and a few from the end of EB. The debris was chiefly massive stones perhaps from the town's earliest wall. They prevented us reaching bedrock in this pit. The building was probably a palace or temple. The latter identification is based on the pottery found outside the building: a pottery cult stand (patterned after an Egyptian column), a pottery bull's leg and fragments of two jars with serpent motifs. There were two baskets of animal bones with a heavy proportion of beef bones. Inside the building was a jar handle with serpent motif. The structure was in use from MB II B through much of Iron II. The N wall was later than the original building but went with the three floors found in the room. The first, a stone pavement later patched with *ḥúwar*, was 2.8 m. below the surface of the ground. LB sherds including bil-bils, milk bowls and painted ware were found on the floor. Iron II and Iron I

---

[8] Two courses were accidentally removed from this pier before the surveyor got them on the section, and also three courses from the S pier.

[9] See elevation drawing of gateway. Intrusion rocks above city gateway may have belonged to a Turkish tower.

[10] The building was laid on debris containing many rough field stones but large bracing rocks were leaning against the foundation courses. We had to break them with sledge hammers before we could go deeper.

sherds had been found earlier but recent farmers had destroyed the floor levels.

114. At 3.2 m. sections of a second stone and *ḥúwar* floor (8–10 cm.) and ashes were found. At 3.45 m. there was a thinner *ḥúwar* floor and below it painted pottery in ashes. At 3.62 m. the top of the outer face of a wall appeared at the E edge of the pit. It passed under the N wall. Its foundation was at 4.77 m. which is just below the W and S walls proper but above the foundations of the W and S walls. The E wall passed under the N wall. MB pottery was found below the last painted pottery mentioned. (Some MB had appeared with LB a little earlier, especially store-jars.) A large MB II bowl and serpent handles were found at approximately 3.9 m., i.e. the bottom of the W and the S walls proper. This is apparently the floor level of the temple as shown by the drain hole and the beginning of the foundation courses. We did not excavate the NW room except to discover that its S wall, #9 and #10, was not earlier than Iron II and may be even later. The wall separating the SW and SE room was Iron II as the sherds of that period were found in the wall when it was removed. It went down only to 1.86 m. In the N end of the SW room a *ḥúwar* floor was found at 2.23 m. under the surface, and associated with it at 2.1 m. was a very shallow wall (one or two courses only) in the S end of the room. (This wall is not on the plan.) At 2.78 m. a *ḥúwar* floor appeared in both the SW and SE rooms. Apparently at that time the area was a single room. This level was approximately the same as the stone pavement in the NE room. Beneath this floor in the SW and the SE rooms were at least 15 cm. of ashes. No more floor levels appeared in the area but considerable ashes appeared in the debris from 3.10 to 3.75 m. At approximately the top of the foundation courses of the MB II building we found ashes mixed with animal bones, especially beef, a trumpet foot bowl, a V-shaped drinking cup and cult stand, a pottery bull's leg and MB II sherds. Inside the building, i.e. the NE room, at the same level, were the serpent handle and the trumpet-foot bowl. Three other MB II houses were found and they abutted on the town's W wall, §§61, 64, 66.

115. The collective evidence of the four campaigns shows that Bethel was occupied at least in part during MB II A and the whole site was continuously inhabited throughout MB II B and C. The town continued to increase in importance until its fall at the very end of MB II C. The town's defenses which were erected at the beginning of MB II B were so effective that they served Bethel through most of her long history. The best buildings found were the temple just described and the patrician house of the 1957 campaign. The section of the town excavated along the N wall showed traces of enormous fires within MB II B as well as one at its close. In MB II C the same area produced an excellent patrician house. About halfway through the period it was destroyed by a great conflagration but was quickly rebuilt with little change of plan, suggesting that there was no change of population. This building was again destroyed by fire at the close of MB II C, but no similar destruction was found in any of the other areas we excavated. MB II Bethel was a well-to-do community center for local peasants and also a good trading center for semi-nomads, since it was located at a major crossing of N–S and E–W roads. Although MB did produce some excellent masonry the peak of the town's material culture was to come in LB. MB II pottery is treated in Chapter XI and other artifacts in Chapter XVI.

CHAPTER V

BETHEL IN THE LATE BRONZE AGE

116. Bethel seems to have been unoccupied in LB I. The absence of bichrome ware need not be significant, in view of the small amount of such pottery from this general period. But native wares of this LB I period are also missing at Beitîn. It was *c.* 1400 B.C. before the town returned to life. The most striking discovery of the 1934 campaign was a well-built LB II town subdivided into two phases of construction (Pl. 3). The earlier phase was characterized by base-ring and white-slip (wishbone-handled) sherds, and quantities of native painted pottery.[1] The second phase had much less painted pottery and imported ware and was dated in the thirteenth century.

117. The masonry of LB II, particularly of phase 1, was so good that Père Vincent, who had seen more excavations in Palestine than anyone else, declared that it was the finest domestic construction of this age and area that he had ever seen. It was characterized by fine pavements of well-laid flagstones (Pls. 17a, b; 20a) as well as by even commoner floors of thick plaster (Pl. 19a, b). There were superimposed pavements of the two phases with a layer of debris between. There were also examples of two layers of pavements, the upper being a repair of the lower but both belonging to the second phase. Still more remarkable were skillfully constructed stone drains (Pls. 18a; 19a, b). In one place there were two superimposed drains (Pl. 19b).

118. All of Area I was occupied by a single large structure[2] (Pls. 3a; 22a). Around a central court, rooms were grouped in one or two rows. The original building, which dates very late in LB I or early in LB II was destroyed by fire. The reconstruction in LB II followed the original ground plan, varying from it only in minor details. All of 53E, 53W, 54, and 55 was a courtyard. The large square stone in the middle had some practical household use and was not a building element. The pavements in sub 41, 51, 52, and 56W were all of phase 1. Paving stones seemed a little thinner in phase 1 than in phase 2. Locus 52 seems to have been used as a toilet, since there was a roughly rounded pit in the broken virgin rock below the LB foundations, and this contained exclusively LB pottery. There was a *ḥúwar* floor in 62. Along the N side of 63 and also along the small spur wall to the W there was a stone bench, with a jar set in it; the bench continued to the corner of the room as a bin (see plan). The MB walls which were reused in this structure have been described in detail in §§103 ff. Sometime in the latter part of phase 1, the doorway between 51 and 52 was carefully blocked up; presumably at the same time a door was opened in the now destroyed S wall of 52. The blocking up of the doorway between 51 and 60 may be attributed to the same time, since the pavement of 60 in phase 2 was higher than it and was built against it. (The original doorsill here had been a single well-dressed stone.)

The first phase of LB occupation was destroyed by fire in the late fourteenth or early thirteenth century, after Mycenaean pottery had come into use. The burning was especially clear in 59 and 58E, where the maximum thickness was about 0.25 m. Nowhere did it come below a point just above the LB foundations. Between the higher and lower pavements in 51 were remains of this severe conflagration. The rebuilding of this structure followed the general plan of phase 1. In phase 2, however, the wall between 62 and 61 no longer abutted on the wall just W of it but was now bonded in. The doorway in the E wall of 61 was blocked up. The closest parallel to this building is at Megiddo,[3] where the MB city introduced this ground plan but LB improved it. Ta'anach, Beth-shemesh and Gezer also have examples; see *TBM II*, §72.

---

[1] "About a score of base-ring and white-slip sherds were found nearly all belonging to the first phase. Four Mycenaean sherds were unfortunately doubtful, though one comes from a prevailing early context, while two others seem also to belong to the earlier phase. The unpainted local ware of both phases is so fine in texture, for the most part (even in the case of storejars!), that it cannot be confused with the Middle Bronze II, and is as different as possible from Iron I; the closest resemblance in paste is with Hellenistic ware." *BASOR*, No. 56, p. 6.

[2] Part of this building has not yet been excavated.

[3] *Meg II*, Text, Fig. 381, is the best parallel but see also Figs. 382–83. Fig. 380 is MB.

119. Most of the walls in Area II belong to phase 2; the shaded ones (Pl. 3) are phase 1 (Pls. 15a, b; 16a, b). The oldest wall was found in 162 where it lay just as it was after destruction by an earthquake (Pl. 14a). The approximate thickness of its 19 courses, counting from the top down is as follows: 13, 10, 8, 11, 10–12, 8–12, 10, 9, 14, 12, 12, 14, 20, 15 (?), 15, 8, 12, 12, 12 or *c.* 2.28 m. of the original height of 2.5 (?) m. The best preserved room was 161 where the N and E walls were phases 1 and 2, but most of the S and all of the W walls were phase 2 only.[4] In the middle of the N wall there was apparently a broad entrance gate of phase 1. It was blocked by a wall forming the S jamb of a door connecting 159 and 160, (Pl. 18b). This doorway was 1.3 m. wide and the probable threshold of phase 1 was 60 cm. below the W jamb and 30 cm. below the E jamb. On the S we have a phase 2 wall with the W jamb 1 m. inside of the SE corner. The major features in 159 and 160 were the drainage conduits, §§117, 120 (Pls. 18a; 19a, b). The thickness of the plaster floors in these rooms could be easily checked; it varied from 13 to 20 cm., averaging about 15 to 16 cm. except over the covering slabs of the drain and over the threshold, where it was thin. In 171 the rebuilders cleared out the area to a lower level, reusing the earliest pavement. The doorway from 165 to 170 was longest in use, showing three phases; MB II and both phases of LB. 166 contained a table made of two massive stone slabs about 1 m. each in length, set on three stone piers and built against the S wall. Jars were found just NE of it. This was a phase 1 installation, but a stone mortar in the same room and a stamped jar handle (spiral design) belonged to the later phase. Under 167 there is a conspicuous burned level of phase 1; otherwise this burning is not very prominent in Area II. There is a cave under 167.

120. A special feature of Area II was the drainage system. The skilled manner in which LB builders handled drainage problems is illustrated by the two conduits which cross one another in 160 (Pl. 19a). The lower drain, where it emerged from the SW corner of 159, had a height of 29 cm. At the crossing its top was lowered so that the height became only 18 cm. and it continued E at that height. It then ran directly under the upper drain, converging with the latter under the E wall of 159. At a point 1 m. farther E in 160 where one drain was built directly on the other, utilizing the roof slab of the lower as the floor slab of the upper, the height of the lower again averaged 25 cm. The lower drain had been rebuilt. These drains led to a major storm sewer which discharged its water outside the town wall. The fine conduit of 169 is a continuation of that in 160 and 164 and belongs to phase 2. In 164 the floor slabs and S sides are phase 1. The roof slabs and N wall are phase 2. The conduit that runs diagonally across 170 is probably of phase 1. The floors and covers of the drains were thin slabs and the floor slabs were often skillfully fitted together. The stones in the side walls were long and narrow and much thicker. For cross sections of Areas I and II see Pl. 10.

121. Since no digging has been done in the more heavily populated S part of the *tell* it is too early yet to assume that Bethel, like Tell Beit Mirsim and Jericho, was unoccupied during LB I. The masonry of the LB levels excavated demands an early date in LB II, for many MB walls in the various areas studied in the different campaigns were reused in LB. On the other hand, some time must have elapsed after the MB phase, for in the same building were found complexes in which some MB walls were reused and others in which they were not. Oddly enough, a new LB wall was at times built above and just to one side of a good MB wall. Apparently sufficient time had elapsed to allow some wind and water debris to conceal some walls but not others. Naturally we must allow builders some leeway in following familiar plans regardless of surface remains. Somewhere *c.* 1400 B.C. seems to be a likely date for resettlement.

122. The 1954 campaign found a badly destroyed and comparatively thin LB level (Pl. 85) except in 305 where there was a complete olive oil factory §124, (Pl. 89c, d). The most prominent and earliest building feature was in locus 307 where there was a short section of a 1.47 m. wall built on the 1.07 m. wall of MB II (Pl. 88b) which had been destroyed by a conflagration. The new wall ran at a slightly different angle from that of the earlier one. Both are placed on the MB plans so their relationship can be seen more easily. The LB wall was apparently built, at least in part, of stone taken from the town wall. The largest stone used in the wall was 1.4 m. long, *c.* 50 cm. wide and 25 cm. thick. It had been carelessly laid on an irregular bed so that it cracked under the

---

[4] The N and E walls are above MB walls.

weight of the wall above it. The highest section of the wall still standing intact was *c.* 50 cm., but sections of fallen wall were found as far N as we dug. This 1.47 m. wall was almost twice as wide as those of the LB house walls found in the 1934 campaign, except where they had reused MB walls. The details of the building of which it may have formed the N wall are in unexcavated terrain. It was in use through both phases of LB and was destroyed in an intense conflagration; even *mizzi* rocks were cracked. Some Iron I buildings to the N were erected immediately over the irregular debris of the fallen wall. Other adjacent Iron I houses were constructed of large stones collected from the fallen wall.

123. Indeed, LB house walls found in 1954, seem to have served as quarries for Iron I houses. Only fragmentary walls were left and these seem to be the last phase of LB II. Several dressed stones appeared as part of the E wall of 302 (which is just above 303) and there was one course of stone in the N wall of 304 (with a burning above it). There was also a single course of good interlocking foundation stones just under the Iron I wall to the N of 307 and 308. It ran at a different angle, however, from the Iron I wall above it. It was covered with ashes and just N of 303 was the calcined remains of a heavy burning above the stone pavement. (This pavement appears in large extent on the Iron I level plans.) In 307 there was a *ḥuwar* floor N of the 40 cm. wall.

124. The olive-oil factory in 305 was a rewarding feature of the 1954 work in LB (Pl. 89c, d). It consisted of three installations. There was a large stone mortar used to crush the olives, with the major exterior dimension *c.* 1 m. and the major interior dimension *c.* two-thirds as much. Its interior depth was just over 50 cm.[5] The crushed olives were removed from this mortar to a much larger plaster vat somewhat rectangular in shape. Here water was added so that the best olive oil could rise to the surface. The vat was approximately 2 m. × 1 m. with a roughly spherical basin 60 cm. deep except for a slightly lower small collecting basin, which made possible easy removal of the last of the oil. Between the two vats stood a stone bench on which baskets of olives could be placed for sorting and small jars could be placed to be filled with oil. The floor must have been beaten earth, for we were unable to find its exact level. *Zebâr*, the refuse left after the process was completed, was found in considerable quantity N of the factory. This installation seems to have been used in both phases of LB but was discarded by the invading Israelites, who built a house wall directly over the N end of the plaster vat, cracking it.

125. The LB installations found in 1957 were very disappointing (Pl. 92a). The level was thin (30 cm.) and the two phases easily distinguished in 1934 could not be differentiated here. Furthermore, the masonry was so poor it seemed unrelated to other LB installations. At this time and from now on this area of the town seems to have been a slum. The E walls of 407 and 411 were reused from MB but those two rooms were now a single long narrow room. (The wall on the plans is an MB one.) The new thinner W wall of the room, however, was just E of the former MB wall and the new builders were apparently unaware of its existence. A new wall 50–60 cm. wide appeared above the center of the old courtyard, dividing it into 404 and 405. A wall 85 cm. wide formed the E wall of both rooms. Also each room had a stone pavement at the same level although only a little of 405 was preserved. (It does not show on the plans.) There was a new S wall and a stone pavement in 408. The surface level of the stones of the wavy pavement in 403 varies as much as 22 cm. so the pavement might be LB or Iron I. It appears on the Iron I plans. A short stub wall 1 m. long and 30 cm. wide jutted into 406 from the unexcavated area to the E. The LB level was destroyed by an intense fire according to evidence found over all the area dug.

126. The only important building found in the 1960 campaign was the reused MB II B structure which we tentatively identified as a temple. It was only a common house in LB. Its sherds included bil-bils, milk bowls and other painted ware. The area outside the S wall of the city near the spring produced a good variety of local LB painted and foreign sherds.

127. The 1934 campaign had demonstrated that the finest masonry in Bethel's entire history was in LB (especially the first phase of construction) and it also represented the best example of LB work yet found anywhere in Palestine. Only the MB II B temple at Bethel is comparable. The building activity of MB II C which produced the

---

[5] The dotted lines in the drawings of the vats show the relative size of the interiors in relationship to the surface openings.

fine patrician house beside the N city wall was only anticipatory of the still better architecture of LB. Not only the size of the houses but especially the excellent pavements and drainage systems testify to the wealth of the owners. The finds in these buildings tell the same story and are in striking contrast to the succeeding Israelite phase. The first phase of LB II is better than the second although the latter is not too far behind. The destruction of the first town was not cataclysmic. Phase 2 shows that the people who reoccupied the city rebuilt it on almost identical lines. There is no definite clue as to who destroyed the first LB town. There was an earthquake in phase 1 which left its mark in 162 (Pl. 14a). The last LB town was utterly destroyed by a great conflagration and the succeeding Israelite town was strikingly different. Because of the importance of these circumstances it is treated in detail in Chapter X. Pottery is treated in Chapter XI and other artifacts in Chapter XVI.

CHAPTER VI

Bethel in Iron I

128. Sometime about 1240–1235 B.C. the second phase of LB II was destroyed by a tremendous conflagration (Pls. 14b; 24b) which left abundant traces wherever we excavated but which raged with peculiar violence in Area II of the 1934 dig. Burnings of phases 1 and 2 in Iron I are also seen in Pl. 24b. Masonry of phases 1 and 2 above LB appear in Pl. 21b. Phases 1, 2, and 3 appear in Pl. 21a, and all four phases are seen in Pl. 25b. In Area II about 20 m. around the S and W edges of the excavations were filled to an average depth of 1.5 m. with a solid mass of black and ash-filled earth, fallen brick now burned red, and charred and splintered debris. We have never seen indications of a more destructive conflagration in any other Palestinian excavation, a fact which suggests extensive use of wood in Iron I construction at Bethel. The cultural break between LB and Iron I was also more complete than in any other similar break at Bethel except between the sixth and fourth century levels. When we consider the masonry, building-plans, pottery and other remains of the following three phases, which were in all these respects homogeneous, it is clear that we cannot throw a bridge across the break. We are compelled to identify it with the Israelite conquest. For the relation of this historic phase to Joshua's conquest, see §§185 ff.

129. The Iron I levels excavated in 1934 (Pls. 4 and 5) were of high significance, since both their masonry and pottery were sufficiently well preserved to enable us to work out a detailed picture. The cultural drop from LB to Iron I was quite extraordinary, as may be seen by contrasting the crude masonry of Iron I which succeeded the fine LB building that occupied all of Area I (Pl. 22a). Iron I craftsmanship in masonry and in ceramics deteriorated from phase 1 through phase 3 which marks the lowest point in workmanship. All four masonry phases are seen in Pl. 25b. Phase four marks the transition from the judges to the monarchy.

130. The most characteristic feature of Iron I masonry at Bethel was the use of piers. The lower third of a wall was often built of continuous masonry, above which the wall was strengthened by piers of massive stone at more or less regular intervals. A single stone might be set on end or large rocks were stacked one on top of another to form piers (Pls. 22a, b; 23a; 24a; 25a). The piers were located about 1 m. apart, running from less than 1 m. to 1.5 m. The stones used in the piers were of all kinds, from well cut LB lintels and thresholds (foreground of Pl. 22b), to massive undressed native rock, weathered and pitted.[1] The largest number of preserved "courses" in the face of a pier was seven, although the upper five were so thin that their total height was less than that of the two stones of average size below them. Four or five "courses" were usually preserved in a pier. Most piers tapered from the foundations upward (Pl. 22a) but a few reversed the order, tapering from the top downward. Smaller and larger stones were used in the same pier, and occasionally two or three courses of small stones were found between average-sized stones. Field stones filled the interstices between piers (Pl. 25a). The roof beams apparently rested directly on these piers but none was found *in situ*. A large charred beam and smaller wood fragments of a roof were found in 35.

131. By the time of phase 4, the pier technique was no longer in use. It was replaced by a new style of masonry employing extremely small stones neatly fitted together. So far as we know this type of masonry has not been found elsewhere in Palestine. Perhaps it is a Philistine influence as there was a deposit of approximately the same date containing Philistine pottery. In one place the wall was 1 m. wide. The style of architecture was short-lived and *c.* the tenth century B.C. masonry had returned to the normal Palestine pattern and was improving rapidly. On the plans, phases 1 and 3 are shaded.

132. The best of the earliest Iron I construction in 1934 was seen in Area I where the old LB walls were often reused (Pls. 21a, b; 23a). There is nothing exceptionally significant in these rooms except the following: a large charred ceiling beam and smaller fragments of charred timber were

---

[1] These latter piers were often twice as massive as the rest.

found in 35. There were two ovens in 38 with "riders" for saddle querns near by and a pit in sub 43S. In Area II the Iron I walls were not so closely related to the preceding LB ones. For Iron I data in Area III see §§68–69. The most intense burning of phase 1 was in sub 32 where below the pavement there was a 40 cm. layer characterized by white and black ashes with fragments of calcined stone and charred wood. There was another intense burning in 50. The most striking burning of phase 2 appeared in sub 32, where above the broken-collared store-jars on the pavement there were 90 cm. of burning—ashes, calcined stones, and red baked earth. The burning was 70 cm. deep in 50. The E wall of 147 was found just as it had collapsed at the end of phase 2 (Pl. 25b). Phases 3 and 4 were differentiated primarily by pottery rather than by architectural features, although in places phase 4 used the odd small stone building technique described above. For cross sections of Areas I and II, see Pl. 10. The phase-by-phase history of the houses found in the 1954 campaign was more easily differentiated and therefore that area of Bethel will be studied in more detail.

133. The 1954 excavations were highly rewarding in the Iron I levels (Pls. 86, 87a). Burnings and rebuildings made it easy to differentiate the first three building phases of Iron I, even more so than in the 1934 campaign. All three corresponded to TBM B_1 although some B_2 appeared in phase 3. The fourth phase in both campaigns included TBM B_{2-3}. Masonry with small stones was found only in the 1934 campaign.

Major factors of construction found in 1954 differed greatly from those of the areas dug in 1934. The stones of the great fallen LB wall served as a quarry for the building material of phase 1. The large size of these rocks made the building of normal house walls easy.[2] The pier construction so common in the Iron I areas of 1934 did not appear in the new excavations, although features superficially resembling piers were discovered. They appeared in the N wall of 307 and 308. Although of approximately normal size, they were built of small stones forming door jambs separating several doorways between rooms to the N and to the S. It is important to note that neither the parallel wall to the N nor the parallel wall to the S contained any pier construction of any kind. About the time of the transition from Iron I to Iron II (ninth century) the construction technique was changed. Flat semi-dressed stones were used instead of the old field stones, and these were now interlocked for strength.[3]

134. The first building erected after the great burning at the end of LB was represented by 310[4] and 312.[5] The other rooms of that building lie to the W in unexcavated terrain. The constructions to the E abut on this structure. Under 309 and 312 the massive LB fallen wall had been left just as it fell; the Iron I walls were built over it. Loci 303, 305, and 309 have the same continuing S wall which was built in part upon the one good foundation course left from the LB house wall (Pl. 88b), which continued into the unexcavated area to the E. The Iron I wall, however, ran at a slightly different angle and was narrower than the foundation. The N wall of 305 was laid directly over the large LB olive-oil vat which was cracked by its weight (Pl. 88a). At that time 303 and 305 comprised a single room. The lower courses and doorsill of the N wall of 301 may belong to this first phase.

135. The first intact floor levels (303–305 and 308) averaged *c.* 33 cm. above the lowest level of their wall foundations, a figure somewhat similar to the 1934 findings. In 303–305 there were ashes above a *ḥúwar* floor and there was an oven in the SW corner of 303.[6] In 308 ashes lay over a wavy pavement made of stones of various sizes. In 310 there was intense burning at the same level as the floors of these other rooms; in 301 and 302 the rocks were split by the heat of the fire and some were completely calcined. The debris of this first phase of Iron I averaged about 50 cm. in depth, whereas that of the second phase was about 35 cm. and of the third about 30 cm. The burning that marked the end of phase 1 probably came

---

[2] Masonry of the 2nd and 3rd phases was much inferior to that of phase 1.

[3] These units were leaning badly out of line and some upper courses had to be removed for safety.

[4] The S and W walls on the plans, however, show the 3rd phase of Iron I.

[5] All corners of 312 were bonded except the lower courses in the SW corner; even here, however, the upper courses were bonded. The NW corner was rounded, the lower courses more so than the upper one that shows on the plan. This room had no door. It was full of pottery and apparently served for storage. Probably one of its walls was low and this room was only a "pantry" off one of the adjacent rooms.

[6] This oven does not appear on the plan.

not later than early in the twelfth century. The pottery was similar to TBM B₁.

136. The second building phase of Iron I followed at once and probably lasted through most of the twelfth century. A new S wall (Pl. 89a) for 304, 307, 308, and 310 was built, extending almost the entire length of our excavation area.[7] It ended in a doorway near the center of 310. Small and large stones had been mixed together indiscriminately throughout the wall and no foundations had been laid. Actually the lowest courses followed the irregular contour of the debris in which they were laid. A still cruder wall appeared between 301 and 302. The W wall of 308 was also rebuilt.[8] There may well have been a wall between 304 and 307 because the former had a stone pavement and the latter only a *ḥúwar* floor. (The wall appearing on the plans at this point is a phase 3 wall.) The E wall of 305 was laid over a thick burned layer with bricks and plaster intermingled. Although this looks like a pier construction, it is not like anything else found in Iron I, phase 1. We did not tear it down to get construction details since we had located our datum point here. It seemed, however, to have consisted of fragments of walls at the lower level and rock debris above it. In the debris of the floor of 305 was a collared store-jar typical of central Palestine before the fall of Shiloh. At this time 307 and 308 formed a single room with a common *ḥúwar* floor. In the NE corner of 307 was an oven. In the following phase 3 a very crude wall was built directly over this oven. There was also an oven in the NW corner of 304. This second phase of Iron I like the first, was destroyed by fire; it is predominantly from the twelfth century B.C. The pottery was still like TBM B₁ but was the poorest quality found on the site.

137. The third phase of Iron I was still dominated by this poor pottery so characteristic of the period of the Judges, but occasionally sherds of a new form of store-jar appeared along with hand burnishing on the best ware, i.e. TBM B₂. This phase seemed to cover the earlier half of the eleventh century, and perhaps came down to *c.* 1025 B.C. or even later.[9] New walls now appeared on the S and W of 310 and the room shrank in size. Both walls were laid over ashes and the W wall leaned heavily westward. A new wall, which appeared in the S of 311, was probably of phase 3. The new E wall of 304[10] was laid directly in the ashes which covered the stone floor of the earlier phase; it had broken the floor by its weight. In the SE corner of the room two stones of the E wall of the earlier phase 2 were still *in situ*, forming an angle different from that of the new wall. The W wall of 304 (Pl. 89b) was also new and it is of particular interest because of a standing LB *maṣṣebah* which had been incorporated into it.[11] The wall was of very crude work. There were no foundations and the wall was laid directly across an oven of the preceding phase 2. Stones of all sizes were mixed together in the wall. Nevertheless it continued in use well down into the Iron II period. The use of this sacred Canaanite stone as an ordinary building stone shows that in Bethel, at least, the Israelites had no superstitious dread of Canaanite cult objects. Their use of such items was strictly utilitarian; it was just another building stone. There was now a stone pavement in 309. A retaining wall, swinging on a wide arc toward the north, appeared N of 303, 305, and 309. It was built above the earlier N walls and leaned N against debris. N of this retaining wall the area was full of small stones and stone chips, mixed with ash and dirt, which looks like the debris left after the destruction of a heavy stone wall, such as a tower.

138. The general house-plan of the 1954 area seemed to have become fixed in this third phase of Iron I. There were only minor changes from now on in Iron I and Iron II walls.[12]

139. The 1954 campaign was so productive that we were able to divide the fourth phase of 1934 into two distinct sub-phases. Each of these two new phases found in 1954 left more debris than either of the two preceding phases. Phase 4a was marked by pottery changes but not by corresponding architectural differences or burnings. The poorer pottery of the first three phases had disappeared quickly; the volume of burnished ware increased greatly and new forms appeared. The pottery picture here corresponded to the

---

[7] The E–W wall appearing in 314 may have been the S wall of these rooms in phase 1.

[8] In phase 1 it had continued farther southward and its lower courses still appeared under the new S wall. In phase 2, it only abutted on this new S wall. Also the new stones used in phase 2 were smaller than those in the earlier courses.

[9] For the relationship of Bethel to the fall of Shiloh, see §197.

[10] This is also the E wall of 303.

[11] The door at the S end of the wall is phase 4.

[12] In the 1934 campaign the Iron I house plans were not carried across into Iron II as was the case in the 1954 area.

B_{2-3} phase of TBM pottery. The late eleventh and early tenth century is the probable dating for the 4a phase of Iron I.

140. The 4b building phase came in the late tenth century. The pottery of phase 4b is classified as B_3 at TBM. Iron I ceramic ware was then at its best. In phase 4a there was some realignment of walls. In phase 3, 307 and 308 had been a single room but in phase 4a a partition wall divided the area. A new wall appeared in 311 and a stone pavement in 308. There was an oven in 304 and the floor level connected with it extended over the E wall of phase 3. There was apparently a doorway between 303 and 305 but at this point there was only 30–40 cm. of *nârî* limestone debris. The transition from Iron I to Iron II can be told only by the pottery and other finds.

141. The Iron I buildings of 1957, like those of LB had little to add to the Beitîn story (Pl. 92b). The peasants in search of good stones for building their new boundary walls had disturbed much of the Iron I levels. We could not, therefore, differentiate sub-phases of Iron I as in the earlier two expeditions. The best we could do was to confirm some of the building features of earlier digs. In 403, 404, 405, and 408 there was a light burning shortly after Joshua's conquest, probably at the end of phase 1. In 404 there was a stone pavement (Pl. 100b) probably going with phase 2; the pavement in 405 is probably earlier. There was a stone pavement in 403 which may be LB or Iron I. There was a second higher pavement in 403 which was definitely Iron I. The wall between 403 and 404 was much wider than that between 403 and 405. The wall of 403 was in two phases; the lower one 20 cm. to the E of the higher section. The only reused walls of LB were the E walls of 404, 405, and 411. The E wall of 407 in Iron I was thinner than in LB, and its E face was about 20 cm. W of the former E face. Most of these walls of Iron I were either a single stone in width; or if wider, they were rocks of all sizes crudely thrown together. The walls varied in width from 40–80 cm. Masonry containing piers, so characteristic of Iron I in Palestine, was found only once —between 404 and 405 (Pl. 100b). Two piers were semi-dressed and one was rough stone. The tallest was 90 cm. The N wall of 401 and 402 was made of heavy stones doubtless obtained from a breach in the town wall nearby. The other walls of these rooms incorporated many of the large stones in the lower course, but there were smaller stones above them and the latter are shown on the plans. The odd shape of 401 plus its closeness to the town wall seems to imply its use as a silo. It was immediately above LB. The long narrow 402 also must have been a storage area. The E end of 405 seems to have served as a bin behind a low 30 cm. wall. The bottom of the bin is the same as the level of the floor. The walls of 403, with the exception of reused LB on the W, were the poorest found; their faces were unbelievably irregular.

142. The most interesting new feature of Iron I was the N doorway of 409, where long LB stone slabs of differing thickness were reused as door jambs (Pl. 99a). The thin slab on one side was sunk below the doorsill and a heavy slab opposite it rested on top of a smaller stone. The thin door jamb had originally served as a normal LB doorsill. Unfortunately the lintel was missing. 406 was a street. The Iron I objects found in 1957 were less varied and poorer in quality than those of other years. The only Iron I buildings of interest in the 1960 campaign were a house above the old S city wall, §71, one near the *madâfeh*, §148, and what appeared to have been a bakery near the W city wall. Here were a number of whole and broken querns, riders, and pestles plus a great quantity of sherds from storage-jars. Below it was a thick LB burning. Iron I houses of the 1960 campaign are discussed in §71.

143. A summary of the campaigns at Beitîn shows that Iron I had four phases, the first three of which were characterized by changing patterns of building though the pottery remained similar, predominantly TBM B_1. In phase 4 there was a change in ceramics only, i.e. TBM B_{2-3} and especially B_3. Burnings separated each of the first three phases but not the fourth. Masonry patterns were fairly similar in the early phases but the work deteriorated through phase 3. The most unique masonry pattern of Iron I was the pier construction. At one point in phase 4 came a new masonry pattern—the use of extremely small stones neatly dovetailed together; but it did not become common nor last long. In some instances the house plans of phase 3 remained intact well into Iron II but in other areas Iron II had a new layout. The Israelite history of Bethel in Iron I is so detailed that it requires a special section for its elucidation, see §§185 ff. For ceramics see Chapter XII, and for other artifacts, see Chapter XVI.

CHAPTER VII

BETHEL IN IRON II

144. None of the campaigns at Bethel added any significant new information about Iron II masonry. The best type of construction in the early period was somewhat anticipatory of the header-stretcher technique which reached its finest workmanship in the days of Jeroboam II. The poorest type of walls found were the partition ones only a single stone wide. One marvels how these walls ever stood. One significant item in all phases of Iron II was the absence of cisterns. To date we have not found a cistern in either Iron I or II. This is a striking tribute to the town's rich natural water supply. Cisterns did not appear until the Roman period.

145. Practically all Iron II walls studied in Areas I and II in 1934 were on different alignments from those of Iron I (Pl. 6). Iron II walls were missing in more than half of Area I (Pl. 28b) but those remaining were of at least two building phases. The Hellenistic builders sank such deep foundations that they often destroyed much Iron II masonry. Although there was not as much Iron II masonry as we might have liked, fortunately, we found quantities of pottery representing the divided monarchy up to the fall of Samaria. In Area II we had continuous walls of this period (Pl. 27a), and in the E and SE parts there were several successive phases of construction. The walls of 145 were raised in part three times, so that the uppermost part preserved is more than 3 m. above the original foundations (Pl. 25a, upper right). The first phases show in Pl. 27b. Here the pottery made more exact dating possible, so that the lowest phase may be dated in the tenth–ninth centuries, the middle phase may be referred to the eighth and the top phase represents the latest occupation before the town's destruction in the latter part of the sixth century. There were at least two phases of occupation in 139, 142, and 143. The emphasis in Area II was on small rectangular rooms; a more normal type of room complex appeared in Area I; but neither reproduced the typical better-class house of Iron II. A close parallel to these houses seems to be TBM, Pl. 3, NW 23 and the lower rooms just S of it. 150 was a large plaster-lined grain pit containing mostly Iron I and early Iron II sherds. The most important architectural find in this period was in the E section of Area I, where we seemed to have reached the edge of the town, since there was a massive quoin construction suggesting a tower, with some relatively heavy walls S of it. The tower was erected in the eighth century (to judge from the homogeneous pottery) and rebuilt in the seventh. On the inside of the W wall of 47, the Iron II foundation was at the same level as outside, where it was near bedrock. Three phases of construction were clearly seen in the W face of W wall of 47, respectively about 60, 60, and 80 cm. (from top down) in height. For cross sections of Areas I and II see Pl. 10. Pl. 28a shows objects in an Iron II house.

146. In the 1954 campaign only the earlier phases of Iron II building installations were found (Pl. 86b). The farmers had destroyed the upper levels when they dug up this field in search of stones for building their boundary walls. As noted in the preceding chapter, the general house plan of this "campsite" area seemed to be fixed in phase 3 of Iron I and there were only minor changes from that point through Iron II. In 302 there seems to have been a local burning at about the transition into Iron II.[1] A new stone floor was put in and that pavement passed over the former E wall of the room. At the transition to Iron II, 305 had a *ḥuwar* floor but later there seems to have been some pavement in the doorway between 303 and 305.[2] There was a heavy stone pavement in 310. At this time 303 and 304 were the same room. There is a possibility that a tower of the town wall may have been located in 306 and 311.

147. In 1957 we found that sections of many Iron I walls were reused in Iron II (Pl. 92b). The following, however, were new in Iron II: the E wall of 402, the N wall of 411 and the top three wide-angling courses of the E wall of 408. The

---

[1] The only other ash layer was in 304, but it was about 40 cm. higher.

[2] Because of uncertainty about the pavement it is not drawn on the plans.

peasants' work in digging for stones to use in boundary walls had made any detailed study of Iron II history impossible, although there was a wide variety of broken Iron II pottery in the debris. The only house walls of this period found in 1960 were in the former MB II B temple and the rooms beside it in pit 5, §113.

148. The largest building on the site of Beitîn is the *maḍâfeh, ʿIllîyet esh-Sheik*. We dug alongside the outer W wall of the first story to see if the building was erected on earlier walls (Pl. 94b). We found that the building had no previous history. A deep V-shaped trench had been dug and a stone footing 30–40 cm. wider than the wall had been laid as the foundation for the wall proper. More smaller stones were used in the lower courses than in those above ground. The most interesting feature of this test area was an Iron II wall which had fallen during an earthquake. There was also an Iron II wall *c*. 1.20 m. in width—which is wide for that period. Just below the Iron II level a large, almost intact, storejar of Iron I was found *in situ*.

149. During the Divided Monarchy there was a large population at Bethel until about the time of the capture of Samaria when Bethel also was destroyed. Manufacturing seems to have been less important at Bethel than at TBM, where virtually the whole town was devoted to weaving and dyeing in the latter part of the Divided Monarchy. We found only isolated loom weights at Bethel and a single stone dye vat.[3] Any new prosperity of Israelite Bethel must have been in large part due to its cultic significance. Amos testifies to its wealth, and Jeroboam's shrine with its golden calf was a royal sanctuary. Although the search for Jeroboam's temple was a major reason for our work at Bethel, we did not find any clues to its location, §§202–205. It seems likely that it must be above the two major springs of the town and under the present village, or on the hill E of Bethel. If it was S of the town it was destroyed by the great Byzantine reservoir. Jeroboam's blasphemy, however, is especially flagrant to anyone who works day by day in old Bethel, for the Mount of Olives constitutes the major feature of Bethel's S horizon; and of course, beyond the Mount of Olives lay Yahweh's true Holy Temple.

150. We had expected to discover that the Assyrians had destroyed the town and this was confirmed by the absence of pottery finds, §206. The town was probably captured after Hoshea's revolt in 724 B.C.[4] It seems to have remained unoccupied until near the end of the Assyrian period when the shrine was revived to play a part in the religious life of the foreigners whom the Assyrians had brought into this section of the Northern Kingdom.[5] We purchased from the natives a small conoid seal (Fig. 1), with its typical Babylonian motif of the worship of the god Marduk, §206, and this testifies to the influence of the Babylonian colonists or the later Babylonian officials. After the destruction of the Assyrian Empire, Josiah added Bethel to his territory *c*. 622 B.C. Apparently, he destroyed only the cult installations, for we discovered no burning at this time in the areas where we worked. Bethel was not destroyed at the time of Jerusalem's extinction in 587 B.C. and even the murder of Gedaliah does not seem to have brought any Babylonian vengeance on Bethel, §206. Apparently the Babylonians, like the Assyrians, had incorporated it into the Samaria province. The town finally met its total destruction somewhere about the time that Palestine was passing from Babylonian to Persian domination. It may have been destroyed in the third year of Nabonidus (553 B.C.) when a general rebellion is attested for Syria and North Arabia; or it may have been wiped out during the chaotic quest of kingship which followed the death of Cambyses and culminated in the reign of Darius. Somewhere between 553 and 521 B.C. Bethel was completely destroyed.[6] The history covered by the Iron II period is treated in detail in Chapter X. Pottery is treated in Chapter XII, and other artifacts in Chapter XVI.

---

[3] This was above ground in a field E of Area I, Pl. 12.

[4] Cf. especially W. F. Albright's *Archaeology and the Religion of Israel*, (1942), pp. 172 f., and *TBM III* (1943), p. 145.

[5] II Kings 17:24 ff.

[6] The preliminary 1934 report reads as follows: "In part the pottery from the burned houses is identical with that from the latest strata of TBM, Beth-shemesh and other towns of Judah which were destroyed by the Chaldaeans shortly before 587 B.C. In part the types here represented were new to us. . . . A destruction somewhat later in the sixth century is not, however, excluded, and would perhaps explain some strange features about the pottery." As the 1934 pottery was worked up for publication in 1935 it became steadily clearer that the pottery from the burned Iron II houses is to be dated well after the destruction of TBM, Beth-shemesh, Lachish, Gibeah, and other towns of Judah by the Chaldaeans. This conclusion has been confirmed by subsequent excavations and study.

CHAPTER VIII

BETHEL IN THE PERSIAN AND HELLENISTIC PERIODS

151. The destruction of Iron II Bethel had been long in coming but when it did arrive it was catastrophic. Its exact history is lost during the transition years that marked the end of Babylon's power and the early days of the Persian empire. There was, however, only a brief period when the site was abandoned. Under the comparative security of the Persian empire, settlement tended to disregard earlier fortified areas and to develop in valleys and on low exposed spurs. Bethel would scarcely have been an exception, so we may safely assume that occupation was concentrated around the springs S of our main excavations. It was therefore, not surprising that we have no direct evidence for good houses in Areas I and II antedating the late fourth century B.C. Ezra 2:28 lists the joint populations of Bethel and Ai as only 223 and Neh. 7:32 as only 123, §208. Little remained of the first reoccupation except fragments of rude walls, probably sheepfolds. The large stones used in them came from upper courses of the former city wall.

152. Area II of the 1934 campaign showed continuous phases of building from the fourth century B.C. to Roman times (Pls. 7–10; 29a, b). By the time of Alexander the Great, Bethel was back on its feet, and its population continued to grow throughout the Hellenistic, Roman, and Byzantine periods. Coins come to the assistance of the ceramist in Hellenistic Bethel and enable us to distinguish three phases. The first was from Alexander the Great to the Maccabees, climaxing in Bacchides' refortification of the city, §210. The second phase was the Maccabaean period itself and the third was Hellenistic-Roman, closing with the capture of the city by Vespasian in A.D. 69. In 1954, 1957, and 1960, no definite Hellenistic levels could be differentiated, for the peasants had destroyed these walls in working their fields and digging for building stone. The story of the Hellenistic period was essentially the story of Area II; Area I had only scanty remains. Good house planning with large rooms had come in. Phase 1 had more heavy walls than the two later phases; seven walls were over 1 m. in width and some were as wide as 1.35 m. The deep Hellenistic foundations had destroyed the houses of late Persian times.

153. The Hellenistic date of phase 1 Pl. 29a is certain, for a newly minted coin of Alexander the Great was found to one side and below the drain in 122.[1] The drain was preserved for only a little over 5 m. It emerged under the upper NE edge of Area II into Locus 122. It was under the plaster floor (level 97.04) of Hellenistic phase 1, with flat stone cover at level 96.82 and adjacent floor of a drain at 96.63. Below it was a fill, under which at 96.17, was the top of a sixth century pottery deposit. The Alexander coin probably fell into the ditch dug for laying the drain. At all events, it shows that the plaster floor of Hellenistic phase 1 was later than *c.* 330 B.C. In the SW corner of 122 the foundations of the S wall (phase 2) were set in the drain of phase 1 which it completely obstructed. There was also the spout of a Greek lamp which is dated approximately to Alexander's period. Greek sherds from the fourth or early third century B.C. also date two houses N of the city wall. Ten Ptolemaic coins, all dating between 285 and 182 B.C., and four coins of Antiochus Epiphanes (175–164 B.C.), illustrate the first Hellenistic phase, though only a few of them were actually found in stratified deposits. For Rhodian jar handles, see Chapter XIV, footnote 6. Three Ptolemaic coins of silver (dated 211–200 B.C.) were found with four similar Seleucid coins (dated 136–130 B.C.) over the ruined wall of phase 3 between 108 and 109, and under Byzantine foundations, proving that phase 3 came to an end here before the hoard in question was buried (after 130 B.C.). Under the odd fragments of a wall in the N part of 108 was a typical folded-over lamp of the third–second century B.C. Sub 117 contained an interesting installation the exact use of which is uncertain. The SE corner of the room was plastered and to the W there was a bin made by two stone slabs each 50 cm. long,

---

[1] The drain was utilized in connection with a pottery factory; and the prepared potter's clay which we found there was used at once by Bethel's modern potter in the manufacturing of 1934 wares.

40 cm. high and 15 cm. wide, running N and S. There was a 25 cm. space just to the W and beyond that was a second bin or trough, which ran E and W. The stones to the S were in length 35, 35, and 37 cm.; those to the N were 40, 35, and 35 cm. The trough itself was 20 cm. in diameter. There was a little pavement W of 124 in which intact jars were found. There was no burning to mark the end of phase 1, but since it came in the early Maccabaean period it is presumably related to Bacchides' fortification of the town about 160 B.C. The statement by Josephus (*Ant.* XIII, 1, 3) that Bacchides fortified Bethel, without apparently having had to storm the town, would explain the absence of any traces of burning and the presence of extensive indications of rebuilding. To this period belong, probably, the ruins of a large tower,[2] Rujm Abū ʿAmmâr, on the ridge NE of Bethel which may have served as part of the Seleucid system of communications by fire signals, §6.

154. Phase 2 is illustrated by four coins of Antiochus Sidetes (137–129 B.C.) together with some Seleucid coins of uncertain date, and by 18 coins of the Jewish kings, all between 125 and *c.* 70 B.C.[3] A number of phase 2 walls were built directly on phase 1 walls.[4] Thinner walls give one of the clues of the transition to phase 2. All the old walls of 126 appeared in 101 but were thinner. The thick end wall of 125 became a thin wall in 109. Walls reused without change were the former ones in 110, 111, and 113, and the wall S of 124 and 128. The W wall of 109 was the old W wall of 125 except for doorways at either end. Old 122 and 125 were completely changed; the S wall of 106 was laid in the former drain and a new W wall with a door was built farther to the W. This room was well dated by a Rhodian jar handle. 127 was a grain pit of this period.

155. The shift from phase 2 to 3 gives no archaeological clues to the Roman conquest of Palestine. The town continued its normal pattern and growth in the areas dug. There was an absence of Herodian coins but this was most likely accidental, as normal Herodian pottery appeared everywhere. From Archelaus on there were plenty of coins down to the capture by Vespasian in A.D. 69. In the 1957 campaign, however, Roman military action was seen in the destruction of the NE city gate and the razing of the town wall just W of it, §§48, 211. (The 1954 campaign, like the 1934 one, had found no evidence of military conquest.)

156. In 1934 the 3rd or Hellenistic-Roman phase added new walls in 113 and 121, some of which were reminiscent of the wide walls of phase 1. 110 now had a W wall and 115 and 114 were cut off from 108. 112 now had new E and N walls. The wall of 105 was also of this third phase as were the heavy stones forming the E wall of 106. The E wall of 101 was also of phase 3, as confirmed by two large store-jars and a cooking pot found *in situ* there. There was a clay floor of this phase in 116. Area I had nothing to add to the constructional features of the Hellenistic period. The end of this transition period came with the town's surrender to Vespasian. For cross sections of Areas I and II, see Pl. 10.

157. In Area III there were two massive walls at the N end belonging to two structures, contemporaneous but independent of one another (Pl. 11). The N wall stood to a height of 1.8 m. and was 1.05 m. wide; and its S face was built of courses of large roughly hewn stones, which alternated with courses of smaller flat stones. This alternation was fairly regular in the upper part of the wall. The inner or N face, which was perhaps not intended to be seen, was formed of small stones. The inside of the wall was of rubble held together with lime mortar. The wall was masked at the N by a very rough wall built against it. The S wall (1.7 m. high) was of a somewhat similar construction except that it consisted of two walls running parallel to one another without any space between. This double wall, the components of which are almost equally wide (65 and 70 cm.) had an over-all width of 1.35 m. corresponding to that of the N wall. The S wall also had only one well cared-for face, towards 204, showing that the latter was originally a free space or street between the outer faces of two buildings. The E wall of 204 was very clearly a later partition wall, not bonded in at either end, nor does it interfere with the further course of the main walls eastward. The construction is much poorer than that of the main walls although the two upper courses are solidly built of well-cut blocks of soft *nârî* limestone, probably reused from some important building. This wall was

---

[2] Its size is similar to a tower excavated at New Testament Jericho and which dates to the same period.

[3] Only five of the Jewish coins were in stratigraphic context.

[4] Phase 2 is shaded on the plans.

standing to the height of 1.5 m. but the W wall of 204 had only a single course left. All walls were Hellenistic. The fragmentary walls of 208 and 209 were probably also Hellenistic, although much farther down the slope. 202 was limited on the W by an irregular wall one course high and on the S by a narrow twisted wall four or five courses high. The top of the second wall was on a lower level than the bottom of the first; the area slopes rapidly down to the valley. Both walls apparently form a fence for the Byzantine graveyard in this locus, §164.

158. The 1954 and 1960 campaigns were unable to find Hellenistic house walls within the town, although in 1960 some were found outside it, §174. In 1957 we found a 6 m. section of the N–S wall of a Hellenistic house when cutting a trench through the Hyksos glacis (Pl. 93b). There was also a 2 m. section on an E–W wall of the same house a short distance N of where the N–S wall disappeared. The earliest imported Greek sherds in connection with this wall were fourth or early third century.

159. The Hellenistic period saw Bethel again a prosperous town. The houses were well built although inferior to those of the LB period. Pottery was predominantly native ware with only a small amount of imports. For Hellenistic pottery see Chapter XIV and for other artifacts, Chapter XVI.

CHAPTER IX

BETHEL IN THE ROMAN AND BYZANTINE PERIODS

160. It is impossible to work out a detailed archaeological history of the Roman period because the Beitîn people had destroyed almost all Roman house walls in cultivating their orchards. Coins, historical and literary references date the first Roman phase from Pompey to Vespasian. The second phase closed with Constantine the Great. There was no evidence that Pompey's attack on Jerusalem caused any temporary abandonment of the city. There was no sign of any burning or destruction. There was an absence of Herodian coins but this was most likely accidental, because there was a normal amount of Herodian pottery. From Archelaus until the town's capture by Vespasian in A.D. 69, there were plenty of coins.

161. The only definite signs of Roman conquest were found in 1957 at the NE gate of the city and the adjacent N wall, §§48 ff. Time permitted only preliminary study at this point. The NE gate was destroyed almost down to pavement level and the few sherds found were colorless and could be dated no closer than sometime between Pompey and Vespasian. Just W of the gate the upper section of the N wall had been removed and a Roman house built over the lower courses, §§173–174. There were no signs of burning in the Roman rooms still standing inside the walls. Josephus tells of Vespasian's occupation of Bethel in A.D. 69. He established a Roman garrison in the town and then left Palestine to become emperor.[1] In the second revolt Hadrian's officers also placed a garrison here in order to capture Jewish fugitives.[2] In each case that part of the population which had fled before the Romans took the town seems to have returned shortly afterwards. The excellent water supply demanded a repopulation of the site. Bethel continued to grow throughout the Roman and Byzantine periods, reaching its maximum population and prosperity in Byzantine times.[3]

162. The following loci contained both Roman and Byzantine material (Pl. 9). In Area I of 1934, the pit in 8 was Roman and held a procurator coin from Nero's time along with Byzantine sherds. The pit in 6 contained sherds from the second–third centuries A.D. and one coin each of the following: John Hyrcanus, Caponius, and the First Revolt. A Tyrian silver drachma was found under the pavement of 6. An early Roman lamp was found in the wall between 6 and 8. The other constructions in Area I were Byzantine.

The most interesting feature in Area I was a cellar (3E) with a staircase running W from the corner. The well-dressed stone pier at the end of the free wall is unusual. It is a finely dressed column about 1.5 m. in height and approximately 37 cm. square. The floor was covered with broken two-handled Byzantine store-jars with ribbed surfaces. The rest of the cellar contained the mixed debris of a fill. (The W section of Area II was also a fill whose sherds covered all periods of the city's history from EB to Byzantine.) The ground immediately under the beaten earth floor of this basement yielded chiefly Iron II and Iron I sherds. Under the stairway itself, Hellenistic sherds were found. The W wall of 18 was a later addition to the building although well bonded into the earlier structure. The new foundations were much shallower.[4] The silo in 2 was the latest addition. There was a fine niche still intact in 8. The walls of 12 and 13 were in good *opus spicatum*.

163. The only new room in Area II was 117. Room 101 had new walls to the E and W. The grain pit in it, although Byzantine, also contained Arabic sherds of the eighth–ninth centuries; so 101 may be the installation which remained longest in use. Two Herod Agrippa coins were found under the wall between 101 and 109. The bottoms of eleven large store-jars were found *in situ* in 117. There was a Byzantine pavement in 116. For cross sections of Areas I and II, see Pl. 10.

---

[1] Josephus, B. J., IV: ix, 9.

[2] Lama, R., ii, 3 (Midrash Ekhah).

[3] This Byzantine period ran from about A.D. 350 through the eighth century.

[4] What was apparently the stone pavement of a street passed the front of this house; but since it was uncertain, it was not put on the plans.

164. Along the E edge of Area III (Pl. 11) there was a small Byzantine cemetery. Grave A was that of a woman and contained one iron ring, two small glass vases, three glass bracelets, two large octagonal sequins, and 19 beads. Grave B was not opened. C held the body of a very tall man, but there were no objects. D was that of a child and contained two anklets, two beads and an iron ring 7 cm. in diameter which rested on the chest of the skeleton. E contained a child's skeleton and 12 beads. F contained a child's skeleton with two anklets. In G was the skeleton of a woman and two beads. In 1960 we found a Byzantine intrusion grave in an MB II B ḥaram area §112. This grave was the only Byzantine find except for a great number of sherds.

165. On June 15, 1954, we began work on a completely new area in Beitîn,[5] digging in the two small fields just E of the mosque (Pls. 87b; 90a-d). We chose this site on the chance that Jeroboam's temple might be in that general area, since holy places often have a tendency to remain in a common area. No evidence of the temple was found here. In the field farther from the mosque, part of a large gateway still above ground, 339–340, had attracted our attention. No walls of any significance were found S of the gate, only some pavement (340) in front of the E gate-jamb. Since the Beitîn–Deir Diwân road was immediately N of the gateway, excavation in that direction was impossible. The gateway itself (N of 339–340) was of good workmanship but only a little of it remained. The ground had been turned over to a considerable depth by cultivators, so that the sherds were in reverse order:[6] surface to 80 cm. were more Roman than Byzantine (plus a little Iron I). The next 70 cm. were more Byzantine than Roman. The reason for this phenomenon was before us every day as we drove into Bethel. One farm was being completely turned over to a depth of more than a meter. Across the field was a string of workmen turning the land upside down. If one had not seen the day laborers actually at work one would have thought that some American road building machine had done the work—so deep and so accurate was the trench. Since similar pottery in great quantity was being found in the field beside the mosque, and walls were negligible, we abandoned work near the gateway at a 2 m. depth and concentrated on the field alongside of the mosque.

166. In the surface debris of these fields were six architectural units from the Byzantine church (Pls. 79:7–12; 90d). Another find was the cone or lower unit of a large Roman mill of the type used in a large bakery (Pl. 79:13; 90d). The height of the cone was 43 cm. and the diameter of the base was 55 cm. Another architectural unit was found in 1957. For details see §§365, 368.

167. We began work in the field alongside of the mosque, starting at the extreme S edge of the field where a house wall was still *in situ* above the ground and where a sixth century Byzantine store-jar was soon uncovered (Pl. 74:7). This area was predominantly cisterns, with four large ones close together (Pl. 87b). Until this time no cisterns had been found in Bethel. The exceptionally fine water supply just S of the town had made them unnecessary until the heavy increase in population during the Roman period. In Byzantine times an even more prolific population demanded still more water and an enormous reservoir was built in the valley just S of the city. It was 314 × 217 feet.[7] Edward Robinson spoke of it as one of the largest reservoirs he had seen in the whole country. It now serves as the threshing floor of the village.

168. The cistern 331–332 was excavated as deeply as was safe (Pl. 90a). A second cistern 333 C (Pl. 87b), whose S and E walls ran beyond the mosque area, was excavated only up to that boundary point. A third cistern, about 40 cm. under the pavement of 334 (Pl. 87b) was opened only far enough to see that the original vault had collapsed and had been replaced by a corbelled arch built with massive stones.[8] The two largest stones that sealed the cistern were 150 × 70 cm. and 170 × 60 cm. The cistern was filled with earth to within a meter of these stones. The fourth cistern just E of 331, was in good condition but we had no time to clear it. The area 333 was debris, without any differentiating walls or floors. The upper pottery was mixed Roman and Byzantine. Below that came a mixture of Iron II and Iron I; but from 2.5 m. down the pottery was all Iron I.

---

[5] All Roman and Byzantine walls in the campsite Area had been destroyed by the peasants when they built their new boundary walls, so there was no Roman or Byzantine evidence from that area.

[6] Some *zebâr*, olive refuse, was mixed with the sherds.

[7] E. Robinson, *Biblical Researches in Palestine*, Vol. I, p. 449.

[8] This cistern level is shown on the plan just E of 334.

169. The vault of cistern 331–332[9] had collapsed, although sections of it which carried the spring of the arch were still intact (Pl. 90a). The stairway which led down into the cistern descended at the NE corner (Pl. 87b). It was a very narrow stairway which went southward for the first four steps; then it turned westward and the steps widened until it reached the cistern itself. The W wall of the cistern had been built against debris. We did not have time to check the details of the E wall except at the stairway. There was a small amount of Byzantine pottery, but most of the ware was Roman. The earliest was first century A.D. In Byzantine times a very heavy foundation course had been laid on the debris in the cistern and upon it a good Byzantine wall was raised, which was an integral part of the Byzantine complex to the N. The small cistern 333 C which extended W beyond the mosque area, contained chiefly Byzantine pottery but mixed with it were some Hellenistic and Roman sherds that were part of a fill.

170. All the heavy walls and all the pavements (Pl. 90b) that were excavated in the mosque area belonged to the last Byzantine phase, probably the sixth–eighth centuries,[10] and may be a part of a monastery, because they are so close to the church. More excavating, however, must be done before a definite answer can be given. Locus 336 is a paved floor or courtyard. A S section of the heavy pavement in 335 was removed and it was discovered that this heavy pavement had been laid on a bedding of stones averaging about 15 cm. in diameter. The pottery beneath was predominantly sixth–seventh centuries A.D., although a Ptolemaic silver coin was found with it. There was a *ḥuwar* floor in 334 about 60 cm. below the stone pavement. On this floor were several varieties of potter's clay. Perhaps this explains the cistern in the same room as part of a potter's factory. The only sign of fire in this Byzantine building was in 338 where there had been a fierce burning. The stone paving here was at times 20 cm. thick. A door socket, not *in situ*, was found under the pavement. This building is probably what Edward Robinson refers to when he speaks of " the foundations of a much larger and earlier edifice built of large stones " within which there was a Greek church.[11] The Byzantine churches on the ridge E of Bethel are described in §6.

171. In the E section of 338 we went down through the pavement, sinking a test pit (335) to get the early history of the site. No walls or floors were encountered but the following sherds were found: some Iron II with hole-mouth jars predominant and a considerable amount of Iron I, especially the wide burnishing at the end of the period. LB was represented by a few bases, MB II by good burnished ware and flat bottom store-jars, along with combed ware—the combing running very fine to average. EB had cooking pot rims and inverted plate rims characteristic of the end of that period. Since no building remains had been discovered, a second test pit was sunk in the same room but along the S wall.[12] Under the pavement was a little mixed Byzantine and Roman pottery. At 90 cm. there was a burning with most of the pottery Iron I, although mixed with it were some early hole-mouth and ring-burnished sherds of Iron II. At about a meter there was a second and very destructive burning. Below it was Iron I$_1$ pottery. A little below this was a house wall in the W end of the trench. At 170 cm. below the Byzantine stone pavement there was a *ḥuwar* floor. Then we found a little LB followed by MB and EB in about the same variety as at the E end of the room. Below this was virgin soil.

172. In 1954 we were called to see a new hole which had suddenly appeared in the courtyard of the *maḍâfeh* just in front of the main entrance to the building. It was made by the collapse of part of the high vault in a long chamber dating to Roman or Byzantine times. The area was too dangerous for excavations as we had no shoring material. The Roman gate in the S wall has been treated in §76.

173. In 1957 we found a Roman house built directly over the lower courses of the N wall of MB II B (Pl. 93b). Since this house was still in use in Byzantine times, that section of the city wall which it covered was left intact. Immediately to the E and to the W of this house all the stones of the MB town wall had been removed to construct the new Byzantine city wall. The N wall and a portion of the E wall of this Roman-Byzantine

---

[9] 331–32 was originally a single Roman cistern.
[10] Everything else shown on the plans under this top level was cisterns.
[11] E. Robinson, *ibid.*, p. 449.
[12] This test pit had a maximum width of 130 cm. It is not shown as a special feature on the plans.

house on the wall remained. Just N of this house, and abutting on it, is a second house with two rooms preserved. All these walls are represented primarily by foundation courses which were sunk in a trench and then wedged in on either side by extra stone. Here and there courses of the wall proper remain. The walls of the two houses overlap slightly; the earlier house seems to be the S one. The walls were laid in native soil, not on debris.

174. A third and much larger contemporary Roman building lies just W of these houses. Only a 10 m. section of a N–S wall of this larger building remains. Just E of this wall is a 6 m. unit of an earlier Hellenistic building uncovered in the trench which we had cut to study a cross section of the glacis of the MB II B wall. N of both these walls is a short E–W wall of earlier Hellenistic date and beyond it is a silo. This E–W wall seems to have been reused by the builders of the large Roman building. Inside the NE gate of the city, is a crude house wall of Roman date (hatched wall on Pl. 92b). The W end is laid in dirt and the E end climbs over a jumble of rock. Apparently by the time of this wall, the NE town gate had been abandoned. The Roman gate on the S side of the city is described in §76. In 1960 a small early Roman room (Pl. 103a) was found while looking for N city wall.

175. The Byzantine city gate at the NE corner of Beitîn and the city street leading S from it have been described in detail in §§77 ff; see also §43. Our present knowledge of the archaeological history of Beitîn closes with the Byzantine period.

CHAPTER X

THE HISTORY OF BETHEL

176. This history of Bethel is derived from three major sources: the archaeological excavation of the site, the Bible, and secular historical records. The first is the only evidence for pre-Abrahamic Bethel. An abundance of excellent springs near the top of the mountains along the great north–south watershed ridge road of Palestine made natural camp sites for nomads pasturing their flocks. A second important feature of Bethel in that early camping phase was the great open air shrine where the bare mountain top served as an altar for transient worshippers, §§83–89 ff. This sanctuary of El became so important that it gave its name to the site; Bethel remained constant to its original deity. This high place goes back at least to Chalcolithic times, as demonstrated by the Chalcolithic water jar from c. 3500 B.C. found there with some sacrificial animal bones in it still intact. Such an important shrine drew migrant shepherds to bury their dead.

177. By 3200 B.C. a village had grown up just south of the high place. It covered the area excavated in 1934 and appears to extend both to the south and the east, §82. Bethel was later apparently replaced by Ai (et Tell), only a mile and a half away. Ai remained the key citadel of this part of Palestine from c. 2900 to c. 2500 B.C. The present evidence from Beitîn leaves that site unoccupied during Ai's prosperity, and it was not until that city's destruction that Bethel was again occupied. Only four Khirbet Kerak sherds come from the end of this time span.

178. Sometime c. 2400 B.C. sherds similar to TBM " J " level appeared south of the high place and beside the springs in the mosque area. Since these sherds all represent cheap pottery, Bethel may have been a refugee settlement, §92. The city's other name was Luz, which may be derived from *Laudh*, meaning " place of refuge." (Luz also has the alternative meaning " almond," and this area is still ideal fruit and nut country.) It may be well to pause here and discuss the problem of the names Bethel and Luz.

In the detailed boundary descriptions of Ephraim and Benjamin in Joshua, both Bethel and Luz are mentioned.[1] The language might imply that the two were separate but adjacent sites. If so, then perhaps the term " Bethel " in Genesis was applied to the Abrahamic sanctuary on the ridge east of town and " Luz " was applied to the town itself. Genesis 28:19 may lend emphasis to such a view, as the term *māqôm*, " place," is used for Bethel but ʿîr, " town " for Luz. Or the two designations Luz and Bethel may follow the analogy of Rome and the Vatican, Luz being the secular town and Bethel the holy site. A third possibility is that Luz was the name of the first town on the site and Bethel the name of the second town founded after the site of Ai had been abandoned. The use of the name " Bethel " by the community for the second foundation would be a definite appeal to the ancestral god El for his blessing, lest the second city meet a like fate. Or again, the geographer may simply have been clinching his place names by using both of the historic designations.

At least by EB times tombs of important personages were located not only on the ridge east of Bethel, especially toward the south end, but also east toward Ai.[2] From one of these tombs c. 300 m. or so west of Ai, one can today get the same excellent view of the Jordan valley that Abraham did.

The first EB settlement lasted from c. 2400 to c. 2200 B.C. Then the site was unoccupied during the twenty-second and twenty-first centuries when much of Palestine was almost depopulated by nomadic irruptions from the east, §§40, 92.

179. Bethel sprang to life again in MB I, about the nineteenth century B.C. There were substantial buildings of such nature that the site must have been fortified, §§93 ff. No city walls, however, have yet been found. The great stones around the foundation of the beautiful MB II B building, tentatively identified as a temple, may well have come from such a city wall. The

---

[1] Josh. 16:2; 18:13.
[2] One was c. 3 m. square built of stones from 60 cm. to 1.25 m., and still standing 4 or 5 courses high.

MB II B city wall was doubtless built of stones from this missing wall. The only major structure identifiable in the MB I city was the temple, which was erected directly upon the original mountain top shrine, §§96 ff.

It is now time to take up the patriarchal narratives of Genesis, for they seem to fit best into MB I and II. The Abrahamic story has him encamped on the ridge east of Bethel and there he built his altar. Since Abraham was a caravan leader and feudal war lord leading his men in alien territory, it was only natural that he would have to camp outside the city.[3] The key question has been whether or not Bethel was a holy site at that time. The question is now definitely answered in the affirmative, for we have not only the original Chalcolithic high place, but the temple that succeeded it in MB I. So Bethel was both a city and a shrine before Abraham's day. Also on the ridge east of Bethel, we have found an old Canaanite altar with microlithic flints at its foot, thus giving a dating far earlier even than Abraham, §91.

180. Archaeological work at Bethel throws no special light on the Jacob story,[4] although certain geological formations near the city might theoretically suggest a ladder.[5] The importance of Jacob's experiences here at Bethel, however, cannot be over-estimated, and the term " Bethel " takes on added significance because of his new use of the term. The terms Luz and Bethel fit the history of Jacob just as accurately as they did the earlier people here; for Jacob indeed found this place (Luz) " a refuge " from Esau, and the gracious vision of God that he had here caused him to acknowledge this place as his sanctuary—Bethel. The use of the *maṣṣebah* here is demonstrated by one pillar found *in situ* on the ridge east of Bethel, §91, a second large one used as a door jamb in an Iron I house and what appears to be the remains of a third near the old open-air shrine.

181. The old Canaanite designation " Bethel " implied an *important* sanctuary site sacred to the god El. It is parallel to Beth-anath, Beth-dagon, Beth-horon, Beth-lehem, Beth-shemesh, etc. The whole tenor of the Jacob story, however, is that Jacob's God is different from any and all Canaanite deities; this is especially clear in the Jabbok episode and in the burial of foreign gods and amulets at Shechem.[6] Bethel now became the place where God had uniquely revealed himself to both Abraham and Jacob. Deborah, Rebekah's nurse, was buried under an oak below Bethel. The country was still heavily timbered as late as Joshua's conquest.[7] The enormous amount of ashes found in the houses at Bethel leads us to believe that more timber was used in the houses here than in less timbered areas.

182. The history of the MB II A city (eighteenth century B.C.) is not yet well understood. There was an occupation near the north wall of the MB II B city but it does not seem to have extended very far along the west wall. The temple above the high place may have been in use as late as MB II A but this is still uncertain. There was also an occupation along the later MB II B city wall on the south side of the city, §100.

183. Bethel became a major town in MB II B. The new city wall, built *c.* 1650 B.C., gave Bethel such excellent defense that it continued to be used throughout its long history with only slight modifications until the Samaritan revolts *c.* A.D. 500, §78. Sections of the north, south, and west city walls still remain, as well as the northeast and northwest gates. There is good but not conclusive evidence for gates on the south and west sides of the city. The east wall of the city was found under a paved street in Beitîn, but it was not dug up. Two major periods of house construction mark the MB II B era, and each of these two phases had burnings over at least parts of the area. The masonry of this period was good and is seen at its best in the city wall, a temple, and a patrician house. There were also a few brick houses showing foreign influence. An earthquake in the earlier phase had left some collapsed walls. For all details of MB II B, see §§101–115. MB II C also had two phases of good building. A new section of the city's west wall was the last major construction work shortly before the city's capture, probably by the Egyptians *c.* 1550 B.C., §67.

184. The site then seems to have been unoccu-

---

[3] Gen. 12:8; cf. 13:3–4. *BASOR*, No. 163 (October, 1961), pp. 36–54, W. F. Albright, *The Biblical Period from Abraham to Ezra*, Ch. I.

[4] Gen. 28:10–22; 31:13; 35:1–16.

[5] We often saw an Arab workman use a stone for a pillow. One night we even took a time exposure by moonlight of the *mukhtâr*'s son asleep with his head on a stone about the size of an ancient saddle quern, §5.

[6] Gen. 32:24–32; 35:4.

[7] Josh. 17; 15, 18.

pied until *c.* 1400 B.C. when the city made an excellent comeback, Chapter V. Within the old city walls houses of better construction than those of any earlier period filled the area. There were two LB phases; the earlier was slightly superior to the latter phase, i.e. the thirteenth century. Patrician houses had increased in size, flagstone pavements were numerous, and skillfully constructed drains were fairly commonplace. This is the only period at Bethel when a good drainage system was found. The houses yielded better finds than previously and formed a striking contrast to the poverty of the following Israelite days. An olive oil factory was the only industry found. The prosperity of the city is witnessed by the enormous amount of burning which marked its destruction at the hands of the invading Israelites.

185. The books of Joshua and Judges bring a wealth of historical data to help us understand the complicated story of Iron I Bethel. It was the key town along the Benjamin–Ephraim border. It was not only large enough to have minor communities under its jurisdiction,[8] but it gave its name to the hill country around.[9] The major geographical term " Mt. Ephraim," included the lesser " Mt. Bethel."[10] There was a Bethel–Shechem highway[11] and in the same passage Shiloh is located in terms of Bethel, thus making Bethel the more important of the two cities at that time.[12] Bethel was the terminus of a road from Jericho, a road so important that it served as the boundary between the tribes of Ephraim and Benjamin. This was the route used by Joshua.[13] Roads led from Bethel to the Mediterranean, via Aijalon to the Philistine coast, and via Gophna to the plain of Sharon. In the early days of the Judges, the ark was located for a time at Bethel. Indeed, Phinehas, the son of Eleazar, was still high priest at that time.[14] Bethel was also one of the three towns on Samuel's circuit judgeship.[15]

186. The Jericho and Ai narratives present knotty problems to the students of Joshua's military campaign, but the over-all conquest itself is now one of the most striking findings in all of Palestinian archaeology. The study of Joshua's conquest has taken on new significance since the excavations at Hazor began in 1955.[16] Now the conquest narrative has archaeological confirmation at Jericho, Bethel, Eglon (Tell el-Ḥesī), Debir (TBM), Lachish (Tell ed-Duweir), and Hazor. The Hazor evidence is especially valuable, not only because it was the key city in the northern phase of Joshua's conquest but because it was the largest and the most important city in Palestine. It was then *the* city of Palestine. Furthermore the pottery found at Hazor is ideal for dating the conquest. One of the major criticisms against a thirteenth century date for the conquest had been the small amount of Mycenaean pottery found in the towns excavated to date.[17] Hazor is a complete reversal at this point, for Yadin's report says ". . . we found the floors of these houses littered with Mykenean pottery as well as many other vessels and objects of local make, all dating back to the last phase of the Late Bronze Age, i.e. the thirteenth century B.C.! In other words here was definite proof that the last city in the big enclosure met its end about the same time as the actual conquest of the country by Joshua, according to the date given by most scholars."[18]

187. Meanwhile Lachish had already furnished a parallel date although Mycenaean pottery had played only a minor part in determining it. At Lachish a broken (but nearly complete) hieratic vase inscription was found dated in the fourth year of one of the immediate successors of Rameses II, probably his son Merneptah.[19] Thus the destruction of Lachish took place about 1234 B.C.

188. The pottery and other finds from Tell Beit Mirsim (Debir, Kiriath-sepher) tell the same story as Lachish except that the destruction of the LB town may have been slightly earlier.[20] The

---

[8] I Chron. 7:28; II Chron. 13:19.
[9] I Sam. 13:2; Josh. 16:1 (?).
[10] Judg. 4:5.
[11] Judg. 21:19; cf. 20:31.
[12] Nearby towns, such as Beth-aven (Josh. 7:2) and Ai (Josh. 12:9), are located in terms of Bethel.
[13] Josh. 16:1–2; 18:13. John Garstang, *The Foundations of Bible History, Joshua and Judges,* pp. 149 ff.
[14] Judg. 20:18, 26–28; 21:2–4.
[15] I Sam. 7:16.

[16] *Hazor I, II,* and *III* by Y. Yadin, Y. Aharoni, R. Amiran, T. Dothan, I. Dunayevsky, J. Perrot.
[17] This criticism was valid because some of the native Palestinian pottery forms at the end of LB and at the beginning of Iron I, are closely related, the latter being a development of the former. Other evidence besides pottery was used by the archaeologists who emphasized the thirteenth century date.
[18] *Bib. Arch.,* Vol. XIX, p. 9.
[19] Albright, *The Biblical Period,* p. 16.
[20] Albright, *Recent Discoveries in Bible Lands,* p. 88.

excavation of Bethel proves that somewhere between *c.* 1240 and 1235 B.C. a terrific conflagration completely wiped out the Canaanite city. Here is one of the thickest ash levels yet reported in Palestine. At Bethel all expeditions found a much smaller amount of LB II pottery than normal. A number of rooms yielded no pottery or any other objects. The city seems to have been plundered much more thoroughly than was usual before it was given over to the torch. The quantity of finds at Hazor toward the end of the conquest contrasts strikingly with the picture in an earlier phase of the same conquest of Bethel.

189. The new evidence from Hazor, plus restudy of the findings at Lachish, TBM, and Bethel, compels a new evaluation of all the Jericho evidence. Furthermore, the work of Miss Kenyon has produced some new material in the tomb area, and the study of the disintegration of the mound has been helpful. A few tomb findings now prove that Jericho was inhabited at the close of LB, confirming Père Vincent's statement about the presence of such pottery on the site at the time of the German excavations.

190. The problem of the disappearance of the walls of Jericho is somewhat similar to that of the walls of the first LB city at TBM.[21] In the latter case the city wall is missing but the houses are there and a street runs on a line approximately concentric with the city wall.[22] In both towns the walls were apparently of mud brick and in both cases they have disappeared through wind and rain erosion. In Iraq *tells* have been denuded by wind and rain to a depth of 5 m. Jericho is in a strong wind zone where the air currents of cold Mt. Hermon, 9000 feet above sea level, are sucked down to the hot Dead Sea, 1300 feet below sea level. These same winds furnished the draft for Solomon's smelters in the Wadi Arabah. The erosive action of rain on mud brick was well demonstrated during one of the British expeditions at Jericho when the excavations were flooded and had to be pumped out. It should also be noted that at Tell es-Sultan there are today no longer any remains of the city of the Moabite King Eglon (Judges 3:13) or that of David's day (II Sam. 10:5). The cuneiform tablet found by Bliss at Tell el-Ḥesī and belonging to the Amarna correspondence was restudied by Albright in 1942 and it now gives us historical data which practically demands a thirteenth century date for the Israelite conquest of the town of Eglon.[23]

191. This over-all archaeological picture of Joshua's conquest is reflected in the Merneptah stele, *c.* 1233 B.C. This inscription has long been one of the major points of evidence for the Rameside date of the Exodus, and the new archaeological findings confirm and greatly elucidate it. The Bethel-Ai phase of Joshua's campaign presents some difficult problems, Josh. 8:1–29; 12:9. Et-Tell (Ai) is being excavated by Professor Joseph A. Callaway, and final conclusions on the problem should await his final report.

192. The Israelite invasion came just at the transition from LB II to Iron I, §§75, 195. In those cities where the Israelites settled there was a complete and striking cultural change, Chapter VI. Canaanite feudalism with "lord and serf" passed away and a form of democracy with its "first, chosen from among equals" took its place. The house of the patrician disappeared and the house of the common man replaced it. The best masonry at Beitîn was LB II and nothing was worse than some Iron I phases except the hovels or sheepfolds of the early Persian period.

193. The contents of the houses were as strikingly different as the buildings themselves. In contrast to the wealth and culture of LB, there was now little variety and little quantity. Craftsmanship in ceramics reached its lowest point in the early part of Iron I. The preliminary Bethel report says of it, "Such monotonous pottery we have never seen elsewhere. If collared store-jars and cooking pots were eliminated, the number of remaining types would be insignificant."[24] This is in striking contrast with the wide variety of native and imported wares in LB II. Bone spatulas took the place of LB copper ones; beads at times were made of pottery. Iron did not become commonplace in Palestine until about the end of Iron I. In religion there was also a distinct change. Canaanite temples disappeared in the conquered cities. At TBM the cult objects of LB were discarded and a stone lion was found on its end in an ancient pit. In Bethel a Canaanite *maṣṣebah* was used as common building stone.

---

[21] Albright, *TBM II*, §70.
[22] The LB II stone wall at TBM encircled the same general plan of the previous town, thus giving strong evidence of the existence of an earlier mud-brick wall.

[23] *BASOR*, No. 87, pp. 32–38.
[24] *BASOR*, No. 56, p. 12.

serving as a door jamb in a house. No superstitious dread here. On the other hand a few figurines of the mother-goddess and lamps with seven wicks were found in the early Israelite levels. No unique Israelite cult objects of any kind were found.

194. To appreciate the complete cultural and religious change brought by the Israelites one need only turn to such cities as Megiddo, Taanach, and Beth-shean, which were not captured by Joshua (Josh. 17:11–12). The excavations of these cities show a Canaanite culture and cult continuing unchanged by Joshua's conquest.

195. Where we uncovered the walls of the LB city we found two points where the Israelites had breached the walls. On the south side of the city an Iron I house had been built partly on the stub of the old city wall and partly on c. 1.75 m. of ash and brick debris from the upper courses. One unit of the west wall was breached but repaired and reused. It was the houses, however, that showed what a conflagration had consumed the city. 1 to 1.5 m. of ashes, charcoal, brick, and earth are not uncommon. The city must have used more than the normal amount of wood in its construction. (It was in a forested area.) Also there must have been exceptionally heavy supplies of grain on hand. We know the Israelites were forced to go out into the desert to bypass Edom and Moab so there must have been a season of long and heavy rains to give them pasturage there. This, of course, meant a period of exceptionally heavy crops in the Bethel area. The Israelites moved into the captured city and made it the central sanctuary of the tribes.[25] But the Israelites of Bethel were soon to be plunged into the relative anarchy of the period of the Judges.

196. The history of Bethel in the days of the Judges presents some difficult problems of chronology but the following interpretation seems to be the most logical in the light of our present knowledge. The story of the extermination of the tribe of Benjamin seems to date very early in the period of the Judges.[26] Note that although Joshua was dead, Phinehas, son of Eleazar, was still high priest, and the ark was located at Bethel.[27] Bethel itself was a Benjaminite city[28] but on the border between Benjamin and Ephraim. As the ark was here, the city was sacrosanct in *civil* war, for the ark was the focus of the Israelite amphictyony.[29]

197. This civil war seems to have sparked a Canaanite revolt, and one of the first victims of that revolt may have been Bethel. Just as the Philistines struck at Shiloh, which was the amphictyonic center of Israel in their day, so the Canaanites may have struck earlier at Bethel. The excavations demonstrate that Bethel was destroyed early in the days of the Judges and this destruction stands out in all the areas dug. It was probably at this crisis that the ark was removed north to Shiloh, which had already played its part in the war with Benjamin.[30] I Sam. 10:3, however, shows that Bethel was still a holy place. The only reference in the first chapter of Judges to Benjamin describes its inability to capture Jerusalem. This again shows how powerless Benjamin was at this time, especially since Judah did capture Jerusalem in this chaotic free-for-all between Canaanites and Israelite tribes in this early period of the Judges.

198. Archaeological evidence shows that Israel quickly recaptured Bethel and this episode seems to be referred to in Judges 1:22–26. The first chapter of Judges now enables us to fit together the episodes of the civil war with Benjamin and Joseph's conquest of Bethel. In Judges the conquest of Bethel is attributed to the house of Joseph.[31] This is perfectly understandable, for if Benjamin had been reduced to a minor role by civil war, then the house of Joseph must have recaptured the key border city of Bethel from the Canaanites in order to secure its own southern frontier.[32] A further chronological clue to these two episodes is the action of the Canaanite inhabitant of Bethel, who had been captured by the Ephraimite spies. He went north to Hittite territory and built a town, calling its name "Luz" (Judges 1:22–26). The time element between Joshua's conquest of the town, the Israelite civil war, the Canaanite reconquest of Bethel, and the Ephraimite conquest of this rebuilt Canaanite town was so short that the attraction of the old

---

[25] Judg. 20:18, 26–28; 21:2.
[26] Judg. Chs. 19–21.
[27] Judg. 20:18–28; 21:2–4.
[28] Josh. 18:22.

[29] Judg. 20:18; 21:2–4.
[30] Judg. 21:12–25.
[31] I Chron. 7:28 also lists Bethel as an Ephraimite town.
[32] For the problem of Bethel's relationship to the tribes of Benjamin and Ephraim see J. Kaufmann, *The Biblical Account of the Conquest of Palestine*, pp. 7–22.

Canaanite name " Luz " still dominated this clan leader. Assuming this Ephraimite conquest of Bethel, it is easy to see why the famous shrine was considered Ephraimite territory by Jeroboam I.

The capture of Israelite Bethel by a revived Canaanite confederacy, followed by its recapture by the house of Joseph, which in turn was followed by the period of Philistine oppression over Israel, may explain why Bethel knew nothing but poverty until the period of the monarchy. The days following Joshua's death seem to have been more perilous for early Israel than had been realized. It is the old story of a military genius who had no successors. The necessity for " saviours " for Israel now becomes more significant than ever. The charismatic judge was Israel's only hope. It is at this time (*c.* 1125 B.C.) that Deborah, the prophetess, was judging Israel " between Ramah and Bethel in Mt. Ephraim."[33]

199. The next military crisis was the Philistine invasion of the central ridge of Palestine. It struck at Saul's residence at Gibeah and went beyond it to Geba[34] in order to control the road to the Jordan. The hill country of Bethel is referred to in connection with Saul's part in the campaign[35] and the Philistines sent a raiding party beyond it to Ophrah.[36] Bethel seems to have escaped destruction in this crisis. There was only one place in the city where there was a burning at this time. Most important of all, Philistine pottery was rare; none was found in the 1954 or 1960 campaigns. Bethel entered into an era of peace at the end of the Philistine crisis in the highlands. For the dating of the archaeological phases covering the book of Judges, see Chapter VI.

200. After this rapid resume of Bethel's archaeological history, we shall study its political history, beginning with Samuel. After the destruction of Shiloh, Samuel became the key figure in Israelite history, working on a circuit judgeship at Bethel, Gilgal, and Mizpah.[37] Bethel is here assigned a political pre-eminence which was doubtless due to its now being reckoned as belonging to Ephraim. Bethel might also have revived some of its prominence as a former amphictyonic center, for Shiloh was in ashes and the ark was in Philistia. Saul, however, was soon made king and political power shifted south to Gibeah. The only reference to Bethel in his reign has already been discussed. David's kingship was a still heavier blow to Bethel's claims, for Jerusalem under David became a unique combination of church and state. Bethel's historic religious priority had to yield to the new ecclesiastical power. Bethel is not mentioned by name under either David or Solomon.

201. Archaeologically, however, Bethel tells the story of the nation's prosperity under both rulers. Building improved quickly, leaving behind the pier construction of the earlier phases of Iron I and the brief phase of small-stone walls. Meanwhile the pottery art took on new activity: new forms appeared and various techniques of burnishing were developed. It was a period of solid prosperity. David's control of iron enabled him to divert use of the metal from nearly exclusive emphasis on weapons to the manufacture of tools and implements. The iron plowshare, with its deep plowing, now revolutionized the tilling of the soil; and increasing crops were alone responsible for a great increase in Israel's population. As nearly as archaeology can interpret the story, Bethel's growth was the result of improved farming and increased commerce.[38]

202. Jeroboam I inaugurated the next phase of Bethel's history by making it Israel's chief sanctuary, a rival to Judah's Jerusalem.[39] Dan was Bethel's sister sanctuary in the north but it was never Bethel's equal. Bethel was a royal sanctuary,[40] and this shrine must have been, at least in some sense, a true rival of Jerusalem. The religious associations of the site were ideal, for both Abraham and Jacob had major religious experiences here. The ark also was stationed here at one time. The shrine brought wealth and craftsmen to the city. Jeroboam needed new clergy and that meant a new population influx.[41] With the resurgent sanctuary in full swing and with the king's special blessing, Bethel seemed destined for a prosperous future.

203. Unfortunately none of the archaeological campaigns recovered any data directly related to

---

[33] Judg. 4:5.
[34] I Sam. 13:2–3.
[35] I Sam. 13:2.
[36] I Sam. 13:17.
[37] I Sam. 7:15–16.

[38] At a later date, it was Hiel of Bethel who rebuilt Jericho.
[39] I Kings 12:26–33.
[40] Amos 7:13.
[41] I Kings 12:31–32.

this cult center, except for an inscribed South Arabian seal from the ninth century B.C.; it must have belonged to the head of an incense caravan (see *BASOR* No. 151, pp. 9–16, and No. 163, pp. 15–18). Until the temple is found it is not wise for a serious historian to speculate about it. One factual item, however, is important: surprisingly few finds of a cultic nature have been found in any of the Iron II houses of the town.

204. We found no sign of a destruction by Abijah, who captured Bethel shortly after the new sanctuary was founded.[42] It was presumably Abijah's plan to spare the town and incorporate it into his territory.[43] Bethel was too close to Jerusalem, so Abijah established a more northern and a much better line of defense—Baal-Hazor to the east and the Ṣarida valley to the west. Baasha took Bethel back, but only temporarily, for Ben-Hadad of Syria compelled him to go north to defend Galilee. Asa then also moved north and his reformation[44] must again have demoted the Bethel shrine, for certainly the Temple could not tolerate this shrine as a rival. Solomon's temple had to be pre-eminent. Jehoshaphat regarrisoned the Ephraim cities that his father had captured[45] and also involved Ephraim in a second reformation.[46] Exactly when Bethel was returned to the Northern Kingdom is unknown, though it may have been under Jehoash of Israel. Jeroboam II again made it his royal sanctuary, and the shrine was restored to its original prominence before the days of Amos.

205. The attitude of Elijah and Elisha to the Bethel sanctuary is obscure. It is significant, however, that there was a school of the prophets here at Bethel when Elijah and Elisha were en route to the former's translation at the Jordan,[47] although the youth of the community is said to have had no respect for the returning prophet.[48] The historical data just summarized implies that Bethel was not an Israelite sanctuary during their prophetic ministry but had been incorporated into Judah. Furthermore, there is no record of Jehu's reformation at Bethel. It is significant also that only a few female figurines of the Jezebel snow-man type were found in the excavations.

206. The city was captured by the Assyrians, probably in connection with Hoshea's revolt in 724 B.C., §150. It seems to have lain in ruins for some time. The shrine was revived to play a part in the religious life of the Babylonian, Syrian, and Phoenician colonists whom the Assyrians brought in to replace the Israelite leadership. Former Bethel priests were recalled after marauding lions had become a major problem in the sparsely settled countryside.[49] After the fall of Assyria Josiah moved north to fill the political and religious vacuum. Although he exacted fearful vengeance on the sanctuary and the tombs of its priests, he seems to have spared the town itself.[50] In the excavated areas we found no evidence of destruction or even of minor rebuilding. We also discovered that Bethel had been spared by Nebuchadnezzar when he destroyed Jerusalem, §150. Bethel had evidently been incorporated into the Assyrian province of Samaria which, of course, then became a Babylonian province. Thus the town was not involved in the revolt of Judah. Note that Bethel was partly occupied by Babylonian colonists whom the Assyrians had planted there.[51] The presence of Babylonian worshippers in Bethel is perhaps illustrated by a small agate conoid seal (Fig. 1) of the sixth or fifth century B.C.,[52] which depicts a worshipper standing before an incense altar. Behind the worshipper is the symbol of the god Marduk. The murder of Gedaliah at Mizpah does not seem to have affected Bethel, and the city appears to have had several decades more of life. Finally Bethel was destroyed in a great conflagration either at the hands of the Babylonian Nabonidus or shortly afterwards at the hands of the Persians, perhaps in the chaotic period preceding Darius, see §150.[53]

207. The Iron II material which we found at Bethel matches well with the Biblical narrative. There is only one catastrophe in the life of the town, when it was captured by the Assyrians.

---

[42] II Chron. 13:19.
[43] For one interpretation of this period of Bethel's history see *JBL*, LXXV, pp. 222–23.
[44] I Kings 15:12–14; II Chron. 15:8 ff.
[45] II Chron. 17:2.
[46] II Chron. 19:4.
[47] II Kings 2:2–3.
[48] II Kings 2:23–24.

[49] II Kings 17:27–33.
[50] II Kings 23:15 ff. Josiah brought to Bethel the ashes which he had collected from vessels used in the worship of Canaanite deities in the Jerusalem temple area.
[51] II Kings 17:24, 30.
[52] This seal was not found in the excavations but was purchased from one of the inhabitants of Beitîn.
[53] See §150 and Albright, *The Biblical Period*, p. 62.

Iron I and Iron II walls were sometimes on the same alignment and sometimes completely different. Masonry varied from good to bad. Rebuilding was all local and done at various times. There was no major change of plan at any time. Some refortification of the north wall dates from the eighth and some from the seventh century. Absence of cisterns was a striking feature of the site; they were made unnecessary by the excellent springs. The ravages of earthquakes were noted at several points. We did not find any major industry in the town. The only dye vat found was in an orchard (Pl. 12b). Whatever new wealth it had must have come from its cult center.

208. After the destruction of Bethel at the shift of world power from the Babylonians to the Persians, §150, the site lay in ruins for only a brief time, §151. A few crude walls, built of stones taken from the old city wall, testify to the earliest reoccupation, but these were more likely sheepfolds than houses. The data in Ezra and Nehemiah parallel the archaeological finds. In Ezra's census (2:28) the men of Bethel and Ai total only 223; in Neh. (7:32) only 123. Bethel was the northernmost town listed with the Benjaminites in Neh. 12:31 ff., but it was not listed at all among the people rebuilding the walls of Jerusalem.[54] The tiny post-exilic village was doubtless close to the springs beneath the built-up area of modern Beitîn. In Zech. 7:2 there is no reference to the sanctuary of Bethel although some translators and commentators erroneously so interpret the passage.

209. We have no literary references for the early Hellenistic period, but the archaeological evidence is good, §§152 ff. There were two major Hellenistic phases and then a transition into the Roman period. The Hellenistic houses were well built although inferior to those of LB. The better buildings were in phase 1. Hellenistic houses were found even outside the N city wall. The pottery was predominantly good native ware with only a small amount of imported pottery from the fourth or early third centuries. Coins covered a fair section of this period and Rhodian jar handles the closing phase, Chapter XIV, footnote 6. We found one coin of Alexander the Great, but none of succeeding years until the time of Ptolemy Philadelphus. Ptolemaic coins continued through Ptolemy V (205–182 B.C.). Seleucid coins began with Antiochus Epiphanes (175–164 B.C.).

210. I Macc. 9:50 and Josephus *Ant.* XIII, 1, 3, inform us that Bethel was one of the towns fortified by Bacchides, and part of this work is tentatively identified in the tumulus Rujm Abū ʿAmmâr on the ridge northeast of Bethel, §6. Hellenistic sherds of the second century B.C. are abundant there. This tumulus looks like one at the Hellenistic-Roman Jericho which contained ruins of this same period and was probably also built by Bacchides.[55] Maccabaean coins include some of John Hyrcanus and Alexander Jannaeus as well as later imitations. Rhodian jar handles also belong in this period. The Maccabaean period was a prosperous one.

211. At some time in the early Roman phase of the town the northeast gate was destroyed and part of the north wall leveled, but it is uncertain whether this was the work of Pompey or Vespasian, although the probabilities favor the latter, §§48 f. Then a Roman house was built over the wall. The town itself has not yielded any evidence of burning at this time. The foundation of a probable Roman city gate at the south side of the town by the upper spring was found. No coins of Herod the Great were discovered, but since Herodian pottery was common the town must have been occupied during this period. Absence of coins is probably accidental, since there is no evidence of the city's abandonment. From the time of Herod Archelaus on, coins are common. Roman houses followed the general pattern of Hellenistic ones.

212. The New Testament makes no specific reference to Bethel although it continued to be a key town and was increasing in population. In the first Jewish Revolt, Bethel was one of the last towns captured by Vespasian before he left Palestine to become emperor of Rome. He established a Roman garrison at Bethel.[56] In the second revolt, Hadrian placed a guard at Bethel to arrest Jewish fugitives.[57]

213. Archaeologically speaking, the Roman period saw such a great expansion in the population of the town that cisterns were introduced for the first time in its history, §§167 ff. They were large community cisterns close to the town's

---

[54] In early Maccabaean days it was still the most northerly city of Judaea. I Macc. 9:50.

[55] *AASOR*, Vols. XXIX-XXX, §§18–20, 23.
[56] Josephus, B. J., IV: ix, 9.
[57] Lam. R., ii, 3 (Midrash Ekhah).

largest spring, where they could be easily filled in the winter. They were not in private houses. Few significant building remains have been preserved, for the peasants have dug deeply in planting their orchards, but a vast amount of broken pottery is to be found almost everywhere. It covers all phases of the Roman period as well as the transition to Byzantine times. The Roman city extended as far south as the mosque.[58] The Roman cisterns at this point preserved the finest assortment of Roman sherds from the site, although not many jars could be reconstructed.

214. In the fourth century A.D. Eusebius called Bethel a large village and the Pilgrim of Bordeaux also mentioned it, §10. Bethel continued to be a holy place, for it was probably in this century that an important Byzantine church was built at Khirbet el-Maqâṭir, perhaps marking an identification of the site of Jacob's dream. About the sixth century another church, supposedly on the site of Abraham's sanctuary, was erected at what is now called Burj Beitîn. Within the city itself near the great spring was a Byzantine church.[59] Just east of it was a large building which, according to location and construction, may well have been a monastery, §170. A few Byzantine house walls are found here and there on the *tell* but the Byzantine phase is represented primarily by pottery rather than by buildings. East of the *tell* proper lies one of the main streets of that town, with the northeast Byzantine gateway, and a section of the east city wall (Pl. 120). This new city wall tells the story of the city's experience with the warlike Samaritans, §78. The pottery demonstrates that the city was occupied through the Byzantine period. Only a very small amount of Islamic pottery was found in the excavated areas. The ruins of the great reservoir just south of the mosque still testify to the importance of the Byzantine city.

---

[58] This was the southernmost point of the dig. The city may have extended farther.

[59] Clermont-Ganneau thinks that a cornice of the apse is Crusader. *Archaeological Researches in Palestine*, Vol. II, p. 284.

CHAPTER XI

Bethel Pottery in the Chalcolithic, Early, Middle, and Late Bronze Ages

215. The Bethel pottery will be studied primarily for its relationship to the pottery researches done at Tell Beit Mirsim,[1] New Testament Jericho, and Khirbet en-Nitla.[2] The following general procedure will be employed. First, the most important features of Bethel's pottery will be compared with TBM ware.[3] Although the final two volumes on TBM (the Bronze Age and the Iron Age) were written after the Bethel campaign of 1934 and the conclusions from the study of the Bethel pottery were reflected in those volumes, the detailed picture of that pottery in comparison with TBM is now presented for the first time. Second, Bethel ware of special interest will be compared with that of such other important sites as Megiddo, Lachish, Hazor, etc. Third, rare forms will be compared with other digs where parallel or related pottery is found.

Since the TBM publications close their comparative study with the Babylonian destruction of that site, the Bethel pottery of the sixth century constitutes a new ceramic unity. Dr. Lawrence A. Sinclair reviews it in Chapter XIII. Pottery vessels of the Hellenistic and early Roman periods will be studied in detail by Dr. Paul W. Lapp, an authority in those fields, in Chapter XIV. Professor J. L. Kelso will compare sherds of the Roman and Byzantine period with pottery found at New Testament Jericho and Khirbet en-Nitla in Chapter XV.

216. In the 1934 campaign Bethel yielded few intact and complete vessels,[4] and therefore it was necessary to employ an unusually high proportion of fragmentary vessels and single sherds in pottery study. In the later campaigns only a few intact pieces were found, but Mahfouz Nassar, a *formatore* of the Palestine Archaeological Museum, was able to reconstruct a fair number of new forms. The pottery drawings of the last three campaigns are usually published only if they add something new to the 1934 picture. The relationship of all the pottery to the various levels in which it was found has been treated in detail in previous chapters describing each excavation level.

Chalcolithic

217. The Late Chalcolithic pottery (*c.* 3200 B.C.) found at Bethel in 1934 was in the virgin red earth,[5] but it was well distributed over the *tell* area excavated (Pl. 30). It is similar to the Chalcolithic of Tulûl Abū el-ʿAlâyiq (Herodian Jericho) (*AASOR*, XXXII-XXXIII, Pls. 21–36) which is the other terminus of the E–W road from the Jordan valley to the N–S ridge road at Bethel. §82. In excavating the old Canaanite high place in 1960 the earliest pottery found was a Chalcolithic jar (Pl. 81:1) which was dated by Père de Vaux *c.* 3500 B.C., §§87, 247.

Early Bronze Age

218. In 1957 one Neolithic sherd and four Khirbet Kerak sherds, both black and red (EB III A), were found in the glacis of the W wall of the city, §92. In 1954 sherds found in the test pits near the spring Ain el-Baḥr in the S section of the site were similar to level J at TBM (*c.* 2400–*c.* 2200

---

[1] The exhaustive study of all significant Palestinian pottery related to TBM ware was made by W. F. Albright and is published in the following books, *AASOR*, Vol. XII, *The Excavation of Tell Beit Mirsim*, Vol. I, *The Pottery of the First Three Campaigns*—hereafter referred to as *TBM I*. *AASOR*, Vol. XIII, pp. 55–127, *The Excavation of Tell Beit Mirsim*, I A, *The Bronze Age Pottery of the Fourth Campaign*—hereafter referred to as *TBM I A*. *AASOR*, Vol. XVII, *The Excavation of Tell Beit Mirsim*, Vol. II, *The Bronze Age*—hereafter referred to as *TBM II*. *AASOR*, Vols. XXI-XXII, *The Excavation of Tell Beit Mirsim*, Vol. III, *The Iron Age*—hereafter referred to as *TBM III*.

[2] Similar pottery studies of New Testament Jericho and Khirbet en-Nitla were made by J. L. Kelso and D. C. Baramki in *AASOR*, Vols. XXIX-XXX, *Excavations at New Testament Jericho and Khirbet en-Nitla*, Ch. II.

[3] The TBM conclusions are especially valuable as the actual pottery itself from the various sites discussed was usually available in the Palestine Archaeological Museum. No photographs and drawings can ever take the place of the pottery itself in comparative studies.

[4] Pottery is "intact" if unbroken, "complete" if completely reconstructed from fragments.

[5] For the significant difference between red and black earth, see *AASOR*, Vol. XVII, §17.

B.C.).[6] In 1957 and 1960 similar sherds were found in the fill over the high place and also in the glacis of the MB II B city walls both to the N and to the W. They were also found in the NW corner of the site. No vessels could be reconstructed from any of these EB sherds.

Middle Bronze I*

219. Characteristic MB I pottery at Bethel is much like that of TBM levels, I–H. Although the MB I pottery of 1934 corresponded mostly to TBM level I (eye),[7] later digs showed a larger proportion of pottery similar to that of level H. Pottery of the MB I type has been found all over Palestine except in South Transjordan. In recent years Nelson Glueck found scores of sites from the latter part of MB I in the Negeb of western Palestine. This pottery is derived from the caliciform ware of Syria which was in use from not later than 2100 to *c.* 1850 B.C. at Hamath on the Orontes. The Danish expedition has published its studies of the levels of this period aggregating four meters in thickness.[8] Ruth Amiran has a good article on "The Pottery of the Middle Bronze Age I in Palestine."[9]

220. The Bethel ware is nearly always thin and free from grit. It tends to show a red or creamy cross section, although other color patterns do appear. The slip is normally a creamy grey. Its dominant decorative features are incised designs with emphasis on horizontal bands in both large and small ware. The latter also has a combination of horizontal and wavy bands. The large jars, at times, show delicate combing. High on the shoulder of store-jars there are often rows of incised dots, dashes, saw-tooth patterns, fingernail imprints, etc. Another common decorative feature is vestigial ledge-handles.

221. The store-jars found at Bethel are normal MB I ware, characterized by a slender ovate body with flat base.[10] The flaring neck and mouth join the body at a relatively sharp angle and the shoulder is decorated with combing or incised decorations or both. The necks were often made separately on a wheel but their lines blended well with a handmade body. The exterior junction is usually excellently finished although the vase, Pl. 31:4, shows some carelessness. The interior junction, however, is often left unsmoothed. The decoration around the neck in Pl. 31:8 may be an adapted external collar-lap from this neck junction. In Pl. 48:3 the neck is indented from the shoulder and this indentation is highly accented with what looks like a fingernail decoration, although it was actually made by a tool. The wavy neck in Pl. 48:11 is probably due to wet clay which sagged before drying.[11] The shoulder decoration here is the same as in TBM I A, Pl. 21:4.[12] Unlike TBM ware Bethel showed no vestigial conical knob-handles (except in 1960). The paste of Bethel store-jars is similar to that of TBM ware.[13] It is in striking contrast to that of Bethel's hole-mouth jars, Pl. 48:4, 6, which seem to be a hangover from EB both in form and paste. The small ovoid jar, Pl. 48:7 has a close parallel, except for neck and rim, in a jar from Beit Sahur.[14] Pl. 31:1 is also similar to one of the Beit Sahur jars. The delicate combing of MB I, in contrast to the coarser EB, is shown in the Bethel sherds, Pl. 31:7. This general ovoid form is fairly common at Gibeon, which is on the main road from Bethel to the Mediterranean, but the proportions of the Gibeon ware usually differ from those of Bethel (Pl. 48:7). The closest Gibeon forms are Figs. 56:4 and 64:1, "The Bronze Age Cemetery at Gibeon," J. B. Pritchard. The proportions of similar Jericho ware are still farther removed from those of the Bethel ware than the Gibeon pottery.

222. The caliciform bowl Pl. 48:9 is similar to TBM I A, Pl. 3:1. The decorative pattern of bowl 8 is similar to TBM I, Pl. 5:12, 13, except

---

* Miss Kathleen M. Kenyon prefers the term "Intermediate Early Bronze–Middle Bronze Age."

[6] Inverted bowl rims and pattern combing were most common.

[7] The relevant chronology of TBM and Bethel is clearest in the case of the folded or "envelope" ledge-handles which are characteristic of *TBM I* (eye) but not of H. The best homogeneous collection of early EB I A masses of folded ledge-handles was found by Nelson Glueck at Tell Umm Gharbi in the S middle Jordan Valley, *AASOR*, Vol. XXV-XXVIII, part 2, Pl. 93–97, esp. no. 93.

[8] On this pottery see: G. E. Wright, *BASOR*, No. 71, pp. 27–34; Albright in *BASOR*, No. 95, pp. 6, 7; *TBM I*, pp. 8 ff.; *I A*, pp. 62–67; *II*, p. 14; Kathleen Kenyon, *Excavations at Jericho*, Vol. I, Ch. 4; Nelson Glueck, *BASOR* No. 138, pp. 7 ff.; No. 142, pp. 21 ff.; No. 145, pp. 15 ff.; No. 149, pp. 10 ff.; see also Glueck's, *Rivers in the Desert*, pp. 70 ff.

[9] *Israel Exploration Journal*, Vol. 10, pp. 204–25.

[10] Pl. 48:1–3, 5, 10–11; sherds, Pl. 31:1–11, 16, 20–24.

[11] *TBM I A*, Pl. 2:5,7 show wavy external neck lines but these seem purposeful rather than accidental.

[12] See also Bethel, Pl. 31:4.

[13] *TBM I A*, §7.

[14] G. E. Wright, *BASOR*, No. 71, pp. 27 ff., Fig. 1.

that the Bethel swirls are closer together. If one can judge from sherds only, the Bethel caliciform bowls and cups are similar to those of TBM. Ledge-handles are on Pl. 31:12–15.

The one unique sherd Pl. 31:17, is of greyish creamy ware with minute grits. The notches, made by a pointed stick, remind one of the surface of some Tell el-Yahūdîyeh juglets of MB II. This resume of MB I pottery is based upon the finds of the 1934 campaign. The 1954 and 1957 expeditions found fewer MB I sherds and these presented no new features. The 1960 campaign found many MB I sherds above the high place and in the temple fill (Pl. 113), but again no significant pottery information was added to that gained from the study of the 1934 finds.

Middle Bronze II

223. The 1934 campaign produced only a little MB II A pottery and that belonged to the end of that period. Later campaigns increased this percentage and at the close of the 1960 campaign along the S city wall we seemed to be reaching an MB II A level. The 1934 pottery was MB II B and C with the latter the more common. According to Kathleen Kenyon's classification, our MB II A is her MB I and our MB II B is her MB II A, while our MB II C is her MB II B. *Digging up Jericho*, pp. 186 ff. (cf. Fig. 9).

224. There are four varieties of lip profiles in Bethel store-jars Pls. 49:1, 3, 5–6, 8–9, 11–13; 51:15. The oldest representative seems to be 49:11, which may be an unpainted derivative of MB II A (*TBM I A*, Pl. 4:13). Pl. 51:15 presents a second variety. Here is a sort of funnel neck like *TBM I A*, Pl. 7:5, although the Bethel lines are more graceful. Elaborate profile necks are found in *Meg II*, Pls. 27:3; 35:1–2; 43:1, levels XII–X, covering MB II B–C. The similar profile rims of Bethel belong in two categories. Pl. 49:1, 3, shows a small secondary decorative roll just below the heavy roll rim.[15] *TBM* has examples from the D level, Vol. I, Pls. 41:10; 45:8. *Beth-zur* has it in Pl. VI:15; as does *Tirzah*, *R. B.*, LVIII: p. 402, Fig. 5:1. *Meg II* runs one or more supplementary decorative rolls in Pls. 27:3; 35:1. In the other profile rim the potter converted the rolled lip into a concave overhanging ledge with a smaller decorative ridge below it, Pl. 49:5–6, 8, 12–13; 51:27. This pattern is fairly common at *TBM I*, Pl. 45:4; *I A* Pls. 11:3–7; 14:5, 10; also at *Beth-zur*, Pl. VI:16–17, 19–20 and *Jericho I*, Figs. 196:3; 213:4. Earlier types from the eighteenth century are *Meg II*, Pls. 27:8; 28:1. *Hazor I*, Pl. C:9 is somewhat like Bethel's Pl. 49:5. Photos of various rim profiles appear on Pls. 32:3, 5, 7; 33:9–10; 34:3–4, 6–8, 10. Pl. 49:14 has a small flat bottom, normal for MB II store-jars but this jar is unusual because it carried a buff slip. The conclusions in *TBM I*, §§28, 29 and *TBM I A*, §28 hold good for Bethel store-jars.

225. Tall vases with wide mouths and bodies,[16] roughly in the form of a convex cylinder are represented on Pl. 51:7, 18, 21, 25. There are parallels in *TBM I A*, Pl. 10:1, 4; *Meg II*, Pls. 18:6, 26, 18–19 and *Taʿannek*, fig. 85. Similar jars but with an emphasis on an inverted rim are on Pl. 51:2, 12, 23. The rim in *Hazor I*, Pl. CI:18 is like Bethel's 51:21. Pl. 51:16 is hard to identify—a nondescript form. It is somewhat like *Meg T*, Pl. 13:15 which is a tiny funnel but with similar neck and sides.

226. Bethel has the two distinctly different types of MB II cooking pots. There is an old handmade flat-bottom type with a plastic band below the rim or on it, Pls. 34:16–18; 50:23; 51:14,[17] and the finer wheel-made vessel with the rounded bottom.[18] Bethel did not have the earlier type of cooking pot with steam holes above the band. Pls. 33:5, 11, 17, 19–21; 34:1–2, 12–15; 50:1–14, 16,[19] 18–19, 22, represent this new form with the rounded bottom which was just coming into production at Bethel and its form had not yet been standardized as it was in LB. The large variety of forms and the relative percentage of grit show that this experimental period lasted for a considerable length of time. Some of these cooking pots were exceptionally large, as that illustrated in Pl. 50:18 which has a rim diameter of 48 cm., and the one in Pl. 50:7 with a rim diameter of 52 cm. The new cooking pot was usually shallow but there was also a deep variety. Pl. 50:1 is similar to the fine photo in *Lachish II*, Pl. LVI A, 362.

---

[15] The groove top of the rim in Pl. 49:1 is matched in *Meg II*, Pl. 36:1.

[16] *TBM I A*, §33.
[17] Bethel did not have the earlier type with steam holes. *TBM I*, §36, *I A*, §§35, 42.
[18] *TBM I A*, §42.
[19] Late in MB II.

227. Bethel does not add much that is new to the repertory of TBM carinated bowls[20] except a beautiful low form with an unaccented rim, Pl. 49:4. It has the same shape as the lower three-quarters of a normal MB carinated bowl, *TBM I A*, Pl. 12:1. The Bethel example is a little shallower. Why the Bethel potter chose to omit the flaring mouth remains a puzzle. Pls. 49:7, 50:20; 51:26, show the more common carinated forms.[21] The first is a later form than *TBM I A*, Pl. 8:14, for the Bethel example no longer shows a sharp metallic carination; cf. *Meg T* 23:4. The second is still later for the carinated form has now become wavy. The third is a forerunner of one of the most common LB bowl forms at Bethel, cf. *Hazor I*, XCV:2, CXIV:8, *Meg II*, Pls. 28, 37, 44. Trumpet-foot bases of carinated bowls are hard to classify, whether they belong to tall vases with relatively narrow mouth or wide-mouthed chalices, Pls. 32:18; 33:14 (upside down); 51:1, 3–6, 8–11, 13, 17*. The taller are probably early rather than late. Pl. 51:17* is unusual in having horizontal burnishing both inside and outside. Note the various ways in which turning was done on these feet.

228. The largest carinated jars, Pls. 32:23–24; 52:1*–2, look like jardinieres and are related to *TBM* ware. The larger Bethel example is carinated with a shape much like *TBM I*, Pl. 41:9, but with decoration on a continuous high glossy burnishing. *Meg II*, Pl. 52:4 is a later relative with handles,[22] but it lacks the fine lines of the Bethel pieces. The major decorative band is the same as *Meg II*, Pl. 52:5 but Megiddo adds a smaller band at the top of the handles. These pieces are from Meg's stratum IX, which dates them later than the Bethel ware.

229. Bethel adds little new information on the shallow bowls so common in MB II,[23] Pls. 49:2, 15, 16*, 17*, 18, 19*; 50:15, 17; 51:19*; 52:3*, 4**, 5*, 7**. Pl. 50:17 is late in MB II. Pl. 52:4 has the rim highly burnished and painted red; the bowl was burnished inside at right angles to the rim. Bethel rims are usually plain[24] or slightly inverted and form a contrast to the Megiddo bowl rims which tend to be both inverted and everted. Pl. 49:2 appears to have a flat base instead of the usual disc base, but it is matched in *Meg T*, Pls. 24:14; 35:15. Pl. 51:20 is a late example of an MB II A form. Pl. 50:21 looks like an early variety of LB ware and it may be LB; see *TBM I*, Fig. 8 at extreme right. Pl. 51:19 is parallel to *Hazor I*, CI:5, cf. C:16; CI:4. Photos of bowl sherds appear on Pls. 33:2–3, 4*, 16**; 34:5*, 20–21*. Miscellaneous burnished sherds are Pls. 32:6*; 33:13; 34:22*. Ring-bases are Pls. 32:15*, 17; 33:1*. Disc-bases are on Pls. 32:13; 34:19. Pl. 49:10 is a concave disc-base, not beveled as in LB.

230. Bethel's MB II pottery was so badly smashed that handles, bases, and rims constitute a heavy percentage of sherds that can be identified. Thus the presence of jugs is known chiefly by their rims, Pl. 32:2, 8, and that of juglets is quickly recognized by handles. Pl. 32:16*, 20*, 21, 22* shows the familiar triple handles in burnished ware but of poor quality both in clay and craftsmanship.[25] Pl. 32:21 belongs to the familiar Tell el-Yahûdîyeh ware with double handle and a small knob where the handle meets the rim. Pl. 32:19 is the neck and handle of an elongated juglet but of poor quality.[26] The handle meets the neck just below the rim. Pl. 33:6–7* has similar juglet handles. Pl. 33:8 is a large jar or pitcher handle with incised herring-bone decoration—a rather uncommon place for such decoration in MB II. In §348 there is the description of scarab impressions on MB II store-jar handles.[27] Pls. 33:18; 34:23–24 are normal store-jar handles with thickening and prolongation where the lower end fits into the side of the jar. Pl. 32:10, 14 is MB combing but not of the best quality.

231. Sherds add a little information on painted ware. As at TBM,[28] this shows up at the very end of MB II. Pl. 34:25**, 30**–31**, 35**, has painting on burnishing after the better MB tradition. No. 35** is an unusual painted piece as it belongs to the tall jar form of Pl. 51:7. Pl. 34:26–28, 32–34, is painted but not burnished. No. 29 may be the neck of an incense burner.

---

[20] *TBM I*, §§33–34; *I A*, §§29–30.
[21] Pl. 51:24* may belong here.
[22] Stratum IX.
[23] *TBM I*, §35; *I A*, §34.
* Signifies burnished ware. Burnishing will be treated in the text only when it is of unusual importance.
** Signifies that the ware is both painted and burnished.

[24] A plain rim is neither inverted nor everted.
[25] *TBM I A*, §31.
[26] *TBM I*, §32; *I A* §46.
[27] Cf. *BASOR*, No. 136, pp. 20–21.
[28] *TBM I A*, §35.

Incised relief decoration at Bethel, Pl. 33:22–35 is either cut directly into the jar or into a rope-like moulding. Such decoration is primarily but not exclusively on store-jars. Nos. 24 and 28 are unusual in that they are on bowl rims. The latter employs rows of oblique notches but the former is apparently derived from the careless working of a herring-bone pattern or combing. Pl. 32:4* is from a deep straight-sided vessel with everted rim; Pl. 33:15 is a peculiar vessel with flat sharp edged rim and horizontal combing. Pl. 33:12 is a disc with two holes made from a potsherd. It may be a bull-roarer. No.† 510 is a pottery game piece 4.1 cm. dia. × 1.4 cm. No. 645 may be a pottery knob 2.7 cm. dia. No. 634 is a pottery spindle whorl 2.6 cm. dia.

232. The detailed study of Bethel pottery shows a light occupation of the site in MB II A, but the city had a large population throughout MB II B and C. Indeed, LB forms were showing up before the city's capture shortly after 1550 B.C. The MB city was substantial but not wealthy. The very finest wares are not common but the pottery is of good quality. (The later 1960 dig produced the best variety of MB II A sherds.)

Late Bronze

233. The areas excavated in all the campaigns showed no evidence of occupation in LB I. But in LB II A the city suddenly came to life. The first level of LB occupation at Bethel (fourteenth century) produced good ceramic ware, but the second level (thirteenth century) showed some decline in quality although its pottery is much superior in craftsmanship to most Iron I_1 ware. Painted pottery played an important part in LB ware and continued to emphasize certain MB features. Only a little foreign pottery was found and that usually in phase 1. There were about a score of base-ring ware and white-slip (wishbone-handled) sherds. Four Mycenaean sherds were found, although only one was in a definite phase 1 context. Pottery from phase 1 is shown on Pls. 52:6, 8–23; 54:15. Pottery from phase 2 is shown on Pls. 53:1–15; 54:1–14. The following are of uncertain phase Pls. 53:16–30; 54:16–17 and 55:1–5, 7–8.

234. Only fragments of LB store-jars of Bethel were found.[29] The vertical neck of the store-jar with the thickened everted rim appears in Pls. 37:15; 53:22. The handle is smooth and oval in section, Pl. 37:17. The LB II rounded base Pl. 52:12 is intermediate between the flat base of MB II and the normal knob-base of LB. Pl. 54:7 is a broader LB II base with incipient knob. Pls. 37:25; 53:19; 55:2 (probably late in LB II) have the true knob but are not as pronounced as much LB ware elsewhere.[30]

Cooking pots were already fairly well standardized in form in phase 1 of LB II,[31] as seen in Pls. 52:14, 18–19, 21; 54:15. Pls. 53:25, 28–30; 54:16–17; 55:1, 3, 5, 8 are LB cooking pots but it is uncertain whether they belong to the upper or lower phase. The largest diameters in phase 1 ran 56, 40, 38 cm. Those of uncertain phase tended to run 32, 30, 28 cm.

235. Good carinated bowls continue from MB into the first phase of LB II.[32] Pl. 52:9 shows excellent carination; Pl. 52:17 is very fine clay but the form is not equal to the ware. In phase 2 the typical LB carination is continued in Pl. 53:3, 10, 15. 53:20 is a degenerate carinated form. More often the arc above the carination tends to straighten out, Pls. 53:1–2, 4–7, 11; 54:4–5, 8, 14. Pl. 53:24, 27 was LB but the context made it uncertain whether the ware was early or late. It was more likely early, as the form is modified MB. In LB II the carinated bowl normally tends to shift from a disc base or a bevelled ring-base to a plain, flat base, or a convex or concave one.

In depth the bowls still run shallow to average; none was high. *Meg II* shows about the same shifts, with some flat bottoms coming in earlier, especially in high ware. *Hazor I* has a wide collection of all types of bowls. Their LB II carinated bowls also tend to straighten out above the carination. Their bases tend to be better than the similar type at Bethel. Pl. 53:21 is a small fragment but looks like the rim of our MB jardinières, see Pl. 52, 1, 2. If not, then it is the rim of a store-jar, but it is very thin for a store-jar. Pl. 53:23 is like the rim of a later tall four-handled crater of *Meg II*, Pl. 69:15 (VII A–VI A).

236. Bowls without carination are very com-

---

† Is the abbreviation of number and refers to the number given the object in the expedition's record book. Such No. items do not appear on any of the plates unless so specified in the text.

[29] *TBM I*, §48; *I A*, §53.
[30] See also photos Pl. 37; 25, 28.
[31] *TBM I*, §55; *I A*, §54.
[32] Cf. *TBM I*, §§50–51; *I A*, §52.

mon.[33] Phase 1 is represented by Pl. 52:6, 8, 15–16, 20, 22; phase 2 by Pls. 53:8–9, 12–14; 54:1, 2, 6, 12. The following are of uncertain context, Pl. 53:16, 18, 26. Extremely shallow bowls were not as common as in MB II. The majority of bowls carry on the MB ratio of height to diameter. Pl. 52:15, 22 have decidedly steeper sides than the MB II form. The high wavy rim and shoulder profile and several handles (Pl. 54:3) appear first in LB and continue in Iron I. For complete bowls see *TBM I A*, Pl. 16:14, 16. A larger bowl with wavy rim-shoulder profile is *TBM I*, Pl. 47:13. Bases for Bethel LB bowls of the first phase were usually well made. In the second, however, they usually deteriorated to simple flat or rounded bases. Concave bases in phase 1 are shown on Pl. 52:6, 8. A high outcurving ring-base of phase 2 found in the final LB burning is Pl. 54:13; somewhat related is Amman Tomb Fig. 6:13 (*PEFA VI*). For photos of ring-bases see Pl. 37:18, 19. The excellent sharp bevelling of LB, as in 19, is characteristic and does not seem to occur elsewhere.

For disc-bases see Pl. 37:26–27 where wheel marks are quite pronounced as in the last of LB. The distinctly inverted rim as on Pl. 37:16, 20 is more characteristic of phase 1 than 2; the plain rim or only very slightly inverted rim is more characteristic of phase 2. Pl. 52:20 has an unusual LB profile for the under edge of a shallow bowl, suggesting a vestigial carination; it carries a cream slip on the inside. It looks like an imported piece. We have not found a parallel. Pl. 37:22, 24 has knobbed barhandles, which are an LB characteristic. They go back to similar barhandles pierced longitudinally for a cord. It is the source of the typical straight barhandles of Iron I as seen in LB at Ugarit.

237. The knife-pared elongated juglet of LB[34] appears at Bethel, Pl. 52:11. This is a local imitation in brownish buff of the original white clay juglets. The thrower's marks show fast strong work, unusual in so small a vessel. Phase 2 examples of elongated juglets are Pl. 54:9, 11. Pl. 52:13 of the earlier level is the fatter, round-bottom juglet which runs from MB II on through LB and into Iron I. It is LB II in *Hazor I* (Pl. XCVI:17). The clay and craftsmanship usually give the clue to which period they belong. The fatter pointed juglet with carinated shoulder and trefoil lip, Pl. 55:7,[35] comes from a general LB context. It is matched in an LB tomb at *Gezer III*, Pl. LXIV:8 although the juglet is less graceful than the Bethel one.

238. The large jug on Pl. 54:10 from the second phase of LB differs from the average LB ware in straightness of the neck and the small space between neck and handle. The small sherd Pl. 52:23 may be a rim from one of the typical jugs of LB, see *Meg II*, Pl. 39:13 and Pl. 48:17 (IX). Bethel's jug, however, is unpainted.

239. The two-handled lentoid (pilgrim) flask with its handles springing upward and arch-wise, Pl. 52:10, fits into the detailed description of this type in *TBM I*, §57. The Bethel piece is from the first phase of LB II. *Meg II*, Pl. 70:9 shows a later example with similar neck and rim details.

240. Bethel follows the general pattern of native painted ware, except that the variety of patterns represented is below normal. In Pl. 35 there are concentric circles on bowls and jugs. In some cases at right angles to the circles are patterns of wavy lines between straight lines. Also there are thin lines equally spaced in small ware. Pl. 36 adds checkerboard patterns and also thin lines equally spaced and at right angles over concentric circles on a jug. In phase 1 of LB the more common painted sherds are about equally divided between those which have the paint directly applied to the clay, and those where slip or burnishing precede the painting. Paint on burnishing and paint on unburnished slip are less common; paint on a wash is very rare.

241. On Pl. 37 the wishbone-handled ware presents the following patterns; grey ware with light green slip, light grey slip, greyish blue slip and white passing into a light blue slip. There is also a light grey ware with white slip and a reddish brown ware with yellow grey slip. There was one imitation wishbone handle. A few base-ring fragments appear on Pl. 38:1–11, including an imitation piece (9). Pl. 37:11–14 has small Mycenaean fragments. Pl. 37:10 is a Greek lekythos sherd from the second half of the fifth century, see §320. No. 715 is a stamped jar handle Pl. 72.

242. To summarize, the LB pottery at Bethel was normal Palestinian ware with a minimum of foreign pottery. It presented no new forms except

---

[33] *TBM I*, §§50–54; *I A*, §52.
[34] *TBM I*, §56.

[35] See also Pl. 37:21 for photo of trefoil lip on small jug.

for several unique pieces. With the destruction of Bethel by Joshua the Bronze Age had run its course and the Iron Age took over with Israelite influence now dominating everything.

1954 Campaign

243. The campaigns of 1954, 1957, and 1960 confirmed the pottery findings and conclusions of the 1934 expedition. In 1954 more pottery came from the new test area near the mosque than from the dig on the 1934 campsite. The pottery of the mosque area is over-whelmingly Roman and Byzantine. It will be treated in Chapter XV. Sherds from EB IV, MB I and MB II were found, but no forms could be reconstructed until LB. Pl. 73:1 is an LB handmade bowl of light brown ware and was found when cutting through the 147 cm. LB wall. The closest related forms are from *Hazor I*, Pl. XC:12, CXLIII:29 (LB II) but these are thrown ware. No. 1115* is a typical LB lamp (fragment) 18×5 cm. Only one Mycenaean sherd was found although there were several base-ring and wishbone-handle sherds.

1957 Campaign

244. The 1957 campaign added one Neolithic and four Khirbet Kerak (EB III A) sherds and later wares. There are some new forms beginning with MB II for the Bethel picture and also some complete forms where only fragments were known before. MB II forms are as follows: Pl. 77:2 is a tan-grey four-handled store-jar with combing extending from the neck to the bottom of the handle. The form is found at *TBM I*, Pl. 41:12 and *TBM I A*, Pl. 6:1 but the latter has better handles. *Jericho I*, Figs. 183:1, 2; 196:2 have the same form but the handles differ. The first and last have two handles and the second has the four handles in sets of twos. *Beth Shemesh*, p. 131:696 has only two handles. Pl. 77:3 is the lower half of another store-jar. Both of these Bethel jars are seventeenth–sixteenth century.

245. Pl. 77:6 is one of the finest MB II bowl forms although it lacks burnishing or painting and is over-fired. It is grey on the outside and buff inside. Pl. 52:4 is only a slightly different rim but it is highly burnished and painted red.

---

* Pottery which bears a number (the record book number of the excavations) is not unique enough to be drawn but is significant in getting an over-all picture of the pottery story.

Similar forms appear at *TBM I A*, Pl. 10:9, *Hazor I*, Pl. CXIX:10, *Tirzah, R.B.*, LIX, Fig. 2:6 and *Jericho I*, Figs. 148:1, 218:2 but the Bethel base is finer work than any of these parallels. Pl. 77:5 is a light buff bowl with light burnishing on the outside. It lacks the fine lines of the preceding piece and is much too thick. *Meg II*, Pl. 38:3 is also poor work but *Meg II*, Pl. 29:24 shows this form at its best. Compare also *Jericho I*, Fig. 115:1 and *Hazor I*, Pl. XCIV:2. Pl. 77:4 is MB II although this form is normally associated with LB. It is pinkish buff ware with a burnished slip in buff. Pl. 77:7 is an unusual rim pattern. The closest example found is *Hazor I*, Pl. CXII:13. Pl. 77:1 is a pinkish buff pitcher with a combing design, the most graceful form found in our Bethel campaigns. It is apparently an imported piece as it has no Palestine parallel. No. 2187 is a broken lamp with a maximum dia. of 12 cm. No. 2132 is a loom weight, 10.3 cm. high and 7 cm. wide. There are three special jar handles: No. 2103 is on Pl. 72; No. 2174 is an incised equal-angled cross and No. 2189 is an illegible Hyksos seal.

246. LB produced a beautiful vase of pinkish ware with delicate black lines, Pl. 77:8. It is doubtless an imported piece. Its closest Palestinian relative seems to be *Ain Shems IV*, Pl. LVI:14 (LB II). Pl. 77:10 seems to be a new juglet form but from a very common family. The neck is unusually wide and straight and the body halfway between the rounded and the elongated varieties. It is an over-fired grey unburnished piece. *Meg T*, Pl. 48:4 is its closest relative. Pl. 77:9 is a poorly made buff bowl. Pl. 77:11 is the only " cup and saucer " fragment found at Bethel. It is like *Hazor II*, Pl. CXLVI:8, 13 (LB II) but the Bethel piece has a ring-base. Pl. 77:12 is the fragment of a goblet or chalice but no parallel was found. It is buff ware with two bands in brown paint, 2.5 mm. wide and spaced 7 mm. apart. It came from a mixed MB–LB context but it is most likely an LB piece. No. 2183 is a fragment of a colander or strainer 9×6 cm. and 1.6 cm. thick. One sherd each of Mycenaean and wishbone-handled ware were found. Four new painted patterns were found.

1960 Campaign

247. In this campaign we worked along the city walls and therefore we found no great variety

of pottery forms although we did find a considerable number of vessels that could be completely or largely reconstructed. The oldest vessel found in any campaign was Pl. 81:1, which Père de Vaux identified as Chalcolithic, cf. *Lachish IV*, Pl. 56:26. The clay of this handmade piece contains a large amount of quartz. The exterior of the pot is buff but the interior is reddish brown. The exterior of the jar is partly smooth. The handles blend well into the walls. Although the jar was found below the east door of the high place temple, it was so close to bedrock that it must be identified with the high place rather than the temple. It contained a fragment of a skull with the eye ridges of a small animal and a bone fragment probably of a femur.

248. MB I pottery is represented by sherds only, see Pl. 113*. MB II finds are as follows: Pls. 81:2 and 119a (No. 3143) is a ceramic cult object which is probably imitative of a pillar of an Egyptian temple. It is a grey clay with a white slip on the exterior. The vessel has very thick walls for MB II ware. No Palestinian parallels were found. It was discovered just outside the building near the NW gate which we are tentatively identifying as a temple. Found near it was a graceful, delicate drinking cup, Pl. 81:5. The clay is excellent and finished off with a good burnishing, but the vessel was slightly warped in firing. The foot is missing. No Palestine parallels were found. Near it was a beautiful shallow trumpet-foot bowl, Pl. 81:3. It is rose-colored ware made of a good clay but slightly over-fired. A slip covered the interior and extended just slightly over the rim. It is better craftsmanship than *TBM I A*, Pl. 10:8; cf. *Hazor I*, Pl. CXIX:10 (MB II) and *Meg II*, Pl. 45:12 (XII–X). Other MB II pieces from other areas were as follows. Pl. 81:4 is a very large but graceful elongated juglet. Its grey to buff surface is pitted by over-firing. The neck is unusually thin and the thrower's marks on the interior show only toward the top of the piece. It is somewhat like *Hazor I*, Pl. CXX:7 (MB II). There are two very small bowls. Pl. 81:8 is a good form but with excessively thick walls and an unfinished base. Its EB ancestor can be seen at *et Tell*, Pls. LXV:9, 1525, LXXV:1387, and its LB descendant at *TBM I*, Pl. 47:1. Pl. 81:6 belongs to a family found in both MB and LB. The closest parallel is LB I (*Meg T*, Pl. 49:14). The Bethel piece is buff ware with a stringcut base. It is quick throwing and well fired but the clay was of only mediocre quality. (Pl. 81:7 is out of place here: it is Iron II.)

249. The 1960 campaign gave us three excellent forms in MB II store-jars, Pl. 82:4 being a greyish buff to pink. It is over-fired giving some lime pitting. It is well thrown, a four-handled jar with thin combing bands, one around the neck and a second around the shoulder at the top of the handles. Bethel's closest relative is *Jericho I*, Fig. 183:2; cf. also Fig. 196:3, a two-handled jar. *TBM I A*, Pl. 6:2, has the same general form as Bethel but the latter has a more complex rim and only 4 handles. There is also another quite similar Bethel store-jar No. 3114, except that its rim is less complex and the combing is between the tops of the handles which are in pairs spaced 24 cm. apart on opposite sides of the jar. Pl. 82:1 is somewhat similar to *TBM I A*, Pl. 6:1 but the Bethel form narrows toward the bottom and has only 2 handles; cf. also *Jericho I*, Fig. 206:5. The jar was made with very fast throwing and the thickness of the walls varies more than shown in the drawing. The combing is fine and delicate. The ware is slate grey with a pinkish buff. No. 3123 is the upper section of a jar similar in form to Pl. 82:1 but is exceptional in that it is made of a cooking pot clay although it is well thrown and a little thinner than normal. Pl. 82:2 is the most narrow of MB II jars. It is buff to pinkish buff with thin combings wider spaced at the handles than elsewhere. It is good clay, well thrown and well fired. The upper part of the jar is somewhat like *Meg II*, Pl. 18:2 (XIII A) but the Bethel lower section is much longer and narrower. For a variety of patterns used in MB combings, see Fig. 2. Pl. 119a (No. 3090) is a 10 cm. section of a jar handle with two serpent patterns running lengthwise on the handle. The same plate shows a serpent motif on the base of a store-jar. They were found with other cult objects.

250. Pl. 119b (No. 3102) is a jar handle with a good scarab seal impression, see photograph. No. 3087 is a jar handle with an illegible Hyksos seal impression. No. 3093 is a small potsherd stopper or plug, 1 cm. thick with an upper dia. of 2.4 cm. and a lower dia. of 1.8 cm. No. 3046 is an unfinished pottery spindle whorl 3.9 cm. in dia. The hole had been started on each side but not bored through. From the front steps of the

---
* A few sherds are earlier.

U-shaped city gate came No. 3100, an MB II potsherd shaped as a playing piece. It was a crude circle with a maximum dia. of 5.1 cm.

251. The only LB store-jar, Pl. 82:3, is a large fragment found with milk bowl sherds. The exterior is a slate color and the interior a pinkish buff. It is excellent clay well thrown and well fired. We can find no exact parallels. The bowl, Pl. 82:7 is hard to match but is somewhere between *Ain Shems IV*, Pl. LVIII:36 (LB) and *Meg T*, Pl. 37:1 with handles (LB I). The latter is much better craftsmanship. The Bethel piece is of good clay of a light chocolate color with a red core. It is well thrown but only partially smoothed on the exterior. Pl. 82:5 is somewhat like *Lachish II*, Pl. XXXIX:68, which has handles. The clay contained limestone grits which had popped in over-firing. The exterior color was pink, the inside buff; the interior was fairly well smoothed but the exterior was irregular due to rings made by the limestone grits in throwing. Pl. 82:6 seems to be an LB descendant of an MB II piece. The ware is a poor clay badly blistered by over-firing. The closest parallel to Pl. 82:8 is *Lachish II*, Pl. XLIB:104. This ware is white to grey with a whitish slip. It is made of excellent clay and is well thrown. It is smoothed on the inside but only partially so on the outside. The bottom is well smoothed.

CHAPTER XII

Bethel Pottery in Iron I and Iron II

Iron I

252. The Iron I pottery of Bethel falls into the same three patterns as at Tell Beit Mirsim, where it was divided into pre-Philistine,[1] Philistine,[2] and post-Philistine.[3] As there is little Philistine pottery at Bethel the following phraseology will be used. Bethel's Iron I$_1$ corresponds to TBM's pre-Philistine, I$_2$ to Philistine, and I$_3$ to post-Philistine. At Bethel the shift from Iron I$_1$ to I$_2$ was characterized not so much by Philistine pottery as by the introduction of burnishing[4] and a few new forms.

253. Bethel's Iron I$_1$ pottery was predominantly poor, getting progressively worse through the second and third building phases. There were, however, some good LB forms and good LB texture appearing in the first phase of Iron I$_1$. The overwhelming amount of Iron I$_1$ pottery, however, was of poorly worked clay and often the throwing was inferior. An accurate drawing will usually show the contrast between LB and Iron I$_1$ when the same forms are used. Cooking pots and collared store-jars with profiled rims constituted the bulk of the sherds. The remainder of the sherds represented a good variety of forms, including painted ware. With the coming of I$_2$ the quality of the clay and the craftsmanship improved quickly and in I$_3$ the pottery represented the best craftsmanship. More new forms were introduced and more varied burnishing techniques were developed.

254. Iron I store-jars belong in two rim categories: (1) the jar with a high collar, shifting to a profiled rim with a roll above and a ridge below and (2) a later jar with heavy rolled rim which tends to be concave on the under side. The first was used throughout the first three phases of building. The second then came into use and continued through Iron I$_2$ and Iron I$_3$. The collared rim appeared in abundance in contemporary Ai and Tell en-Naṣbeh, as well as in the first Israelite occupation of Gibeah (Tell el-Fûl); it was abundant in Beth-zur in the S and in Shechem in the N. At TBM and Beth-shemesh in the Shephelah it appeared, but was not common. It appeared in Meg stratum VI, but not in V; see *Meg II*, Pl. 83:1, 4. All examples listed are from VI (loci 1735 and 1729, with 1727, 1747, and 1774). The range of distribution is stated as VIIB-VI, but the earlier pieces were presumably only fragments. "Now, this type of pottery, which first appeared during the first half of the twelfth century, lasted until after the Philistine destruction of Shiloh, *c*. 1050 B.C. . . . In the period of Saul at Gibeah a new type of rim displaced the collared rim, which accordingly went out of use there well before 1000 (the minimal date for Saul's death). This same new rim appears at Bethel, Tell en-Naṣbeh, and other sites in the following phase, so it was widely distributed and drove out the collared rim between 1050 and 1000, presumably in the third quarter of the eleventh century."[5] The profiled rim appears on Pls. 56:1-22;[6] 61:1. Photos appear on Pl. 40: 19-20, 23-24, 30-31, 35. Nos. 19 and 24 show finger prints along the edge of the rim. This decoration also appears on jar handles Pl. 40:1-2. Incised decoration is on handles Nos. 3, 6, 10. No. 42 is a plain handle. Although the early rim appeared in various profiles they have not yet furnished any clue to closer dating within the period of their use. The new lower heavy rolled rim appears on Pls. 40:26; 41:18, 22, 27, 30-31, 34, 37; 56:23-26; 57:1-5; 61:2-8. (Pl. 41:36 is a related rim of a much smaller jar.) The knob base of LB store-jars continued in use for some time into Iron I but was then replaced by the slightly rounded base of Pl. 57:7-11.

255. The Iron I cooking pot is usually indistinguishable from its LB predecessor.[7] It appears on Pls. 40:33; 41:25; 57:12-22; 58:1-26; 59:13; 61:9-10. Pl. 59:12 was from a mixed context

---

[1] *TBM I*, §§76-79.
[2] *Ibid*., §§80-86.
[3] *Ibid*., §§80-92.
[4] Pl. 40:28*-29*, 32*, is at the end of I$_1$. TBM also has a little burnishing at the end of Iron I$_1$.
[5] W. F. Albright, *Archaeology of Palestine* p. 118.
[6] Pl. 57:6 may also belong here.
[7] *TBM I*, §55, §§76-79; *III*, §22.

and may be LB. Pl. 58:17 was found in the burning of the first building phase. Pls. 58:13; 59:13 are tenth–ninth century B.C. Pl. 61:10 is from a mixed Iron I and II context; 61:9 is a transitional form going into the Iron II cooking pot. Pls. 57:18; 58:20 show the handles on these cooking pots. The most common diameter of Bethel cooking pots in Iron I was $c.$ 28 cm. Diameters of $c.$ 26 cm. and $c.$ 30 cm. were approximately equal in number and constituted the second largest group. The smallest cooking pot was $c.$ 22 cm. and the diameter of the largest $c.$ 38 cm.

256. Most Iron I bowls[8] were offshoots of LB forms but the Iron I_1 pottery was usually thicker ware made from poorer clays and was often carelessly thrown, with the bases generally left unsmoothed. In the later phases of Bethel Iron I the pottery was improved in all respects. The LB carinated bowl continued on into Iron I but was generally much poorer in quality. Usually the carination was modified into a wavy profile. Pl. 60:4 shows the best work; cf. an inferior piece in *Meg II*, Pl. 74:6 (from VIB, early eleventh century B.C.). Poorer work at Bethel is seen in Pls. 59:16–17, 21; 60:7. Pl. 60:3 is the high bowl characteristic of Iron I at Bethel; it was at its best toward the end of Iron I at Bethel. It was common among sherds where it can be recognized by the sharp angle of the wall as it springs from the base. *TBM I*, Pl. 50:7 is a good example of this bowl. Another form with more prominent carination, situated much lower on the vessel, is shown on Pls. 59:15; 60:11, 15. Pl. 59:11 is the lower part of one of these bowls. Pls. 59:15 and 60:11 seem to have had seven handles. The closest example is *Meg II*, Pl. 85:4, but the latter is painted and shallower; cf. also *Meg I*, Pl. 32:167 and *Meg T*, Pl. 70:13 (4 handles). Naṣbeh forms are not as close. Pl. 60:9 is the base of a very large bowl perhaps of this variety. Another modified carinated bowl is Pl. 60:8 with an inverted-everted rim; cf. the similar bowl-rim in Meg II, Pl. 78:17. Pl. 59:20 looks like an Iron I variety of a large LB bowl similar to the larger bowl *Meg II*, Pl. 69:15 (VIIA, twelfth century). The Bethel bowl may possibly be from an LB context. The rim of a carinated bowl with a very sharp angle appears on Pl. 60:18. Pl. 60:13 may be a very small bowl but it is more likely a jeweler's crucible. Philistine craters were represented by only three sherds Pl. 38:12–14, although there were some imitations of Philistine ware. Two sherds portray spirals and one shows a swan. Pl. 60:12[9] is a modified form of a Philistine crater with tilted loop-handles, but its only decoration is dark red bands on the outside of the rim and below the handles. *Ain Shems I*, Pl. XXXIII:18, 19 also has two lines as decoration on the body of the bowl. It also appeared in the twelfth–eleventh century levels at Hazor. Pl. 60:10, 14 may belong to the same bowl form.

257. Iron I shallow bowls usually had a plain rim and were a little taller than those of LB. Pl. 61:18 is typical Iron I ware. Pl. 59:14 has the same coarse clay but good throwing. Pl. 60:5 is better clay but poor throwing. It appeared at *Tirzah R.B.* LIX, Fig. 8:10. Pl. 61:17 is an odd piece. The interior had an excellent contour but the outside seemed to have been purposely roughened. Pl. 59:19 is such poor work that it is uncertain whether this form belongs in the category of shallow bowls or carinated ones. Pl. 59:18* has good clay and excellent throwing (slightly everted rim), hand-burnished inside. It is I_2 or later. Pl. 60:6 is an imported faience piece. It had a light blue slip over a cream core, which was not well levigated.

The inverted rim, so often found in LB bowls, has at times become a part of the bowl in Iron I, Pl. 60:1–2, 16. Pls. 41:15*; 60:17* show the pinched button-rim of a bowl horizontally hand-burnished inside and on the rim, I_3. Pl. 40:17 shows a spatulate bar-handle with a vertical hole. Pl. 40:7–8 has a square horizontal handle with a vertical hole. Other photographs dealing with bowls are Pl. 40:13, 18, 22*, 25, 27, 36, 38*, 39, 41.

258. The libation chalice was an LB form that continued over into Iron I increasing in quantity but usually deteriorating in esthetic value in the process. It is represented on Pls. 55:6, 10; 59:10; 61:11. The wavy edge pattern was not too common but occurs at *Meg II*, Pl. 87:6 (VI). The low foot of Pl. 55:9 is more characteristic of LB than of Iron I. It was probably Iron I_1. The stem of Pl. 55:12 is common in Iron I.

259. Pl. 59:1*, 2*, 3 presents three forms of Iron I juglets. The first two are especially valuable because of their close dating; No. 1 is tenth–

---

[8] *TBM I*, §§53–54, §76 ff.; *III*, §22.

[9] *TBM I*, §§80–86.

* Signifies burnished ware. Burnishing will be treated in the text only when it is of unusual importance.

ninth century B.C. and No. 2 is about tenth century. Both have chordal burnishing on the bottom and vertical burnishing above. No. 1 is similar to *Ain Shems I*, Pl. XXXVIII:22. *Meg T*, Pl. 74:5 is similar in form; it is Iron II and unburnished. No. 2 has the same form as *Ain Shems I*, Pls. XXXVIII:26; XXXIX:7, but the latter are not burnished. Pl. 61:12 is a beautiful example of the spherical long-neck juglet with button-base. The surface was pinkish buff. It came from a late context. *Meg I*, Pl. 5:136 is a similar form but with less emphasis on the button-base. Pl. 41:32 is the forerunner of the most common Iron II juglet. Pl. 40:37 is a photo of a juglet bottom and 40:11* is a handle.

260. The only Mycenaean pottery that was imitated in quantity by Israelite potters was the squat juglet with two lug-handles.[10] The Iron I variety tends to be taller than LB. In Pl. 59:5 the decoration is in parallel bands as in *TBM I*, Pl. 47:9; but both its form and painting are inferior to LB varieties. It is earlier, however, than the juglet Pl. 59:4 where the height is exaggerated and the body is in an egg shape. It is plain ware lacking the earlier painting and the later black burnishing. Photos of tilted lug-handles appear on Pl. 40:4, 9, 14.

261. Iron I had several varieties of pitchers that came over from LB.[11] There is a spherical variety Pl. 55:16, 19, cf. *TBM I*, Pls. 45:21; 47:10. No. 19 seems to be imported ware and carries alternate bands of red and black over a white slip; *Meg I*, Pl. 6:147 is in part related to the Bethel piece. No. 16 is unpainted local ware and of poorer craftsmanship; it is like *Meg II*, Pl. 73:1. Pl. 55:18 is also spherical but with wider neck and trefoil rim;[12] it was probably early in Iron I. Pl. 59:8 is a modified sphere with bulging shoulder; it came from an LB–Iron I context; the form was more LB than Iron I. Pl. 55:15 is a wide mouth pitcher. The plain lip was uncommon in Iron I but common in Iron II. The handle, however, was a typical I$_3$ pattern. For other jug handles see Pl. 59:6–7; photo Pl. 40:3, 5. Pl. 41:33 is the fragment of a jug with sharp edged rim.

262. The most important jug fragments found were Philistine. They constitute the shoulder and neck (including a strainer spout) of a Philistine beer-jug, Pls. 38:15a–15b; 59:9. The decoration was black and red lines on a white wash, the horizontal lines in red and the vertical and semi-circular in black. This pattern was unusual in beer-jugs where the metopees usually portray swans, spirals, diamonds, etc.[13] Pl. 40:15–16 is a strainer spout; in No. 15 there is a dark red line on the edge of the spout. Pl. 40:12 is the usual strainer, not a strainer spout.

263. Parts of three lentoid (pilgrim) flasks were found in Iron I, Pls. 55:14, 17; 61:19–20.[14] The last had LB texture but was thick ware. Its grey clay suggests that it was an imported piece. Pl. 55:14 has its closest parallel in *Naṣbeh II*, Pl. 76:1745, where it is dated Iron II. The Bethel piece, however, was beautiful imported ware whereas the Naṣbeh piece was a local imitation. Pls. 41:28; 55:17, have their closest parallel in *Lachish III*, Pl. 103:677. Examples of Iron I painted sherds are on Pl. 39.

264. The lamp Pl. 55:11 must be late in Iron I for its form is much closer to Iron II.[15] It lacks the rounded foot of Iron I and only rarely does the narrow rim appear at that time. The lamp Pl. 40:40 has a slightly rounded base; the one on Pl. 41:35 marks a transition between the round and the flat bottom.

265. Pl. 55:13 is difficult to interpret since the bottom is missing and a hole had been pierced in the side. It may belong to the hole-mouth category as in *Naṣbeh II*, Pl. 24:393 (p. 140), which had two holes pierced in it. The hole-mouth jar, however, was not commonly found in Iron I. See also *Jericho, S. & W.*, Pl. 31: A, 1. *Meg T*, Pl. 65:19 represents another possible bottom for our fragment.

266. The most interesting pottery jar handle is Pl. 44:7. The decorated head band is below the center of the jar handle and the chin is as low as the shoulder of the jar. The eyes, ears, nose, mouth, and chin are all carefully delineated but give the appearance of a mask rather than portraiture. No exact parallel has been found although handle decoration in Iron I was not too uncommon. It is dated *c.* 1100 B.C. Pl. 72 has

---

* Signifies burnished ware. Burnishing will be treated in the text only when it is of unusual importance.

[10] *TBM I*, §§62, 65, 68, 83, 85, 96.
[11] *TBM I*, §58.
[12] Pl. 40:34 is a trefoil rim.

[13] *Rumeileh III*, Fig. 2:15, has part of the same painted design but on a similar shaped perfume juglet.
[14] Pl. 61:19–20. These are front and side views of the same flask.
[15] *TBM I*, §93.

seven incised jar handles: Nos. 315, 386, 388, 415, 468, 481, 482. Nos. 161 and 378 are jar handles with a crude "Y" impression. From a mixed Iron I–II level comes a jar handle, No. 334, which bears the impression of a small piece of closely woven cloth.

267 There are two small kernos fragments Nos. 102, 422. The former is like *Gezer III*, CLXXV: 9. No. 244 is the cup of a crude canteen. No. 277 is a small pottery stopper with a hole for a string. Worked potsherds are represented by a pendant, a spindle whorl and a two-holed button No. 325. It is too small to be a bull-roarer. No. 304 is a limestone potter's wheel 15.8 cm. dia. and with an 11.6 cm. pivot.

Iron II

268. Iron II pottery of Bethel adds little new to the ceramic story beyond that already learned at TBM, although it does confirm that information.[16] TBM was destroyed by Nebuchadnezzar's troops in 597 B.C., but Bethel was spared destruction for another half century or more. Bethel's pottery, therefore, in these later years is significant for it marks a transitional phase between Iron II and Iron III. While most of this new sixth century pottery is rooted in Iron II forms, the modifications in these forms are more numerous than those which preceded the destruction of Jerusalem, and it is therefore necessary to treat this new pottery as a separate group. This study is presented in Chapter XIII by Lawrence A. Sinclair.

269. Iron II pottery which preceded the destruction of TBM has been treated in such detail in the TBM volumes that remarks on the Bethel pottery will be reduced to a minimum. Much of Bethel's pottery is fragmentary and therefore exact detailed comparisons are difficult. But if one uses the general forms of both sites and does not press exact sizes and decorative details, then Bethel presents only a few forms which are new. The ring-burnished bowl is the major better pottery form at both sites and Bethel follows the same general story as TBM.[17] Plain bowls tell the same story. One special Bethel feature is the use of the inverted-everted rim as in Pl. 63:1–2, 5, 13. A second difference is the use of a shallower bowl at Bethel, Pls. 62:13–14; 63:5, 17. The only new form is Pl. 63:8. It is somewhat similar to *Meg I*, Pl. 32:163–164 (V) but the lip differs. Ring-burnished bowls are found in Pls. 62:1, 3, 4, 6–19; 63:1–3, 5–6, 8–9, 12–13, 15–24. Burnishing details are given in the descriptive listing of the plates. Plain bowls are found on Pls. 62:2, 5, 20; 63:4, 10–11, 14, 26. Pl. 63:26 is Iron I or early Iron II; Pl. 63:5 is early in Iron II; and Pl. 62:19 is ninth century.

270. The cooking pots, Pl. 65:1–2, 4, 6, 8, are similar to the TBM forms but Pl. 65:3, 5, 7 are not.[18] Nos. 3 and 7, however, are like *Meg I*, Pl. 39:8. Bethel juglets, Pl. 61:13–15, represent the transition from Iron I to Iron II. Bethel juglets, Pl. 65:9–12, 14–17, are normal Iron II examples similar to TBM.[19] Pl. 65:18 may be as late as sixth century B.C. The jugs or pitchers, Pl. 65:19–20, are similar to TBM.[20] The latter was early in Iron II. The small amphora, Pl. 64:19, has a rim pattern which differs from TBM but is something like *Naṣbeh II*, Pl. 27:447.[21] The water decanter neck Pl. 64:17 is probably sixth century. Its closest example is *Hazor I*, Pl. LXXII, 7 (IV-V). The lamps Pl. 65:21, 23 add nothing new to the story of Iron II ware.[22]

271. New Bethel forms without TBM parallels are as follows. Pl. 65:13 is a small carinated vase with graceful lines. It seems to be Iron II but no close parallel has been found, unless it is related to such forms as *TBM I*, Pl. 67:21, or *Gezer III*, Pl. CLXXIX, 23, both of which are much poorer pieces. Pl. 65:22 seems to be a pottery ointment jar, probably imitating an alabaster form. It is paralleled at *Meg I*, Pl. 9:34, p. 165, §34, and at *Gerar*, Pl. LIX: 75p. A few sherds of Samaria ware were found but no vessels could be reconstructed. No Assyrian forms, such as were found at Samaria, were present at Bethel. Pl. 72 has four examples of incised or impressed jar handles, Nos. 231, 235, 387, 493. The only other items were a spindle whorl 4.2 cm. dia. No. 7 and a flat pendant 7.4 × 7.2 cm. No. 478, probably ninth century B.C. (Eight incised jar handles came from a badly mixed Hellenistic–Iron II context. No. 103 was an incised cross on the shoulder of a jar below the handle. No. 389 was an incised

---

[16] *TBM I*, Ch. VI; *III*, Ch. IV-V.
[17] *TBM I*, §117; *III*, §160.
[18] *TBM I*, §109; *III*, §155.
[19] *TBM I*, §§112–13; *III*, §§153–154, 158.
[20] *TBM I*, §111; *III*, §150.
[21] *TBM I*, §108; *III*, §156.
[22] *TBM I*, §119; *III*, §161.

sherd with a cross in a circle *c.* 10 cm. dia. These two were from a mixed Hellenistic–Iron I context.)

1954 Campaign

272. The campaigns of 1954, 1957, and 1960 confirmed the Iron I findings of the 1934 dig. The 1954 campaign demonstrated still more clearly the deterioration of pottery in the second building phase. The first phase had carried over some good LB characteristics but these were completely missing after that phase. One complete store-jar Pl. 73:15 was from the eleventh or tenth century, the context favoring the earlier. *Meg I*, Pl. 17:86 shows a slightly later form of this jar. Pl. 114:11 (No. 1150) is a unique seal impression on the handle of a store-jar.

273. Bowls with inverted rims were better represented in 1954. Pl. 73:14 is a light brown bowl with a continuous burnishing. Pl. 73:13 is a rich reddish brown with a burnishing which looks something like that of MB II. Pl. 73:12 is buff. The clay was poor and the grits showed in the throwing circles; the throwing, however, was fast work and fairly good. The last two were from the same locus. The form on Pl. 73:14 is somewhat like that of Iron I bowls with bar-handles. Pl. 63:1 seems to be a sixth century B.C. version of Pl. 73:12, cf. also *Hazor II*, Pl. LIV:4 (VIII). Pl. 73:4 has an unusually thick rim. The color was a deep rich red with widely spaced hand-burnishings. It is tenth–ninth century. Three examples of a new Bethel type appear in Pl. 73:2, 6, 9. Pl. 73:6 is an excellent tenth century piece in a rich red color and burnished in a two-fold pattern. The bottom is burnished in parallel lines but the side burnishings run around the bowl. *Meg II*, Pl. 89:10 (V A) has something of the same form but a different finish; cf. also a later variety in *Meg I*, Pl. 28:97 (V–IV) and *Samaria III*, Fig. 4:10, 11 (III). Bethel, Pl. 73:9 is a well-thrown dark tan piece but only a little burnish remains. Pl. 73:2 is also a dark tan piece of good clay and well thrown, cf. *Meg I*, Pl. 28:98. The more common Iron I bowl is represented on Pl. 73:8, 11. The former was sand colored with a light buff burnishing, which had largely disappeared. The exterior throwing was poorly done but the interior was well finished. The LB ancestry is well seen in *Meg T*, Pl. 37:9. Pl. 73:11 is pinkish red with specks from over-firing. It was unburnished. *Meg I*, Pl. 28:106 is a better form of this vase. Pl. 73:5 is a shallow bowl with exaggerated everted rim. The clay was poor, the throwing was good except for a careless thick bottom. The color was tan. *Naṣbeh II*, Pl. 53:1182 is somewhat similar. We also excavated an early ring-burnished bowl similar to Pl. 62:8 and another ring-burnished piece similar in form to the unburnished *TBM I*, Pl. 62:3.

274. Pl. 73:3 is an unburnished juglet, a poor piece of throwing, and over-fired. It was early in Iron I. We found an excellent black burnished juglet with perpendicular strokes similar to *TBM I*, Pl. 51:11 except that the walls of the TBM jar were thinner. We also found an all-over burnished juglet similar to Pl. 61:12 but of poorer workmanship. The shoulder of a jar imitating a Philistine beer jug was found but the craftsmanship was wretched with excessively thick walls especially at the neck. No true Philistine sherds were found. Pl. 73:7 is a light buff chalice for which we cannot find an exact duplicate elsewhere. Pl. 73:10 is the base of a trumpet-foot chalice. It is fine pinkish buff ware and shows a better form of craftsmanship than the related *Meg II*, Pl. 90:8, a tenth century piece. The finest jug is Pl. 74:4 (No. 1125). There was also the top of a similar jar in surface debris. *Beth Shemesh*, p. 181, No. 478, is the closest relative in general form to this jug, but it has no spout. *Meg I*, Pl. 19, No. 111 has a similar spout and handles, but the neck is wider. Unfortunately the lower section of this jar is missing. Most spouted jars in this general form have a flat base.

275. There are four lamps, Nos. 1063, 1064, 1065, and 1094. All were broken and none shows any unique features. The diameters are 13 to 14 cm. but the heights run 3, 5, 4.5 and 3.8 cm. No. 1062 is a pottery spindle whorl, 5.8 cm. in dia. and No. 1088 is a pottery bull-roarer, 5 cm. in dia. No. 1033 is a broken pottery bead 12 mm. in dia. No. 1101 is an inscribed sherd of a store-jar with a pattern formed by three equidistant straight lines intersecting three other equidistant straight lines at right angles.

276. Iron II added only a few new interesting pieces. Pl. 74:8 is an open mouth cooking pot with a unique treatment of the handles. It was also exceptionally large having a body dia. of 46.7 cm. Pl. 74:3 is a ninth century modification of an Iron I bowl represented by Pl. 73:6, 9. It was good clay and well thrown but lacks burnish. It

was a pinkish buff piece probably ninth century B.C.; cf. related forms in *Samaria III*, Fig. 17:4, 5 and *Hazor I*, XLIX:1. We also excavated a ring-burnished bowl similar to Bethel, Pl. 62:8 and a ring-burnished piece similar in form to the unburnished *TBM I*, Pl. 62:3. Pl. 74:1 is a heavy shallow bowl but better worked than Pl. 63:14. Pl. 74:2 is a small kohl mixing bowl. Pl. 74:5 is a much more delicate pitcher body than Pl. 65:19. No. 1013 is a fragment of a drinking bottle in animal form. Only a few sherds of Samaria ware were found. Nos. 1001 and 1153 were lamps found in debris. Both are broken but in each case there was a high foot. No. 1080 is a typical Iron II loom weight with a diameter of 3.3 cm. For pottery figurines, and a doll's leg see "artifacts," Chapter XVI.

1957 Campaign

277. From Iron I comes Pl. 78:11 an excellent example of a store-jar; cf. *TBM I*, Pl. 50:11 and *Lachish III*, Pl. 94:466. The latter has a lower rim. This Bethel piece was found almost intact and standing upright in place. This over-fired jar is buff above the handles and a greyish-tan below. A pinkish-buff jar with thickness varying from 1 to 1.25 cm., Pl. 78:12, is similar to *Meg T*, Pl. 73:7. A complete banquet bowl appears on Pl. 78:6. It is hand-burnished on the rim and inside to about the bottom of the handle and then radial-burnished to the center. It is about tenth century. An Iron II modification of this Bethel form is seen on Pl. 62:2. There were two complete well-designed chalices. Pl. 78:8 is pinkish-buff ware with a painted pattern in red. *Meg II*, Pl. 90:8 has a similar but unpainted form. Pl. 78:10 is a pinkish-buff unpainted piece whose bowl is similar to *Naṣbeh II*, Pl. 69:1575 but the Bethel foot is much more delicate. There were also two bowls from broken chalices. Pl. 78:7 is buff ware burnished on the inside. For similar forms see *Ain Shems IV*, Pls. LXI:45, LXIV:34. Pl. 78:9 is a pinkish-buff piece from surface debris. It seems to be an Iron I form, cf. *Lachish III*, Pl. 99:597, but the Lachish example is shallower than Bethel. There are two stamped jar handles. No. 2024 shows the impression of a deer in a forest. No. 2045 is a cooking pot handle with an incised pattern like a Roman cross. No. 2122 is a sherd probably from Iron II which has an incised pattern looking very much like "XII."

278. The most interesting pottery find of the 1957 campaign was the large store-jar, Pl. 78:13. It was packed tight with sixty-two rocks and upon them was a broken juglet, Pl. 78:4. Many of the rocks were larger than a baseball and some were two or three times that size. We have no explanation for this filling. The large jar was standing upright in the remains of an LB fire. Three walls of the room were Iron I reused in Iron II but there was a new fourth wall for the Iron II phase. In the debris around the jar Iron I and Iron II sherds were found. In debris near the top of the jar Hellenistic and Roman sherds were found. The latter probably came from the peasants' plowing of the soil which could also explain why the top of the jar is missing. The closest relative of the zir is *PEFA* VI, Fig. 10, which is dated Iron I. The small juglet in the Bethel jar, however, is much more likely Iron II. The big zir was apparently an Iron II vessel which was placed in a hole dug into the lower levels of Iron I and LB. No Iron I jar would likely have remained intact up to the Hellenistic period. Nearby but higher was a Hellenistic cooking pot.

279. Definitely Iron II are the following: Pl. 79:1 is a beautiful grey ring-burnished water decanter, cf. *TBM I*, Pl. 59:4 and *Naṣbeh II*, Pl. 39:735. Pl. 79:2 is the neck and shoulder from a pinkish-buff decanter with four painted lines between the lip and the first ridge on the neck and two painted lines below the handle, cf. *Samaria III*, Fig. 5:1 (*c*. ninth century). Pl. 79:4 is a large pointed bottle. It was buff ware with the center two lines in red and the other lines in brown, cf. *PEFA VI*, Fig. No. 22:99 dated about 650 B.C.; *QDAP*, XIII, p. 98:31, which is earlier; and *Tirzeh, R.B.*, LVIII, Fig. 12:13. Pl. 79:5 is a rich deep red bowl with the inside of the bowl and the outside of the rim ring-burnished. The rim is heavier than Pl. 63:27. The craftsmanship was poorer than *TBM I*, Pl. 66:5, or *TBM III*, Pl. 20:2. Pl. 79:3 is the bowl of a slightly over-fired, tan-colored pitcher and therefore it is difficult to identify it exactly. *Meg I*, Pl. 6:155 represents more delicate workmanship in this same general pattern. There were three lamps, all broken. No. 2019 had a high foot, Nos. 2194 and 2267 had low ones. Pl. 115:16 (No. 2093) is a pottery bull-roarer or button in the form of an elipse; the two holes are lengthwise. There was one sherd which was an imitation of Samaria ware. No. 2023 was a jar handle with equal armed cross.

1960 Campaign

280. Iron I was represented by bowls only. Pl. 83:8 is a brownish-buff banquet bowl with a pink core. The clay was only fair. The throwing was good although the vessel was not smoothed inside or out. The handles were well integrated into the vessel. The ware was slightly over-fired. Although the general form is common, the exact rim was not found. Pl. 83:6 used a clay which contained both limestone and quartz particles. It was over-fired. The interior was well smoothed but the exterior only partly so; the base was well smoothed. The color ran from pink to red. *Lachish II*, Pl. XLIIIB:151, seems to be an ancestor of the Bethel form and *TBM III*, Pl. 23:3 is an Iron II descendant. Pl. 83:3 is an unusual piece because the clay was the cooking pot type and the walls were very thick. On the other hand the ware was well smoothed both inside and out and there was a good bevel on the ring-base.

281. Pl. 83:4, 5, 7 are excellent small bowl forms of a common family. Pl. 83:7, which looks more like LB than Iron I, has beautiful lines and a well beveled ring-base. The clay, however, was poor and the sand showed in the thrown rings on the exterior. The ring-base also was not smoothed. The interior and rim, however, were well smoothed. Pl. 83:5 is a buff to pinkish-buff piece slightly over-fired. The bowl had been burnished on the inside and perhaps over the rim but it was so badly worn that the type of burnishing could not be determined. Pl. 83:4 is like *Ain Shems IV*, Pl. LXVI:12, and *Naṣbeh II*, Pl. 55:1238. It had a buff exterior and pinkish-buff interior. It was good clay, well thrown and seemed to have been burnished inside. It may be Iron II.

282. There were store-jars where at least the upper halves could be reconstructed. Pl. 83:1 marks the transition from Iron I to Iron II. This pinkish-buff piece was of excellent clay and the craftsmanship was good. Note the slight ring under the collar. The handles blended well into the sides and the jar was well fired. *Meg I*, Pl. 21:126 (V), has the same general form but lacks the refinements of the Bethel piece. Definitely Iron II are the following. Pl. 83:2 is grey to pinkish-buff and has faint traces of two thin lines below the handles. The throwing was good but the piece was slightly over-fired causing some pitting. There are two banquet bowls. Pl. 84:4 is pinkish-red. It had a good form although the bottom was too thin at the shock point. The handles fitted well into the pattern. The bowl was originally ring-burnished. Compare *Hazor I*, Pl. LXXI:13, which is poor craftsmanship and without handles. Pl. 84:5 is a form for which we could not find duplicates. Its surface is tannish-buff and grey. It was good clay but slightly over-fired. The throwing was good, the interior smoothed, and ring-burnished. Only the upper section of the exterior was smoothed. Pl. 81:7 is a common Iron II saucer form. It was buff ware, with interior smoothed and the exterior left rough. Pl. 84:3 is a well-made Iron II pitcher. The color varies from buff to pink and the piece was slightly over-fired. The rim was slightly misformed by pressure inward. It had an excellent beveled ring-base and the handle was well placed. It is similar to *TBM I*, Pl. 58:5, but better craftsmanship than TBM. Pl. 84:1 is a large unique jar but apparently a descendant of a form such as *Meg I*, Pl. 21:125 (V). The exterior ran from grey to greenish-buff; the interior was pinkish-buff. The clay was of mediocre quality with sand and a small quantity of larger grits and the piece was slightly over-fired. The design of the vessel was good and although the walls were thick they were well fashioned and the foot was good. It came from a mixed context of Iron II and later. Pl. 84:2 is a canteen for which no parallel has been found. It was also from the same mixed context. The dotted lines represent the end view and the decorative lines are in a reddish paint. No. 3026 is a broken pottery loom weight 8 cm. in diameter.

CHAPTER XIII

BETHEL POTTERY OF THE SIXTH CENTURY B.C.

Lawrence A. Sinclair

283. The sixth century B.C. pottery from Bethel, when compared to the pottery forms of the immediately preceding and subsequent periods, appears as transitional between the two. This pottery can be characterized as degenerate Iron II. The repertoire of types includes bowls of various sizes, cylindrical jars, rims of large jars, water pitchers, and juglets.

284. The most significant locus from this stratum (sub 104) contains a variety of bowls and juglets, Pl. 64:4, 7, 12, 13, 14, 16, 18. Bowl No. 7 has a light brown surface and a dark brown core, with minute grits. Its disc-base also appears on a more rounded bowl, No. 13, from this locus as well as on a bowl, Pl. 64:10, from locus 136. A flat-based bowl with a body form similar to No. 7 appears at Beth-shemesh[1] in tomb 14, dated by Wright to the sixth century B.C. The surface of bowl No. 10 shows discoloration by smoke, from the conflagration which destroyed the sixth century B.C. level at Bethel. The surface of No. 13 shows the same discoloration. No evidence of burnishing appears on the surface of these bowls, in contrast to the spiral-burnished forms in Tell Beit Mirsim, stratum A, and other contemporary sites of Judah.[2] Note the form, similar to No. 10, from Lachish, dated 700–500 B.C.[3]

Bowl No. 4 has a well-levigated brown core with a buff surface. The sides appear heavier than those of No. 7 and the rim is formed into a more pronounced lip. Moreover, this bowl rests on a ring-base. Bowl No. 12 from the same locus, as well as bowls Nos. 6 and 9 (Pl. 64) from locus 123 and locus 129 respectively, has a ring-base. A ring-base similar to No. 12, with a reddish-brown core, appeared at Beth-shemesh, Tomb 14, dated sixth century B.C.[4] A burnished bowl standing taller than No. 6 was found in an eighth century B.C. context at Lachish, Tomb 1002, layers 1–5.[5] Our bowl, No. 6, without burnishing and squatter in shape seems to be typologically later. The red surface of No. 9 shows evidence of burning during the destruction of the sixth century B.C. town.

285. Two juglets, Nos. 16, 18, form part of the assemblage of pottery from locus sub 104. No. 16 is the body of a juglet with a black, vertically burnished surface. The body of a juglet of similar size but with a buff surface was uncovered at Beth-shemesh in stratum IIc[6] which ended about 587 B.C. This form appears at the end of the seventh–beginning of the sixth century B.C. at Lachish.[7] The buff juglet corresponds to No. 18 at Bethel, which has a brownish buff surface, vertically burnished. A black juglet with a similar form came to light in Tomb 14 at Beth-shemesh,[8] but it is not the same size and it has a more pointed bottom than does our juglet. None of these is typical of the Iron II black or buff juglets found in large numbers at Tell Beit Mirsim[9] or in other Iron II strata of Palestine, but the Bethel examples represent a degeneration of the Iron II dipper juglets.

286. The last form from locus sub 104 is bowl No. 14 with grey-buff surface and dark grey core. A larger bronze bowl with a similar body shape but displaying an everted rim appeared in stratum II at Beth-shemesh.[10] This comparison suggests that the Bethel bowl could be an example of pottery imitation of metal forms. Similar pottery bowls were found at Samaria,[11] with and

---

[1] *AS IV*, Pl. LXVIII:27, reddish-brown ware.
[2] *TBM III*, pp. 152 ff.
[3] *L III*, Pl. 98:570. Tufnell follows Wampler's date for this type of bowl. See *L III* text, p. 276.
[4] *AS IV*, Pl. LXVIII:21.
[5] *L III*, Pl. 79:23. See my remarks on the dating of Tomb 1002 in *Annual*, Vol. XXXIV-XXXV, pl. 22, n. 46.

[6] *AS IV*, Pl. LXVI:40.
[7] *L III*, Pl. 88:31, in an assemblage from Tomb 114 dated to the first half of the sixth century B.C. (*L III*, p. 190). We are not happy with Miss Tufnell's date for the end of the tomb, about 550 B.C. The horizon of Tomb 114 agrees with Tomb 109 and the first phase of 106 dates toward the end of the Iron II age. Burnishing is still found on most of the ware, and the forms are in many cases classic Iron II; note the decanters, lamp and juglets. We should date Tomb 114 together with Tombs 109 and 106 to the end of the seventh or beginning of the sixth century B.C.
[8] *AS IV*, Pls. LXVIII:4 and XLVIII:11. Dated late sixth century B.C.
[9] See *TBM I*, Pl. 68:1–32, *AS V*, p. 145, and *TBM III*, Pls. 18:1–9, 70:1–15.
[10] *AS IV*, Pl. LXVI:47.
[11] *SS III*, Fig. 18:4. The bowl drawn, Fig. 19:5, has a more pointed edge than the Bethel bowl and has been burnished.

without burnishing, associated with Periods V–VI. This type of bowl has its beginning in the eighth century B.C. and continues until the sixth century B.C.

287. The typological study of sixth century B.C. pottery from locus sub 104 indicates that some of the forms have affinity to the preceding period, but are not typical. We seem to have degenerate Iron II forms.

The pottery of sub 104 is the best locus group from this stratum. We have several other homogeneous loci (129 and 136) but none with the variety and number of pieces of sub 104. Therefore the remainder of this study will emphasize typological grouping of the pottery forms.

288. Let us return to the study of the bowls. The rim of No. 9, Pl. 64, can be classified with No. 3 of the same locus and No. 5 from locus 136. The ware of Nos. 9 and 3 may be described as red-surfaced with well-levigated, dark grey or dark brownish cores, while No. 5 has a reddish-buff surface. No burnishing is evident on these bowls, which appear to be typologically related to the red burnished bowls of Iron II. A bowl with ware and profile similar to No. 5, but with handles, appears in level IIb at Beth-shemesh.[12]

Bowl No. 8 has a profile with a slight exterior ribbing differentiating it from the three Bethel bowls just mentioned above. A similar but squatter form comes from Beth-shemesh,[13] level IIb. On the other hand, the bowl from Anthedon,[14] level 449, sixth century B.C., may be compared to our rim.

As yet bowl No. 11 from locus 136 has no exact parallel in published excavation reports. Its grey ware was smoked by fire during the conflagration of the sixth century B.C.

289. Next we turn to the analysis of the large thickened rim bowls represented by examples from the 1934 and 1957 excavations. Two examples, Pl. 64:1, 2, from locus 129 of the conflagration level were found in 1934, and four examples, Pl. 80:6, 1, 8, 7, from loci 401, 403, 404, 407, respectively were found in 1957. Note the handles on the bowls from the 1934 material in contrast to forms from 1957 without handles. One immediately recognizes typological relationship between our bowls and spiral burnished bowls of Iron II found in large numbers at Tell Beit Mirsim, stratum A.[15] The technique of spiral burnishing appears at the beginning of Iron II[16] as a substitute for painted decoration.[17]

290. The bowls show a variety of surface treatment. Bowl, Pl. 64:1, has a red surface with traces of burnishing; No. 2, from the same locus 129, has a similar red surface which was smoked from the conflagration but shows no burnishing. This is significant, in spite of the fact that the bowl is reconstructed from two fragments that do not fit. Pl. 80:6 from the 1957 campaign has burnishing on the rim but not over a red slip, while Pl. 80:8 appears with the red slip but unburnished as do the remaining examples from this campaign.

Dr. Albright[18] concluded from the evidence at Beth-zur, excavated in 1931, that spiral burnishing ceased to be used in the sixth century B.C. Engberg[19] thinks that Albright's conclusions were confirmed at Megiddo. From the study of the Bethel material we can now date the end of spiral burnishing in the first half of the sixth century B.C. Evidence from the excavations at Lachish and Samaria fit into this scheme. Tomb 106 at Lachish was used for burials during the seventh–sixth centuries B.C. and during the third-fourth centuries A.D. Bowl 70[20] of the first period in the tomb is spiral burnished and smaller than most of the Bethel bowls. A similar date is assigned to bowl 72,[21] which is analogous to bowl 70 but shows no evidence of burnishing. Kenyon, in commenting on the burnished bowls from Samaria,[22] suggests that all are seventh century B.C. in date.

291. Thanks to the efforts of James L. Kelso in 1957 and the excavators of Hazor we are now able to trace the typological sequence which resulted in the heavy-ribbed or smooth-sided bowl so characteristic of Iron III (Persian Period).[23]

---

[12] *AS IV*, Pl. LXVI:19.
[13] *AS IV*, Pl. LXVI:4.
[14] *Anthedon*, Pl. XXXII: 16L⁴.

[15] *TBM I*, Pl. 60 (bowls with handles), Pls. 61–63 (bowls without handles), and *TBM III*, Pls. 22, 23, 72.
[16] Albright, *TBM I*, pp. 85–86, *TBM III*, pp. 152–54. See my discussion of the pertinent material since 1943, *Annual*, XXXIV–XXXV, pp. 29–30.
[17] See my remarks, *op. cit.*, pp. 25–26.
[18] *TBM I*, pp. 85–86.
[19] *MI*, p. 165.
[20] *L III* (plate) Pl. 80.
[21] *Op. cit.*, Pl. 80.
[22] *SS III*, p. 127, reference to Fig. 11:1–7.
[23] Examples of this type of bowl have appeared at Afula, Anthedon, Hazor, Lachish, Megiddo, Samaria, Tell Abū Hawâm, Tell Jemmeh, Tell en-Naṣbeh, and Tell Qasîle.

The thickened rim of Iron II forms an inverted profile, Pls. 64:1, 2, and 80:8; the profile is the same as that of Iron II bowls, but the bowls are not burnished or a straight profile with an angle a little below the rim. Pl. 80:6 from locus 401 has typical Iron II burnishing inside and over the rim. The form changes with the lowering of the thick part of the rim to a position at the side, Pl. 80:4, 7, with the top edge blunted to form the rim. Note Pl. 80:4 has a sharp edge. Pl. 80:7 has lost the inverted profile and is very similar to Iron III forms. A bowl slightly deeper but with a pointed rim like Pl. 80:4 was found in the Adoni-Nur Tomb, Amman,[24] dated late seventh–sixth century B.C.[25] Subsequent changes in the bowl take two directions: one obviously leads to the characteristic heavy open Iron III bowl with either smooth or wavy sides; the other leads to the type with a thick band of clay encircling the bowl just below the rim, Pl. 80:1. A parallel to the latter type was found at Hazor in stratum II of Area B,[26] dated to Iron III. It is quite possible, on typological grounds, to assign Pl. 80:1 to Iron III.

On the other hand, Pl. 80:1, of buff ware with a ring-base, does not correspond to good Iron III forms, which have a heavy flanged foot. The wavy outside profile makes its appearance early in the period.

It appears from the above discussion that the Iron III[27] bowl derived its form from the Iron II type with the transitional forms appearing at Bethel.

292. An unburnished pinkish-buff surface describes Pl. 80:5 found during 1957 in surface debris. It has some resemblance to those on Pl. 64:4, 7, and is probably of the same class. A little later example (Iron III) comes from Samaria;[28] on the other hand, a similar form but showing a heavier rim was found at Amman, in the Adoni-Nur Tomb,[29] dated late seventh–early sixth century B.C.[30]

Pl. 80:2 from room 406 and Pl. 80:4 from the same locus show no trace of burnishing over the red surface. The flat base gives way to a graceful wavy profile ending in a flaring rim. Earlier spiral burnished bowls of like form have been published from Tell Beit Mirsim[31] and Lachish,[32] dated to late Iron II. A similar bowl with some trace of burnishing came from Tomb C at Amman,[33] which should be dated in the sixth century B.C.[34] The Bethel bowl appears as a later and more degenerate form with no burnishing and a simple base.

Another bowl from room 407, Pl. 80:9, has a buff surface, burnished inside. (See above discussion of Pl. 80:7 from this locus.) This is very typical of Iron II, as may be illustrated by Tell Beit Mirsim, stratum A examples and Megiddo examples.[35] This typological relationship with Iron II should cause no difficulty; one expects some pottery from the earlier period, particularly at Bethel, where there was a continuous occupation of the site during the seventh and sixth centuries B.C.

293. One-handled juglets, of which we have two from room 403, Pl. 78:1, 2, are next to be considered. The first can be described as a burnished, one-handled, round-mouth juglet with red surface. An earlier form, with more rounded bottom than our examples, but with the ridge where the neck joins the body, appeared at Tell Beit Mirsim, stratum A.[36] A form at ʿAthlît,

---

[24] *PEFA*, VI, Fig. 21:71.

[25] The pottery of the Adoni-Nur tombs agrees substantially in date with that from Amman, Meqabelein, and Sahab. Sinclair, *Annual*, XXXIV-XXXV, pp. 42, 52, and Landes, *BA*, XXIV, pp. 75, 82–85.

[26] *Hazor I*, Pl. LXXIX:20. Note additional examples of bowls, nos. 17–27, and *Hazor II*, Pl. LXXV:20–23.

[27] There are several variations within the class of Iron III bowls. Some have smooth sides instead of a wavy profile, while others have a flat base instead of a flanged ring base. Their chief characteristics are heaviness and coarseness. They all appear to have been thrown on a wheel, but it is doubtful that they received later refinement by the turner. (See Kelso and Thorley, *TBM III*, pp. 96–97, for a discussion of the two techniques.) This can characterize most of the locally made pottery in Palestine during Iron III. We cannot draw definite conclusions for the history of the country at this time, but unrefined pottery fits into the picture of the early post-exile period.

[28] *SS III*, Fig. 12:2, from Period VIII and associated with Fig. 12:13, a typical heavy bowl of Iron III.

[29] *PEFA*, VI, Fig. 21:64.

[30] See above, note 25.

[31] *TBM III*, Pl. 21:4, stratum A. Note this form has a slight concave base.

[32] *L III*, Pl. 98:560. The type drawn is from building 505 destroyed in 587 B.C.

[33] *ADAJ*, Vol. I, Fig. 1:2.

[34] Harding dates the contents of the tomb to the early eighth century B.C. *Ibid.*, p. 37. See now *Annual*, Vol. XXXIV-XXXV, p. 52.

[35] Notice numerous examples scattered in *TBM I*, Pls. 64–65. *TBM III*, Pls. 24–25. At Megiddo the type drawn (*M I*, Pl. 24:28) is from stratum III but has a distribution throughout strata IV-I. Engberg (*M I*, p. 169) mentions that this type is displaced by the form drawn Pl. 23:5–9 in stratum I.

[36] *TBM I*, Pl. 68:41.

Burial I[37] does not have the ridge sharply distinguished.[38] A somewhat later type may be seen among the pottery at Lachish,[39] Tombs 109 and 114 from the late seventh–early sixth centuries B.C.[40] and at Tell en-Naṣbeh.[41] It has a wet-smoothed surface. Our Bethel examples, particularly Pl. 78:1, have burnishing but are degenerate Iron II in form.

294. A second type of one-handled juglet is represented by Pl. 78:3 from over the wall between rooms 408 and 409. This small piece has a burnished buff surface. A slightly larger and less refined juglet was found at Tell en-Naṣbeh in Cistern 49 dated to the seventh century B.C.[42] but a late seventh century–early sixth century B.C. date is more likely.[43] Its light brown surface exhibits a close vertical burnishing. A similar form with a different style handle, more rounded than ours, was found at Lachish in Tomb 114.[44]

The deep red slip on jug, Pl. 78:5, is highly burnished. Our closest parallels in form are from Amman, Tombs A and C,[45] dated to the late seventh–early sixth centuries B.C.[46] A general resemblance to the trefoil jugs of Iron II[47] can be noted, but we do not have the mouth of our jar and most of the trefoil jugs have a ring-base. It seems probable, however, that the Bethel form may be degenerate from Iron II trefoil jugs.

295. The first of the large jars for discussion are those which resemble Iron II forms, with royal stamps on the handles. Two jars, Pl. 80:10, 12, from room 407 show a buff to brown or pinkish-buff surface and the characteristic four handles, but no royal stamps.[48] Their relationship to the Iron II forms is unmistakable, but the Bethel jar, Pl. 80:12, shows a tendency toward a base blunter than the typical Iron II jars, and the neck of Pl. 80:10 is shorter and straighter.

Several varieties of large jars were found in room 403. An interesting jar, Pl. 80:11, with brownish-buff surface, has a very low neck, almost to the point of disappearance. In fact it is this feature which distinguishes it from the " hole-mouth " jars of Iron II and Iron III. This jar remains unique, since exact parallels are wanting. Another jar rim from locus 403, No. C*, stands in sharp contrast to Pl. 80:11, with a high neck and moulded rim. No exact parallel can be cited. A third rim decorated with spiral burnishing seems to be part of a general class of large jars which would include a rim from Tell en-Naṣbeh.[49] A later form, from Period IV, appeared at Gibeah.[50]

296. Cylindrical jars or " hole-mouth " jars may be classified in two groups: (1) those which have a thickened rim, often flat on top, sometimes convex or slanting, ribbed or plain and usually of soft ware; (2) those which have an inturned rim

---

[37] *QDAP*, 6, Fig. 4:3 (p. 139).
[38] Cf. *TN II*, p. 87. Wampler lists the form from ʿAthlit as comparative material for the Tell en-Naṣbeh forms 781 in Pl. 41, which has a ridge where the neck joins the body. I, too, noted this form before I looked at Wampler's list, but decided that it did not have a ridge and was more characteristic of the Iron II juglets.
[39] In *L III* the type drawn, Pl. 88:292, is from the courtyard (106) of the Solor Shrine, but similar forms are listed from Tombs 109 and 114. The juglet drawn has traces of burnishing. Moreover, the Shrine was built in the Iron III period and was continuously used for several centuries afterwards. Therefore, this juglet seems out of context. On the other hand, a similar juglet, but without burnishing, appeared at Tell Abū Hawâm, stratum II (*QDAP*, IV, p. 15, no. 9); its form is very much like our Bethel no. 235. A later development, with the handle attached to the neck midway between the shoulder and the rim, was found at Samaria (*HES I*, p. 285; Fig. 162:6a; *HES II*, Pl. 67c), and another one in Strip I, Cistern 7 (*HES I*, p. 291, Fig. 167:6a), grouped in *HES II*, Pl. 65, with forms which may be dated to the fourth century B.C. with possible extension into the third century B.C. *Annual*, XXXIV-XXXV, p. 38, n. 14a.
[40] See above note 7.
[41] *TN II*, Pl. 41:781.
[42] *TN II*, Pl. 38:675 and p. 124.
[43] In Cistern 49 such forms as a top of a decanter (*TN II*, Pl. 40:749), a one-handled juglet (*ibid.*, Pl. 42:827), and a flask (*ibid.*, Pl. 76:1445) were also found and indicate a date toward the end of Iron II.
[44] *L III*, Pl. 87:277. For the date of Tomb 114 see above n. 7.
[45] Tomb A, *QDAP*, IX, p. 72:33–34, 36; Tomb C, *ADAJ*, I, Fig. 1:26–30 (p. 39).

[46] See above n. 34.
[47] I do not have a complete list of all trefoil jugs, but will mention those at Megiddo (*M I*, Pl. 3:83–85, 89, strata IV-II), Samaria (*SS III*, Fig. 10:15–16; 22:7, 9, Periods III-VI), and Lachish (*L III*, Pl. 86:241).
[48] For a general discussion of the royal stamp before 1960 see *Annual*, XXXIV-XXXV, pp. 32–33, and literature there cited. Now see Yadin, *Bulletin*, No. 163 (1961), pp. 6–12, who argues that the jar handles bear the names of four defensive zone centers where army food stores were located.
* No. C was lost in the mail and therefore does not appear in any plate drawing.
[49] *TN II*, Pl. 67:1512, dated after 600 B.C. *Op. cit.*, p. 40.
[50] *Annual*, XXXIV-XXXV, pl. 25:21, dated to the early Hellenistic Age, from second half of the fourth century B.C. to c. 200 B.C.

meeting the exterior wall without a projection and usually hard, well-fired ware. The rims are usually the same thickness as the walls of the jar.[51]

A study of the cylindrical jars found in Palestine at Beth-shemesh, Gibeah, Hazor,[52] Lachish,[53] Megiddo, Ramat Raḥel, Samaria, Tell Beit Mirsim, Tell Jemmeh,[54] Tell ej-Judeidah, Tell Zakariya substantiate Albright's earlier conclusions that this type is common in the ninth through sixth centuries B.C., becoming rare in the fifth century B.C.[55]

297. All of the cylindrical jars at Bethel belong to our first class, Pl. 66:3–6, 9–13. The plain rims Pl. 66:3, 9, are easily distinguished from the ribbed type, Pl. 66:4–6, 10–12, and provide the basis for two sub-groups within our class.

Five miscellaneous large jars make up the group for our discussion. The ware of Pl. 66:1 from locus 101 consists of a drab grey core with black and white grits under a dark red surface. Wheel marks are evident on the inside. No exact parallel can be located in published archaeological material. Pl. 66:2 appears without handles, in contrast to No. 1. The ware also indicates a difference between the two; No. 2 has a hard light brown core with white grit and buff surface. Again we have no exact parallels of form, but locus sub 119 is immediately below the Hellenistic I phase. We can also date Pl. 66:7 on the basis of stratigraphy to the sixth century B.C. Typologically, our jar seems to be grouped with similar four-handle jars from Tell Beit Mirsim, stratum A.[56] Note that the rim of our jar has a plain profile, in contrast to the more elaborate jar from Tell Beit Mirsim. The jar drawn on Pl. 66:13, likewise, has no exact parallel in published material. It has a cream slip outside, buff color inside and a light brown core. It seems to be in the same general pottery horizon of the Iron Age (Tell Abū Hawâm[57] and Tell Jemmeh[58]), but the locus 6 has mixed pottery, Hellenistic to Byzantine.

298. Large ridge-necked jars are next for discussion. In this general class the forms range from a vertical neck with a ridge, Pl. 66:14, to a rim with a slanting ridge on the shoulder, Pl. 67:8. Some of the forms are reminiscent of Iron II or even earlier.[59] The ridged, vertical-neck jars can be divided into several groups. The rim in Pl. 66:14 parallels Pl. 67:17 in form and almost in ware. No. 14 has reddish buff surface, drab-grey core and small grit, while No. 17 has a buff surface, red ware with unlevigated grey core. A more rounded ridge than found on Nos. 14 or 17 characterizes a second possible grouping of forms. Included would be Pl. 66:15; Pl. 67:12, 14, 19, with some questions about No. 12 which has a sharp outer edge around the rounded top of the rim in contrast to the blunt edge on Nos. 15, 14, and 19. Even the ware of No. 12 is different, creamy buff surface, greyish-brown core with small grits while Nos. 15, 14, and 19 have dark grey cores with reddish or buff surfaces. They are grouped here because they are found on the same locus. A third group would include Pl. 67:2 and 3 from locus 129. The ware of No. 2 has been described as drab with a buff surface smoked by fire; that of No. 3 is very hard and red with reddish-buff surface. The last of the vertical-necked ridged jars are Pl. 67:10, 15, 18. No. 10 has a buff slip over red ware. Red surface, grey core with minute grits characterize No. 15, while No. 18 has a buff surface and core.

Parallels are found at Megiddo, especially in III and II,[60] at Tell el-Farʿah (near Nablus) in

---

[51] Cf. my previous discussion *Annual*, XXXIV–XXXV, pp. 31, 32, 37. Note that at Gibeah Pl. 23:8–14 (Groups 2 and 3) are characteristic of our new Class 1, and Pl. 23:6, 7 (Group 1 but redefined) are representative of our new Class 2.

[52] See also *Hazor II*, Pl. LXI:1–13, all from VIII.

[53] Jar (*L III*, Pl. 97:540) from building R/Q/S, 15–16:10–21 at Lachish represented only by a sherd from Room 17. Room 11 contained Hellenistic pottery, providing the date of the building, but one sherd is not sufficient evidence to extend the "hole mouth" jars into the Hellenistic period. Another jar at Lachish (*L III*, Pl. 97:539) came from the Bastion associated with the ostraca. On *L III*, p. 146, a jar has been dated with G 12/13:1–8 which is contemporary with Megiddo stratum I. Megiddo's occupation must have ended *c.* 450 B.C. (*Annual*, XXXIV–XXXV, p. 43, n. 37) as probably did the Lachish building. We are not surprised to find an occasional cylindrical jar in the early part of the fifth century B.C.

[54] For a redating of Iron age levels at Gerar, see Albright, *TBM I*, pp. 74–5, 79, 84, 85, 87; *TBM III*, pp. 23–33, 80, 81, 144 (n. 1), 151, and Wright, *AS V* pp. 138, n. 15; 139, n. 20, and 143, n. 38.

[55] *TBM I*, p. 79, and *TBM III*, p. 147.

[56] *TBM III*, Pl. 13:1, 2, 4.

[57] *QDAP*, IV, Pl. XXXVI:174.

[58] *Gerar*, Pl. LV:46g; Level 189.

[59] See my discussion of the Iron I form and evidence of late Iron Age development, *Annual*, XXXIV–XXXV, p. 23.

[60] *M I*, Pl. 14:70, 76, 77. No. 70 is from stratum IV, but there are four examples listed from III. The jar (no. 70) was found in 315 located on the grid—R12. It is interesting to note that on *M I*, Fig. 121 (aerial photograph) no loci are

level 2[61] and at Tell en-Naṣbeh, stratum I.[62] Clearly our jars are a continuation of Iron II forms.

299. The jars with slanting-ridge on the shoulder can be classified according to several groupings. The jars on Pl. 67:4, 5, 13, show just the beginning of a slanted profile with a neck ridge. No. 4 has a grey to pink surface, drab core, well levigated except for occasional coarse quartz grits. A buff surface and well-levigated grey core characterize No. 5. No. 13 has the same buff surface but has a brownish-grey core. Another grouping of this type of jar includes Nos. 1 and 16 on Pl. 67. This group is characterized by a very noticeable slanted-ridge profile, and a ridge on the neck. Both have a buff surface and brownish or dark red-grey core. No. 1 comes from locus sub 108 as does Pl. 67:5. The body of these jars may be seen in Pl. 67:6. They are large, with a sharp angle at the shoulder from which extends the loop handles. Jar, Pl. 67:11, seems to be next in order, representing a slightly different profile from those discussed above. It has a red surface over a hard reddish-buff coarse paste. The last of the series, Pl. 67:8, shows a very pronounced slanting. This two-handled jar has a reddish-buff ware and a surface decorated with rows of circular protuberances and of incised shallow grooves.

Parallels to these jars are difficult to find. A rim similar to Pl. 67:1 appears at Samaria[63] in Iron II. Typologically later forms are also found at Samaria.[64]

The large jar, Pl. 67:9, is made of a hard red ware with grey core. An exact parallel to the rim appeared at Tell en-Naṣbeh[65] and is dated on the basis of the Bethel find. Our jar seems to be more advanced than the Iron II forms from stratum II at Beth-shemesh.[66] Our jar was found with Pl. 67:6 in locus 145.

The rim of a large jar, Pl. 67:7, is shallow with broad grooves extending over the shoulder. It has a red ware, grey core with minute grits and a light red surface. On analogy with other decorated forms we would expect protuberances on the shoulders. No exact parallel can be found and there is some question about the date of the jar.

300. A funnel, Pl. 80:3, with the tube part missing was found during the 1957 campaign in room 403. It has a red, unburnished surface. No exact parallels are known, but similar funnels appeared at Tell en-Naṣbeh.[67] Wampler[68] comments that "all of the TN examples seem to fall within the period *ca.* 750–450 B.C. Of the twenty-three examples, all but two were wet smoothed. One of these was burnished spirally, the other horizontally." The earliest appearance of funnels in Palestine seems to be at Megiddo during the Late Bronze Age.[69] They are more common, however, during the Iron Age with examples from Anthedon,[70] Beth-shan, and Gibeon. Later appearances are noted from Qumran, period II,[71] and Gerasa.[72]

301. The pottery of the sixth century B.C. from Bethel is related to Iron II forms of Palestine, but not typical of classic shapes of that period. In fact, with discontinuation of burnishing and deviation in form from earlier styles, our pottery appears sub-standard in comparison to that of Iron II. It is certain that Bethel was occupied in the sixth century B.C. because of the similarity between the pottery of our conflagration level and that of Tomb 14 at Beth-shemesh and tombs of the Transjordan.[73] The lack of characteristic Persian Period forms means that we cannot date the destruction of Bethel beyond the end of the sixth century B.C. when such forms presumably began to make their appearance. The exact

---

marked, but the remains of the walls in the western half of the grid square R12 are the same as outlined on Fig. 71 assigned to III-II. No. 76 was chosen for an example from stratum II of which four more exist along with ten from III and seven from IV. Some of the loci are clearly Iron I, indicating that the grouping of sherds in the Megiddo volume does not differentiate clearly between Iron I and Iron II forms. The example for no. 77 was drawn from III material and is very common at this time.

[61] *RB*, Vol. 59, Fig. 9:6.
[62] *TN I*, Fig. 58:3B, C. Dated by Wright (*TN I*, p. 225) eighth–fifth centuries B.C.
[63] *SS III*, Fig. 11:25, Period VII, Fig. 21:12, E 207.
[64] *HES I*, Fig. 160:2, "early deposits and from cistern 3 at the Basilica."
[65] *TN I*, Fig. 58:2, p. 226. See also p. 225.

[66] *AS IV*, Pl. LXV:4–12.
[67] *TN II*, Pl. 77:1776, 1777.
[68] *Ibid.*, P. 51.
[69] Engberg, *Megiddo Tombs*, p. 155.
[70] Petrie, *Anthedon*, Pl. XXXVIII:92c.
[71] *RB*, Vol. 63 (1956), p. 561, Fig. 5:11, 12. Note the handle on no. 11.
[72] Kraeling, *Gerasa*, Fig. 43:X30 from Tomb 10 dated first–second centuries A.D.
[73] The pottery of Tell en-Naṣbeh is contemporary with the Bethel collection, but probably extends beyond Bethel in time. Wright, *TN I*, p. 186; Albright, *The Biblical Period*, rev. ed., p. 86.

historical event related to the end of Bethel is not clear. It is possible that the town was destroyed by Nabonidus in 553 B.C. during his campaign into Syria[74] to quell a revolt,[75] or by Cyrus 539–538 B.C.[76]

---

[74] Oppenheim, *Ancient Near Eastern Texts* (ed. Pritchard), p. 305.

[75] Albright, *Archaeology and the Religion of Israel*, 3rd ed., p. 173; *BASOR*, no. 120 p. 25.

[76] See Cyrus' Cylinder (*Ancient Near Eastern Texts*, p. 316), which mentions king of the west who brought tribute to him in Babylon. We are not sure, however, when Cyrus captured these countries, before or after his conquest of Babylonia. In any case, by 538 B.C. he controlled all of Syria and Palestine to the Egyptian border.

CHAPTER XIV

Bethel Pottery of the Late Hellenistic and Early Roman Periods

Paul W. Lapp

302. The pottery shown on Pls. 68–72:1–9 belongs typologically to three distinct horizons.[1] As is typical of this period, it does not come from stratigraphically homogeneous groups. With few exceptions its provenience is a series of imported fills in which only the latest material is of significance for dating the fill and associated installations.[2] Since during the Bethel campaigns analysis of the pottery of this period had not advanced to the stage of precision necessary to isolate the latest forms in a given group or layer, the pottery is discussed by type, following the order of *PCC*.[3]

303. Most of the material comes from the 1934 campaign and was designated Hellenistic or Hellenistic-Roman by Albright. The former included material assigned to the first two phases he distinguished and the latter to the third phase.[4] By correlation of numismatic and literary evidence these phases were dated as follows: Phase 1, late Persian to 160 B.C.; phase 2, 135–63 B.C.; and phase 3, 4 B.C.—A.D. 69. Pottery of this period from the subsequent campaigns can be assigned typologically to these same horizons.

304. The discussion below will detail the remarkable correspondence between the dates assigned the three ceramic horizons on typological grounds and the last years of the three phases Albright distinguished. That he was able to distinguish Early Roman pottery (Hellenistic-Roman) from Late Hellenistic—and in a few instances even between second and first century B.C. forms—is an indication of his exceptional discrimination. Such precise analysis was not matched in the next quarter-century of Palestinian excavation.

305. Although a typological analysis using the *PCC* Corpus framework generally agrees with Albright's 1934 analysis, no significant addition or modification of the *PCC* Corpus is required from the Bethel material. Six vessels assigned a specific phase are represented in the Corpus from contemporary deposits at other sites.[5] The rest of the material can most reliably be assigned one of the three phases by comparisons with the *PCC* Corpus.

306. The only significant change in Albright's chronology demanded by comparisons with the *PCC* Corpus is a lowering of the *terminus post quem* for phase 1. This is indicated by the total lack of fourth or third century B.C. ceramic forms.[6] This is another instance of the sharpening of chronological conclusions based on numismatic grounds by ceramic evidence. The fact that not a single example of the rounded jar rim, which dominates third century deposits, appears at Bethel should take precedence over the coins of Alexander and the Ptolemies in determining the beginning of phase 1.[7] To be sure, ceramic groups tend to represent the end of a phase of occupation,[8] but the complete absence of any ceramic evidence for over a century of occupation is highly improbable.

307. Close parallels to practically all the Bethel Hellenistic and Early Roman forms are found in the rather small corpus of forms for the period provided in *PCC*. This fits well with what has

---

[1] The following analysis is made exclusively on the basis of drawings. The pottery was not at the writer's disposal.
[2] Cf. *PCC*, pp. 57–59 and esp. n. 10, for a more detailed methodological discussion.
[3] Cf. *PCC*, pp. 140–43.
[4] *BASOR*, 55, p. 24. Cf. *BASOR*, 56, pp. 14–15.
[5] Pl. 69:10, 11; 70:1; 71:1, 3, 7.
[6] *PCC*, p. 104, states that the earliest Hellenistic pottery from Bethel belongs to the late third century B.C. Increased precision based on Nancy Lapp's study of the third century B.C. pottery from Balâṭah makes it preferable to lower the *terminus post quem* for the group to about 200 B.C. although certain individual forms could belong to the late third century.
The Rhodian jar handles, Reg. Nos. 48, 58, (Pl. 47:7, 9) and 418, should be noted in this connection. The sketched shapes of the first two with sharply squared handle bend could not predate the second century B.C. They are a later development of the third century B.C. form illustrated by Virginia Grace, "Stamped Amphora Handles Found in 1931–1932," *Hesperia* III, Pl. 11:5. The first and third contain names that appear in Miss Grace's post-180 B.C. group (DAMAINETOS and PAUSANIAS). *Ibid.*, p. 219, Fig. 2.
[7] For examples of coins indicating an earlier horizon than related ceramic groups cf. *PCC*, p. 92, n. 312; p. 95, n. 335; R. de Vaux, *L'archéologie et les manuscrits de la Mer Morte* (London, 1961), p. 53. Ptolemaic coins were still circulating in Palestine in the first decade of the second century B.C. Cf. *BASOR*, 161, pp. 45–46.
[8] Cf. *PCC*, p. 12.

been observed about a *koine* development of local ceramic forms in this period.[9] The lack of any imported sigillata is also a strong confirmation of the gap in occupation from the beginning of the Roman occupation until the turn of the era.[10]

308. *Jars.* Well over half of all the rims collected from the Hellenistic strata at Khirbet eṭ-Ṭubeiqah and Balâṭah were rims of jars. This was also true at Beitîn. Publication of a large number of these rims is therefore justified.

Pls. 68:1—69:9 contain rims that may be assigned to phase I. Pl. 68 contains examples of the "squared" rims from the 1934 campaign. They find their closest parallels in Beth-zur II (175–165 B.C.),[11] a horizon contemporary with that assigned the end of phase 1 by Albright. They may be considered typologically in three groups. First are rims with short, vertical outside profile Pl. 68:1–10. Next are those with outside rim line slightly everted Pl. 68:11–17. Finally, there are rims with slightly concave outside profile Pl. 68:18–25. All of these rims are out-turned, most of them rather sharply. They have small diameters of about 10–12 cm. Their shoulders tend to evert sharply just below the rim leaving a very short neck. They develop from a rounded and less everted jar rim which is characteristic of the third century B.C. at Balâṭah but which is developing into the rims here illustrated about 200 B.C. Pl. 69:3–9 are examples of the "squared" rim from the 1957 campaign.

309. Pl. 69:1 shows a less common development of the third century rounded rim. The form remains somewhat rounded but is more everted and drawn to a point. It belongs with the *PCC* class of "rounded" rims and has its closest parallels in the first half of the second century B.C.[12] Pl. 69:2 seems to be a rim from a different jar type than the preceding rims because of its larger diameter. It might be related to an example from the *PCC* Corpus from a contemporary context at Samaria, but that has a smaller diameter.[13] Closer parallels are provided by two unpublished examples from the 1960 campaign at Balâṭah, also from contemporary deposits.[14]

310. Pl. 69:10–23 contains jar rims that may be assigned to phase 2. A slightly later jar from Qumran Ib provides an excellent parallel to the jars illustrated on Pl. 69:10 and 11.[15] The rims of Pl. 69:10a and 12 are similar to Pl. 69:1, but they belong to jars of less heavy ware, a later characteristic. The rim, Pl. 69:11a, is similar to phase 1 "squared" rims, but it is more outturned than most, and its outside profile line is more everted than any examples illustrated from phase 1. It is very similar to the *PCC* example.[16] Note also the slight shoulder break near the upper handle attachment and the very similar handles in both Beitîn and Qumran jars. A parallel to the general shape of the body occurs in the contemporary Bethany Cistern 61.[17]

311. The phase 2 development of the squared rim consists of a lengthening of the rim into the distinct collar that characterizes Pl. 69:13–23. In this same development the eversion of the rim has been lost and the rim projects vertically from a rather sharply outturned shoulder. Good parallels to these rims are found in Bethany Cistern 61 (75–50 B.C.) and Qumran Ib (50–31 B.C.).[18] Transitional forms seem rare, and there seems to be a definite chronological gap between examples from phase 1 and those from phase 2.[19]

312. In phase 3 the lengthening of the collar continues as can be seen in Pl. 70:2 and 3 from the 1957 campaign. These examples also have thickened, everted tips absent from the phase 2 examples. No precise parallel can be cited for Pl. 70:1, which is assigned to phase 3 by the excavator. Perhaps it is related to the form of a large footed jar having Corpus parallels from

---

[9] Cf. *PCC*, p. 56, n. 1, and p. 224.

[10] Importation of sigillata probably began after 63 B.C. (cf. *PCC*, p. 223, n. 21) and apparently ceased shortly after the beginning of the Christian era (cf. *PCC*, p. 226, n. 29).

[11] *PCC*, Corpus 11.2. A–D. Parallels are cited by *PCC* Corpus number only. A comprehensive list of parallels may be located through the Corpus.

[12] *PCC*, Corpus 11.3.C.

[13] *PCC*, Corpus 11.3.D.

[14] Pottery Reg. No. 955 from Phase 2a (ended *c.* 190 B.C.) and No. 3175 from Phase 1 (ended *c.* 150 B.C.).

[15] *PCC*, Corpus 11.3.H. This parallel should be stressed in connection with Père R. de Vaux's continued insistance upon the unique character of the Qumran Ib forms. *Op. cit.*, pp. 13–14.

[16] This has been classed with the "rounded" rim type and represents the latest development of that type. It is easily confused with the "squared" rim of the second century B.C., but that type develops into the longer collared type in the first century B.C. *PCC* Corpus Type 11.3 should be considered a catch-all for vestigial and dying forms of the rounded rim, separated from the main line of development.

[17] *PCC*, Corpus 11.1.C.

[18] *PCC*, Corpus 11.2.E–F.

[19] Contrast, e.g., Pl. 68:21–23 with 69:22.

Qumran locus 89 and Ib.[20] Rims of Pl. 70:4–23 belong to a type of jar which originated in the first century B.C. and seems to have gradually replaced the collared rim jar in popularity in the first century A.D. Pl. 70:4 is a 1934 example assigned to the Hellenistic period. It could represent an early appearance of the jar, paralleling an example from Bethany Cistern 61,[21] but more likely it should be placed with the 1957 examples, Pl. 70:5–23, which belong typologically with phase 3. The shaving of the rim is especially characteristic of the first century A.D. jar and cooking pot rims. Thickened, everted rim tips also seem to characterize many first century A.D. rims of this type. Numerous parallels from first century A.D. contexts are cited in *PCC* Corpus 12. C–H. These rims are usually ridged at the base of the neck and should not be confused with the collared rims Pl. 69:2 and 3 of the same period. This variety of rims should not be forced into a homogeneous group from about A.D. 70 but probably spans the period A.D. 1–70, the shorter necks tending to be early. Pl. 69:24 represents another type of jar common in the first century A.D. The complete form may be seen in an example from Qumran II.[22]

313. *Jugs*. Pl. 70:25–32 represent jug forms from phases 1 and 2, all from the 1934 campaign. In a few instances it is difficult to distinguish jug and jar rims, especially when dealing only with drawings. Occasionally a jar has a typical jug rim,[23] but usually jug rims are easily distinguished by their longer necks, their thinner and more finely levigated ware, and their form.[24] The heavy more rounded rim, Pl. 70:26, belongs to phase 1, as its parallels indicate.[25] Pl. 70:27 could be assigned to phase 1, but its thinner ware and close parallels in the Beth-zur cistern[26] make it a likely transitional form between phases 1 and 2. The other forms belong to phase 2. The nearly complete jug, Pl. 70:25, provides a parallel to a Beth-zur cistern jug (140–100 B.C.), but its sharper base indicates a date closer to Bethany Cistern 61, which contains the earliest sharp base of this jug type from a well-dated context.[27] The rim, Pl. 70:32, belongs to the same horizon. Pl. 70:28–31 are rims of the type common in the Beth-zur cistern.[28] These continued to be popular in the early first century B.C.

314. *Flask*. A flask from the 1934 campaign, 71:1, is assigned to phase 3. The typological development of the flask in the first centuries B.C. and A.D. is difficult to trace. The closest *PCC* Corpus parallel is from Qumran Trench A, considered of the Qumran Ib horizon.[29] Similar examples from Tulûl Abū el-ʿAlâyiq and the Jerusalem North Wall excavation show that the phase 3 attribution is undoubtedly correct.[30]

315. *Crater*. The rim of a crater from the 1957 campaign, Pl. 71:2, can be assigned to phase 3 on the basis of first century A.D. parallels at Herodian Jericho and Qumran.[31]

316. *Cooking Pots*. Cooking pots from phases 1 to 3 are illustrated on Pl. 71:3–9. These pots are from the 1934 campaign except Nos. 5 and 9, which were unearthed in 1960. Belonging typologically to phase 1 are Nos. 4 to 8. Pl. 71:4 was assigned to Iron II, but with a notation questioning the date. It has a good parallel from the Beth-zur cistern (140–100 B.C.),[32] and its grey core and slightly heavier ware suggest the somewhat earlier date of phase 1. The globular cooking pot, Pl. 71:5, does not have a good *PCC* Corpus parallel.[33] Its general shape and ware make its attribution to phase 1 quite certain. Unfortunately, it does not come from a chronologically significant context and therefore should not be added to the Corpus. Pl. 71:6 belongs with the shallow cooking pots with lid device that were fairly common in the second century B.C. but rare thereafter. A fairly good parallel comes

---

[20] *PCC*, Corpus 13.A.
[21] *PCC*, Corpus 12 (p. 152, read Type 12 for Type 11) A–B.
[22] *PCC*, Corpus 14.1.B.
[23] *PCC*, Corpus 11.3.B.
[24] The "squared" jug rim (*PCC*, Corpus 21.1.H, M), which first appears in the second century B.C., must be carefully distinguished from the "squared" jar rim of the same period. This can easily be done in most instances by observing thickness of ware, length of neck, and levigation. This jug rim becomes more popular in the later second and first century B.C., by which time the "squared" jar rims have developed into collars. The sharply outturned outside profile line of Pl. 70:27–30 is characteristic of jugs, not jars (contrast Pl. 69:11a).
[25] *PCC*, Corpus 21.1.A.
[26] *PCC*, Corpus 21.1.F–G.

[27] *PCC*, Corpus 21.1.H and M.
[28] *PCC*, Corpus 21.1.F–G.
[29] *PCC*, Corpus 29.F. Cf. p. 52.
[30] *PCC*, Corpus 29.G.
[31] *PCC*, Corpus 45.3.
[32] *PCC*, Corpus 71.1.D.
[33] Cf. *PCC*, Corpus 71.1.H for a similar pot with a more everted neck and similar rim from a later second century B.C. context.

from Room 1 of the Hellenistic House at Balâṭah (150–100 B.C.).[34] There is no reason to limit the type to the second half of the second century, but this could be a transitional form between phases 1 and 2. Pl. 71:7 is a cooking pot from a mixed context from which a coin of Ptolemy Philadelphus was recovered. Albright has correctly assigned it to phase 1. The nearest chronologically significant parallel is from Beth-zur (175–165 B.C.).[35] The similar cooking pot, Pl. 71:8, was discovered on the phase 2 floor and was assigned by Albright to that phase. There is no stratigraphic evidence for this form in the first century B.C., and it belongs typologically with Pl. 71:7. It could be considered a transitional form between phases 1 and 2, but attribution to phase 1 seems preferable.

317. The cooking pots, Pl. 71:3 and 9, belong respectively to phases 2 and 3. The former was recovered in the 1934 campaign and assigned to phase 2. It has a good contemporary parallel from Bethany Cistern 61.[36] Pl. 71:9, from the 1960 campaign, has the typical first century A.D. shape, which is more squat than the earlier globular pots. An example from Quran II (A.D. 50–68) provides a good parallel.[37]

318. *Lamps*. The available evidence does not seem sufficient to assign the lamps, Pl. 72:1–5,[38] to a specific phase. All can be assigned to either phase 1 or 2. Lamps with the ray motif and related types, Pl. 72:1–4, can be associated with Howland's Type 48. He considers this "the standard type of second century B.C. decorated lamp."[39] Examples from Gezer and Beth-zur indicate that these lamps were also used in Palestine in the second century B.C., since neither site was occupied in the first century B.C.[40] Yet, probably because of limited evidence, the only stratified Palestinian parallels belong to the first century B.C.[41] A similar situation exists in the case of the folded lamp, Pl. 72:5. It must have been in common use in the second century B.C. at Beth-zur, for example, but the only stratified examples come from first century B.C. contexts.[42] Howland suggests that his rayed Type 48 A "flourished for more than a century with no appreciable changes in shape or decoration."[43] This is apparently what must be said of these Hellenistic types in Palestine.

319. *Unguentaria*. The three fusiform unguentaria, Pl. 72:6–8, are from the 1934 campaign and were attributed to phases 1 or 2. On the basis of stratified parallels it is possible to assign Nos. 6 and 7 to phase 1 and No. 8 to phase 2. The former belong with the heavy ware unguentaria with stratified examples from the first half of the second century B.C.[44] The last has distinctly thin ware and belongs with the thin ware unguentaria of the first century B.C.[45] Pl. 72:9 is a sketched example of a piriform unguentarium from the 1934 campaign. This form began to appear in Palestine about the beginning of the Christian era and has many parallels contemporary with phase 3.[46]

* * *

SUPPLEMENT BY J. L. KELSO

320. In 1934 there was a small fragment of a Greek lekythos, No. 101, Pl. 37:10, which Iliffe dated to the second half of the fifth century B.C. It is reddish-buff ware with a creamy to reddish-buff slip and bears a brown to black decoration. The spout of a glazed lamp, No. 19, was dated by John Howard Young to the fourth century B.C. either just before or after Alexander the Great. In 1960 the latter also identified two sherds (each from a different house N of the city wall) to the fourth or early third century B.C.

---

[34] *PCC*, Corpus 72.1.H. The unpublished example, No. 1064=1066, is a closer parallel.
[35] *PCC*, Corpus 71.1.F.
[36] *PCC*, Corpus 71.1.K₁.
[37] *PCC*, Corpus 71.1.N₂.
[38] These lamps are sketched, not drawn to scale.
[39] R. H. Howland, *Greek Lamps and their Survivals* (The Athenian Agora, Vol. IV; Princeton, 1958), p. 158.
[40] *PCC*, pp. 10, 109–110.

[41] *PCC*, Corpus 83.2.
[42] *PCC*, Corpus 81.2.
[43] Howland, *op. cit.*, p. 158.
[44] *PCC*, Corpus 91.1.
[45] *PCC*, Corpus 91.2.
[46] *PCC*, Corpus 92.

CHAPTER XV

Bethel Roman and Byzantine Pottery from the Mosque Area, 1954

321. Most Roman and Byzantine pottery found in the 1954 campaign came from the mosque area. Only a few vessels could be reconstructed from sherds found in the fields because the soil had been turned upside down for more than a meter's depth and Byzantine and Roman sherds were hopelessly mixed §165. Sherds taken from the cisterns were similarly mixed. All of Pls. 75 and 76 represent the reconstructed vessels. Since there was no stratification these vessels can be dated only by typology. Pl. 74:7 was dated A.D. sixth century by Father Sallers. Pl. 74:6 was from a newly opened Roman tomb found on the E hillside just below Beitîn. The drawing does not show the fine ribbing on the shoulder. The jar is A.D. first century. This tomb was originally Iron II as the hillside in front of the tomb was covered with Iron II sherds.

322. A detailed study of the large quantity of sherds from the mosque area shows that the Roman pottery types of Bethel are surprisingly like those of New Testament Jericho.[1] This was to be expected as an important road connected Bethel and Jericho. Indeed, only Jericho's Roman types 4, 6, 11, 15, 16, 17, 23, 24, 25, 33, and 35 are missing. Since several of these types are rare at Jericho, their absence at Bethel is not surprising. It is interesting, however, to note that the mosque area at Bethel did not produce some of the common Jericho types; there are no unguentaria of type 17, pilgrim bottles of type 25, lids of type 33, or store-jars of type 24. In the Roman types found at Bethel there is often a modification in form from those of Jericho. Through the years the walls of several types of bowls became thicker. The sharp-edged rims of type 2 lost their sharpness and the projecting ridge became wider, thus producing a forerunner of the wide, flat edges of the Byzantine period. In type 9 and several others, the carination rounded out into a full curve. Most of this pottery came from cistern 1, and there is no way by which the ware can be identified by stratification as to the Early or Late Roman phase. Some Hellenistic influence was seen in cooking pots and in ointment jars of type 18, but most of the ware was definitely later than Hellenistic. The trend from Roman into Byzantine is plain. The excellent thin ware of Early Roman constituted the smaller percentage of material finds. The ware became thicker and the skill used in throwing it deteriorated. A few forms not found at Jericho appear, the most common of which are the casserole and the jar stand.

323. The Roman pottery forms of Bethel and Herodian Jericho are closely related but the Byzantine pottery of Bethel and Nitla[2] are by no means so closely related, although Nitla is only 3 km. E of Jericho. Jerusalem is a much closer relative of Bethel's pottery in Byzantine times than is Nitla. The Byzantine types common to Bethel and Nitla are Nitla's Byzantine types 1, 5, 6, 7, 9, 10, and 11. Many of the Nitla Arabic[3] forms are simply a continuation of Byzantine forms and of this group types common to both sites are types 13, 14, 16, 17, 19, 21, 22, 25, 27, 28, 29, 32, 33, 34, 36, and 38.

---

[1] *AASOR*, Vols. XXIX–XXX, pp. 20–31.

[2] *AASOR*, Vols. XXIX–XXX, pp. 32–35.
[3] *AASOR*, Vols. XXIX–XXX, pp. 35–41.

CHAPTER XVI

Bethel Artifacts other than Pottery

324. The Beitîn farmers in planting their orchards and in digging for building stone disturbed the original levels in numerous places. Many of the objects we found came from a mixed context. Some of the best finds came from surface debris. These are not discussed or pictured unless their forms are characteristic of only one archaeological period, i.e. Iron II. In the listing of the objects we first discuss those from a definite level and then those from a mixed context.

325. Byzantine objects from a clear level are rare. No. 34 is an iron pruning hook 12.5 cm. long. No. 41 is a pottery loom weight, truncated pyramid, 8 cm. high, quadrilateral top and base. No. 43 is a limestone spindle whorl 2.4 cm. dia. No artifacts other than pottery and coins come from a definite Roman level. From a mixed Roman-Hellenistic level comes an ostracon with the incised letters ΘE Pl. 42:3 (No. 121), and an egg-shaped glass bead 2.4 cm. dia. × 1.8 cm. with variegated eyes, Pl. 46:2 (No. 30). There is a complete bone spatula 13.7 × 2.4 cm. with one end rounded and the other pointed (No. 178) and also a poorer one 19 cm. long (No. 85).

326. From the Hellenistic level there is a store-jar handle showing the impression of a Hellenistic gem 95 × 73 mm. (No. 636). It shows a male figure walking, probably Mercury. (The seal was stamped upside down in relationship to the jar). Another seal impression (1.4 cm. long) of a closely related pattern appears twice on the rim of a jar (No. 783). On a jar handle (No. 75) there is a third impression 2 × 1 cm. apparently of a similar pattern, but it is poorly stamped; the left side of a seal did not print. No. 389 is an inscribed sherd 12.1 × 8.5 cm. with a cross inside a circle. No. 377 is a whittled bone point *c.* 9 cm. long. Bronze is represented by half an earring (No. 373), a small wire ring 2 cm. dia. (No. 84) and a 6.7 cm. fragment of a kohl spatula (No. 357). Iron is represented by two broken spear points *c.* 12 and 14 cm. long (Nos. 55 and 155), an iron rod 8 mm. dia., now in six fragments (No. 156), and a large-headed nail 4.4 cm. long (No. 56), There are two beads. One is a short barrel of red coral 4 mm. dia. × 8 mm. No. 367, and the other is a small irregular bead of blue paste 4 mm. dia. × 6 mm. No. 374. Stone is represented by No. 365 which is apparently a granite gaming piece 2 cm. dia. × 4 mm., No. 23 a limestone spindle whorl 2.7 dia. × 1.4 cm. and No. 95 one foot of a large basalt tripod mortar.

327. From a mixed Hellenistic-Iron II level come the following objects. There is an undecorated bronze fibula No. 28, which is almost identical with *Naṣbeh I*, Pl. 111:30, dated there to seventh or sixth century B.C.; see also *Bethel*, Pl. 46:20. Pl. 46:16 (No. 295) is a bronze earring. This form is found in Iron I and II as represented in *Gerar* XX:40–46, *PEFA VI*:Pl. V:199–204 and *Lachish III*, Pl. 57:42. There are two bronze kohl sticks: a complete one 14.4 cm. long (No. 73) and a broken one 10.2 cm. (No. 76). There is a bronze pin with head intact 6.2 cm. long (No. 80) and a 5.2 cm. needle fragment No. 398. A well-preserved, three-bladed, socketed bronze arrowhead appears on Pl. 46:28 (No. 180). The same form is found at Samaria where it is more Hellenistic than Iron II, *Samaria III*, Fig. 110:3 ff. At Amman it appears *c.* 650 B.C., *PEFA VI*, Pl. VII:30 and p. 70. At Gerar it appears as early as the ninth–eighth century B.C., *Gerar*, Pl. XXIX:14, 19. It is also from the Iron levels of *Lachish III*, Pl. 60:53; cf. *Naṣbeh I*, Pl. 104:8, *QDAP*, II, Fig. 14: C and page 56. No. 60 is a complete iron nail 11.3 cm. long; No. 276 is only the head fragment of a spike 3.2 cm. dia. No. 44 is an irregular shaped fragment of lead 9.7 × 8.5 cm.

328. There are two complete bone spatulas: No. 179 is a scimitar shaped one 9.9 × 2.8 cm., and No. 279 is another with one end pointed and one rounded 11 × 2.4 cm. No. 82 is a bone spindle whorl 2.9 cm. dia. × 1 cm. Nos. 170 and 274 are broken bone awls. The beads are varied in form and material. Three are glass: No. 99 is plane-conical 8 mm. dia., No. 126 is short oblate 1 cm. dia., and No. 45 is a tiny cylinder 5 mm. dia. Two beads are stone: No. 226 is marble (?) barrel disk 1.3 cm. dia. × 6 mm. and No. 633 is grey stone in standard barrel form 1.2 cm. dia.

329. There are two stoppers for store-jars. No.

220 is a roughly shaped limestone one 10.7 cm. dia. × 7.1 cm. and No. 396 is a well-fashioned chalk one with a groove through the center.[1] Its height is 15.2 cm., the diameter of the upper portion is 15.2 cm. and that of the lower portion 9.4 cm. No. 275 is a steatite spindle whorl 1.9 cm. dia. × 9 mm. Pl. 64:15 (No. 459) is a basalt tripod mortar. It is apparently an Iron II piece for it is similar in form to No. 421 of that period and its dimensions run 26.3 cm. dia. × 13.8 cm. No. 300 is a fragment of another basalt mortar 10 cm. high. No. 165 is a basalt rubbing stone 4.3 × 3.1 cm.

From a mixed Hellenistic-Iron I context comes a steatite scaraboid (No. 183). The flat surface portrays a fish above four stars (?). It is 1.5 × 1.3 × 1 cm. (high). There was also a two-pronged deer antler, No. 219, which is 14 × 9.1 cm.

Iron II

330. A scaraboid Pl. 44:4 (No. 548) portrays a stylized spider. It was found in a ninth–eighth century context. The face of this black stone scaraboid is concave, the back is flat and smooth and the stone is pierced longitudinally. There is also a basalt seal cylinder 1.7 dia. × 2.9 cm. (No. 514). It is divided into five panels covered with unintelligible patterns of straight lines, arcs, circles, and dots.

There is a small ostracon Pl. 47:10 (No. 3) with two incised letters (פד). The letters may have belonged to the name Pedaiah. They are to be dated to the seventh century B.C. The sherd is reddish-grey with white grits and the surface is buff.

331. All figurines from this level are fragmentary. The most interesting is a head 5.2 cm. high and 3.7 cm. wide (No. 96). It looks somewhat like a Sumerian head but is crudely fashioned. It is hollow rather than solid as is characteristic of Iron II ware. Pl. 45:15 (No. 59) is a typical Iron II figurine. There are also two fragments (Nos. 40 and 467) in which only the pillar of the figurine remains. Animal figurines are represented by eight fragments, all small. The best preserved is Pl. 45:16 (No. 740) where the proportions of the bull are better than usual and the tail is represented. Among other items there are three torsos (Nos. 57, 221, 754), two forequarters (Nos. 242, 480), and two legs (Nos. 218, 808).

332. Numerous bone items of various usages come from this level. Pl. 45:5, 6, 8, 9 (Nos. 401, 311, 432, 186) shows very common Iron II pendant forms. The second is roughly rectangular toward the lower section where there are four rows of five circles. The third has three rows of four circles; the last four rows of three circles each. There is a well-polished kohl stick 9.9 cm. long, thickened at one end and flattened at the other (No. 577) and a well-fashioned spindle whorl 4.9 cm. dia. (No. 576). Pl. 45:12 (No. 292) is probably one side of a sword or dagger handle. Good parallels are *Meg I*, Pl. 99:10, (V), and *Gerar*, Pl. XXXIII:29. Pl. 45:10 (No. 393) is a paddle-shaped bone, but no parallels were found. Pl. 45:3 (No. 605) is a spatula highly polished on both sides. It is tenth or ninth century. There are also two other complete spatulas; No. 160 is 9.6 × 2.5 cm. and No. 483 is 14 × 2.1 cm. There are nine broken spatulas. No. 660 is a whittled bone fragment 4.5 cm. long which has all the appearances of a worked flint tool. No. 598 is a broken bone tube, perhaps a tool handle, 9.6 cm. long. No. 622 is a bird-bone needle 4.2 cm. long and No. 323 is a large astragalus.

333. Bronze fibulae are represented on Pl. 46: 19, 20, 21 (Nos. 74, 77, 78). All are forms common to Iron II. The first is best represented at *Gezer III*, Pl. CXXXIV:1, 7. The second is paralleled in *Naṣbeh I*, Pl. 111:30 where it is dated seventh–sixth century B.C. and *Gerar*, Pl. XVIII: 12, where it is dated *c.* 800 B.C. The third is paralleled in *TBM III*, Pl. 64:5, where it is dated not far from 900 B.C.; *Naṣbeh I*, Pl. 110:22; *Gerar*, Pl. XVIII:6, where it is dated about 800 B.C.; *PEFA VI*, Pl. VII:19, 21, dated there *c.* 650 B.C., *QDAP*, 2 Fig. 13, "Dual Monarchy into Hellenistic Times." There is a complete kohl stick on Pl. 46:27 (No. 330) that is 16.7 cm. long. No. 309 is a fragment of a bronze pin. The only weapons are two bronze arrowheads. Pl. 46:33 (No. 187) has its closest parallel in *Meg I*, Pl. 80:56. The other (No. 551B) is an asymetrical form due to corrosion 7.9 × 1.9 cm. No. 530 is a small lump of copper slag.

334. Iron is represented by the following items. The only weapons are javelin points or arrowheads. No. 291 is 9 × 2.1 cm.; No. 557 is 9.2 × 1.4 cm.; No. 558 is 6.2 × 1.4 cm.; No. 578 has a broken point but is still 6.1 cm. long. There are

---

[1] *Gezer III*, CXCI:13 has a similar groove.

fragments of five arrowheads.[2] There are also fragments of two knife blades; No. 473 is 6 cm. long and No. 623 is 5 cm. There are two interesting tool points. No. 157 is 9 cm. long; No. 164 is 9.4 cm. long. Each is a four-sided pyramidal shape, the former being 1.2 cm. square at the base and the latter 1.5 cm. No. 531 appears to be a small section of pipe with only a third of the arc preserved. No. 289 is a small roughly edged triangular fragment of iron. There are three fragments of rods or tools.[3]

335. Beads from a definite Iron II level are twelve in number. The truncated convex bicone form is represented by two carnelians; No. 174 is 7 mm. dia. × 5 mm. and No. 397 is 1.1 cm. dia. × 8 mm. No. 189 is the same form in silver colored glass 9 mm. dia. × 5 mm. There is also a short truncated convex bicone in variegated glass 1.8 cm. dia. No. 619. There are three examples of a barrel disk; No. 190 is blue glass 1.2 cm. dia. × 4 mm., No. 283 is black paste, 2.1 cm. dia. and No. 318 is stone 9 mm. dia. × 4 mm. No. 529 is a standard barrel in a light green paste 1.7 cm. dia × 1.1 cm. and No. 173 is a long barrel in brown quartz 8 mm. dia. × 1.5 cm. No. 188 is a small cylinder 4 mm. dia × 8 mm. in agate and No. 166 is a blue paste cylinder with two bands 5 mm. dia. × 1.1 cm. No. 400 is a large spherical ivory bead 2.3 cm. dia.

336. Pl. 45:18 (No. 725) is a beautifully decorated and polished limestone cosmetic palette. No. 419 is a slightly chipped flint palette. The depression is smaller than usual and the only decoration is six small holes. Its dia. is 8.4 cm. and its height 2.7 cm. No. 540 is a small stone loom weight 2.2 cm. dia. Nos. 282 and 399 are poorly made spindle whorls. The former has a dia. of 2.1 cm. and the latter is 3.3 cm. No. 399 seems to be carved from a fossil. No. 553 appears to be a small weight of a light red stone with a polished base, roughly rectangular in form 2.5 cm. × 1.4 cm. high. There are two flints: No. 171 is a sickle edge and No. 738 is probably a sickle point. There is a complete basalt tripod mortar No. 421 with 26.5 cm. dia. × 12.7 cm. high.

337. The following items come from a mixed Iron II–I context. Pl. 45:4 (No. 110) is a thin decorated circular bone inlay. No. 313 is a bone needle 2.6 cm. long and No. 532 is a triangular-shaped bone awl 6 cm. long. No. 609 is three astragali from a common locus. Pl. 46:22 (No. 230) is a bronze fibula. Its closest parallel is *PEFA VI*, Pl. VII:20, where it is dated *c.* 650 B.C. There are four fragments of rods or tools, each averaging *c.* 6 cm.[4] There are five beads. Two are spherical in form; No. 317 is glass 6 mm. dia. and No. 320 is a steatite 1.7 cm. dia. No. 314 is a stone narrow barrel 6 mm. dia. × 3 mm. Pl. 46:7 (No. 116) is a carnelian long, convex, bicone 1 cm. dia. × 2.1 cm. No. 198 is a large irregular steatite sphere *c.* 2.5 cm. dia. No. 109 is a steatite spindle whorl 3.1 cm. dia. × 2 cm. No. 199 is a pumice stone polisher 9 × 3.1 × 2.3 cm. There are two weights (?), one of limestone 9.1 × 7.3 cm. No. 200, and one of flint 4.3 cm. dia. × 2.3 cm. No. 392. No. 158 is a pear-shaped limestone mace head 7.16 cm. dia. × 8.4 cm. Pl. 61:16 (No. 515) is a basalt mortar.

Iron I

338. From phase 1 comes a paste scarab with hawk design Pl. 44:2 (No. 442). From phase 1 or 2 comes a paste scaraboid with a boat and lotus pattern Pl. 44:3 (No. 445). The human form appears in five pottery items from the Iron I levels. No. 104 is a broken astarte plaque in which the body is better proportioned than in most Palestinian plaques. The closest parallels are *Ain Shems IV*, Pl. LI:17 and *Gerar*, XXXV:2, but the latter is LB. No. 243 is a broken Astarte plaque with the feet portrayed in typical Egyptian style. Pl. 45:13 (No. 560) is a torso. Pl. 45:14 (No. 328) is a Baal figurine (broken), apparently a pottery imitation of a metal figurine of Baal holding a shield, *Meg T*, Pl. 153:8. Note the thin body, the uplifted arms and a necklace. The only other figurine No. 333 is a fragment of a torso. Although the pottery context is Iron I the figurine looks like an Iron II form. Pl. 44:7 (No. 638) is a jar handle shaped in the fashion of a human head, §266.

339. The best carved work in bone is the top of a broken spindle Pl. 45:2 (No. 191). There is also the top fragment of a bone handle 4.1 cm., No. 644, whose decoration is two sets of three lines each cut at right angles to the cylinder with a diagonal line connecting the two units. A bone

---

[2] Nos. 307, 405, 408, 409, 472; Nos. 406, 407, and 413 may possibly be arrowhead fragments.
[3] Nos. 177, 427, 502.

[4] Nos. 316, 336, 338, 372.

8.2 cm. long (No. 195), probably served as a whistle as there is one hole near the middle of the bone. No. 735 is a beautifully worked bone ring 1.8 cm. dia. There are four bone pendants, all undecorated and crudely made. No. 227 is 7 × 1.7 cm.; the hole is near the smooth end and the opposite end is broken off. No. 228 is 7.2 cm. long. It is 1.8 cm. wide at the end where the hole is pierced. The opposite end tapers toward a point. No. 486 is a broken pendant 3.9 cm. long with the hole now near the center. No. 245 is a simple crude flat bone 7.3 × 2 cm. with a hole at one end. No. 455 is the largest bone spatula, 18.8 × 4.3 cm.; it is flat at the narrow end and pointed at the wider end. No. 541 is curved, polished on both sides and pointed at both ends. It is 11.3 × 1.8 cm. There are fragments of two other spatulas with wide pointed ends. No. 536 is 6.8 × 2 cm. and No. 734 is 5.8 × 2.1 cm. No. 358 is the narrow pointed end of a spatula 9.4 × 2.8 cm. Five bone needles run in length, 8.4, 6.3, 4.5, 4.3, 4.2 cm.[5] Three awls run 9.3, 7.8, and 7.4 cm.[6] One locus yielded thirteen astragali No. 527. There is one forked animal horn 7.6 cm. long No. 561, but its fauna identification is uncertain.

340. The finest bronze object is an excellent twelfth century socketed spearhead Pl. 46:35 (No. 613). Its closest parallel is *TBM II*, Pl. 41:22 where it is LB. This particular form of socketed spearhead seems rare, *QDAP*, II, 1933, Pl. XXXIV:914. There are two complete bronze arrowheads Pl. 46:31 (No. 431) and Pl. 46:32 (No. 539). The former has parallels in *Meg II*, Pl. 174:14 (VIII) and Pl. 176:62 (V). *Lachish IV*, Pl. 25:62 and Pl. 55:43 has this form but it is LB at Lachish. No. 539 has a parallel in *Meg I*, Pl. 81:18 (V). It appears as LB in *Meg T*, Pl. 135:10 and *Lachish IV*, Pl. 55:44. There is also a narrow triangular-shaped arrowhead in fragments No. 662. There is a square-shaped bronze earring two-thirds complete which is 2 × 1.7 cm. No. 240. No. 547 may be the small fragment of another earring. There are two interesting piercing tools. No. 535 is 6 cm. long with a circular cross section in the center. One end has a square cross section and the other end is a point. The major diameter is 7 mm. No. 542 is 7.6 cm. long with a rectangular cross section for the body and a smaller square section for one end; the opposite end is pointed.

The major diameter is 9 mm. There are fragments of three copper pins, the longest 6 cm.[7] There are two irregular-shaped fragments of sheet copper, each *c*. 5 cm. in the longest dimension Nos. 285 and 452. There is only a little iron in the Iron I level. No. 272 is a corroded arrowhead 8 × 1.9 cm. and there is also half of a second arrowhead. There are three narrow iron pieces each about 6 cm. in length from different loci— they may have been tool points.

341. There are two short barrel beads: No. 225 is white paste with green eyes 7 mm. dia. × 5 mm. and No. 294A is carnelian, 7 mm. dia. No. 294B is a long barrel carnelian 5 mm. dia. No. 736A is a small, long bone cylinder 1.6 cm. in length. No. 302 is steatite approximately spherical 1.2 cm. dia. Pl. 46:13 (No. 612) is a small carnelian pendant 1.4 cm. long. No. 573 is a tooth-shaped mottled grey stone pendant 1.9 cm. long.

342. No. 326 is a beautiful striated grey stone 3.5 cm. long but the upper end of this neck pendant has the hole missing. No. 327 is a plain limestone neck pendant 7.2 cm. × 8 mm. No. 545 is a most interesting stone piece. It is 2.6 × 1.8 cm. The long sides are parallel and the ends are concave. What makes the piece unique is that the hole through the center of the stone has the shape of a letter T. Pl. 46:4 (No. 332) is a steatite conoid button. No. 629 is a game piece (?) 3 cm. dia. with a convex top. No. 484 may be a steatite weight 2 cm. dia. × 1.7 cm. No. 284 is a dumbbell shaped pestle 9.8 cm. long. No. 281 may be a quartz weight roughly rectangular 2.1 × 1.7 cm. No. 511 is a limestone rubber 10.9 × 3.5 cm. No. 417 is the small top fragment of a worked pumice stone with the hole intact. No. 304 is a small potter's wheel of limestone, 15.8 cm. dia. × 11.6 cm. high. Nos. 390 and 391 are two crude limestone awls *c*. 10 cm. long. There are five double-edged flint knives Nos. 114, 194 (?), 537, 546, 650.

343. From a mixed Iron I—LB—MB II context comes No. 461, a bone kohl pencil 8.1 cm. long, and No. 451 a spherical bead of black marble 7.5 mm.

Late Bronze

344. One of the outstanding finds of the season

---

[5] Nos. 543, 610, 574, 280, 236.
[6] Nos. 663, 628, 273.

[7] Nos. 298, 290, 319.

was an Astarte seal cylinder, Pl. 43 (No. 513). Unhappily it was discovered in an ancient dump inside the city wall. "The context was MB II—LB—Iron I, allowing a scope of several centuries. It is a seal-cylinder of frit, either made in Egypt for Asiatic consumption or, more likely, manufactured at Gaza or another town under strong Egyptian influence. Facing one another are two deities, each holding a spear, the two of which serve as a frame for the hieroglyphic inscription ʿ–s–t–(a)r–t = ʿAstart. ʿAstart was the Canaanite pronunciation of the name, which became ʿAshtart, ʿAshtarôt in Hebrew and Phoenician, Greek Astarte, as the goddess of fertility was called in Canaan. The cult of this goddess was borrowed by the Egyptians of the New Empire, as we know from many references in Egyptian literary and other texts. She is here represented as wearing the high Egyptian tiara with the feathers of the 'two truths' on each side of it; from her tiara stream the two ribbons which indicated royalty in Canaan, and were frequently attached to the helmet of a god. She wears a long robe, and perhaps holds the ʿankh sign ('Egyptian cross') in her right hand. The costume is that of ʿAnat on stelae of Beth-shan, though the similarity is not quite complete in any one case. Opposite her is the god Baal, wearing a waist-cloth, and brandishing the Egyptian scimeter (khopesh) in his right hand. Scholars who have seen the seal agree with our date, the Nineteenth Dynasty; we may quote the opinions of Rowe, Starkey, Vincent, and Yeivin." *BASOR*, No. 56, pp. 7–8.

Pl. 42:1 (No. 549) is a bone sistrum handle carved in the form of an Egyptian Hathor column and capital. "The carving is good, but the workmanship is unmistakably Palestinian." "Egyptian parallels from Sinai point to about the fifteenth century B.C., a date which would suit the stratification admirably." *BASOR*, No. 56, pp. 8–9. No. 551A is a thin flat oval-shaped bone palette polished on both sides and with its edges slightly sharpened. The maximum length is 6.3 cm. and the maximum width is 2.4 cm. No. 460 is a carved bone cylinder 1.2 cm. dia. × 1.85 cm. No. 471 is a bone handle 9.6 cm. long with 1.9 cm. dia. No. 446 is an end fragment of a bone inlay 6.9 × 2.1 cm. with two nail holes. No. 447 is an 8 cm. fragment of a bone kohl stick. There are four bone spindle whorls. Nos. 586, 720 are 2.4 cm. dia.; No. 597 is 2.2 cm. and No. 492 is 2.5 cm. Two large astragali come from this level: Nos. 465 and 466 and both are from the same locus. No. 611 is a two-pronged stag horn with a maximum length of 24 cm.

345. Bronze objects are well represented in the LB strata. Pl. 46:37 (No. 477) is a knife. No exact parallels were found. Pl. 46:36 (No. 476) is a shorter knife with an upturned point. (Both knives are from the same locus.) Closest parallel of the latter is *Lachish IV*, Pl. 23:5, Pl. 54:44, although the Bethel knife curves higher. Weapons are represented by two flat bladed arrowheads Pl. 46:30, 34 (Nos. 516, 714). The latter comes from the last LB burning. No. 516 has an LB parallel in *Meg II*, Pl. 174:4 (X). *TBM III*, Pl. 62:11, *Gerar*, XXIX:40 and *Lachish III*, Pl. 60:68 have it in the Iron Age. No 714 has a parallel in *Lachish IV*, Pl. 25:59. No. 552 is a broken tang probably from a dagger. Bronze toilet articles are represented by a complete toggle pin Pl. 46:26 (No. 239), and two broken kohl sticks. No. 238 is 9.5 cm. long and No. 241 is 11.4 cm. No. 464 is a small piece of a lead bar 1.7 × 1.5 cm. No. 728 is probably a lump of copper ore.

346. Beads are represented by a spherical form No. 450 in green stone 8 mm. dia. × 7 mm., No. 500 a short melon also in green stone 9 mm. dia. × 7 mm. and No. 501 a short barrel in paste 5 mm. dia. × 4 mm. There is also a broken multitubular haematite bead 1.7 cm. dia. × 2.9 cm., No. 498. The best stone item is a limestone dagger pommel Pl. 45:20 (No. 593). No. 474 is half a granite mace head 4.8 cm. dia. × 2.5 cm. Nos. 394 and 499 are fragments of alabaster rims. The first 3.8 cm.; the second 3.4 cm. wide. No. 554 is half of a beautifully carved basalt bowl with an inverted rim and ringbase. Its diameter is 35.5 cm. and its height 8 cm. No. 603 is a flint sickle edge. No. 564 is a flint knife.

347. From a mixed LB–MB II context are the following items. Pl. 44:1 (No. 620) is a steatite scarab. It portrays Horus on an *nl* sign, looking to the left; before him are two Uraei. The elytra is not marked.

There are two bone handles, No. 602, 6.4 cm. long and No. 649, 3.4 cm. long. No. 462 is a broken bronze pin or kohl stick 10.5 cm. long. No. 491 is a paste bead in scaraboid form 8 mm. dia. × 1.4 cm.

Middle Bronze II

348. No. 94 is a Hyksos scarab impression on

an MB II jar handle. It apparently represents a stylized man standing with one leg upraised. *BASOR*, No. 136, pp. 20–21, described another scarab impression. No. 454 is a fragment of a seal impression on bitumen from an MB II context, 2.8 × 2.2 cm. The design is small concentric circles close together, similar to those used on bone inlays. Bone items from this level are as follows. Pl. 45:11 (No. 630) is a flat inlay with ten incised circles irregularly arranged and showing traces of a black pigment within the circles. This irregular design is unusual but see *Meg I*, Pl. 99:1. The front side of the Bethel inlay is polished, the back shows the natural structure of the bone. Pl. 45:7 (No. 581) is the best bone object, an oval pendant decorated with two rows of incised circles still showing traces of a light blue pigment. Both sides are polished; the front is slightly convex, the back is flat. This pendant had doubtless served as the lid of a perfume box. No similar example has been found in Palestine. No. 596 is a flat bone button 1.7 cm dia. There are two spindle whorls; No. 606 dia. 2.8 cm., and No. 641 dia. 2.7 cm. Nos. 631 and 643 are broken awls.

349. No. 550 is a bronze dagger. The length including the stub of the tang is 18.5 cm., maximum width 4.5 cm. The blade narrows only slightly and ends in a broad curve. The MB II level has six beads. No. 575 is a spherical light blue faience 4 mm. dia. Pl. 46:3 (No. 448) is a stone cone 1.4 cm. base dia. × 8 mm. No. 193 is a steatite (?) standard sphere 1.4 cm. dia. Pl. 46:8 (No. 569A) is a short melon faience piece 9 mm. dia. and No. 569B is a white paste short barrel 6 mm. dia. Pl. 46:9 (No. 621) is a large light green faience bead in a long truncated bicone form 2.4 cm. long.

350. The MB II level has the following stone objects. No. 453 is a green quartz game piece (?), roughly rectangular in form 2.5 × 1.8 cm. No. 642 is an alabaster game piece, a tall cone 3.6 cm high, dia. 1.6 cm. No. 544 is irregular in shape (2.1 cm. high), but it is polished as if it might be a weight. No. 444 is a flat spindle whorl dia. 3.7 cm. × 9 mm. No. 632 is a flint sickle edge. Nos. 192 and 604 are fragments of double edged flint knives.

Middle Bronze I

351. From the MB I level come a flint knife No. 485 and a basalt ring No. 572, 4.7 cm. dia. × 1.6 cm.

352. From a mixed MB I–EB context come two carnelian long-barrel beads Pl. 46:5, 6 (Nos. 646A, 646B). The first is 1.1 cm. long and the second 1.4 cm.

* * * *

Surface Debris and Graves

353. The following items are from surface debris. The majority of them were considered important enough to photograph and the objects usually give a clue to the level from which they originally came. Pl. 45:13 (No. 560) is an uncommon Astarte form. The clay, however, is typical of Iron I. No. 122 is a stylized lion's foot of a figurine or a vessel. It looks like Iron II ware. Pl. 45:1 (No. 2) is a typical MB II bone inlay, the leg of a small jewel box. Pl. 46:17 (No. 616) is a circular bronze earring. Pl. 46:29 (No. 31) is a bronze rhombic arrowhead. It is probably Hellenistic cf. *Samaria III*, Fig. 110:15–17. Pl. 46:10, 11 (Nos. 727, 169) are both short-barrel carnelian beads. Pl. 45:17 (No. 54), a limestone macehead, is probably LB. Its length is 6.7 cm., its width 5.8 cm. and its greatest thickness 5 cm. From surface debris but with Iron II sherds comes a stone dagger pommel Pl. 45:19 (No. 10) and Pl. 44:6 (No. 101) an inscribed weight. Pl. 46:18 (No. 719) is a bronze ornament. Pl. 46:24 (No. 744) is a bronze needle. Pl. 44:5 (No. 661) is a basalt conoid seal portraying two animals. It is 3.1 dia. × 3.2 cm. and is pierced horizontally.

354. From Grave A comes a glass bracelet Pl. 46:15 (No. 201). From Grave D is a twisted bronze bracelet Pl. 46:14 (No. 209). From Grave E, Pl. 46:12 (No. 117) comes a string of tiny paste beads, mostly light blue but with some dark blue and gilded. Since a silver Arabic coin was attached, the string is probably Arabic. From Grave F, there are two bronze bracelets, Pl. 46:1, 25 (No. 213); one has a punctured design in zigzag pattern. Most graves were Byzantine.

1954 Campaign

355. In 1954 the surface debris from the campsite area of the 1934 dig was badly mixed because the farmers had dug deeply to find stone for the

building of new boundary walls. Iron II was the first undisturbed level. The pottery figurines are fragmentary. No. 1011 is an Astarte torso 6 cm. high. No. 1004 is the rear half and tail of a bull somewhat like Pl. 45:16. Nos. 1008 and 1028 are the front halves of animals, probably bulls. Nos. 1014 and 1023 are legs of horses or bulls. From this level are the following bone objects. Pl. 114:9 (No. 1025) is a bone pendant with a row of five dots. (The dots do not show in the photo.) The pendant is similar to Pl. 45:6. No. 1026 is the upper half of a pendant 4 cm. × 8 mm. Pl. 114:10 (No. 1072) is a bone pendant with an interesting pattern. Pl. 114:16 (No. 1068) is a spatula. No. 1021 is a broken spatula 11.8 cm. long.

356. From a good Iron II level come the following beads. No. 1033 is a short barrel, pottery, 11 mm. dia. × 12 mm. No. 1047 is a short barrel, agate, 14 mm. dia. × 11 mm. Metals are represented by the following items. No. 1015 is a fragment of a bronze ring. No. 1020 is an iron plowshare (broken) 22.6 cm. × 6.5 cm. No. 1031 is a broken iron arrowhead, 7.4 × 2.2 cm. No. 1024 is an iron fragment 19.5 × 1.2 cm. No. 1069 is another iron fragment 4.5 cm. long.

357. Stone is represented by the following items. Pl. 114:19 (No. 1027) is a pumice stone; the upper portion is pierced with a hole. No. 1067 is a sandstone whetstone in the form of a truncated cone 9.3 cm. × 4.9 cm. No. 1066 may be a flint weight 6.1 cm. dia. × 5.6 cm. Pl. 114:8 (No. 1029) is a polished black stone pendant. No. 1157 is a good limestone roof roller 55 cm. long with a diameter of 20 cm.

358. From a mixed Iron II–I context come the following. Pl. 114:5 (No. 1061) is a bone spindle whorl. No. 114 is a bird bone awl 5.6 cm. long. No. 1056 is 22 small astragali, all found in one locus. No. 1075 is a semi-circular bronze bucket handle. Its length is 15 cm. Pl. 114:17, 18 (Nos. 1152, 1096) are iron arrowheads, as is No. 1097 which is 9.3 cm. long. No. 1074 is a flint awl 5 cm. long and pointed at both ends. No. 1052 is one end of a broken whetstone 3.5 cm. × 1.3 cm.

Iron I

359. From a clear Iron I context come two figurines, both late in Iron I. No. 1054 is the head and neck of a horse, 4.5 cm. long. No. 1112 is similar but with very prominent eyes; the fragment is 7 cm. long. Pl. 114:12 (No. 1073) is a red stone (pebble). The decoration is a bird (ostrich) before a plant. The work is not Egyptian. No. 1012 is a frit scarab from the latest phase of Iron I. The pattern is not clear. Pl. 114:11 (No. 1150) is a jar handle with a large interesting stamp impression. We found no parallels.

360. Bone objects are as follows. Pl. 114:13 (No. 1051) is the lower section of a pendant decorated with 5 dots to a row. No. 1083 is a broken spatula 13.5 × 1.7 cm. No. 1116A is a broken kohl stick 6.2 cm. long. Iron I has the following beads. No. 1046 is a carnelian oblate disk 18 mm. dia. × 9 mm. No. 1070 is a topaz (?), long cylinder 8 mm. dia. × 18 mm. No. 1076 is a carnelian short barrel 7 mm. dia. × 8 mm. No. 1082 is a carnelian oblate disk 2.2 cm. dia. × 8 mm. No. 1100 is a short barrel of stone 9 mm. dia. × 8 mm. No. 1087 is a carnelian pendant 1.5 cm. long; the top is 4 mm. wide, the bottom 7 mm.

361. Bronze objects are as follows. No. 1045 is four fragments of a bronze bracelet and No. 1086 is three fragments of another bronze bracelet. Pl. 114:2 (No. 1050) is a wire ring where the ends overlap. Pl. 114:4 (No. 1091) is a ring. No. 1044 is a bent wire 9.3 cm. long. No. 1103 is an iron hammer 20 × 9 cm. Pl. 114:15 (No. 1058) is an iron arrowhead; No. 1057 is an iron fragment 6 cm. long.

362. Stone objects are as follows. Pl. 114:1 (No. 1090) is a limestone dagger pommel. No. 1049 is a finger-shaped limestone pestle 7.4 × 1.7 cm. Pl. 114:6 (No. 1098) is a worked cylinder of bituminous limestone with grooved sides, perhaps a playing piece. Pl. 114:7 (No. 1116B) is a thin worked stone found with other toilet articles; it is 3.6 cm. long. No. 1043 is a circular stone with socket in the center 6 cm. dia. × 3.1 cm. Pl. 114:14 (No. 1089) is a pumice stone in the unusual form of an hour glass 5.6 cm. high. No. 1048 is a broken quartz spindle whorl 2.6 cm. dia. × 2.3 cm. Rubbing stones have the following dimensions. No. 1102 is 4.2 × 2.6 cm., No. 1042 is 7.8 × 3.9 cm. and No. 1084 is 9.5 × 6.5 cm. There are many large sling stones; the greatest diameter is 9 cm. No. 1081 is two fragments of bitumen.

363. From an Iron I–LB context comes No. 1071, a moss agate short barrel bead 12 mm. dia.

× 10 mm. and No. 1053 a great quantity of zebar (refuse left after the extraction of olive oil). LB artifacts are represented only by sling stones. These are much smaller than the Iron I variety; one was only 5 cm. in diameter.

364. Jewelry from the MB II level are a well-finished bronze ring Pl. 114:3 (No. 1106), the fragment of a bronze toggle pin No. 1110, and two beads. No. 1107 is a faience oblate spiral gadrooned, 1.3 cm. dia. × 1.1 cm. No. 1113 is a carnelian short barrel 8 mm. dia. × 7 mm. No. 1108 is two small sea shells. The only tools are 5 awls (No. 1109) made from bird bones and a flint sickle tooth (No. 1111) 3.8 × 2.6 cm.

* * * *

365. The artifacts from the mosque area are from badly mixed debris, §321 ff., and therefore only the following unique items are listed, all on Pl. 79. Nos. 10 and 11[8] are altar columns from the Byzantine church. No. 9[9] is a column base with a slot for the chancel screen. No. 8[10] is a fragment of a column base. Nos. 7 and 12[11] are decorative fragments, the latter in linear pattern, the former in floral design. All the above are limestone. No. 13[12] is a basalt cone, the lower unit of a Roman mill used for making flour. ("M" designates all material from the mosque area.) The architectural items seen by Sternberg at Bethel are shown on pp. 8–9 of his article on Bethel in *ZDPV*, Vol. 38 (1915).

366. Interesting coins from the first century A.D. included those of the procurators Marcus Ambivius, Annius Rufus, Valerius Gratus, Pontius Pilate. There are also coins of Herod Agrippa I and of the first revolt.

1957 Campaign

367. In the 1957 campaign only commonplace objects were found as we worked near the city walls which are always a plundered area.* There was one important exception which was a unique pottery seal (ninth century B.C.) with an early Arabic inscription Pl. 118 (No. 2295), which was found in mixed debris just outside the W wall of the city. It was used to seal the incense bags shipped out of Arabia and sold at Bethel and Jerusalem. The seal was so unique that its study was given 7½ pages in *BASOR*, No. 151, pp. 9–16. Its significance is well summarized in the last paragraph of that report. "The importance of this stamp for South Arabian and Palestinian studies can hardly be overstated. As perhaps the earliest South Arabian inscription known (except for rock inscriptions), it provides an invaluable peg for the study of South Arabian palaeography. Of equal importance is the light it sheds on relations between Palestine and South Arabia. Since it is the earliest (possibly even the first) South Arabian object found in Palestine, it proves that contact had already been established between Israel and South Arabia early in the first millenium B.C., no more than two centuries and possibly only a few years after the visit of the 'Queen of Sheba' to Solomon. While this substantial historicity of this event has been increasingly accepted in recent years, this object carries us closer to that period than most scholars had dared hope. Moreover the fact that it was found at the temple city of Bethel enables us to define the nature of this contact with reasonable probability."

An almost identical seal was later found by A. Jamme in the famous Glaser collection of squeezes in Tübingen. It had been found in central Hadhramaut. Thus we have two business documents by the same company covering sales territory between South Arabia and Palestine. *BASOR*, No. 163, pp. 15–18.

In the same debris with the incense seal came the foot and leg of a jointed pottery doll Pl. 115:1 (No. 2229). The leg is 9.2 cm. long and the foot is 2.6 cm. It looks something like *Gerar*, Pl. XXXVI:9 and *Meg II*, Pl. 206:49. Nearby was a frit scaraboid Pl. 115:4 (No. 2228).

368. In the surface debris near the maḍâfeh was a well-preserved limestone Byzantine capital Pl. 79:6 (No. 2247). Above the beautiful lathed-turned work was a square abacus.

369. The first undisturbed level of the campaign that yielded artifacts other than pottery was Iron II, from which came the following items. There are two bone pendants, both broken, which are typical Iron II forms. No. 2041 is the lower half of a pendant 4.5 × 1.2 cm. with three dots showing in each row of the design. Pl. 115:11 (No. 2072) has four dots to a row but the dots are only

---

[8] Pl. 79:10 = M2, 79:11 = M1.
[9] Pl. 79:9 = M3.
[10] Pl. 79:8 = M 166.
[11] Pl. 797 = M 168, 79:12 = M 167.
[12] Pl. 79:13 = M 4.

* We have not compared these artifacts with finds from other excavations except in a very few instances.

in the lower half of the pendant. It is broken at the hole. No. 2106 is a broken curved bone handle, 9.5 × 3.2 cm. There are four broken spatulas, 8, 6.4, 6, 4.5 cm. long (Nos. 2081, 2109, 2206, 2203). The widest is 2.6 cm. and the narrowest 1.8 cm. There are two complete bone needles Pl. 115:7 (No. 2205) and Pl. 115:9 (No. 2227). The latter is perfect workmanship; note the delicate eye. There are three broken awls. No. 2115 is 2.8 cm. long, No. 2131 is 11 × 4 cm. and No. 2223 is 7.2 × 1.2 cm. There are two small astragali No. 2048 and one large one No. 2077. From the same locus comes another large one and eleven small ones No. 2021.

370. Bronze objects from Iron II are represented by No. 2025, a bracelet 5.8 cm. dia., No. 2162 a ring 2.3 cm. dia., and No. 2037 a fragment of an earring 1.7 cm. dia. Iron objects are as follows. No. 2204 is a broken arrowhead 6.2 × 1.4 cm. No. 2087 is three thin nails, 9, 8.2, and 6 cm. long and No. 2133 is probably another nail 5.8 cm. long. No. 2063 is an iron fragment, perhaps part of a pruning knife 7.8 × 2.3 cm.

371. There are two beads. No. 2221 is a lump of amber 1.9 × 1.5 cm. No. 2222 is a short oblate black stone 6 × 7 mm. No. 2207 is a cowrie shell used as a bead 1.8 × 1.3 cm. Stone objects are represented by No. 2184, a small fragment of a typical Iron II limestone palette with concentric circles on the rim, No. 2009 a basalt pestle in cylindrical form 7 × 4.2 cm., No. 2076 a cone-shaped limestone pestle 3.1 × 3.5 cm., and No. 2055 a haematite weight (?) 2.2 × 1.4 cm. There are three limestone rubbing stones. No. 2017 is elliptical in form 9 × 6 cm., No. 2018 is triangular 9 × 7.5 cm. and No. 2084 is dome-shaped 7 cm. dia. × 5.5 cm. No. 2166 is a good rectangular whetstone 8.2 × 3.2 × 1.5 cm.; No. 2118 is a broken whetstone approximately half that size.

372. From a mixed Iron II–I context comes No. 2030 a bronze ring 2.8 cm. dia.; the wire forming the ring is looped over across the front of the ring. There are two broken iron arrowheads; No. 2143 is 6.6 × 2.3 cm. and No. 2275 is 6.4 × 1.9 cm. Because of the length of the fragments they may be javelin points.

373. The following objects come from the Iron I levels. Pl. 115:12 (No. 2119) is a broken pottery stamp with a design in irregular squares 3 × 2.6 cm. (The design does not show in the photo.) No. 2082 is a 5.6 cm. fragment of a bone spatula. No. 2129 is a bone awl 4.4 × 2 cm. From a single locus come four astragali No. 2035. No. 2225 is an iron javelin point 7.5 × 1.8 cm. and No. 2134 is an iron arrowhead 5.8 × 1.8 cm. Both are in poor condition. No. 2026 is an iron fragment 6.5 cm. long probably from an iron ring.

374. Beads from the Iron I level are as follows. No. 2034 is stone long cylinder 1 cm. dia. × 3.1 cm. No. 2053 is a very thin round bone 8 mm. dia. There are three short barrels. No. 2091 is carnelian 9 mm. dia. × 6 mm. No. 2114 is stone 10 mm. dia. × 7 mm. No. 2120 is frit (?) 14 × 11 mm. There are only three stone items from Iron I. Pl. 115:15 (No. 2016) is a flint awl. No. 2033 is a flint sickle tooth and No. 2224 is a whetstone 7.8 × 3.8 cm. From a mixed Iron I–LB context comes half of a dome-shaped haematite weight 2.7 cm. dia. × 2.2 cm., Pl. 115:14 (No. 2121).

375. Late Bronze has some interesting bone objects. Pl. 115:3 (No. 2163) is a well-finished scimitar-shaped bone inlay. No. 2107 is the fragment of a bone hair ornament in a leaf pattern. The maximum length is 4 cm. and the width 3.1 cm. No. 2022 is two-thirds of an animal bone 10 × 4 cm. with a square hole in what was the center of the original piece. It is probably a drill holder; compare *Meg II*, Pl. 285:1, 2. (The *Meg* pieces are almost identical with No. 3027 found in surface debris in 1960.) Pl. 115:8 (No. 2027) is a thin bone awl as is No. 2080 which is 6.2 cm. long. There are two large astragali No. 2052 and one large one No. 2056.

376. No. 2169 is a broken bronze bracelet, original dia. 5.7 cm. No. 2083 is half of a bronze bucket handle including the section fitting into the bucket. The original diameter of the arc of the handle was 17 cm. No. 2161 is the rounded portion of a bronze tweezer 3.5 × 1.2 cm. No. 2102 is a narrow bronze javelin head or arrowhead 7.8 cm. long. No. 2218 is a truncated convex carnelian bead 1.1 cm. dia. × 1.4 cm. No. 2124 is the foot of a large shallow basalt mortar 8.2 cm. high. No. 2182 is a broken cone-shaped basalt pestle 4.9 cm. dia. × 8.5 cm. No. 2058 is a rectangular rubbing stone 6.5 × 3.8 × 2.8 cm. No. 2051 is a badly worn flint knife 6.3 cm. long. No. 2105 is a few olive seeds that came for a mixed LB–MB II context.

377. In the Middle Bronze II level we found only two bone objects, a broken awl 5 × 1 cm., No. 2167, and a large astragalus No. 2098. Bronze objects are more common. There are

three complete bracelets. No. 2090 is 5.4 cm. dia.; No. 2146 is 3.9 cm. and Pl. 115:2 (No. 2186) has a diameter of 5.9 cm. One end is finished with a five-sided knob, the other end is corroded. Pl. 115:5 (No. 2111) is an almost complete bracelet 5.6 cm. dia. One end is finished with a snake's head. No. 2170 is half a ring 2 cm. dia. No. 2135 is a 4.2 × 3.1 cm. fragment from the center of a knife blade. No. 2276 is about three-fourths of the bottom of a bronze bucket 14.4 cm. dia.

378. No. 2089 is a short barrel stone bead 8 mm. dia. × 1 cm. No. 2171 is a truncated convex bicone stone bead 8 mm. dia. × 6 mm. Stone objects are as follows. No. 2096 is a cone game piece 7 × 3 cm. Pl. 115:6 (No. 2071) is a flat triangular black and white striped stone with maximum dimensions 2.5 × 2.8 cm. Flint is well represented as might be expected in MB II. No. 2088 is a broken knife 5 × 2.4 cm.; No. 2172 is also a knife fragment 5.8 × 3.1 cm. Pl. 115:13 (No. 2179) and Pl. 115:17 (No. 2181) are excellent oval flint scrapers. Sickle teeth are as follows. No. 2104 is 4.6 × 3 cm. No. 2168 is 4.4 × 4 cm. and No. 2175 is 4.8 × 3.5 cm. No. 2151 is a flint awl 6.3 × 3.7 cm.

1960 Campaign

379. The artifacts other than pottery found *in situ* in the 1960 campaign were few although there was a considerable number of items found in the debris of the areas where the Byzantines had robbed the city wall and where the Arab farmers had dug deep to aerate the soil. None of the ten coins found was *in situ* although one is of special interest. No. 3006 is a bronze coin of the procurator Antonius Felix from A.D. 58–59; cf. Reifenberg # 136. Pl. 119c (No. 3063) is a stone scarab which looks like Neo-Babylonian work. It portrays a tree with a man standing on each side of it. The scarab came from mixed debris which would permit this dating but the debris also contained earlier material. The only other related Babylonian object from Bethel was a small conoid seal (Fig. 1) which we purchased from a local farmer. It presented a stylized Babylonian motif of the worship of the god Marduk, §206.

The only items from a clear Hellenistic level are beads. No. 3015 is faience, short barrel 11 mm. dia. × 11 mm. No. 3037 is carnelian, short barrel 9 mm. dia. × 7 mm. The only item from an undisturbed Iron II level is No. 3130, the fragment of a basalt mortar which is 28 cm. dia. × 10 cm. From a mixed Iron II–I context comes No. 3060, a fragment of a bronze bracelet 7.2 cm. long × 3 mm. wide, also No. 3062 an oval pumice rubbing stone 10 × 7.4 cm. and No. 3067 a stone spindle whorl 4.4 cm. dia.

380. From the Iron I level come the following items. No. 3064A is a bronze earring 1.6 cm. dia. × 2 mm. in thickness. No. 3071 is a broken bone spatula 5 × 2.2 cm. No. 3064B is a flask-shaped stone pendant 1.5 cm. long × 8 mm wide. No. 3066 is a triangular-shaped flint arrowhead or javelin point 5.4 cm. long × 3.8 cm. at the base. No. 3065A is a flint arrowhead 2.2 × 1.2 cm. There are three sickle teeth; No. 3068 is 4.2 × 3.1 cm., No. 3074 is 3.1 × 2.8 cm. and No. 3080 is 4.5 × 2.8 cm. Pl. 116:6 (No. 3073) is a flint scraper. Sling stones are very common; the maximum diameter is 9 cm. From a mixed Iron I–LB context comes No. 3082 the leg of a pottery bull figurine 6.8 × 2.2 cm. and No. 3081 a pottery spindle whorl 7.5 dia. × 1.6 cm. There are also three small faience oblate beads, No. 3078, 7 mm. dia. × 5 mm., 7 mm. dia. × 6 mm., 5 mm. dia. × 5 mm. No. 3077 is a rubbing stone or weight 11.8 cm. dia. × 7.5 cm.

381. From LB come two small bronze javelin heads. No. 3083 is 13 × 2 cm. No. 3084 is 10.7 × 2.1 cm. No. 3027 is a natural bone with a square hole in the center, probably a drill holder. Although found in surface debris it is almost identical with No. 2022 of 1957. Stone items are as follows. Pl. 116:7 (No. 3054) is a fan-shaped flint scraper. No. 3055 consists of three broken flint knives: 5.3 × 3.3 cm., 4.2 × 1.8 cm., 3.7 × 2.2 cm. and a sickle tooth 3.4 × 2.5 cm. There are also two other sickle teeth. No. 3038 is 3.8 × 4.2 cm. and No. 3039 is 4.5 × 4.6 cm. Pl. 116:9 (No. 3099) is a water polished stone in something of a cone shape 3.1 cm. high with a base 3.6 cm. It may have served as a weight.

382. The MB II level was rich in artifacts. Pl. 119a (No. 3101) is a delicately fashioned pottery bull's leg found with several other cult objects. Pl. 119c (No. 3007) is a scarab. It shows a man or monkey protected by a winged snake (uraeus?) confronting a griffon.

383. From the floor of the U-shaped gateway comes Pl. 115:10 (No. 3019) the upper part of a decorated bone spindle. No. 3051 is the 6.8 cm.

section of a bone pin 4 mm. diameter. No. 3094 is an 11.5 cm. section of an animal bone; there are three carved lines at right angles to the axis at one end of the bone averaging *c.* 1.5 cm. dia. There are also two crude bone awls, Nos. 3023 and 3085. No. 3057 is a gazelle horn 23 cm. long × 1.5 cm. wide.

384. There are two flint arrowheads Pl. 116:12, 13 (No. 3020). There are two sickle teeth. No. 3047 is 5.5 × 3.7 cm. and No. 3053 is 4 × 2.6 cm. Pl. 116:8 (No. 3044) is a limestone axe and No. 3045 is the lower half of another limestone axe 6.8 × 4 cm. No. 3043 is a limestone pestle 9 × 5.4 cm. Pl. 116:14 (No. 3091) is a rectangular limestone loom weight with a hole at the top. No. 3089 is a limestone rubbing stone 5.6 × 4 × 3.5 cm. No. 3096 is a granite one 9.4 × 6.8 × 5 cm. Pl. 116:4 (No. 3092) is the small fragment of the rim of an alabaster bowl; the diameter of the bowl is *c.* 24 cm.

385. Beads from MB II consist of the following. No. 3010 is quartz oblate 12 mm. dia. × 5 mm. No. 3012 is faience oblate 4 mm. dia. × 2 mm. No. 3059 is faience short barrel 13 mm. dia. × 11 mm. No. 3086 is sandstone long cylinder 10 mm. dia. × 22 mm. The following are probably MB II. No. 3029 is stone short barrel 7 mm. dia. × 7 mm. No. 3040 is faience short barrel 9 mm. dia. × 7 mm.

386. From MB I comes No. 3104, the leg or horn of a crude animal figurine 6.5 cm. long × 1.7 cm. wide. Pl. 116:10 (No. 3103) is a fan-shaped limestone scraper. Pl. 116:1 (No. 3021) is a flint spearhead.

387. From the open air sanctuary site (MB I–Chal.) come the following interesting flint forms. Pl. 116:2 (No. 3154) is a razor. Pl. 116:11 (No. 3155) is a crude hand axe. Pl. 116:3 (No. 3153) is an excellent adze. Pl. 116:5 (No. 3151) is a javelin head. No. 3152 is a broken spear point 6.2 × 3.8 cm.

CHAPTER XVII

BETHEL FLINTS FROM EARLY CANAANITE HIGH PLACE AND MIDDLE BRONZE I TEMPLE ABOVE IT

James L. Swauger

Provenience

388. The provenience for these items is the early Canaanite high place and Middle Bronze I temple above it. Since the flints came from mixed debris there is no point of location horizontally or vertically for any piece. No opportunity therefore exists to judge the items other than typologically.

Methodology

389. The items were washed and then sorted into general categories: obvious tools, doubtful tools, spalls, chips, lumps, and the like, by my son, John. I went over his assignments and made such readjustments as I deemed necessary. Each piece was numbered and then subjected to individual close scrutiny including observation under a microscope, when necessary.

The remarks below are based on a final observation of the collection. All but ten of the 692 stone pieces are flint.

Terminology

390. The terminology of my descriptions is as follows:
- a *lump* is a relatively small mass of stone without regular form;
- a *core* is the form produced when pieces have been knocked off a lump or a pebble as tools are manufactured whether the intent be to use the pieces knocked off as tools or to use the core itself as a tool;
- a *spall* is a piece of stone chipped off from a lump or a core by a blow; in general I separate such chips into several divisions, and when I say spall, I mean a relatively thick piece;
- a *flake* is also a piece of stone chipped off from a lump or core or other base shape by a blow, and in that sense is a spall, but when I say flake, I mean a relatively thin piece;
- a *chip* is also a piece of stone sliced off from a lump or core or other base shape by a blow, and in that sense is a spall and a flake, but when I say chip, I mean a tiny piece;
- a *sliver* is a thin, fragile, longitudinal chip or flake;
- a *blade* is a thin, longitudinal, usually parallel-sided flake suitable for use as a tool either as produced when struck from a core, or with secondary shaping;
- a *scraper* is a tool used for scraping; usually it is made from a flake or is a flake used as a scraper;
- *rind* is the outer " skin " of a lump of stone or a core; and
- *serrate*, of course, means toothed like a saw.

General Remarks

391. Many of these pieces were struck from prepared cores, i.e. ideally the maker deliberately shaped a lump of stone into a rough cylinder with a striking platform at right angles to the long axis of the core. When the striking platform was struck (usually quite close to an edge) with a blow whose force traveled parallel to the long axis of the core, a flake was detached from the core. By experience and training, a good flint worker struck off flakes whose size and general shape had to a large extent been determined by him as he prepared the core.

Such objects in this collection as 323, 324, and 512 are not ideal cores but the methodology of their use was much the same, i.e., glancing blows struck off flakes or spalls. I'm not sure that 401 through 403 are really cores, but they have certainly been battered with glancing blows and, I suspect, rolled so that the edges of chipped areas are rounded. In any event there are no large objects that can be called cores.

392. Numerous pieces exhibit a bulb of percussion, the conchoidal swelling produced as a spall or flake broke away from its parent core. Many of the pieces were struck from pebbles. Numerous examples exist of which a few illustrating the typical rounded profile along one edge of such a type are: 544, 545, 555, 574, and 585. Particularly with the pieces struck from pebbles, but also with tools, spalls, and flakes as 1, 184, 227, and 409, segments of the original surface of the lump from which pieces were struck remain. These I call rind.

393. While it is perfectly obvious that the

serrated edges of such tools as the sickle blades 1 through 7 were deliberately manufactured, I am not sure that serrated edges of many of the pieces in the collection were the result of meaningful manipulation by their makers. Experiments conducted by Birgitta L. Wallace and myself* prove that sometimes perfectly fine looking serrated edges and " secondary chipping " of the sort employed in shaping edges are produced by use of a simple blade tool in cutting bone or wood, or, in the instance of a thin fragile blade, even in cutting fresh meat. The same sort of result is sometimes achieved by pieces knocking against each other in a storage tray. Serrated items I do not dignify as tools are neglected in this fashion because I am not sure the edges were deliberately manufactured.

394. Having no knowledge of flint sources near Bethel, nor indeed in the Near East, I can say nothing about possible sources of the flints in this collection. In color they run the gamut from dark grey through light tan and bluish grey. Particularly interesting as color variants are 397 through 426, mottled warm greenish brown flints; 470 through 475 and 621 through 624, warm light grey flint with white rind; and 392 through 396, deep brown flint.

395. These flints are not from a macrolithic paleolithic culture, nor are they Natufian or Tahunian. They are Neolithic or later.

396. The following are the items I thought interesting or intriguing. Nos. 1–7 are tools, sickle blades, implements with which to cut grain. The theory is that grain grasped into a bunch was drawn across the toothed edges of these implements or that the tool was used to saw across the strands of the bunch. Nos. 1, 2, 4, and 7 are backed, i.e. the edge opposite the toothed edge is not worked to a blade edge nor a serrated edge, but left blunt. Nos. 3, 5, and 6 are serrated on both edges although the serration of one edge of 6 is questionable and, indeed, 3, 5, and 6 are in character different from the chunkier, sturdier 1, 2, 4, and 7. It is possible that 3, 5 and 6 are not true sickle blades but only serrated blades. It is possible that if these two groups represent two types of sickle blades some chronological placement of them in relation to each other is possible, but I have no guide to permit me to do so. Nos. 1–4 and 6, 7, show result of use in cutting grain because of a shining band called " varnish " along the main serrated edge.

No. 11, a blade, shows serrated edges, but I think the serration was produced accidentally. It is a Y-ribbed blade; in other words, the core from which it was fashioned was shaped in such a way that objects struck from it have a Y-shaped rib along their backs. No. 12, on the other hand, was struck from a core which gave single-ribbed blades. No. 5 is a fine example of a parallel-ribbed blade, i.e. there are two ribs on its back, and they run parallel to each other. I do not know that ribs of all three kinds were not sometimes knocked from the same core, particularly as early shaping to produce facets giving, let us say, the parallel-sided blades, might well produce single-ribbed, Y-ribbed, or multiple-ribbed blades. But there are ribs of several different kinds on blades in the collection.

397. No. 16 is a chunky piece that might well have been a scraper although I see no signs of use as such. No. 26 is a puzzler. I classify it as a broken blade, finely serrated along one edge, but the teeth look accidental to me. They do, however, exhibit varnish, a factor normally found with much-used deliberately shaped tools. No. 61 is another blade with varnish along a finely serrated edge. I think these serrations accidental. No. 37 is roughly awl-shaped, and I should not be surprised if its use as an awl or punch did not result in its teeth. No. 78 is interesting. It looks as if an attempt had been made to use a section from the edge of a striking platform. Nos. 122 and 123 are examples of spalls that may well have been used as tools.

398. Nos. 163, 184, 467–475, 620–624, and 679 have very white rind. Body color of the objects varies from light green to deep tan. No. 180 is a thin, translucent flint spall, the only piece of its kind in the collection. No. 229 is a spall with a chisel edge. This may be accidental as I see no signs of its use as a chisel, plane, or scraper, all reasonable employments.

No. 318 is all that is left of a core. Nos. 323 and 324 were also cores, not classic, but lumps from which chips were knocked off that were made into tools. Nos. 355 through 361, 364–372 are a series of triangular cross-sectioned flint objects that I call spalls but that might be parts of tools.

---

* James L. Swauger and Birgitta L. Wallace, "An Experiment in Skinning with Egyptian Paleolithic and Neolithic Stone Implements," *Pennsylvania Archaeologist*, XXXIV, No. 1, April, 1964; pp. 1–7, 7 Figs.

Edges such as that of No. 369 are in some instances finely retouched.

399. No. 378 is of a shiny green flint, the only one of its kind in the collection. Nos. 392 and 393 are very dark brown flint. Nos. 400 through 426 continue in the brown range but vary from a quite light color to a medium brown. These are distinctly different in color and consistency from most of the rest of the collection. It differs also in that many of its members, 403, 405, 406–408, 411–413, 416, 417, 422, 425, and 426 exhibit to a greater or lesser degree the sheen known as " desert varnish " and attributed to exposure to scouring by sand whipped across them by wind. In any event, they differ markedly from other stone in the collection. The varnish suggests they were surface materials, but that is a suggestion only, since the varnishing could have occurred years earlier and the items subsequently been buried. Nos. 401, 402, and 403 are tiny cores. No. 411 can be called a heavy, much used and/or rolled triangular cross-sectioned blade. Nos. 412 and 426 are scrapers. No. 427 is an odd stone, almost glassy, and non-flint.

400. The series of 442 through 457, and 459, 460, is a group exhibiting the rounded shoulders or backs peculiar to objects struck from boulders. No. 445 has a very shiny " interior " surface somewhat like a desert varnish. Its edges have been deliberately worked. Some of these as 456 and 457 are large spalls from which other spalls were chipped as the stone was worked down to give smaller pieces. No. 486 is a banded stone, flint, I think, very shiny, with the bands giving a sort of mottled effect on one side. It is the only one of its kind in the collection. Nos. 645 and 655–657 are a set of bulky objects with triangular cross-sections that might well have been knives. No. 659 is a used tool, a blade. Teeth along one edge were deliberately produced.

Catalogue of Pottery Plates

Plate 48 MB I

		Reg. No.	Date	Prov.	§ Ref.
1	Jar, greyish buff ware, hard minute grits outside, reddish buff, greyish buff inside, band of sharp parallel combing	438	8–14	Pit	221
2	Jar, fine paste, half pink, half brown, surface creamy buff outside, grey buff inside	584	8–24	Sub L 56	221
3	Jar, red ware, gritty, grey in center (coarser than the typical MB I ware) buff surface, raised rouletted band (like applied scales, certainly not done with the finger, but with some tool)	530	8–25	L 53 bedrock	221
4	Hole-mouth jar, brick-red ware with white and grey grits (like EB ware), surface red inside and mostly blackened outside	448	9–8	Sub 162	221
5	Base of jar, pastel red gritty ware, surface red inside, buff outside	494	9–3	L 166 near bedrock	221
6	Hole-mouth jar, coarse gritty brown ware (like EB ware) surface reddish buff outside, dark brown inside	569	8–28	L 62	221
7	Ovoid jar, greyish drab ware, buff surface	809	8–17	L 52 S bedrock	221
8	Caliciform vase, hard red ware, surface buff outside, light red inside	614	8–17	L 55	222
9	Caliciform vase, hard red ware, inside edge buff, surface red inside, buff outside, band of combing	613	8–17	L 54	222
10	Jar, brownish buff ware, buff surface, row of oblique notches, band of parallel combing	446	8–28	L 62 bedrock	221
11	Jar, hard drab ware, light buff surface, horizontal and oblique bands of combing	418	8–24	Sub 58 N	221

Plate 49 MB II

		Reg. No.	Date	Prov.	§ Ref.
1	Jar, drab ware with minute white grits, buff surface, wheel combing on shoulder	419	8–17	L 56	224
2	Bowl, reddish grey ware, light red surface, traces of red slip	412	8–18	L 208	229
3	Jar, greyish brown ware, reddish brown surface	435	8–15	L 61	224
4	Bowl, brownish buff ware, well levigated, minute white grits, buff surface	696	8–23	L 58	227
5	Jar, hard drab ware, minute white grits, buff surface	433	8–16	Area I, corner of Tower	224
6	Jar, drab ware, minute white grits, buff surface	434	8–31	Sub 161	224
7	Bowl, reddish ware, grey in center, buff surface	501	8–28	L 62	227
8	Jar, reddish buff ware, fired through, small white grits, light reddish buff surface	309	7–11	I West	224
9	Jar, hard drab ware, minute white grits, buff surface	524	9–1	L 161	224
10	Base of jar, drab clay with minute grits, reddish buff inside, buff slip on outside, traces of vert. burnish	507	8–28	L 62 bedrock	229
11	Jar, reddish buff ware, well levigated, buff surface, typical MB II paste, occasional dark grits	432	8–15	L 61	224
12	Jar, greyish brown ware, well levigated, buff surface	595	8–8	L 31	224
13	Jar, fine greyish brown ware, brownish buff surface	594	9–8	Sub 163	224
14	Base of jar, fine greyish brown ware, brownish buff surface inside, creamy buff slip outside and on base	589	8–27	L 52 N	224
15	Bowl, fine brown ware, light buff surface	499	8–31	L 167	229
16	Bowl, light brown ware, light red surface, ring burnished inside	557	8–8	L 31	229
17	Bowl, red ware, creamy buff slip both sides, wheel burnished on inside, occasional lines of burnish outside	437	8–17	L 63	229
18	Bowl, reddish brown ware, fairly well levigated, buff surface, no slip, wheelmarks visible inside and out	38	8–3	L 37	229
19	Bowl, light brown ware, grey in center, minute white grits, creamy buff slip inside, wheel burnished, outside without slip with wheelmarks and occasional lines of burnishing	491	8–29	L 63	229

Plate 50 MB II

		Reg. No.	Date	Prov.	§ Ref.
1	Cooking pot, reddish brown ware, many grits, light brown surface with white grits	348	8–23	L 58 N	226
2	Cooking pot, light brown ware grey in center, few grits, reddish brown surface	528	8–24	Sub L 51	226
3	Cooking pot, fine tan paste, reddish buff surface, smoked	560	8–18	L 65	226
4	Cooking pot, brown ware, blue grey grits, surface red inside, brown buff and smoked on outside	558	8–22	L 205	226
5	Cooking pot, light brown gritty ware, reddish brown surface	529	8–31	Sub 161	226
6	Cooking pot, red brown ware, grey core, white grits, surface red inside, reddish buff outside	486	8–24	Sub 51(?)	226
7	Cooking pot, brownish grey ware, grey core, white grits, surface dark red buff, smoked	487	8–17	L 52	226
8	Cooking pot, red gritty ware, grey in center, red surface	350	8–23	L 58 N	226
9	Cooking pot, dark greyish brown ware, large white grits, brown surface, smoked	574	8–31	Sub 165	226
10	Cooking pot, reddish buff ware, grey in center, red surface with white grits	349	8–23	L 58 N	226
11	Jar, red gritty ware, surface reddish buff inside, buff outside	485	8–25	L 60	226
12	Cooking pot, red ware, grey in center, small grey grits, red surface	37	8–23	L 58 N, Sub #3	226
13	Cooking pot, brown ware, white grits, red brown surface, smoked	484	8–31	L 166	226
14	Cooking pot, brown gritty ware, light brown surface showing white grits, traces of brown slip	442	8–15	L 56	226
15	Bowl, red ware, well levigated, minute white grits, pinkish buff surface, creamy slip, smoothed inside and overlapping a little outside	377	8–28	L 63	229
16	Cooking pot (late MB II), brownish buff gritty ware, reddish brown surface, smoked	512	8–23	L 58	226
17	Bowl (late MB II), brownish grey ware, fairly well levigated, buff surface, smoked outside	376	8–24	L 147	229
18	Cooking pot, reddish brown gritty ware, red surfaces	531	8–30	Sub 155	226
19	Cooking pot, very dark brown ware, medium coarse grits, dark tan surface, smoked to black	591	8–24	L 63	226
20	Bowl, buff ware, well levigated, surface red outside, buff inside	445	8–31	E of 150	227
21	Bowl, red ware, grey core, red to buff surface	424	8–24	L 51	229, 245
22	Cooking pot, grey gritty ware, reddish brown surface	502	8–13	L 130	226
23	Cooking pot, coarse ware, outside half grey, inside half buff, shining grey grits, surface grey outside, buff inside, vertical notches on outside of rim	586	8–4	L 33	226

Plate 51 MB II

		Reg. No.	Date	Prov.	§ Ref.
1	Trumpet base, fine paste, from red brown near outer edge to grey on inner edge, light buff surface	609	8–15	L 57	227
2	Vase, grey ware, red surface, grey on inside	504	8–31	Sub 161	225
3	Trumpet base, grey ware red at edges, buff surface	513	8–24	L 51	227
4	Tr. base, hard reddish drab ware, surface light red inside, creamy buff outside	536	8–23	II, pit	227
5	Tr. base, drab ware, light buff surface	410	8–31	Sub 161	227
6	Tr. base, fine light brown ware, buff slip inside and out	600	8–23	L 58	227
7	Vase, fine red ware, grey in center, red surface	416	9–1	Sub 162	225, 231
8	Tr. base, buff ware, creamy surface, traces of buff slip	411	8–20	E of 58	227
9	Tr. base, fine pink ware, surface pink buff outside, pink inside	590	8–31	L 167	227
10	Tr. base, fine tan ware, grey core, pinkish buff slip	582	8–31	Sub 161	227
11	Tr. base, reddish buff ware, pink buff surface	596	9–1	Sub 167	227
12	Vase, fine reddish ware, minute grits, red surface	415	9–1	Sub 162	225
13	Tr. base, fine greyish brown ware, surface red outside, pink inside	573	8–31	L 166	227
14	Pot, greyish brown ware, coarse white grits, dark buff surface	606	8–16	L 55	226
15	Chalice (?), fine reddish buff ware, minute grits, reddish surface	505	8–31	L 153?	224

		Reg. No.	Date	Prov.	§ Ref.
16	Pot, fine reddish buff ware, buff surface	490	8–15	L 58	225
17	Tr. base, light brownish buff ware, brownish buff surface, horizontal burnishing on outside and on inside of foot, smoked	426	9–1	L 61 S	227
18	Vase, fine red ware, minute white grits, reddish buff surface	552	9–1	Sub 166 W	225
19	Bowl, pale brown grey ware, pink surface, traces of wheel burnishing outside	549	8–31	L 160	229
20	Pot, reddish buff ware, reddish buff surface	526	8–28	L 63	229
21	Vase, fine buff ware, buff surface	601	9–1	L 161	225
22	Bowl, fine light brown ware, creamy slip, burnished centripetally inside and horizontally outside	572	9–7	Sub 168	
23	Vase, fine grey ware, red at edges, minute white grits, pink buff surface	588	8–31	Sub 161	225
24	Bowl, red ware, grey core, reddish buff surface continuously wheel burnished outside and on inside of rim	414	8–21	L 207A	227
25	Vase, fine pink ware, pink surface	598	8–31	Sub 162	225
26	Bowl, medium fine reddish buff ware, pink buff surface	592	8–31	L 167	227
27	Jar, fine light brown ware, reddish buff surface on inside, buff on outside	568	8–31	L 166	224

Plate 52 Figs. 1–5 and 7 are MB II; Figs. 6 and 8–23 are LB phase 1

		Reg. No.	Date	Prov.	§ Ref.
1	Jar, reddish buff ware, minute white grits, light buff slip, continuous high glossy burnishing, notches on slightly raised bands bordered by raised lines	403	8–14	Sub 60 trial pit	228, 235
2	Jar, reddish drab ware, minute white grits, light buff surface, not burnished, incised notches also on rim	402	8–24	L 147	228, 235
3	Bowl, buff ware, surface buff outside, inside red slip burnished horizontally (prob. by wheel)	413	8–31	L 166	229
4	Bowl, fine paste, inside half pink and outside half buff, surface buff outside, pink inside, with rim painted red and highly burnished, bowl originally burnished inside at right angle to rim	580	8–16	L 55	229, 245
5	Bowl, brick red ware, light red surface, horizontally burnished inside on very thin red slip	509	8–31	L 166	229
6	Bowl, buff ware, minute grits, light buff surface	508	8–27	L 52 N	236
7	Bowl, drab to grey ware, red near inner edge, minute grits, light red slip inside, creamy buff slip outside, wheel burnished inside and out, dark red band on rim inside and out, another red band near center	492	8–23	L 58	229
8	Bowl, greyish buff ware, reddish buff surface	518	8–27	W of 60	236
9	Bowl, brick red ware, red surface	421	8–24	L 63	235
10	Neck of pilgrim flask, hard light brown to grey ware, buff surface, smoked	430	8–31	Sub 162	239
11	Juglet, knife pared, brownish buff clay, minute grits, buff surface	439	8–25	L 60 above LB I thresh.	237
12	Base of jar, medium coarse dark grey ware, surface buff outside, grey inside	578	9–1	L 63	234
13	Juglet, reddish buff paste, well levigated, fine grits, pinkish buff surface	341	8–27	L 60	237
14	Cooking pot, red gritty ware, dark red surface	420	8–17	L 54	234
15	Bowl, fine tan paste, light buff surface	550	8–25	L 60	236
16	Bowl, grey ware, surface red inside, reddish buff outside	517	8–25	L 60	236
17	Bowl, very fine tan paste, buff surface	610	8–24	L 51	235
18	Cooking pot, red ware, dark grey in center, white grits, red surface smoked outside	481	8–27	L 63	234
19	Cooking pot, fine dark red brown ware, surface red buff inside, red brown outside	548	8–24	L 63	234
20	Bowl, greyish buff ware, surface light red on outside, creamy slip on inside	436	8–27	L 52 N	236
21	Cooking pot, red ware grey core, white grits, red brown surface showing white grits	547	8–31	Sub 162	234
22	Bowl, fine grey ware, minute white grits, buff surface, coarse	577	8–25	L 60	236
23	Jar, fine light red ware, light buff surface	555	8–31	L 166	238

Plate 53 LB (Figs. 1–15 are phase 2; Figs. 16–30 phase uncertain)

		Reg. No.	Date	Prov.	§ Ref.
1	Bowl, buff ware, minute white grits, buff surface	346	8-23	L 58 N	235
2	Bowl, dark brown well-levigated ware, buff brown surface	358	8-23	L 58 N	235
3	Bowl, red ware minute grits, buff surface (found under piers of I₁ #3)	408	8-23	L 58	235
4	Bowl, greyish ware with minute grits, buff surface, uneven base (found as Fig. 3)	407	8-23	L 58	235
5	Bowl, reddish brown ware, few grits, reddish buff surface	562	8-23	L 58 N	235
6	Bowl, reddish brown ware, fine white grits, reddish buff surface	316	8-23	L 58 (as Fig. 3)	235
7	Bowl, red ware, minute white grits, pinkish buff surface	345	8-23	L 58 N	235
8	Bowl, hard reddish buff ware, buff surface	409	8-23	L 58 (as Fig. 3)	236
9	Bowl, red ware, surface dark red and coarse outside, reddish buff and smooth inside	356	8-23	L 58 N	236
10	Bowl, red ware, minute white grits, red surface	359	8-23	L 58 N	235
11	Bowl, brown ware, coarse grits, light brown surface	347	8-23	L 58 N	235
12	Bowl, tan paste, surface buff outside, pink buff inside	583	8-23	L 58	236
13	Bowl, reddish buff ware, well levigated, fine grits, reddish buff surface	355	8-23	L 58 N	236
14	Bowl, light brown ware, coarse grits, buff surface	2	8-23	L 58	236
15	Bowl, buff ware, minute white grits, buff surface	360	8-23	L 58 N	235
16	Bowl, brown ware, medium fine, surface buff outside, pink buff inside	575	8-23	L 58	236
17	Bowl, fine red ware, pale red surface	566	8-28	L 51	233
18	Bowl, asymmetrical, pink surface red ware	556	8-23	L 58	236
19	Base of jar, coarse but hard grey ware, light yellow surface outside, grey inside	521	8-21	L 156	234
20	Bowl, reddish buff ware, reddish buff surface, blackened inside	522	8-25	L 152?	235
21	Storage jar, light brown ware, well levigated, minute black grits, buff surface	146	8-18	L 146	235
22	Jar, brownish buff ware, fairly well levigated, buff surface	34	8-17	L 52	234
23	Jar, dark buff ware, reddish buff surface	425	8-14	L 38	235
24	Bowl, fine red paste, surface reddish buff inside, buff outside	581	8-14	L 38	235
25	Cooking pot, brick red ware, grey core, reddish brown surface	535	8-24	W of 146	234
26	Bowl, fine red ware, red buff surface	579	8-17	L 52	236
27	Bowl, reddish buff ware, grey in center, minute white grits, buff surface	180	8-15	L 55	235
28	Cooking pot, dark grey gritty ware, surface red inside, brown to grey outside	503	8-15	L 55	234
29	Cooking pot, dark grey gritty ware, brown surface	444	8-30	Sub 153	234
30	Cooking pot, dark grey ware, white grits, red brown surface, smoked	543	8-30	Sub 148	234

Plate 54 LB (Figs. 1–14, phase 2; Figs. 15–17, phase uncertain)

		Reg. No.	Date	Prov.	§ Ref.
1	Bowl, pinkish buff ware and surface, fairly well-levigated clay, fine grits	353	8-23	L 58 N	236
2	Bowl, greyish brown ware with grits, buff surface	46b	8-15	L 58	236
3	Basin, handled, fine red ware, minute white grits, light red surface	476	8-23	L 58	236
4	Bowl, grey-brown ware, buff surface, skew	215	8-15	L 58	235
5	Bowl, red ware, minute white grits, surface partly red, partly buff	562	8-17	L 58	235
6	Bowl—no description	357	8-23	L 58 N	236
7	Jar-base, fine light brown to grey ware, light buff surface	454	8-23	L 58	234
8	Bowl, pinkish buff surface	354	8-23	L 58 N	235
9	Juglet, greyish buff ware with fine white grits, buff surface, pronounced wheel marks on the outside	318	8-23	L 58 N, Sub #3	237
10	Jar, dark buff ware, grey in center, well levigated, reddish buff surface, darker on inside	428	8-30	Sub 155	238
11	Juglet, dark grey ware, reddish brown to dark grey surface, partly smoked, pronounced wheel marks on outside	315	8-27	L 52 N, below Iron I foundations	237
12	Bowl, reddish buff ware, buff surface	559	8-23	L 58	236
13	Base of large bowl, fine dark grey ware, greyish buff surface, smoked on outside	468	8-24	L 151, LB II burning	236

		Reg. No.	Date	Prov.	§ Ref.
14	Bowl, pinkish buff ware and surface, well-levigated clay	41	8 23	L 58, Sub #1	235
15	Cooking pot, light brown ware, grey core, reddish buff surface, smoked	556	8–25	L 60	234
16	Cooking pot, dark brown ware, white grits, brown surface, smoked	480	8–15	L 58	234
17	Cooking pot, brownish grey ware, fairly well levigated, few grits, dark reddish brown surface, smoked	49	8–27	L 52 SE, below #2 foundations	234

Plate 55   Iron I (Figs. 1–5, 7–8 are LB)

		Reg. No.	Date	Prov.	§ Ref.
1	Cooking pot, brown ware, dark grey in center, very fine grits, brownish buff surface, smoked	489	8–23	L 58 N	234
2	Base of large jar, dark grey ware, not well levigated, reddish buff surface. (From base and texture probably late in LB, found in region of Astarte Cylinder)	364	8–9	L 207B	234
3	Cooking pot, dark brown ware, white grits, surface reddish brown inside, dark brown outside, smoked	479	8–15	L 55	234
4	Cooking pot, reddish brown ware, dark grey in center, surface red-buff inside, dark red-brown outside	607	8–25	L 60, below LB 2 pav.	234
5	Cooking pot, brown ware, black in center, white grits, brown surface, smoked, red on inside	443	8–30	Sub 153	234
6	Bowl of libation chalice, medium fine black ware, coarse surface buff inside and outside	599	8–21	L 146	258
7	Juglet, slightly skew, pinkish buff surface	555	8–23	L 51	237
8	Cooking pot, dark grey ware, red surface	482	8–16	L 52	234
9	Foot of libation chalice, buff to grey ware, coarse grits, buff surface	520	8–9	L 201	258
10	Bowl of chalice, coarse black ware, coarse buff surface	493	8–21	Sub 144S	258
11	Lamp, dark grey ware, not well levigated, buff surface	438	8–14	Sub L 32	264
12	Body of libation chalice, buff ware, grey in center, reddish buff surface	477	8–20	L 144	258
13	Large pot, hard red ware, grey in center, white grits, reddish buff surface wet smoothed, hole pierced through wall	404	9–1	E of 155	265
14	Juglet, import ware, fine light red paste, surface light red inside, light buff outside, dark red bands of decoration	554	8–31	E of 150	263
15	Jug, buff ware, grey in center, reddish buff surface	496	8–9	S of 202	261
16	Jug, brownish buff ware, white grits buff surface	639	8–31	E of 150	261
17	Neck of pilgrim flask, greyish brown ware, core of handles black, small grits, red-brown surface, red slip continuously burnished	242	7–12	L 4	263
18	Jug, dark grey coarse ware, pink surface, skew rim	378	8–8	L 208	261
19	Jug, well levigated buff ware, some grits, creamy buff slip, alternating bands of red and black	129	7–24	I SW	261

Plate 56   Iron I Store-Jars

		Reg. No.	Date	Prov.	§ Ref.
1	Grey ware pink at edges, coarse, light buff surface with grits	31	7–24	Sub L 6	254
2	Coarse grey ware, buff surface showing large white grits	16	8–9	Sub 207A	254
3	Coarse buff ware, buff surface	143	8–9	Sub 207A	254
4	Brownish red ware, coarse grits, reddish buff surface with white grits	372	8–8	L 207	254
5	Grey ware, small grits, buff surface showing large white grits	158	8–3	L 41	254
6	Dark grey ware, coarse grits, greyish buff surface	233	8–3	L 41	254
7	Reddish brown ware, grey in center, small and large grits, buff surface	18A	8–9	Sub 207A	254
8	Dark grey ware, coarse grits, buff surface	370	8–9	Sub 207A	254
9	Gritty grey ware, reddish buff surface	247	7–12	L 3	254
10	Dark grey ware, very coarse grits, surface buff outside, reddish buff inside	497	8–20	Sub 133	254
11	Dark grey ware, coarse grits, buff surface showing large white grits	384	6–16?	L 57	254
12	Grey ware, coarse dark grits, reddish buff very rough surface	369	8–9	L 207A	254

Catalogue of Pottery Plates

		Reg. No.	Date	Prov.	§ Ref.
13	Grey ware, buff at edges, grey grits, buff surface	124	8–7	L 42	254
14	Coarse grey ware, buff surface	19	8–7	L 42	254
15	Coarse grey ware, reddish buff surface	371	8–7	Sub L 25	254
16	Grey ware, coarse but infrequent grits, buff surface	817	8–7	L 42	254
17	Dark grey ware, coarse, reddish buff surface with white grits	37	8–9	L 207A	254
18	Coarse grey ware, pink buff surface	17	8–7	L 42	254
19	Coarse grey ware, pinkish buff surface	29a	8–15	L 53	254
20	Coarse grey ware, reddish buff surface	227	8–9	Sub 207A	254
21	Dark greyish brown ware, coarse grits, pinkish buff surface, double finger impressions on rim	43	8–3	L 33	254
22	Coarse black ware, buff surface	238	7–20	L 119	254
23	Light grey ware, coarse black grits, reddish buff surface	157	7–30	L 113	254
24	Coarse greyish red ware, reddish buff surface	115	7–21	I Sub center	254
25	Coarse dark grey ware, grits of flint and quartz, surface yellowish buff outside, light pink on inside (late Iron I)	66	7–12	I East	254
26	Light buff ware, dark grey in center, buff surface	488	8–31	L 167	254

Plate 57   Iron I

Store Jars Figs. 1–11

		Reg. No.	Date	Prov.	§ Ref.
1*	Light reddish buff ware, grey core, reddish buff surface	452	8–15	N of L 43	254
2*	Reddish buff ware, grey core, reddish buff surface	539	8–30	E of 150	254
3*	Hard grey ware, buff surface	36	7–23	L 5	254
4*	Grey ware, fine paste, light pinkish buff surface	30	7–24	L 6	254
5	Dark grey ware, coarse grits of quartz, buff surface with white grits	305	7–12	L 18	254
6	Buff ware, grey in center, coarse, some grits, pinkish buff surface	324	8–15	L 50	254
7	Coarse grey ware, buff surface	308	8–3	L 32	254
8	Hard grey ware, reddish surface, wet smoothed	519	9–3	E of 150	254
9	Coarse reddish buff ware, surface red with white grits outside, drab inside	612	9–4	N Silo in 145	254
10	Coarse grey ware, greyish buff surface, showing white grits	518	9–3	E of 150	254
11	Coarse grey ware, pinkish buff surface	307	8–7	Sub wall 26/29	254

Cooking Pots Figs. 12–22

12	Reddish brown ware, coarse grits, red surface smoked	334	8–7	L 42	255
13	Brownish to grey ware, coarse grits, red surface smoked	381	8–7	L 42	255
14	Brownish to dark grey ware, coarse grits, dark red surface, smoked	331	8–7	L 42	255
15	Brownish red ware, black in center, coarse grits, dark red surface, smoked	310	7–24	I Sub center	255
16	Reddish brown to dark grey ware, gritty, brownish red surface, smoked	235	8–7	L 42	255
17	Coarse dark grey ware, white grits, reddish buff surface, slightly darkened below the rim	120	7–23	Sub L 6	255
18	Coarse dark grey ware, reddish brown surface	9	8–9	L 207 B	255
19	Dark grey ware, white grits, brownish black surface	390	8–7	L 42	255
20	Dark grey ware, coarse grits, brownish grey surface, smoked	335	8–7	L 42	255
21	Greyish brown ware, white grits, drab surface, smoked	260	7–30	Sub 113	255
22	No description	236	8–7	L 42	255

* The jars are late in Iron I.

Plate 58   Iron I Cooking Pots

		Reg. No.	Date	Prov.	§ Ref.
1	Grey ware, reddish brown on edges, gritty, brown surface, smoked	96	7–30	Sub 112	255
2	Black ware, coarse grits, grey buff surface, smoked	100	7–30	Sub 107	255
3	Brownish red ware, coarse grits, dark red surface, smoked	380	8–9	L 201	255
4	Coarse grey ware with grits, surface light pink inside, reddish pink outside	221	7–25	Sub L 6	255
5	No description	—	—	—	—
6	Brownish red to grey ware, coarse grits, dark red surface, smoked	382	8–9	L 201	255

	Description	Reg. No.	Date	Prov.	§ Ref.
7	Gritty red to black ware, burnt black on outside, grey on inside	462	8–10	W of 124	255
8	No description	237	8–7	L 42	255
9	Red brown surface, smoked inside, red ware, black in center	306	7–14	L 5	255
10	Dark grey ware, white grits, surface dark reddish brown inside, light buff outside, smoked	470	8–4	L 33	255
11	Brownish red to black ware, coarse grits, dark red surface, smoked	312	8–7	L 42	255
12	Dark brownish ware, white grits, dark red surface, smoked	388	7–24	I Sub center	255
13	Brownish ware, some grits, red surface (context partly tenth–ninth century)	48	8–23	L 145 N	255
14	Brownish red to black ware, coarse grits, dark red surface, smoked	311	8–7	L 42	255
15	Reddish brown ware, black in center, coarse grits, red surface, smoked	48b	8–17	L 41	255
16	Dark grey ware, coarse grits, reddish brown surface	54	8–7	L 42	255
17	Brownish black ware, some grits, red surface, smoked	39	8–14	L 34	255
18	Brownish red to black ware, coarse grits, red surface, smoked	323	8–7	L 42	255
19	Coarse black ware, dark red surface	216	7–24	I, SW (?)	255
20	Gritty red ware, dark grey core, reddish brown surface, prob. two-handled	510	8–20	Silo, Sub 208	255
21	Dark brownish red coarse ware	211	7–18	L 107	255
22	Brownish red to dark grey ware, coarse grits, red surface, smoked	322	8–3	L 40	255
23	Grey-brown ware, coarse grits, red brown surface, smoked	5	8–7	L 34	255
24	Coarse black ware, red brown surface, smoked	408	8–13	L 34	255
25	Red to dark grey ware, coarse grits, brick red surface	232	8–3	L 38	255
26	Brownish grey ware, coarse grits, pinkish buff surface	142	8–7	L 42	255

Plate 59 Iron I

	Description	Reg. No.	Date	Prov.	§ Ref.
1	Juglet, (tenth–ninth century), red ware, grey in center, fairly well levigated, red surface, burnished vertically, chordal burnish on bottom	666	8–21	L 142	259
2	Juglet (c. tenth century), grey-brown ware, dark buff surface, burnished vertically, chordal burnishing on bottom	565	8–21	L 147	259
3	Juglet, dark grey gritty ware, dark grey porous surface	570	8–24	Sub 134	259
4	Juglet, brown ware, buff surface with white grits, tilted oblique lug handles	614	8–29	Sub 123	260
5	Juglet, dark brown ware, well levigated, buff surface decorated with brown bands	600	8–23	S of 146	260
6	Jug, coarse greyish brown ware, gritty surface brown buff outside, red brown inside, white grits showing on surface	540	8–22	L 152	261
7	Jug, grey ware, medium coarse, buff surface	541	8–16	L 41	261
8	Jug, grey ware, gritty, reddish buff surface context LB, a little Iron I	665	8–24	S of 147	261
9	Philistine jug, reddish buff ware, surface reddish buff inside, buff slip outside, horizontal lines in red, vertical and semicircular lines in black	664	9–3	E of 150	262
10	Bowl of libation chalice, grey ware, large white grits, visible also on the light red surface	450	9–1	E of 150	258
11	Base of jar, coarse reddish ware, large grits, red surface	520	9–3	E of 150	256
12	Basin, (possibly LB, Iron I context) dark grey gritty ware, buff surface	8	8–3	L 33	255
13	Cooking pot (tenth–ninth century), dark grey ware, coarse grits, red surface	42	8–24	L 145	255
14	Bowl, dark grey ware, coarse grits, reddish buff surface	136	8–7	L 38	257
15	Large seven handled bowl, dark grey ware, reddish surface, wet smoothed	427	8–24	L 153	256
16	Large bowl, dark grey ware, large grits, pinkish buff surface	533	8–4	L 41	256
17	Bowl, reddish brown ware, grey in center, coarse light red surface	473	8–23	L 153	256
18	Bowl, reddish buff ware, fairly well levigated, red slip, hand burnished inside	35	8–16	L 140 S	257
19	Bowl, (Iron I late?) light brown ware, white grits, surface buff outside, reddish buff inside	559	8–13	L 133	257
20	Large basin, light brown ware, gritty buff surface	7	7–28	Sub 119, wall	256
21	Large bowl, coarse dark grey ware, pink surface	11	8–15	L 57	256

Plate 60 Iron I

		Reg. No.	Date	Prov.	§ Ref.
1	Bowl, coarse dark grey ware, coarse pink surface	366	8–9	L 202	257
2	Bowl, pinkish brown ware, large and small grits, pinkish buff surface	24	8–9	Sub 207A	257
3	Bowl, buff ware, grey in center, white grits showing also on the buff surface. Diameter of rim 18 cm.	458	8–1	Sub 20	256
4	Bowl, fine tan ware, buff surface	608	9–3	E of 150	256
5	Bowl, reddish buff ware, fairly well levigated, some grits, buff surface	375	8–22	L 205	257
6	Bowl, *faience*, creamy core, not well levigated, light blue surface	350	7–30	Sub 113	257
7	Bowl, dark grey ware, coarse surface buff outside, light red inside	423	7–31	L 208	256
8	Basin, coarse grey ware with grits, brownish red surface	153	7–24	Sub L 6	256
9	Base of jar, grey ware, red surface with white grits, wet smoothed	338	8–20	Silo, sub 207A	256
10	Bowl with tilted loop handles, dark grey ware, gritty, red surface, dark red bands on outside of rim and below handles. Cf. Fig. 12 for reconstruction	365	8–15	L 41	256
11	Bowl, probably seven handled, coarse grey ware, light red surface	447	8–15	L 55	256
12	Bowl, reconstructed from Figs. 10 and 14	615			256
13	Bowl, coarse, buff surface	351	8–4	L 32	256
14	Base belonging but not joining to Fig. 10. Cf. Fig. 12	385	8–16	L 41	256
15	Bowl, dark grey ware, coarse grits, red surface with white grits	373	8–20	Silo, Sub 207 B	256
16	Bowl, coarse buff ware, grey in center, buff surface, very rough	27	8–7	L 42	257
17	Bowl (late Iron I), pinched handle, greyish buff ware, greyish buff surface, horizontal hand-burnishing inside and on rim	449	8–23	E of 150	257
18	Bowl, greyish buff ware, coarse, gritty buff surface (pure I_1 context)	231	8–7	L 42	256

Plate 61 Iron I

		Reg. No.	Date	Prov.	§ Ref.
1	Jar, hard reddish buff ware, well baked, light grey in center, minute white grits, buff surface	620	9–1	E of 150	254
2	Drab ware, minute grits, buff surface	422	8–30	E of 150	254
3	Jar, dark grey ware, poorly levigated, reddish buff surface	320	7–21	L 117	254
4	Jar (no description)	663	8–13	L 123	254
5	Jar, buff, dark grey ware, well levigated	202	7–9	Area I	254
6	Jar, pink buff surface, grey core, large and small grits	14	8–11	L 113	254
7	Jar, buff surface, brownish core, minute grits and coarser black grits	277	7–21	Sub L 6	254
8	Jar, buff surface, dark core, not well levigated	75	7–9	Area I	254
9	Cooking pot, red brown ware, black core, white grits, brownish buff outside, reddish buff inside	597	8–18	L 48	255
10	Cooking pot, dark brown outside, red buff inside, white grits	498	8–24	L 152	255
11	Chalice, brownish drab ware, light brown surface	532	8–18	L 146	258
12	Juglet, pinkish buff surface, button base	615	8–29	Sub 123	259, 274
13	Juglet, black surface, vertical burnishing, grey core, fine grits	297	?	?	270
14	Juglet, black surface, spiral burnishing, core dark grey, well levigated, few small grits	130	7–27	III center	270
15	Juglet, pinkish buff surface, rough	571	8–24	L 152	270
16	Basalt mortar, Iron II–I	515	8–17	Sub 133	337
17	Bowl, pinkish buff surface, brown to dark grey core, some grits	640	8–23	L 58	257
18	Bowl, pink surface, core dark grey, coarse	47	8–16	L 50	257
19	Pilgrim flask, surface dark grey, core grey, grits, well levigated	566	8–21	S of 146	263
20	Side view of No. 19				

Plate 62 Iron II Bowls

		Reg. No.	Date	Prov.	§ Ref.
1	Bowl, red ware, red slip, ring burnished inside and on rim	245	?	L 5	269
2	Buff ware, fine white grits, surface creamy buff outside, buff inside	474	8–20	L 134	269–277
3	Brown ware, gritty, surface red inside, buff outside, ring burnish	451	8–20	136 Sub	269–276
4	Red ware, red slip, wheel burnished inside and on upper rim	253	7–11	I center	269
5	Dark grey core, small grits, reddish brown surface, outside strongly marked by wheel, no slip or burnish, disk base	83	7–16	L 18	269

		Reg. No.	Date	Prov.	§ Ref.
6	Red ware, red slip, ring burnished inside and on upper rim	394	7–21	L 13	269
7	Reddish brown ware, small grits, red slip, ring burnished inside	93	7–23	Sub 11	269
8	Reddish brown ware, light grey core, red surface ring burnished in broad strokes	51	8–18	L 47	269, 273, 276
9	Brick red gritty ware, red slip, ring burnish inside and on upper rim	251	7–9	Tr. shaft	269
10	Reddish brown ware, red slip, ring burnished inside and on upper rim	149	7–31	L 203	269
11	Reddish buff ware, minute white grits, creamy slip inside and on upper rim, wheel burnished, outside red and unburnished	32	7–23	Sub 14	269
12	Dark grey ware, buff surface outside, grey inside, wheel burnished inside and on upper rim	187	7–13	L 6	269
13	Brownish red ware, fine grits, red surface, ring burnish as above	122	7–21	Sub center	269
14	Brownish red ware and surface, ring burnished	78	7–12	I East	269
15	Greyish brown core, red surface, wheel burnish in broad strokes	186	7–12	I East	269
16	Dark greyish brown ware with small grits, brown surface with broad coarse strokes inside and outside (ninth century)	?	7–12	I West	269
17	Brownish red ware, white grits, red surface ring burnish inside and on rim	121	7–23	Sub 12	269
18	Brownish red ware with grits, red surface, ring burnished	45	8–18	L 47	269
19	Light brown ware, grey core, minute grits, buff slip, ring burnished inside and on rim	181	7–13	I East	269
20	Reddish buff ware, small white grits, buff surface, no slip nor burnish	495	8–9	Sub 210	269

Plate 63 Iron II Bowls

		Reg. No.	Date	Prov.	§ Ref.
1	Red ware, buff in center, red slip, ring burnished	123	7–23	Sub 14	269
2	Soft buff ware, well levigated, occasional grey and black grits, red slip, ring burnished inside and on rim	53	7–30	Sub 120	269
3	Brownish red ware, grey in center, well levigated, red surface, ring burnished inside and on rim	20	7–25	Sub 11	269
4	Reddish brown ware with grits, pinkish buff surface inside, red outside	28	7–30	Sub 201	269
5	Red ware, dark grey core, well levigated, red slip, ring burnished inside and out with broad strokes	240	7–13	I center	269
6	Red ware, red slip, ring burnished inside and on rim	183	7–11	I East	269
7	Light red ware, minute grits, reddish buff surface, no burnishing	222	7–23	L 18	269
8	Buff ware, grey on inside edge, buff slip, ring burnished inside and on rim	13	7–30	Sub 201	269
9	Brownish red ware, red slip, ring burnished inside and on rim	52	7–27	L 112	269
10	Brick red ware, minute grits, red surface traces of ring burnished on rim	440	8–27	L 145	269
11	Light red ware, minute white grits, red surface, no burnishing	26	7–23	Sub 15	269
12	Hard brown ware, white grits, light creamy buff slip, ring burnished inside and on rim	25A	7–30	Sub 119	269
13	Light buff ware, grey center, red slip, ring burnish inside and rim	21	7–31	L 209	269
14	Reddish brown ware with grits, light red surface, skew	479	8–11	Sub 128	269
15	Reddish brown ware, minute grits, red slip, ring burnished inside	534	7–31	L 209	269
16	Brownish red core, fairly well levigated, dark reddish brown surface, semi-continuous wheel burnishing inside	256	7–13	L 17	269
17	Greyish brown ware, well levigated with minute white grits, outer surface buff, inner surface red continuously burnished, lines of burnishing not distinguishable	276	7–14	L 10	269
18	Buff ware, buff surface, ring burnished inside and out	?	7–11	L 1	269
19	Grey ware, red slip, ring burnished	389	7–23	Sub 14	269
20	Light red ware, red surface, ring burnished inside and on upper rim	138	7–23	Sub 11	269
21	Red ware, reddish brown surface, ring burnished inside and on rim	139	7–18	L 102	269
22	Reddish brown ware, red slip, ring burnished inside and on rim	161	7–21	I	269
23	Brownish grey ware, surface grey inside, buff on rim, grey and buff outside, ring burnished inside and partly on rim	162	7–23	L 28	269
24	Red ware, red surface, ring burnished	184	7–11	Debris	269
25	Reddish buff surface, unburnished. Sixth century? Much Iron II in context but paste here too well levigated	280	7–9	Shaft 2nd $\frac{1}{2}$ m.	269
26	Pale red, coarse paste, pale red surface	571	8–30	N of 145	269
27	Light brown ware, very well levigated, red slip, unburnished	89	7–23	Sub L 20	279

Plate 64 Sixth Century B.C. Bowls, etc.

		Reg. No.	Date	Prov.	§ Ref.
1	Bowl, very hard reddish grey ware, minute white grits, red surface, traces of burnishing	655	8–13	L 129	289–90–91
2	Bowl, reconstructed from two fragments (which did not fit) very hard reddish grey ware, red surface, smoked from conflagration	656	8–13	L 129	289–90–91
3	Bowl, dark brownish grey ware, well levigated, red surface	33	8–10	L 129	288
4	Bowl, brown ware, well levigated, fine grits, buff surface	443	7–30	Sub 104	284, 292
5	Bowl, fine reddish buff ware, surface buff inside, reddish buff outside	467	8–13	L 136	288
6	Bowl, reddish buff ware, well levigated, reddish buff surface, partly smoked from conflagration	651	8–11	L 123	284
7	Dark brown ware, well levigated, minute grits, light brown surface	423	7–30	Sub 104	284, 292
8	Very hard and compact reddish drab ware, buff surface, slightly ribbed on outside	661	8–16	Sub 140	288
9	Dark grey to red ware, red surface, smoked	406	8–13	L 129	284, 288
10	Grey ware, light red surface, smoked from conflagration, wheelmarks on base	425	8–13	L 136	284
11	Grey ware, with minute grits, grey surface, smoked	426	8–13	L 136	288
12	Pinkish brown ware, pinkish buff surface	360	7–30	Sub 104	284
13	No description	80	7–30	Sub 104	284
14	Dark grey ware, greyish buff surface	361	7–30	Sub 104	284, 286
15	Basalt mortar	459	8–13	L 123	329
16	Black well-levigated ware, wheel marks inside, vertical burnishing outside	97	7–30	Sub 104	284, 285
17	Neck of water decanter, very hard and compact reddish drab ware, buff surface, handle has central rib	659	8–25	L 145	270
18	Juglet, brown ware, well levigated, brownish buff surface, burnished vertically	359	7–30	Sub 104	284, 285
19	Jar neck, red ware, grey in center, buff surface, ribbed inside	660	8–25	L 145	270

Plate 65 Iron II

		Reg. No.	Date	Prov.	§ Ref.
1	Cooking pot, red surface	40	8–17	L 133	270
2	Cooking pot, surface reddish brown, white grits	44	8–30	Sub 7	270
3	Cooking pot, dark brown, with white grits	461	8–10	Sub 126	270
4	Cooking pot, reddish buff surface, deep red paste, well made	463	8–1	L 101	270
5	Cooking pot, surface reddish brown, core dark brown, white grits	10	8–17	L 133	270
6	Cooking pot, reddish surface, brick red core, grits	230	7–23	Sub 12	270
7	Cooking pot, burnt surface, dark buff inside, coarse grits	453	?	?	270
8	Cooking pot, surface brownish pink, core reddish grey, grits, wheel marks inside	98	7–23	Sub 11	270
9	Juglet, greyish black surface, vertically burnished	490	8–15	L 123	270
10	Juglet, surface black, core dark grey, vertical burnishing	587	8–25	L 145	270
11	Juglet, buff surface	412	8–11	L 122	270
12	Juglet, surface dark grey vertical burnishing	411	8–13	L 125	270
13	Vase, black surface, fine black paste with white grits	150	8–3	Sub 20	271
14	Juglet, pinkish buff surface, vertical burnishing	519	8–17	L 123	270
15	Juglet, reddish buff surface, vertical burnishing	18	7–13	L 10	270
16	Juglet, buff surface, vertical burnishing, core brown	512	8–17	L 133	270
17	Juglet, surface buff, core brown	458	8–14	L 129	270
18	Juglet, surface brown buff, vertical burnishing, core brown	457	8–14	L 129	270
19	Pitcher, surface reddish brown, core black, gritty	244	7–9	Trial pit	270, 276
20	Pitcher, surface reddish buff, core light brown, coarse grits	90	7–31	Sub 4	270
21	Lamp, buff	362	7–30	Sub 104	270
22	Unguentarium, surface red brown, core brown	440	8–14	L 129	271
23	Lamp, grey, well levigated, unevenly baked	106	7–16	L 15	270

Plate 66 Sixth Century B.C.

		Reg. No.	Date	Prov.	§ Ref.
1	Jar, dark grey ware, with black and white grits, dark reddish brown surface, wheel marks inside	151	7–18	L 101	273–297
2	Jar, hard light brown ware, white and grey grits, buff surface	864	7–30	Sub 119	297
3	Jar, brown ware, large white grits, reddish brown surface showing wheel marks	118	7–23	Sub I	297
4	Red ware, minute white grits, light red surface	301	7–23	Sub 18	297
5	Reddish brown ware, minute white grits, buff surface	155	8–3	Sub L 7	297
6	Brown ware, well levigated, minute grits, pink surface	300	7–13	I L 6	297
7	Hard red ware, grey in center, poorly levigated, coarse grits, reddish buff surface	84	7–28	Sub 108	297
8	Reddish buff ware, well levigated, minute grits, buff surface	417	8–18	L 41	
9	Jar, buff inside and out, fine grits	457	8–18	L 201	297
10	Jar, reddish buff ware, buff surface	527	8–16	L 132	297
11	Jar, fine brown buff ware, light buff outside, reddish buff inside	465	8–14	L 122/125	297
12	Jar, light grey ware, white grits, light red surface	271	7–13	I L 6	297
13	Jar, light brown ware, cream slip outside, buff inside, fine texture	154	7–21	L 6	297
14	Jar, dark grey ware, small grits, light reddish buff surface	107	7–21	Sub 6	298
15	Jar, dark grey surface, coarse clay, large and small grits, red-brown surface	267	7–23	Sub center	298
16	Jar, brown buff inside and outside, gritty paste	587	8–8	Sub 14	

Plate 67 Sixth Century B.C. Jars

		Reg. No.	Date	Prov.	§ Ref.
1	Hard brownish grey ware, minute white grits, buff surface	82	7–30	Sub 108	299
2	Drab ware, buff surface, smoked from conflagration	429	8–13	L 129	298
3	Very hard and compact red ware, reddish buff surface	662	8–11	L 129	298
4	Storage jar, drab ware well levigated, except for occasional grits of quartz, grey surface	6	8–13	L 136	299
5	Grey ware, well levigated, minute white grits, buff surface	163	7–30	Sub 108	299
6	Greyish buff ware, hard with white grits, reddish surface	654	8–25	L 145	299
7	Red ware, grey in center, minute white grits, light red surface, shallow broad grooves on rim and on shoulder	657	8–11	L 123	299
8	Reddish buff ware, light red surface, incised shallow grooves and rows of circular protuberances	652	8–11	L 123	298–299
9	Hard red ware, grey in center	658	8–21	L 145	299
10	Ware dark grey in center, red on edges, buff slip outside, inner surface red	249	7–16	L 18	298
11	Reddish buff, hard but rather coarse paste, red surface	201	7–14	L 10	299
12	Greyish brown ware, well levigated, small grits, creamy buff surface	125	8–4	Sub 7	298
13	Brownish grey ware, coarse grits, buff surface	140	8–4	Sub 7	299
14	Dark grey ware, well levigated, sporadic grits, pinkish buff surface	50A	7–23	I sub center	298
15	Hard grey ware, brick-red at outer edge, minute white grits, red surface	459	8–11	Sub 126	298
16	Hard grey ware, light brown at edges, buff surface	234	8–3		299
17	Red ware, grey core, not well levigated, buff surface	289	7–21	Sub L 6	298
18	Buff ware, minute grits, buff surface	94	7–23	Sub L 12	298
19	Dark grey ware, well levigated with small grits (as in royal jar handles) red surface	95	7–23	I sub center	298

Plate 68 Hellenistic Pottery, phase 1

		Reg. No.	Date	Prov.	§ Ref.
1	Reddish buff, poorly levigated	192	7–10	Area I E	308
2	Light grey core, buff surface, well levigated	156	7–31	L 202	308
3	Buff surface, well levigated	193	7–11	Area I NW	308
4	Buff exterior, grey core, well levigated	147	7–31	L 209	308

Catalogue of Pottery Plates

		Reg.No.	Date	Prov.	§ Ref.
5	Buff surface, well levigated	199	7–12	Area I NE	308
6	Buff surface, grey core, well levigated	225	7–30	Area III	308
7	No description	91	7–21	L 119	308
8	Buff surface, grey core, well levigated, few coarse grits	291	7–31	L 209	308
9	Buff surface, dark grey core, well levigated	191	7–9	?	308
10	Buff, well levigated	190	7–11	Area I, center	308
11	Pink, fairly fine levigation	250	7–18	L 101	308
12	Buff surface, grey core, well levigated	197	7–10	Area I, center	308
13	Buff surface, well levigated	189	7–1	Area I, center	308
14	Buff surface, pinkish buff core, fairly well levigated, fine grits	292	7–28	L 116	308
15	Buff surface, grey core, fairly well levigated	68	7–18	L 6	308
16	Reddish buff, some white grits	220	7–20	L 115	308
17	Buff surface, dark grey core, minute grits	252	7–10	Area I, center	308
18	Buff surface, red core, well levigated	70	?	?	308
19	Buff surface, brownish core, fairly well levigated	285	7–18	L 101	308
20	Grey-brown core, minute grits	169	7–20	L 119	308
21	Reddish buff surface, dark red core, fairly well levigated	313	7–27	Sub 108	308
22	Buff surface, light grey to drab core, well levigated	272	?	Area II NE	308
23	Buff surface, grey core, well levigated	226	7–30	Area III, center	308
24	Buff surface, grey core, well levigated	173	7–16	L 17	308
25	Buff surface, pink core, well levigated, minute grits	296	7–20	L 117	308

Plate 69 Hellenistic Pottery, phase 1 (1–9), phase 2 (10–23)

		Reg. No.	Date	Prov.	§ Ref.
1	Pink buff surface, pink brown core, poorly levigated, minute white grits	294	7–28	L 108	308, 309, 310
2	Grey outer surface, reddish buff inner surface, brown to grey core, fairly well levigated	286	7–20	L 113	308, 309, 312
10*	Reddish buff surface, grey core, fine grits	116	7–27	L 112, phase 2	310
11	Reddish buff surface, grey core, fine grits	131	7–28	L 113 E	310
12	Reddish buff surface, brownish core, fairly well levigated	284	7–18	L 101	310
13	Buff surface, dark grey core, well levigated	278	7–23	Sub 7	310, 311
14	Buff surface, dark grey core, well levigated, minute grits	50	?	?	310, 311
15	Buff surface, greyish buff core, well levigated	288	7–18	L 109	310, 311
16	Buff exterior, well levigated	103	7–19	L 112	310, 311
17	Buff surface, brownish core, fairly well levigated	172	7–19	L 112	310, 311
18	Buff surface, dark grey core, well levigated	160	7–20	L 112	310, 311
19	Reddish surface, brownish red core, well levigated	188	7–19	L 112	310, 311
20	Buff surface, brownish core, minute grits	145	7–27	L 117	310, 311
21	Reddish buff surface, well levigated	?	7–12	L 7	310, 311
22	Buff surface, dark grey core, well levigated	61	7–13	L 18	310, 311
23	Creamy buff surface, reddish buff core, fairly well levigated	214	7–20	L 117	310, 311

* (Missing numbers are from surface debris, 1957.)

Plate 70 Hellenistic and Early Roman Pottery. Roman (1–24); Hellenistic (25–32)

		Reg. No.	Date	Prov.	§ Ref.
1	Buff surface and core, well levigated, minute grits	81	7–17	L 101	312
4	Buff surface, dark grey core, well levigated	?	?	?	312
25*	Buff surface, red brown core, well levigated	283	7–28	L 119	313
26	Reddish surface, dark red core, small grits	228	7–27	Sub 102	313
27	Buff surface, pinkish buff core, fairly well levigated, grits	293	7–21	S of L 119	313
28	Buff surface, dark grey core, well levigated, fine grits	135	7–27	Sub 105	313
29	Light reddish buff surface, red to grey core	456	8–11	L 129?	313
30	Buff surface, grey brown core, minute grits	295	7–28	Sub L 108	313
31	Buff surface, reddish with dark grey core, minute grits	67	7–11	Area I W	313
32	Reddish buff surface, grey core, well levigated, fine grits	290	7–30	Sub L 111	313, 312

* (Missing numbers are from surface debris, 1957.)

Plate 71 Hellenistic and Early Roman Pottery

		Reg. No.	Date	Prov.	§ Ref.
1	Reddish buff, well levigated	102	7–18	L 101	314
2	Crater rim	1957 Surface debris			315
3	Brownish red surface, reddish core, finely levigated	133	8–10	L 127 silo	316, 317
4	Dark red brown surface, dark grey core, black and white grits	?	?	?	316
5	No description	1960 Surface debris			316
6	Dark red surface, red core, well levigated, light ribbing	328	7–30	Sub 103	316
7	Dark red surface and core, well levigated	113	7–28	L 114	316
8	Dark red surface and core	287	7–28	L 116	316
9	Deep red, very thin ware, excellent throwing and firing	3117	6–16	L A, E garden	316, 317

Plate 72a Late Hellenistic and Early Roman Pottery
**   b Stamped Jar Handles, Middle Bronze II–Iron II**

		Reg. No.	Date	Prov.	§ Ref.
1	Lamp	108	7–21	Area I, center	318
2	Lamp	125	7–27	L 101/109	318
3	Lamp	123	7–26	Area III	318
4	Lamp	375	8–10	?	318
5	Lamp	128	7–27	Sub 108	318
6	Unguentarium, dark grey surface, grey core, well levigated, few fine grits	111	7–28	L 109, Sub 3	319
7	Unguentarium, buff surface	168	7–27	L116, under N wall	319
8	Unguentarium, buff surface, dark grey core, well levigated	101	8–10	L 127 silo	319
9	Unguentarium	37	7–17?	L 18	319

(Lower half of plate is stamped jar handles)

Plate 73 LB (Fig. 1), Iron I (Figs. 2–15) 1954

		Reg. No.	Date	Prov.	§ Ref.
1	Bowl, light brown ware, handmade	1131	6–29	L 318	243
2	Bowl, dark tan ware, good clay, well thrown	1003	5–27	Area VI	273
3	Juglet, unburnished buff ware, white grits, poor throwing, overfired	1077	6–10	L 323	274
4	Bowl, hand burnished, deep red ware	1035	5–31	L 313	273
5	Bowl, tan ware, poor clay, thick bottom	1121	6–16	L 322	273
6	Bowl, rich red ware, burnished (see text)	1123	6–10	L 320	273
7	Chalice, light buff ware, poor clay	1037	6–4	L 315	274
8	Bowl, sand colored ware, light buff, burnish almost gone	1085	6–11	L 315	273
9	Bowl, dark tan ware, little burnishing remains, poor clay	1038	6–4	L 315	273
10	Chalice, fine pinkish buff ware, unburnished, overfired	1104	6–17	L 322	274
11	Bowl, pinkish red ware, unburnished, overfired	1039	5–28	Area VI	273
12	Bowl, buff ware, poor clay with grits	1120	6–10	L 320	273
13	Bowl, rich reddish brown ware, burnishing something like MB	1078	6–10	L 320	273
14	Bowl, light brown ware, continuous burnishing	1036	6–4	L 317	273
15	Store-jar, excellent craftsmanship	1151	6–11	L 315	272

Plate 74 Iron I (Fig. 4); Iron II (Figs. 1–3, 5, 8); Roman (Fig. 6); Byzantine (Fig. 7) 1954

		Reg. No.	Date	Prov.	§ Ref.
1	Bowl, heavy shallow ware	1154	5–31	L 317	276
2	Bowl for mixing kohl, red ware, poor clay and craftsmanship	1034	5–29	L 315	276
3	Bowl, pinkish buff ware, unburnished, good clay, well thrown	1060	6–7	L 321	276
4	Jug, imported painted ware with spout	1125	6–17	L 322	274
5	Pitcher	1149	6–22	L 318	276
6	Store-jar, excellent Roman ware, A.D. first century	M 153	7–1	Roman tomb	321
7	Store-jar, good Byzantine ware, A.D. sixth century	M 93	6–18	Mosque L 3	321
8	Cooking pot, see text for special features	1117	6–8	Sub 320	276

Plate 75 Roman, Byzantine 1954, Mosque Area

		Reg. No.	Date	Prov.	§ Ref.
1	Cooking pot, chocolate ware, good throwing, overfired	M 165	6–22	L 3	321
2	Cooking pot, dark red ware, good clay, excellent craftsmanship	M 164	6–22	L 3	321
3	Cooking pot, rich deep red ware, fine clay good throwing	M 97	6–24	L 3	321
4	Cooking pot, exterior black, core buff-pink, good clay and throwing, overfired	M 162	6–23	L 3	321
5	Casserole, mottled red and black ware, good clay, bottom too thin	M 159	6–22	L 3	321
6	Cooking pot	M 98	6–24	L 3	321
7	Casserole	M 100	6–22	L 3	321
8	Casserole	M 161	6–22	L 3	321
9	Casserole (handle missing), chocolate ware, good clay, fast throwing	M 158	6–22	L 3	321
10	Bowl, grey buff ware, good clay and throwing, overfired	M 99	6–24	L 3	321
11	Bowl, pinkish brown ware, fine clay, well thrown	M 111	6–19	L 1	321

Plate 76 Roman, Byzantine 1954, Mosque Area

		Reg. No.	Date	Prov.	§ Ref.
1	Bowl, buff ware	M 95	6–21	L 3	321
2	Pitcher	M 121	6–21	Surface	321
3	Pitcher	M 66	6–29	L 3	321
4	Jar stand	M 36	6–23	L 2	321
5	Jar stand, brownish buff ware, good clay, careless work	M 13	6–19	L 1	321
6	Jar stand	M 14	6–19	L 1	321
7	Bowl, reddish buff ware, good clay, fast work	M 122	6–19	L 1	321
8	Bowl	M 124	?	Surface	321
9	Bowl	M 125	6–23	L 3	321
10	Pitcher neck	M 40	6–23	L 2	321
11	Bowl	M 24	6–21	L 3	321
12	Jar, beige surface, fine clay, handles carefully worked	M 110	6–19	L 1	321

Plate 77 MB II (Figs. 1–7); LB (Figs. 8–12) 1957

		Reg. No.	Date	Prov.	§ Ref.
1	Pitcher, pinkish buff ware, combing decoration, imported ware	2246	7–30	L 403	245
2	Store-jar, tan-grey ware, combing from neck to bottom of handle	2279	8–24	L 413	244
3	Store-jar	2270	8–13	L 403	244
4	Bowl, pinkish buff ware, buff burnished slip	2286	8–6	L 402	245
5	Bowl, light buff ware, light burnishing on exterior	2243	7–30	L 403	245
6	Bowl, grey ware outside, buff inside, overfired	2259	7–13	L 403	245
7	Jar rim	2296	7–30	L 410	245
8	Vase, pinkish buff ware, black lines, imported ware	2237	7–24	L 408	246
9	Bowl, buff ware, poor work	2191	8–10	N city wall	246
10	Juglet, grey ware, unburnished, overfired	2236	7–31	L 402	246
11	Cup and saucer lamp, red ware, fragment	2256	8–26	L 412	246
12	Chalice, buff ware, brown bands	2251	7–30	L 410	246

Plate 78 Iron I (Figs. 6–12); II (Figs. 4, 13); and Sixth Century B.C. (Figs. 1–3, 5) 1957

		Reg. No.	Date	Prov.	§ Ref.
1	Juglet, red burnished ware	2234	7–18	L 403	293
2	Juglet, red burnished ware	2235	7–18	L 403	293
3	Juglet, buff burnished ware, fragment	2240	7–27	L 407/408	294
4	Juglet, pinkish buff ware, unburnished	2289	7–23	L 407	278

		Reg. No.	Date	Prov.	§ Ref.
5	Jug, rich dark red ware, highly burnished all over including bottom	2239	7 25	L 411	294
6	Bowl, hand burnished on rim and inside to bottom of handles then radial burnished to center	2280	8–14	Madâfeh	277
7	Bowl, buff ware, burnished on inside only	2263	7–13	L 403	277
8	Chalice, pinkish buff ware, unpainted	2245	7–30	L 408	277
9	Bowl, pinkish buff ware	2282	7–12	Surface	277
10	Chalice, pinkish buff ware, painted pattern in red	2241	7–29	L 409	277
11	Store-jar, buff above handles, grey below, good workmanship except at bottom	2271	8–26	Madâfeh	277
12	Store-jar bottom, pinkish buff ware	2274	7–29	L 409	277
13	Store-jar, upper half tan-grey, sand colored below	2272	7–23	L 407	278

Plate 79 Iron II (Figs. 1–5) 1957

		Reg. No.	Date	Prov.	§ Ref.
1	Water decanter, grey ware, ring burnished, excellent craftsmanship	2250	7–15	L 403	279
2	Water decanter fragment, reddish buff ware, brown bands	2252	8–6	L 409	279
3	Pitcher, tan ware, slightly overfired	2242	7–29	L 409	279
4	Bottle, buff ware, painted design, center two lines in red and others in brown	2232	7–13	L 403	279
5	Bowl, rich deep red ware, inside bowl and outside rim ring-burnished	2244	7–30	L 408	279

Plate 80 Sixth Century B.C. 1957

		Reg. No.	Date	Prov.	§ Ref.
1	Bowl, deep red ware, unburnished	2258	7–15	L 403	289, 291
2	Bowl, red ware, unburnished	2261	7–15	L 406	292
3	Funnel, red ware, unburnished	2233	7–13	L 403	300
4	Bowl, red ware, unburnished, overfired	2260	7–15	L 406	291
5	Bowl, pinkish buff ware, unburnished	2287	7–22	Surface	292
6	Bowl, pinkish buff ware, wheel burnished over rim	2290	7–25	L 401	289–291
7	Bowl, reddish buff ware	2283	7–22	L 407	289, 291
8	Bowl, red ware unburnished	2284	7–15	L 404	289–291
9	Bowl, buff ware, interior burnished	2265	8–5	L 407	292
10	Store-jar, buff to brown ware, good craftsmanship	2277	8–5	L 407	295
11	Store-jar, brownish buff ware	2273	7–15	L 403	295
12	Store-jar, pinkish buff ware	2278	8–5	L 407	295

Plate 81 Chalcolithic (Fig. 1); MB II (Figs. 2–6, 8); Iron II (Fig. 7) 1960

		Reg. No.	Date	Prov.	§ Ref.
1	Ledge-handled pot, handmade, exterior buff, interior reddish brown, gritty clay	3134	6–28	High place	247
2	Cult object, grey ware, exterior white slip, very thick walls, overfired	3143	7–11	Pit 5	248
3	Bowl, rose colored ware, interior slip and over rim good clay, well thrown, slightly overfired	3144	7–11	Pit 5	248
4	Juglet, grey to buff ware, beautiful form, overfired	3132	6–27	S wall	248
5	Cup, excellent clay, delicate form, slightly irregular from firing	3145	7–11	Pit 5	248
6	Cup, buff ware, quickly thrown, well fired, too thick	3126	6–21	S wall	248
7	Saucer, buff ware, smooth interior, rough exterior	3116	6–16	W garden	282
8	Saucer, good form, too thick	3075	6–30	Ḥaram Area	248

Plate 82   MB II (Figs. 1–2, 4); LB (Figs. 3, 5–8)   1960

		Reg. No.	Date	Prov.	§ Ref.
1	Store-jar, slate grey—pinkish buff ware, fine combing, fast throwing	3125	6–20	S wall	249
2	Store-jar, buff to pinkish buff ware, thin combing, good clay, well thrown, well fired	3127	6–21	S wall	249
3	Store-jar, slate colored exterior, pinkish buff interior, excellent clay, well fired	3146	6–21	S wall	251
4	Store-jar, greyish buff to pink, thin combing bands	3115	6–16	W wall	249
5	Bowl, pink exterior, buff interior, interior smoothed, exterior not, overfired	3118	6–17	S wall	251
6	Bowl, poor clay, overfired, blistered	3142	7–7	S wall	251
7	Bowl, light chocolate ware, good clay, well thrown, red core	3139	7–1	Pit 5	251
8	Bowl, white to grey ware, white slip, excellent clay, partly smoothed on exterior	3138	7–1	Pit 5	251

Plate 83   Iron I (Figs. 3–8); Iron II (Figs. 1–2)   1960

		Reg. No.	Date	Prov.	§ Ref.
1	Store-jar, pinkish buff ware, excellent clay, good craftsmanship, well fired	3112	6–8	W wall	282
2	Store-jar, grey to pinkish buff, faint trace of two thin lines below handles, well thrown, overfired	3133	6–28	Pit 5	282
3	Bowl, cooking pot clay, very thick walls, good bevel on ring-base	3120	6–17	W garden	280
4	Bowl, buff exterior, pinkish buff interior, apparently burnished inside, string cut base	3122	6–18	S wall	281
5	Bowl, buff exterior, pinkish buff interior, burnished on interior and over the rim, overfired, badly worn	3137	6–29	Pit 5	281
6	Bowl, pink to red ware, lime and quartz grits, overfired	3136	6–28	Pit 5	280
7	Bowl, gritty clay shows on exterior, interior smoothed, ring-base beveled but unsmoothed	3124	6–18	S wall	281
8	Bowl, brownish buff ware, pink core, good throwing although not smoothed, good handles	3131	6–25	Pit 5	280

Plate 84   Iron II   1960

		Reg. No.	Date	Prov.	§ Ref.
1	Jar, exterior grey, green and greenish buff, interior pinkish buff, clay mixed with sand or small quartz, design cut into rim, overfired	3128	6–22	Pit 5	282
2	Canteen, dotted lines indicate end view	3065b	6–27	Pit 5	282
3	Pitcher, buff to pink ware, beveled ring-base, slightly overfired	3069	6–28	Pit 5	282
4	Bowl, pinkish red ware, originally ring burnished, overfired	3119	6–17	W garden	282
5	Bowl, tan-buff and grey ware, ring burnished, interior smoothed, exterior only in upper section	3135	6–28	Pit 5	282

MISCELLANEOUS POTTERY OBJECTS

1934

Reg. No.	Date	Description	Provenience	Period	§ Reference
7	7–11	Spindle whorl	Area I	Iron II	271
12	9–1	Bull-roarer	Sub 165	MB II	231, Pl. 33:12
102	7–24	Kernos fragment	L 18	Iron I	267
161	7–28	Jar handle	L 119	Iron II–I	266
231	8–3	Jar handle	Sub 20	Iron II	271, Pl. 72
235	7–30	Jar handle	Sub 104	Iron II	271, Pl. 72
244	8–3	Cup of canteen	L 33	Iron I	267
277	8–4	Stopper with hole for string	L 32	Iron I	267
304	8–4	Limestone potter's wheel	L 32	Iron I	267
315	7–31	Jar handle	L 207	Iron I	266, Pl. 72
325	8–7	Button	L 33	Iron I	267
334	8–7	Jar handle with cloth impression	L 47	Iron II–I	266
378	8–6	Jar handle	Sub 28	Iron II–I	266
386	8–8	Jar handle	L 42	Iron I	266, Pl. 72
387	8–10	Jar handle	Sub 122	Iron II	271, Pl. 72
388	8–7	Jar handle	L 42	Iron I	266, Pl. 72
415	8–10	Jar handle	Sub 113	Iron I	266, Pl. 72
422	8–10	Kernos fragment	?	Iron I	267
468	8–13	Jar handle	Sub 131	Iron I	266, Pl. 72
478	8–13	Flat pendant	L 133	Iron II	271
481	8–14	Jar handle	L 139	Iron I	266, Pl. 72
482	8–14	Jar handle	L 48	Iron I	266, Pl. 72
493	8–16	Jar handle	L 122	Iron II	271, Pl. 72
510	8–18	Game piece	L 61	MB II	231
634	8–30	Spindle whorl	Sub 153	MB II	231
645	9–1	Knob?	L 166	MB II	231
715	9–6	Jar handle	L 166	LB	241, Pl. 72

1954

Reg. No.	Date	Description	Provenience	Period	§ Reference
1033	6–3	Bead	Sub 302	Iron II	356
1062	6–7	Spindle whorl	L 315	Iron I	275
1080	6–10	Loom weight	L 324	Iron II	276
1088	6–11	Bull-roarer	L 323	Iron I	275
1101	6–17	Inscribed sherd	L 322	Iron I	275

1957

Reg. No.	Date	Description	Provenience	Period	§ Reference
2023	6–15	Jar handle	L 403	Iron II	279
2045	6–17	Jar handle	L 404	Iron II	277
2093	6–24	Bull-roarer	L 407	Iron II	279, Pl. 115:16
2103	7–26	Jar handle	L 403	MB II	245, Pl. 72
2122	6–26	Inscribed sherd, " XII "	L 411	Iron II	277
2132	6–29	Loom weight	L 403	MB II	245
2229	8–23	Doll's leg	W wall	?	367, Pl. 115:1

1960

Reg. No.	Date	Description	Provenience	Period	§ Reference
3026	6–15	Loom weight	W garden	Iron II	282
3046	6–17	Spindle whorl	W garden	MB II	250
3081	7–7	Spindle whorl	S city wall	Iron I–LB	380
3093	7–6	Stopper or plug	Pit 5	MB II	250
3100	7–9	Game piece	NW gate	MB II	250
3143	7–11	Cult object	Pit 5	MB II	248, Pl. 81:2, Pl. 119a

Catalogue of Artifacts other than Pottery

ARCHITECTURAL FRAGMENTS (MOSQUE AREA)

1954

Reg. No.	Date	Description	Provenience	Period	§ Reference
M 1	6–8	Limestone altar column	Gate	Byz.	365, Pl. 79:11
M 2	6–8	Limestone altar column	L 3	Byz.	365, Pl. 79:10
M 3	6–8	Column base with slots for chancel screen	L 3	Byz.	365, Pl. 79:9
M 166	6–8	Limestone column base	Surface	Byz.	365, Pl. 79:8
M 167	6–8	Stone decorated with linear pattern	Surface	Byz.	365, Pl. 79:12
M 168	6–8	Stone decorated with floral pattern	Surface	Byz.	365, Pl. 79:7

1957

2247	7–30	Limestone capital with square abacus	Maḍâfeh	Byz.	368, Pl. 79:6

ARROWHEADS*

1934

Reg. No.	Date	Provenience	Period	§ Reference
		BRONZE		
31	7–17	II, NE, Debris	Hel ?	353, Pl. 46:29
180	7–28	L 116	Hel-Iron II	327, Pl. 46:28
187	7–30	L 104	Iron II	333, Pl. 46:33
431	8–14	Sub 45	Iron I	340, Pl. 46:31
516	8–20	L 61	LB	345, Pl. 46:30
539	8–22	L 151	Iron I	340, Pl. 46:32
551B	8–23	L 154	Iron II	333
662	9–4	Silo in L 145	Iron I	340
714	9–6	L 172	LB	345, Pl. 46:34
		IRON		
272	8–4	Sub 20	Iron I	340
291	8–6	Sub 11	Iron II	334
307	8–6	Sub 26	Iron II	334
405	8–11	Sub 112	Iron II	334
408	8–13	L 137	Iron II	334
409	8–13	L 137	Iron II	334
413	8–13	L 136	Iron II	334
472	8–17	L 133	Iron II	334
557	8–21	L 146	Iron II	334
558	8–21	L 146	Iron II	334
578	8–25	L 145	Iron II	334

1954
IRON

1031	6–3	L 317	Iron II	356
1058	6–5	L 315	Iron I	361, Pl. 114:15
1096	6–16	L 322	Iron II–I	358, Pl. 114:18
1097	6–16	L 322	Iron II–I	358
1152	5–28	VI	Iron I ?	358, Pl. 114:17

1957
BRONZE

2102	7–26	L 405	LB	376
		IRON		
2134	7–29	L 409	Iron I	373
2143	7–30	L 409	Iron II–I	372
2204	8–15	Maḍâfeh	Iron II	370
2275	7–27	Maḍâfeh	Iron II–I	372

* Javelinheads are included here, but spearheads are under Tools and Weapons.

JAVELINHEADS

Reg. No.	Date	Provenience	Period	§ Reference
		IRON		
2225	8–26	Maḍâfeh	Iron I	373

1960
BRONZE

3083	7–2	Pit 5	LB	381
3084	7–2	Pit 5	LB	381
		FLINT		
3066	6–25	Pit 5	Iron I	380
3151	7–13	High place	Chal. MB I	387, Pl. 116:5

ARROWHEADS

		FLINT		
3020	6–11	NW city gate	MB II	384, Pl. 116:12, 13
3065A	6–27	Pit 5	Iron I	380

BEADS

1934

Reg. No.	Date	Material	Provenience	Period	§ Reference
30	7–16	Glass	L 18	Rom-Hel	325, Pl. 46:2
45	7–19	Glass	L 107	Hel-Iron II	328
99	7–23	Glass	Sub 11	Hel-Iron II	328
116	7–24	Carnelian	Sub 6	Iron II–I	337, Pl. 46:7
117	7–26	Paste	Grave E	Arabic	354, Pl. 46:12
126	7–27	Glass	Sub 112	Hel-Iron II	328
166	7–28	Paste	Pit in L 109	Iron II	335
169	7–15	Carnelian	I, Debris		353, Pl. 46:11
173	7–28	Quartz	Sub 112	Iron II	335
174	7–28	Carnelian	Sub 109	Iron II	335
188	7–30	Agate	Sub 104	Iron II	335
189	7–30	Glass	Sub 104	Iron II	335
190	7–30	Glass	Sub 104	Iron II	335
193	7–31	Steatite?	L 208	MB II	349
198	7–31	Steatite	L 203	Iron II–I	337
225	8–1	Paste	Sub 20	Iron I	341
226	8–1	Marble?	Sub 14	Hel-Iron II	328
283	8–4	Paste	Sub 25	Iron II	335
294	8–6	Carnelian (2)	Sub 25	Iron I	341
302	8–6	Steatite	L 25	Iron I	341
314	8–7	Stone	L 31	Iron II–I	337
317	8–6	Glass	L 28	Iron II–I	337
318	8–6	Stone	L 30	Iron II	335
320	8–6	Steatite	L 28	Iron II–I	337
367	8–10	Coral	Sub 110	Hel	326
374	8–10	Paste	Sub 115	Hel	326
397	8–11	Carnelian	Sub 128	Iron II	335
400	8–11	Ivory	Sub 128	Iron II	335
448	8–15	Stone	L 62	MB II	349, Pl. 46:3
450	8–16	Stone	L 63?	LB	346
451	8–16	Marble	Sub 41	Iron I–MB II	343
491	8–18	Paste	L 63	LB–MB II	347
498	8–18	Haematite	Sub 136	LB	346
500	8–18	Stone	L 62	LB	346
501	8–18	Paste	L 62	LB	346
529	8–21	Paste	Sub 133	Iron II	335
569	8–24	A Faience / B Paste	L 63	MB II	349, Pl. 46:8 / 349
575	8–25	Faience	L 51	MB II	349

Reg. No.	Date	Material	Provenience	Period	§ Reference
619	8–29	Glass	N of 145	Iron II	335
621	8–30	Faience	Sub 123	MB II	349, Pl. 46:9
633	8–31	Stone	E of 150	Hel-Iron II	328
646	9–1	Carnelian (2)	L 167	MB I–EB	352, Pl. 46:5, 6
727	9–11	Carnelian	II, dump	?	353, Pl. 46:10
736A	8–30	Bone	E of 150	Iron I	341

1954

1033	6–3	Pottery	Sub 302	Iron II	356
1046	6–4	Carnelian	L 315	Iron I	360
1047	6–4	Agate	L 320	Iron II	356
1070	6–8	Topaz?	L 318	Iron I	360
1071	6–8	Moss agate	L 314	Iron I–LB	360
1076	6–9	Carnelian	L 318	Iron I	360
1082	6–10	Carnelian	L 323	Iron I	360
1100	6–16	Stone	L 319	Iron I	360
1107	6–23	Faience	L 318	MB II	364
1108	6–30	Sea shells (2)	L 318	MB II	364
1113	7–1	Carnelian	L 317	MB II	364

1957

2034	7–16	Stone	L 403	Iron I	374
2053	7–18	Bone	L 405	Iron I	374
2089	7–24	Quartz?	S city wall	MB II	378
2091	7–24	Carnelian	L 408	Iron I	374
2114	7–27	Stone	L 403	Iron I	374
2120	7–27	Frit	L 408	Iron I–LB	374
2171	8–6	Quartzite	L 401/411	MB II	378
2207	8–16	Cowrie shell	Maḍâfeh	Iron II	371
2218	8–23	Carnelian	W gate	LB	376
2221	8–26	Amber	W wall	Iron II	371
2222	8–26	Ceramic?	W wall	Iron II	371

1960

3010	5–31	Quartz	NW city gate	MB II	385
3012	6–2	Faience	NW city gate	MB II	385
3015	6–8	Faience	W wall	Hel	379
3029	6–16	Stone	W garden	MB II?	385
3037	6–17	Carnelian	W garden	Hel	379
3040	6–17	Faience	W garden	MB II?	385
3059	6–23	Faience	NW city gate	MB II	385
3078	7–1	Faience (3)	Pit 5	Iron I–LB	380
3086	7–2	Sandstone	Pit 5	MB II	385

MISCELLANEOUS BONE IMPLEMENTS
1934

Reg. No.	Date	Description	Provenience	Period	§ Reference
2	7–10	Leg for small chest	I, NE Debris	MB II (?)	353, Pl. 45:1
110	7–23	Disk frag. incised	Sub 20	Iron II–I	337, Pl. 45:4
191	7–31	Spindle, incised	L 24	Iron I	339, Pl. 45:2
195	7–31	Whistle	L 24	Iron I	339
219	7–30	Deer Antler	Sub 112	Hel-Iron I	329
377	8–10	Point, whittled	Sub 102	Hel	326
393	8–10	Paddle	S of 127	Iron II	332, Pl. 45:10
446	8–15	Inlay	Sub 38	LB	344
460	8–16	Cylinder, carved	L 57	LB	344
471	8–17	Handle	L 52	LB	344
551A	8–23	Palette	Sub 58	LB	344
561	8–22	Animal horn?	L 151	Iron I	339
598	8–28	Tube, Tool handle	L 145	Iron II	332

Reg. No.	Date	Description	Provenience	Period	§ Reference
602	8–28	Tube	L 62	LB–MB II	347
611	8–29	Stag horn	S of L 58	LB	344
630	8–31	Inlay for jewel box	L 161	MB II	348, Pl. 45:11
644	9–1	Handle, incised	E of 150	Iron I	339
649	9–3	Tube	L 164	LB–MB II	347
660	9–4	Tool, whittled	L 145	Iron II	332
735	8–30	Ring	E of 150	Iron I	339

1957

Reg. No.	Date	Description	Provenience	Period	§ Reference
2022	7–15	Natural bone with sq. hole in center	L 403	LB	375
2106	7–26	Handle, frag.	L 409	Iron II	369
2107	7–26	Hair ornament frag.	L 405	LB	375
2163	8–5	Scimitar shape inlay	L 407/411	LB	375, Pl. 115:3

1960

Reg. No.	Date	Description	Provenience	Period	§ Reference
3019	6–10	Spindle	NW city gate	MB II	383. Pl. 115:10
3027	6–16	Natural bone with sq. hole in center	Surface W garden	LB ?	381
3051	6–20	Hair pin (?), frag.	S city wall	MB II	383
3057	6–21	Gazelle horn	S city wall	MB II	383
3094	7–2	Carved bone	NW city gate	MB II	383

FIGURINES—Pottery all but Hathor

1934

Reg. No.	Date	Description	Provenience	Period	§ Reference
		Human figurines			
40	7–12	Fragment, pillar	I, E Debris	Iron II	331
59	7–20	Fragment, female bust	N of 3	Iron II	331, Pl. 45:15
96	7–21	Male head	S of Test Pit	Iron II	331
104	7–24	Astarte Plaque	Sub 6	Iron I	338, Pl. 42:4
122	7–26	Foot of figurine or vessel	III, SW	Iron II	353
243	8–3	Plaque, legs to r.	L 31	Iron I	338, Pl. 42:5
328	8–7	Baal with extended arm	L 44	Iron I	338, Pl. 45:14
333	8–6	Female torso	L 26+1	Iron I	338
467	8–15	Fragment, pillar	L 120	Iron II	331
549	8–23	Hathor, Sistrum handle, bone	L 58	LB	344, Pl. 42:1
560	7–14	Female torso	I, Center	Iron I?	338, Pl. 45:13
638	9–3	Male head on Jar handle	E of 150	Iron I	338, Pl. 44:7
		Animal figurines			
57	7–20	Torso	II, SE	Iron II	331
218	7–26	Leg	L 201	Iron II	331
221	7–28	Torso	L 112	Iron II	331
242	8–3	Torso	L 33–1	Iron II	331
480	8–16	Torso	L 48	Iron II	331
740	9–12	Bull	IV SE	Iron II	331, Pl. 45:16
754	8–13	Torso	L 129	Iron II	331
808	8–25	Legs	L 145	Iron II	331

1954

Reg. No.	Date	Description	Provenience	Period	§ Reference
		Human figurines			
1011	5–27	Female torso	VI	Iron II	355
		Animal figurines			
1004	5–29	Hind quarters	VI	Iron II	355
1008	5–31	Front quarters	L 315	Iron II	355
1014	5–29	Leg	L 315	Iron II	355
1023	6–1	Leg	L 315	Iron II	355
1028	6–3	Front quarters	L 317	Iron II	355

Catalogue of Artifacts other than Pottery

Reg. No.	Date	Description	Provenience	Period	§ Reference
1054	6–5	Horse head	L 318	Iron I	359
1112	7–1	Horse head	L 317	Iron I	359

1960

Animal figurines

3082	7–1	Leg	S city wall	Iron I–LB	380
3101	7–11	Bull's leg	Pit 5	MB II	382, Pl. 119a
3104	7–15	Leg or horn, stylized	NW city gate	MB I	386

FLINT IMPLEMENTS*

1934

Reg. No.	Date	Material	Provenience	Period	§ Reference
114	7–25	Knife, two ribs	Sub 14	Iron I	342
192	7–31	Knife, two ribs	L 208	MB II	350
485	8–17	Knife, two ribs	L 56	MB I	351
537	8–22	Knife, two ribs	L 152	Iron I	342
546	8–22	Knife, two ribs	L 152	Iron I	342
564	8–20	Knife, two ribs	Sub 58	LB	346
604	8–28	Knife, one rib	L 62	MB II	350
650	9–3	Knife, two ribs	L 165	Iron I	342
171	7–27	Sickle edge	L 112	Iron II	336
194	7–31	Sickle edge or knife	L 24	Iron I	342
603	8–28	Sickle edge	Sub 146	LB	346
632	8–31	Sickle edge	L 161	MB II	350
738	9–3	Sickle edge or point	L 137	Iron II	336

1954

1111	6–30	Sickle edge	L 318	MB II	364

1957

2033	7–16	Sickle edge	L 404	Iron I	374
2051	7–18	Knife, badly worn	L 403	LB	376
2088	7–24	Knife, broken	L 403	MB II	378
2104	7–26	Sickle edge	L 407	MB II	378
2168	8–6	Sickle edge	L 401/411	MB II	378
2172	8–6	Knife, broken	L 411	MB II	378
2175	8–7	Sickle edge	L 404	MB II	378
2179	8–8	Scraper	L 403	MB II	378, Pl. 115:13
2181	7–29	Scraper	L 407	MB II	378, Pl. 115:17

1960

3038	6–17	Sickle edge	S city wall	LB	381
3039	6–17	Sickle edge	S city wall	LB	381
3047	6–17	Sickle edge	W garden	MB II	384
3053	6–20	Sickle edge	S city wall	MB II	384
3054	6–21	Scraper	S city wall	LB	381, Pl. 116:7
3055A	6–21	Knives, two ribs (2)	W garden	LB	381
3055B	6–21	Sickle edge	W garden	LB	381
3068	6–27	Sickle edge	Pit 5	Iron I	380
3073	6–29	Ax or scraper	Pit 5	Iron I	373, Pl. 116:6
3074	6–30	Sickle edge	Pit 5	Iron I	380
3080	7–1	Sickle edge	Pit 5	Iron I	380
3153	7–15	Adze	High place	Chal.–MB I	387, Pl. 116:3
3154	7–15	Razor	High place	Chal.–MB I	387, Pl. 116:2
3155	7–15	Ax	High place	Chal.–MB I	387, Pl. 116:11

* For other uses of flint, see (1) Arrowheads, (2) Tools and Weapons.

GAME PIECES, ASTRAGALI, WEIGHTS, RUBBERS

1934

Reg. No.	Date	Material	Provenience	Period	§ Reference
		GAME PIECES			
365	8–10	Granite	Sub 115	Hel	326
453	8–16	Quartz	L 61	MB II	350
510	8–18	Pottery	L 61	MB II	231
629	8–31	Stone	L 153	Iron I	342
642	9–1	Alabaster	L 167	MB II	350
		ASTRAGALI			
323	8–7	Bone	L 30	Iron II	332
465/6	8–16	Bone	L 56	LB	344
527	8–21	Bone (13)	L 152	Iron I	339
609	8–29	Bone (3)	Sub 123	Iron II–I	337
		WEIGHTS			
101	7–23	Limestone	N of 18, Debris	Iron II?	353, Pl. 44:6
165	7–28	Basalt	Sub 106	Hel-Iron II	329
200	7–31	Limestone	L 203	Iron II–I	337
281	8–4	Quartz	Sub 41	Iron I	342
392	8–10	Flint	Sub 113	Iron II–I	337
484	8–17	Steatite	L 59	Iron I	342
544	8–22	Stone	L 148	MB II	350
553	8–23	Stone	L 154	Iron II	336
		LOOM WEIGHTS			
540	8–22	Stone	L 154	Iron II	336
		RUBBERS			
199	7–31	Pumice stone	L 203	Iron II–I	337
284	8–6	Stone pestle	L 26	Iron I	342
417	8–14	Pumice stone	L 34	Iron I	342
511	8–14	Stone	L 38	Iron I	342
		POTTER'S WHEEL			
304	8–4	Limestone potter's wheel	L 32	Iron I	342

1954

Reg. No.	Date	Material	Provenience	Period	§ Reference
		GAME PIECES			
1098	6–16	Bituminous limestone	L 322	Iron I	362, Pl. 114:6
		ASTRAGALI			
1056	6–5	Bone (22)	L 315	Iron II–I	358
		WEIGHTS			
1066	6–8	Flint?	L 320	Iron II	357
		RUBBERS			
1027	6–3	Pumice stone with hole	L 320	Iron II	357, Pl. 114:19
1042	6–4	Limestone	L 316	Iron I	362
1049	6–4	Limestone pestle	L 313	Iron I	362
1052	6–4	Whetstone	L 318	Iron II–I	358

Catalogue of Artifacts other than Pottery

Reg. No.	Date	Material	Provenience	Period	§ Reference
1067	6–8	Whetstone	L 320	Iron II	357
1084	6–10	Limestone	L 323	Iron I	362
1102	6–17	Sandstone	L 322	Iron I	362

MISCELLANEOUS STONE TOOLS

Reg. No.	Date	Material	Provenience	Period	§ Reference
1043	6–4	Stone socket	L 317	Iron I	362
1089	6–15	Pumice stone, hour-glass shape	L 324	Iron I	362, Pl. 114:14
1157	6–3	Limestone roof roller	L 317	Iron II	357

1957
GAME PIECES

Reg. No.	Date	Material	Provenience	Period	§ Reference
2096	7–25	Stone	L 407	MB II	378

ASTRAGALI

Reg. No.	Date	Material	Provenience	Period	§ Reference
2021	7–15	Bone (12)	L 403	Iron II	369
2035	7–16	Bone (4)	L 405	Iron I	373
2048	7–17	Bone (2)	L 405	Iron II	369
2052	7–18	Bone (2)	L 403	LB	375
2056	7–19	Bone (2)	L 401	LB	375
2077	7–23	Bone	L 407	Iron II	369
2098	7–25	Bone	L 403	MB II	377

WEIGHTS

Reg. No.	Date	Material	Provenience	Period	§ Reference
2055	7–19	Haematite	L 402	Iron II	371
2121	7–27	Haematite	L 408	Iron I–LB	374, Pl. 115:14

RUBBERS

Reg. No.	Date	Material	Provenience	Period	§ Reference
2009	7–13	Limestone pestle	L 403	Iron II	371
2017	7–13	Limestone	L 403	Iron II	371
2018	7–13	Limestone	L 403	Iron II	371
2058	7–19	Limestone	L 403	LB	376
2076	7–23	Limestone pestle	L 407	Iron II	371
2084	7–23	Limestone	L 407	Iron II	371
2118	7–27	Whetstone	L 410	Iron II	371
2166	8–5	Whetstone	L 407	Iron II	371
2182	8–9	Basalt pestle, frag.	L 402	LB	375
2224	8–26	Whetstone	Maḍâfeh	Iron I	374

1960
WEIGHTS

Reg. No.	Date	Material	Provenience	Period	§ Reference
3099	7–7	Water-worn stone	S city wall	LB	381, Pl. 116:9

LOOM WEIGHTS

Reg. No.	Date	Material	Provenience	Period	§ Reference
3091	7–5	Limestone	Pit 5	MB II	384, Pl. 116:14

RUBBERS

Reg. No.	Date	Material	Provenience	Period	§ Reference
3043	6–17	Limestone pestle	W garden	MB II	384
3062	6–23	Oval pumice stone	Pit 5	Iron II–I	379
3077	6–30	Stone	Pit 5	Iron I–LB	380
3089	7–2	Stone	Pit 5	MB II	384
3096	7–6	Granite	Pit 5	MB II	384

SCRAPERS

Reg. No.	Date	Material	Provenience	Period	§ Reference
3103	7–13	Limestone	N city gate	MB I	386, Pl. 116:10

NAILS, NEEDLES, PINS

1934

Reg. No.	Date	Material	Provenience	Period	§ Reference
			NAILS		
56	7–20	Iron	L 119	Hel	326
60	7–21	Iron	L 115	Hel-Iron II	327
276	8–4	Iron	Sub 102	Hel-Iron II	327
			NEEDLES		
236	8–1	Bone	Sub 20	Iron I	339
280	8–4	Bone	Sub 33	Iron I	339
313	8–7	Bone	L 31	Iron II–I	337
398	8–11	Bronze	Sub 126	Hel-Iron II	327
543	8–22	Bone	L 134	Iron I	339
574	8–25	Bone	L 139	Iron I	339
610	8–29	Bone	Sub 147	Iron I	339
622	8–30	Bone	L 145	Iron II	332
744	9–12	Bronze	Area II	?	353, Pl. 46:24
			PINS		
80	7–21	Bronze	Sub 14	Hel-Iron II	327
290	8–6	Bronze	Sub 11	Iron I	340
298	8–4	Bronze	L 32	Iron I	340
309	8–7	Bronze	Sub 36	Iron II	333
319	8–6	Bronze	Sub 24	Iron I	340
462	8–16	Bronze	L 60	LB–MB II	347
			TOGGLE PIN		
239	8–3	Bronze	L 37	LB	345, Pl. 46:26

1954

Reg. No.	Date	Material	Provenience	Period	§ Reference
			TOGGLE PIN		
1110	6–30	Bronze	L 318	MB II	364

1957

Reg. No.	Date	Material	Provenience	Period	§ Reference
			NAILS		
2087	7–24	Iron (3)	L 407	Iron II	370
2133	7–29	Iron	L 410	Iron II	370
			NEEDLES		
2205	8–16	Bone	Maḍâfeh	Iron II	369, Pl. 115:7
2227	8–23	Bone	W wall	Iron II	369, Pl. 115:9

PENDANTS

1934

Reg. No.	Date	Description	Material	Provenience	Period	§ Reference
186	7–30	Club shape	Bone	NW of 120	Iron II	332 Pl. 45:9
227	8–1	Natural bone	Bone	Sub 21	Iron I	339
228	8–1	Cylinder fragment	Bone	Sub 14	Iron I	339
245	8–3	Natural bone	Bone	L 32	Iron I	339
311	8–7	Club shape	Bone	Sub 15	Iron II	332, Pl. 45:6
326	8–7	Row of holes	Stone	L 42	Iron I	342

Reg. No.	Date	Description	Material	Provenience	Period	§ Reference
327	8–7	Rectangular shape	Stone	?	Iron I	342
401	8–11	Club shape	Bone	Sub 128	Iron II	332, Pl. 45:5
432	8–14	Club shape	Bone	Sub 122	Iron II	332 Pl. 45:8
486	8–17	Natural bone	Bone	L 59	Iron I	339
573	8–25	Tooth shape	Stone	L 139	Iron I	341
581	8–25	Oval, Inc. circles	Bone	L 58	MB II	348, Pl. 45:7
612	8–29	Club shape	Carnelian	L 152	Iron I	341, Pl. 46:13

1954

Reg. No.	Date	Description	Material	Provenience	Period	§ Reference
1025	6–1	Club shape	Bone	L 315	Iron II	355, Pl. 114:9
1026	6–1	Club shape, frag.	Bone	L 315	Iron II	355
1029	6–3	Club shape	Haematite	L 317	Iron II	357, Pl. 114:8
1051	6–4	Club shape, frag.	Bone	L 318	Iron I	360, Pl. 114:13
1072	6–9	Club shape	Bone	L 320	Iron II	355, Pl. 114:10
1087	6–11	Club shape	Carnelian	L 324	Iron I	360

1957

Reg. No.	Date	Description	Material	Provenience	Period	§ Reference
2041	7–17	Club shape, frag.	Bone	L 406	Iron II	369
2072	7–22	Club shape, frag.	Bone	L 406	Iron II	369, Pl. 115:11

1960

Reg. No.	Date	Description	Material	Provenience	Period	§ Reference
3064B	6–24	Tooth shape	Stone	Pit 5	Iron I	380

SCARABS, SEALS, IMPRESSIONS, OSTRACA

1934

SCARABS AND SEALS

Reg. No.	Date	Description	Material	Provenience	Period	§ Reference
183	7–30	Scaraboid, fish design	Steatite	III, SW	Hel to Iron I	329
442	8–15	Scarab, hawk design	Paste	L 104?	Iron I	338 Pl. 44:2
445	8–15	Scaraboid, boat and lotuses	Paste	?	Iron I	338, Pl. 44:3
513	8–20	Cyl. seal, Astarte	Frit	III, dump	LB	344, Pl. 43
514	8–20	Cyl. seal, unintelligible pattern	Basalt	II, W	Iron II	330
548	8–23	Scaraboid, stylized spider pattern	Basalt	L 154	Iron II	330, Pl. 44:4
620	8–30	Scarab, Horus and Uraei	Steatite	L 52	LB–MB II	347, Pl. 44:1
661	9–5	Conoid seal, stag and lion	Basalt	I, debris	?	353, Pl. 44:5

IMPRESSIONS OF SCARABS, ETC

Reg. No.	Date	Description	Material	Provenience	Period	§ Reference
75	7–19	Gem, human figure	Jar handle	L 107	Hel	326
94	7–21	Scarab, human figure?	Jar handle	L 6	MB II	348
454	8–16	Scarab showing concentric circles	Asphalt seal	L 58	MB II	348
636	8–29	Gem, nude male standing	Jar handle	W of 150	Hel	326
715	9–6	Seal?, spiral	Jar handle	L 166	LB	241
783	8–29	Gems, nude male standing	Jar rim	W of 150	Hel	326

RHODIAN STAMPS

Reg. No.	Date	Description	Material	Provenience	Period	§ Reference
48	7–17	ΕΠΙ ΔΑΜΑΙΝΕΤΟΥ ΔΑΛΙΟΥ	Jar handle	II, NW	Hel	Ch. XIV,[6] Pl. 47:7
58	7–19	ΝΑΝΙΟΣ	Jar handle	L 111	Hel	Ch. XIV,[6] Pl. 47:9
418	8–14	ΕΠΙ ΠΑΥΣΑΝΙΑ ΥΑΚΙΝΘΙΟΥ	Jar handle	Sub 128	Hel	Ch. XIV,[6]
456	8–14	ΝΙΚΑΣ ΙΩΝΩΣ Round rose	Jar handle	IV	Hel	Ch. XIV,[6] Pl. 47:8

Reg. No.	Date	Description	Material	Provenience	Period	§ Reference
			OSTRACA			
3	7–10	Two incised letters	Pottery	I, E debris	Iron II	330, Pl. 47:10
121	7–26	ΘE	Pottery	L 201	Rom-Hel	325, Pl. 42:3
389	8–9	A cross within a circle	Pottery	L 118	Hel	326

1954
SCARABS

1012	5–28	Stylized pattern	Paste	L 312	Iron I	359
1073	6–9	Bird before a plant	Red stone	L 318	Iron I	359, Pl. 114:12

IMPRESSION OF SEAL

1150	6–17	Seal, stylized	Jar handle	L 312	Iron I	359, Pl. 114:11

1957
SCARABS

2228	8–23	Scaraboid	Frit	W wall		367, Pl. 115:4

SEALS

2119	7–27	Stamp, irregular squares	Pottery	L 409	Iron I	373, Pl. 115:12
2295	8–26	Stamp, Arabic inscription	Pottery	W wall	Iron II	367, Pl. 118

1960
SCARABS

3007	5–28	Man before a griffon	?	NW city gate	MB II	382, Pl. 119c
3063	6–23	Tree between two figures	Stone	N city wall	Sixth cent.?	379, Pl. 119c

IMPRESSIONS OF

3102	7–11	Seal	Jar handle	Pit 5	MB II	250

SPATULAE
1934

Reg. No.	Date	Provenience	Period	§ Reference
		BONE		
85	7–21	Sub 6	Rom-Hel	325
160	7–28	Sub 114	Iron II	332
178	7–28	Jar L 101	Rom-Hel	325
179	7–28	L 116	Hel-Iron II	328
279	8–4	Sub 103	Hel-Iron II	328
358	8–10	L 113	Iron I	339
455	8–16	L 123	Iron I	339
483	8–18	L 22	Iron II	332
536	8–22	L 152	Iron I	339
541	8–22	L 151	Iron I	339
605	8–28	L 145	Iron II	332, Pl. 45:3
734	8–30	E of 150	Iron I	339

1954

1021	6–1	L 315	Iron II	355
1068	6–8	L 320	Iron II	355, Pl. 114:16
1083	6–10	L 320	Iron I	360

Catalogue of Artifacts other than Pottery

1957

Reg. No.	Date	Provenience	Period	§ Reference
2081	7–23	L 408	Iron II	369
2082	7–23	L 407	Iron I	373
2109	7–28	L 409	Iron II	369
2203	8–14	Maḍâfeh	Iron II	369
2206	8–16	Maḍâfeh	Iron II	369

1960

Reg. No.	Date	Provenience	Period	§ Reference
3071	6–29	Pit 5	Iron I	380

SPINDLE WHORLS* AND BUTTONS

1934

Reg. No.	Date	Material	Provenience	Period	§ Reference
23	7–14	Limestone	L 10	Hel	326
43	7–18	Limestone	L 110	Byz	325
82	7–21	Bone	L 11	Hel-Iron II	328
109	7–25	Steatite	L 20	Iron II–I	337
275	8–4	Steatite	Sub 103	Hel-Iron II	329
282	8–4	Marble	Sub 24	Iron II	336
332	8–8	Steatite	L 31	Iron I	342, Pl. 46:4
399	8–11	Fossil	Sub 128	Iron II	336
444	8–15	Stone	L 123	MB II	350
492	8–18	Bone	L 62	LB	344
576	8–25	Bone	L 154	Iron II	332
586	8–27	Bone	L 62	LB	344
596	8–28	Bone	L 62	MB II	348
597	8–28	Bone	L 52	LB	344
606	8–28	Bone	L 51	MB II	348
641	9–1	Bone	L 166	MB II	348
720	9–8	Bone	L 172	LB	344

1954

Reg. No.	Date	Material	Provenience	Period	§ Reference
1048	6–4	Quartz, frag.	L 315	Iron I	362
1061	6–7	Bone	L 321	Iron II–I	358, Pl. 114:5

1960

Reg. No.	Date	Material	Provenience	Period	§ Reference
3067	6–25	Stone	Pit 5	Iron II–I	379
3081	7–1	Pottery	S city wall	Iron I–LB	380

* For spindles, see Misc. Bone Implements.

STONE BOWLS, MORTARS AND JAR STOPPERS

1934

Reg. No.	Date	Description	Provenience	Period	§ Reference
95	7–21	Foot of basalt mortar	E of L 110	Hel	326
220	7–27	Limestone jar stopper	L 202 S	Hel-Iron II	329
300	8–3	Basalt mortar fragments	Sub 7	Iron II	329
394	8–11	Alabaster bowl rim	Sub 128	LB	346
396	8–11	Chalk jar stopper	Sub 124	Hel-Iron II	329
421	8–10	Basalt tripod mortar	Sub 122	Iron II	336
459	8–13	Basalt tripod mortar	L 123	Hel-Iron II	329, Pl. 64:15
499	8–18	Alabaster bowl rim	L 138	LB	346

Reg. No.	Date	Description	Provenience	Period	§ Reference
515	8–17	Basalt mortar	Sub 133	Iron II–I	337, Pl. 61:16
554	8–20	Basalt bowl	L 61	LB	346

1954

M 4	6–8	Basalt Roman millstone, lower unit	Mosque L 1	Roman	365, Pl. 79:13

1957

2124	7–27	Foot of basalt mortar	L 307	LB	376

1960

3092	7–5	Alabaster bowl rim	NW city gate	MB II	384, Pl. 116:4
3130	6–25	Basalt mortar frag.	Pit 5	Iron II	379

TOILET IMPLEMENTS

1934

Reg. No.	Date	Material	Provenience	Period	§ Reference
BRACELETS					
201	7–31	Glass	Grave A	Byz.	354, Pl. 46:15
209	7–31	Bronze	Grave D	Byz.	354, Pl. 46:14
213	7–31	Bronze (2)	Grave F	Byz.	354, Pl. 46:1, 25
COSMETIC PALETTES					
419	8–13	Flint	L 129	Iron II	336
725	9–11	Limestone	IV, SE	Iron II	336, Pl. 45:18
EARRINGS					
84	7–21	Bronze	L 113	Hel	326
240	8–3	Bronze	L 40	Iron I	340
295	8–6	Bronze	L 31	Hel-Iron II	327, Pl. 46:16
373	8–10	Bronze	Sub 115	Hel	326
547	8–22	Bronze	L 147	Iron I	340
616	8–29	Bronze	III, Dump	Hel-Iron II	353, Pl. 46:17
FIBULAE					
28	7–16	Bronze	L 14	Hel-Iron II	327
74	7–21	Bronze	N of 3/5 wall	Iron II	333, Pl. 46:19
77	7–21	Bronze	Sub 6	Iron II	333, Pl. 46:20
78	7–21	Bronze	Sub 6	Iron II	333, Pl. 46:21
230	7–31	Bronze	L 203	Iron II–I	337, Pl. 46:22
KOHL STICKS					
73	7–21	Bronze	L 115	Hel-Iron II	327
76	7–21	Bronze	L 6	Hel-Iron II	327
238	8–3	Bronze	L 37	LB	345, Pl. 46:23
241	8–3	Bronze	L 33	LB	345
330	8–3	Bronze	Sub 7	Iron II	333, Pl. 46:27
357	8–10	Bronze	Sub 114	Hel	326
447	8–3	Bone	L 63	LB	344
461	8–16	Bone	L 41	Iron I–LB–MB	343
577	8–25	Bone	L 145	Iron II	332
ORNAMENT					
719	9–8	Bronze	Area II	?	353, Pl. 46:18

1954

Reg. No.	Date	Material	Provenience	Period	§ Reference
			BRACELETS		
1045	6–4	Bronze	L 316	Iron I	361
1086	6–11	Bronze	L 324	Iron I	361
			KOHL STICKS		
1116A	7–7	Bone	L 320	Iron I	360
1116B	7–7	Stone	L 320	Iron I	362, Pl. 114:7
			RINGS		
1015	5–31	Bronze	L 315	Iron II	356
1050	6–4	Bronze	L 316	Iron I	361, Pl. 114:2
1091	6–15	Bronze	L 320	Iron I	361, Pl. 114:4
1106	6–23	Bronze	L 318	MB II	364, Pl. 114:3

1957

Reg. No.	Date	Material	Provenience	Period	§ Reference
			BRACELETS		
2025	7–15	Bronze	L 404	Iron II	370
2090	7–24	Bronze	City wall, N	MB II	377
2111	7–27	Bronze	N city wall	MB II	377, Pl. 115:5
2146	7–31	Bronze	N city wall	MB II	377
2169	8–6	Bronze	L 407/411	LB	376
2186	8–9	Bronze	N city wall	MB II	377, Pl. 115:2
			COSMETIC PALETTES		
2184	8–9	Limestone, frag.	L 402	Iron II	371
			EARRINGS		
2037	7–16	Bronze	L 406	Iron II	370
2162	8–5	Bronze, frag.	L 407	Iron II	370
			RINGS		
2030	7–15	Bronze	L 403	Iron II–I	372
2170	8–6	Bronze, frag.	L 403/407	MB II	377
			TWEEZERS		
2161	8–5	Bronze, frag.	L 407	LB	376

1960

Reg. No.	Date	Material	Provenience	Period	§ Reference
			BRACELETS		
3060	6–23	Bronze	Pit 5	Iron II–I	379
			EARRINGS		
3064A	6–24	Bronze	Pit 5	Iron I	380

TOOLS AND WEAPONS

1934

Reg. No.	Date	Material	Provenience	Period	§ Reference
\multicolumn{6}{c}{AWLS}
170	7–27	Bone	L 203	Hel-Iron II	328
273	8–4	Bone	L 33	Iron I	339
274	8–4	Bone	Sub 104	Hel-Iron II	328
390	8–8	Limestone	L 42	Iron I	342
391	8–8	Limestone	L 42	Iron I	342
532	8–22	Bone	L 47	Iron II–I	337
628	8–31	Bone	L 151	Iron I	339
631	8–31	Bone	L 161	MB II	348
643	9–1	Bone	L 162	MB II	348
663	9–4	Bone	Silo in L 145	Iron I	339

DAGGERS

| 550 | 8–23 | Bronze | L 58 | MB II | 349 |
| 552 | 8–23 | Bronze tang | L 146 | LB | 345 |

DAGGER HANDLES

10	7–12	Stone	I, E	Iron II	353, Pl. 45:19
292	8–6	Bone	Sub 11	Iron II	332, Pl. 45:12
593	8–22	Limestone	L 62	LB	346, Pl. 45:20

KNIVES

473	8–17	Iron, fragment	L 133	Iron II	334
476	8–17	Bronze	L 52	LB	345, Pl. 46:36
477	8–17	Bronze	L 52	LB	345, Pl. 46:37
623	8–30	Iron	L 145	Iron II	334

MACE HEADS

54	7–20	Limestone	II, SE corner	LB (?)	353, Pl. 45:17
158	7–28	Limestone	L 119	Iron II–I	337
474	8–17	Granite, fragment	L 58	LB	346

* For other uses of flint, see ARROWHEADS

PRUNING HOOK

| 34 | 7–18 | Iron | L 101 | Byz. | 325 |

SPEARHEADS

55	7–20	Iron	L 119	Hel	326
155	7–27	Iron	Sub 108	Hel	326
613	8–29	Bronze	Wall L 146/7	Twelfth cent B.C.	340, Pl. 46:35

TOOL POINTS

157	7–28	Iron	L 119	Iron II	334
164	7–28	Iron	Pit in 109	Iron II	334
535	8–22	Bronze	L 152	Iron I	340
542	8–22	Bronze	L 151	Iron I	340

MISCELLANEOUS IRON PIECES

156	7–27	Iron rod (8 frag.)	Sub 108	Hel	326
531	8–21	Iron pipe (?)	L 113	Iron II	334
289	8–6	Iron triangular fragment	Sub 11	Iron II	334

MISCELLANEOUS COPPER AND LEAD

44	7–18	Lead fragment	L 104	Hel-Iron II	327
285	8–6	Sheet copper frag.	L 32	Iron I	340
452	8–16	Sheet copper frag.	Sub 41	Iron I	340

Reg. No.	Date	Material	Provenience	Period	§ Reference
464	8–16	Lead bar	L 56	LB	345
530	8–21	Copper slag	Sub 134	Iron II	333
728	9–11	Copper ore (?)	II	LB	345

MISCELLANEOUS STONE PIECES

545	8–22	Stone with "T" shaped hole	Sub 134	Iron I	342
572	8–25	Basalt ring	L 51	MB I	351

1954

AWLS

1074	6–9	Flint	L 323	Iron II–I	358
1109	6–30	Bone (5)	L 318	MB II	364
1114	7–1	Bone	L 317	Iron II–I	358

DAGGER HANDLES

1090	6–15	Limestone	L 324	Iron I	362, Pl. 114:1

HAMMERS

1103	6–17	Iron	L 322	Iron I	361

PLOUGHSHARE

1020	5–31	Iron	L 315	Iron II	356

WIRE

1044	6–4	Copper	L 315	Iron I	361

MISCELLANEOUS ITEMS

1024	6–1	Iron fragment	L 315	Iron II	356
1057	6–5	Iron fragment	L 314	Iron I	361
1069	6–8	Iron fragment	L 320	Iron II	356
1075	6–9	Bronze Bucket handle	L 323	Iron II–I	358
1081	6–10	Bitumen frag.	L 320	Iron I	362

1957

AWLS

2016	7–13	Flint	L 401	Iron I	374, Pl. 115:15
2027	7–15	Bone	L 403	LB	375, Pl. 115:8
2080	7–23	Bone	L 407	LB	375
2115	7–27	Bone	L 410	Iron II	369
2129	7–29	Bone	L 409	Iron I	373
2131	7–29	Bone	L 407	Iron II	369
2151	7–31	Flint	L 402/405	MB II	378
2167	8–6	Bone	L 401/411	MB II	377
2223	8–26	Bone	W wall	Iron II	369

BUCKETS

2083	7–23	Handle, bronze	L 407	LB	376
2276	8–7	Bottom, bronze	L 404	MB II	377

Reg. No.	Date	Material	Provenience	Period	§ Reference
			KNIVES		
2135	7–29	Bronze, fragment	L 407	MB II	377
			PRUNING HOOKS		
2063	7–22	Iron	L 402	Iron II	370
			MISCELLANEOUS IRON PIECES		
2026	7–15	Ring ?	L 403	Iron I	373

1960

Reg. No.	Date	Material	Provenience	Period	§ Reference
			AWLS		
3023	6–13	Bone	NW city gate	MB II	383
3085	7–2	Bone	Pit 5	MB II	383
			AXES		
3044	6–17	Limestone	W garden	MB II	384, Pl. 116:8
3045	6–17	Limestone, frag.	W garden	MB II	384
			SPEARHEADS		
3021	6–11	Flint	NW city gate	MB I	386, Pl. 116:1
3152	7–13	Flint	High place	MB I–Chal.	387

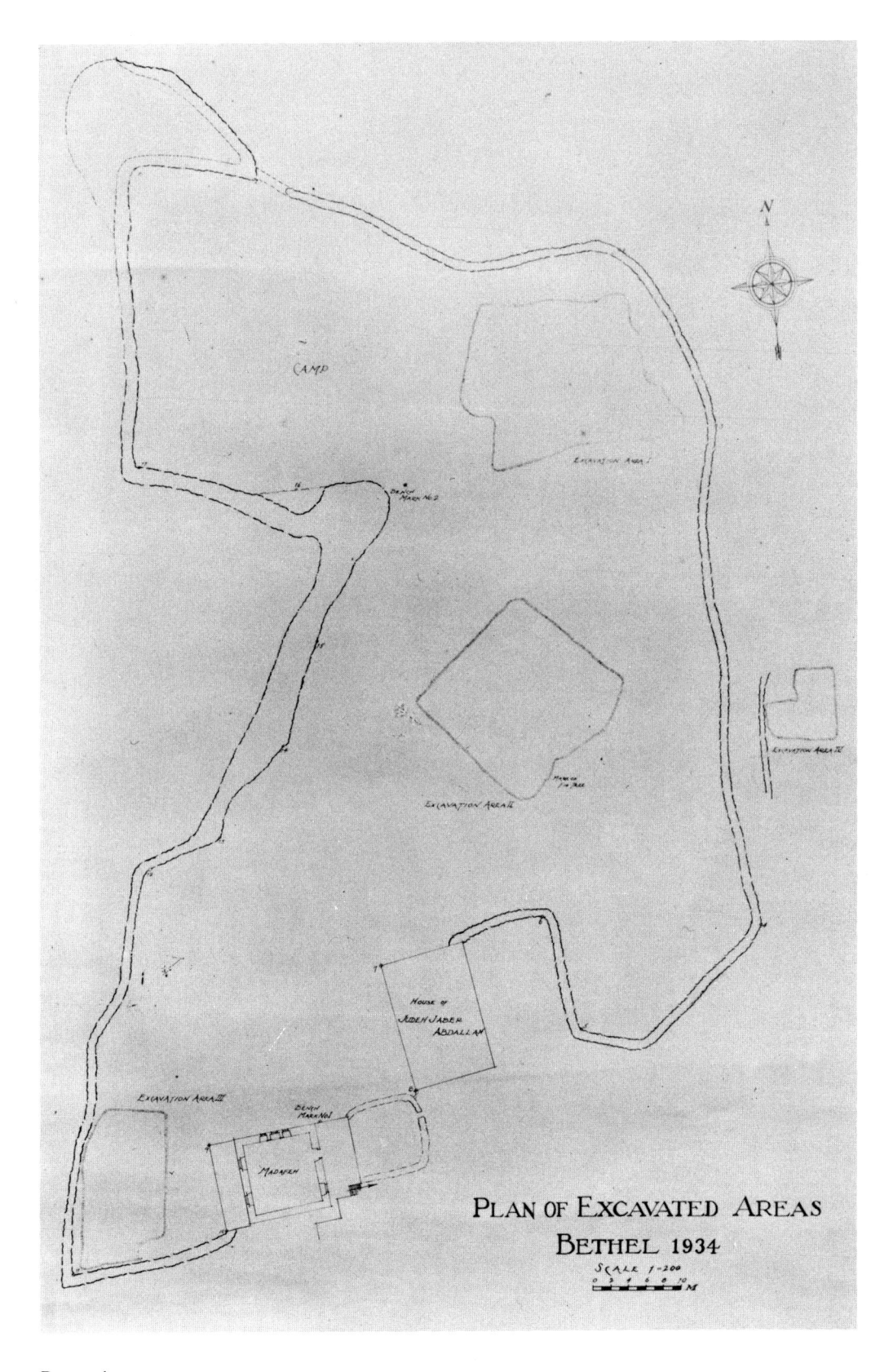

PLATE 1

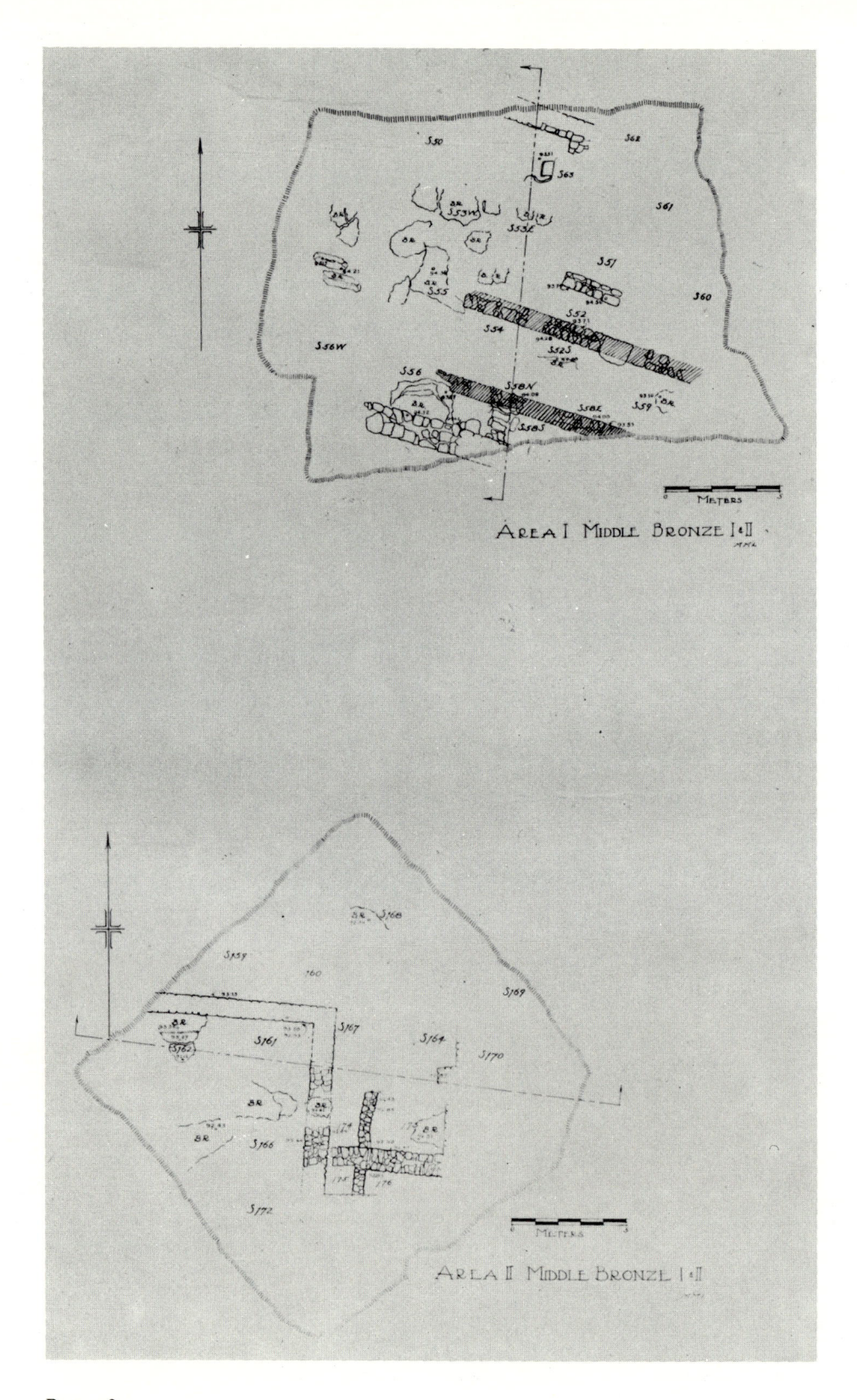

PLATE 2

AREA I LATE BRONZE
PHASES 1 & 2

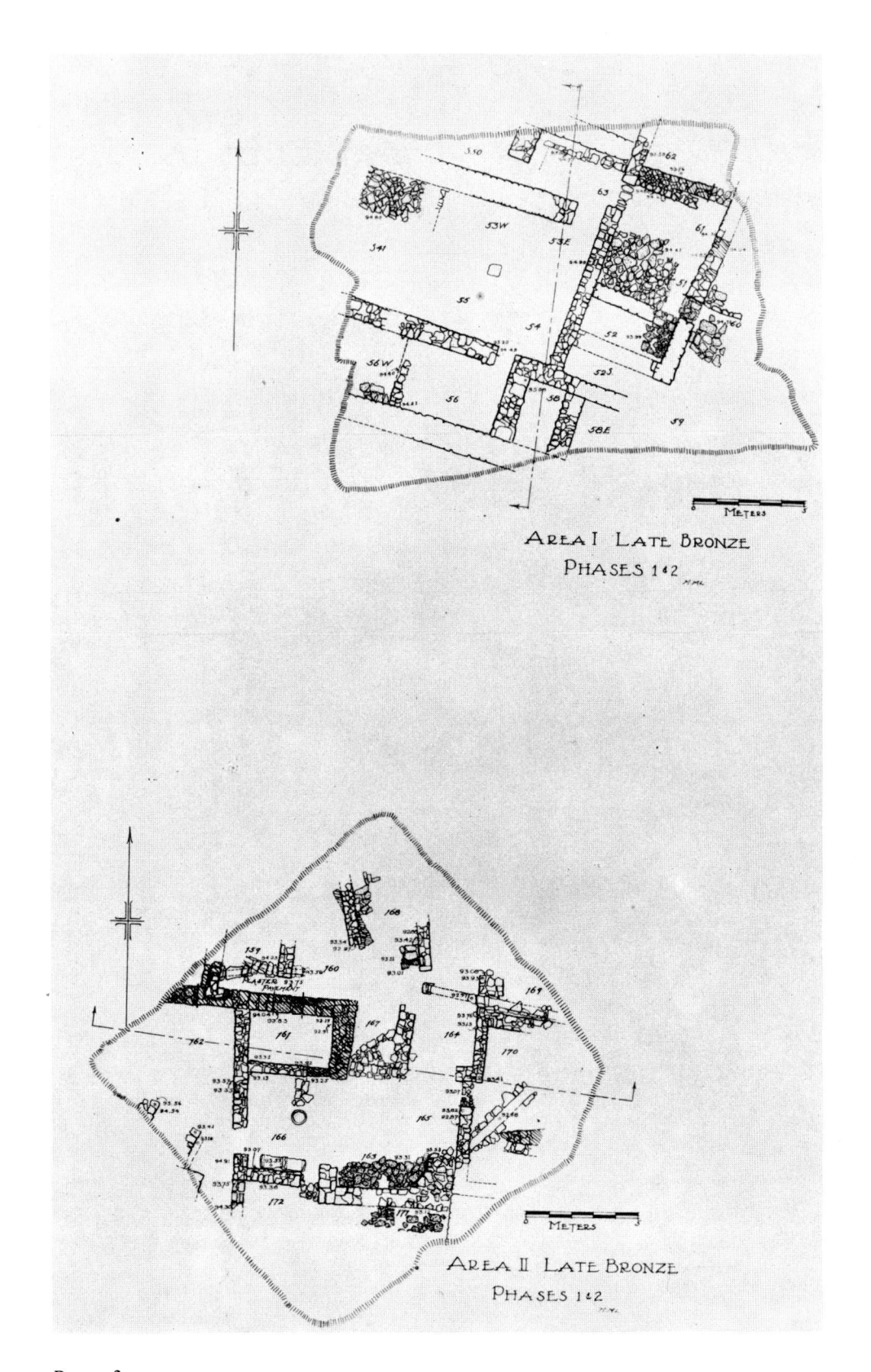

AREA II LATE BRONZE
PHASES 1 & 2

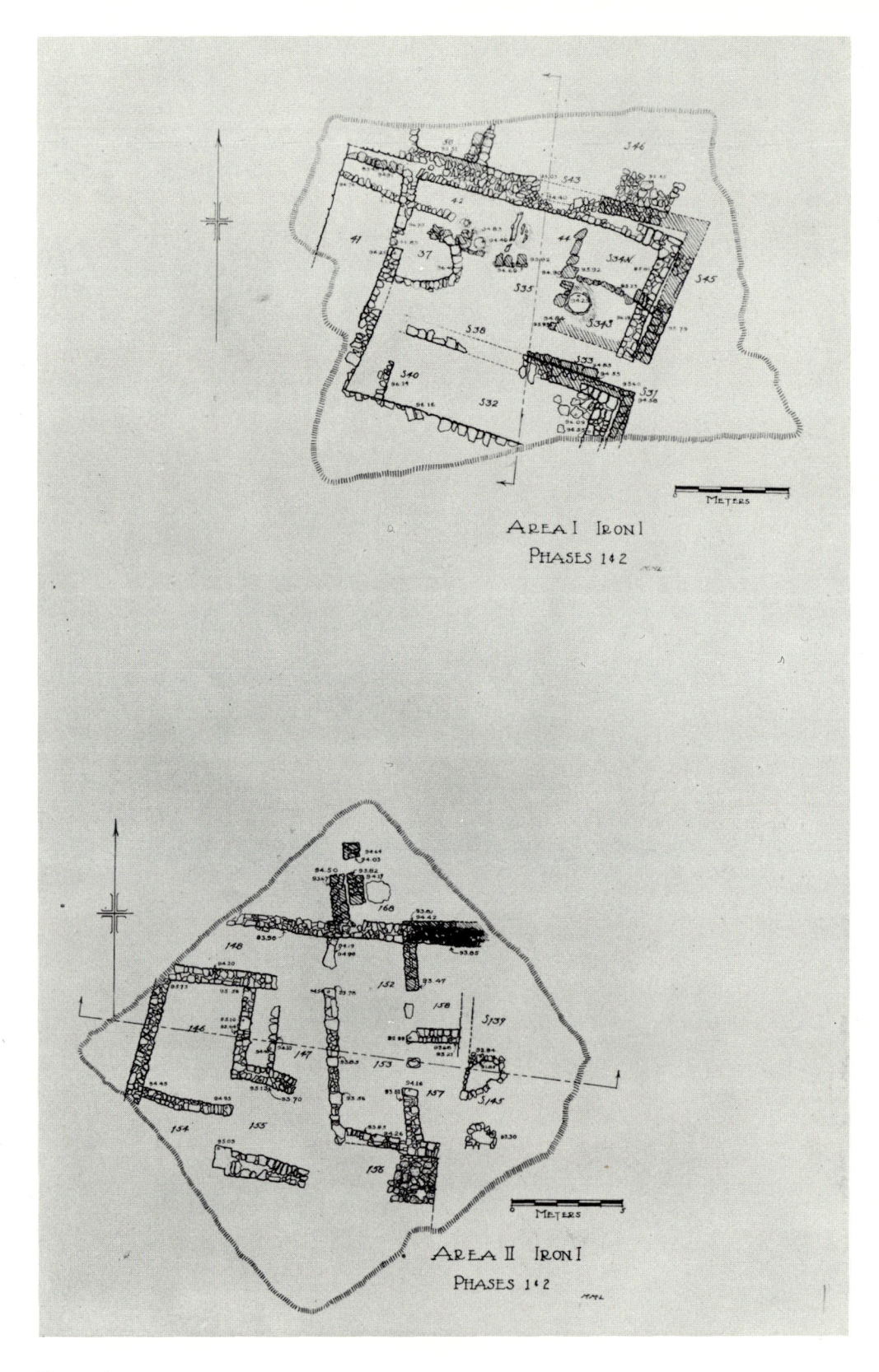

PLATE 4

AREA I IRON I
PHASES 3 & 4

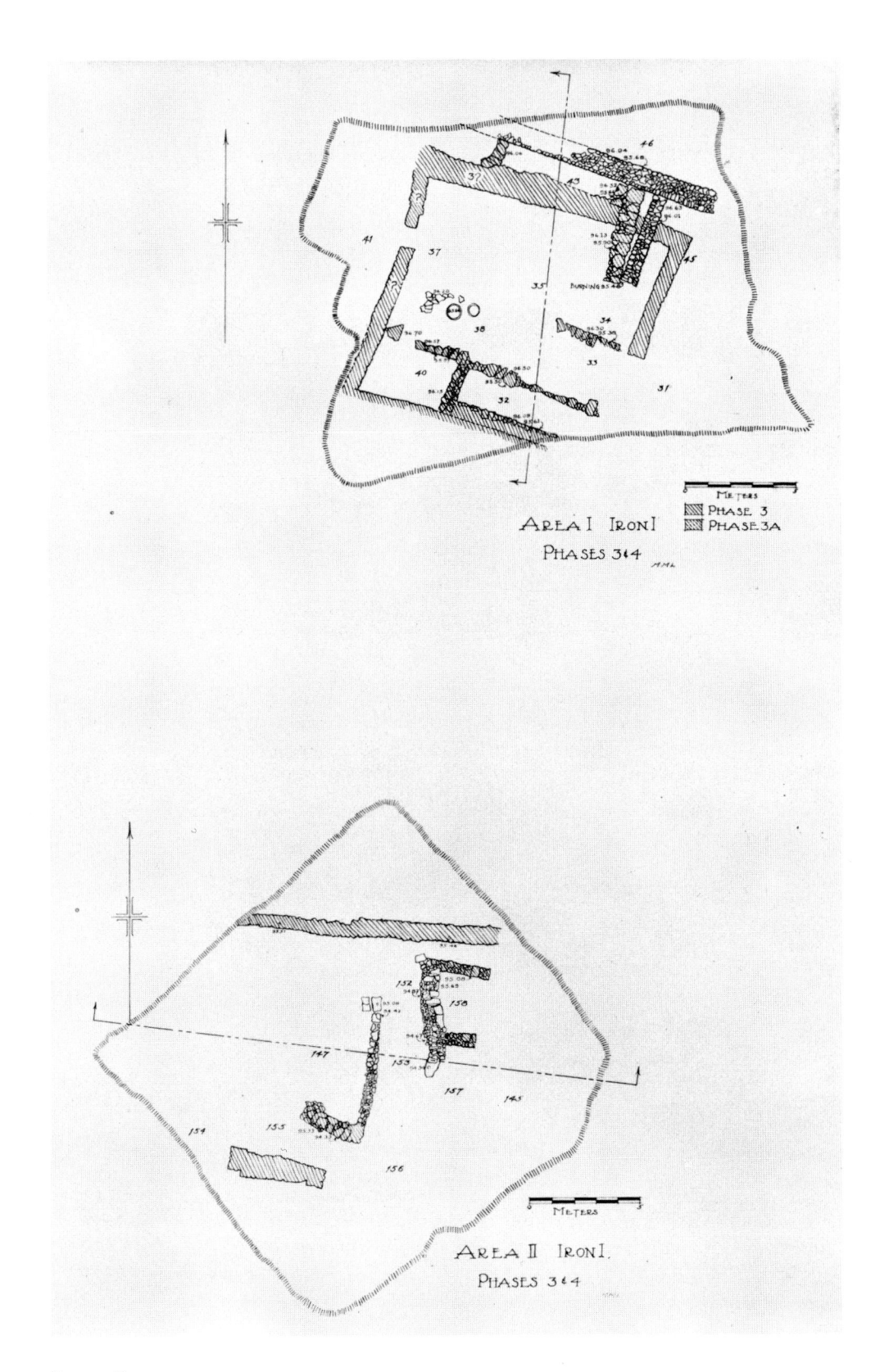

PHASE 3
PHASE 3A

AREA II IRON I
PHASES 3 & 4

PLATE 5

AREA I IRON II

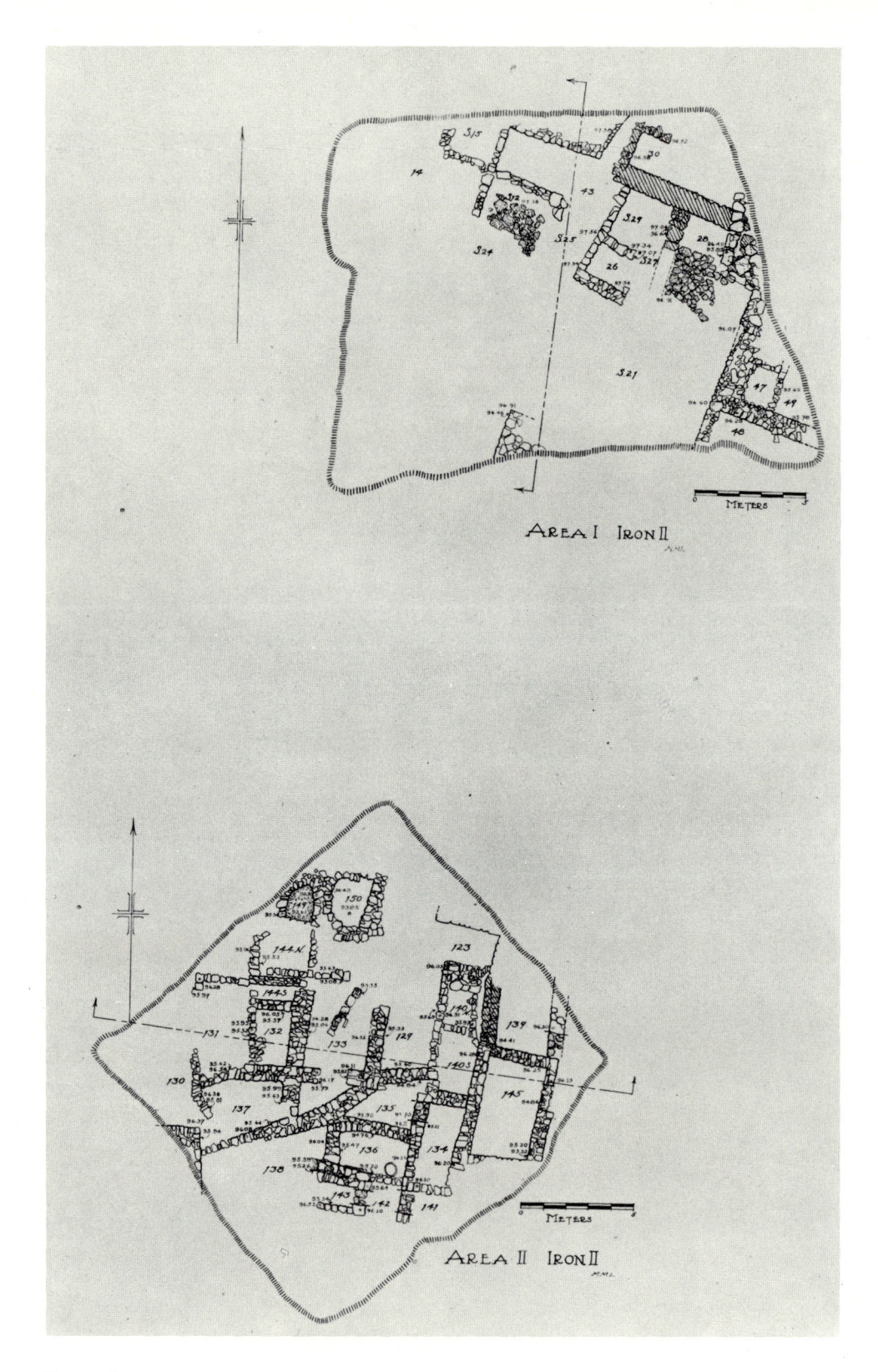

AREA II IRON II

PLATE 6

AREA I
PERSIAN & PHASE 1 OF HELLENISTIC

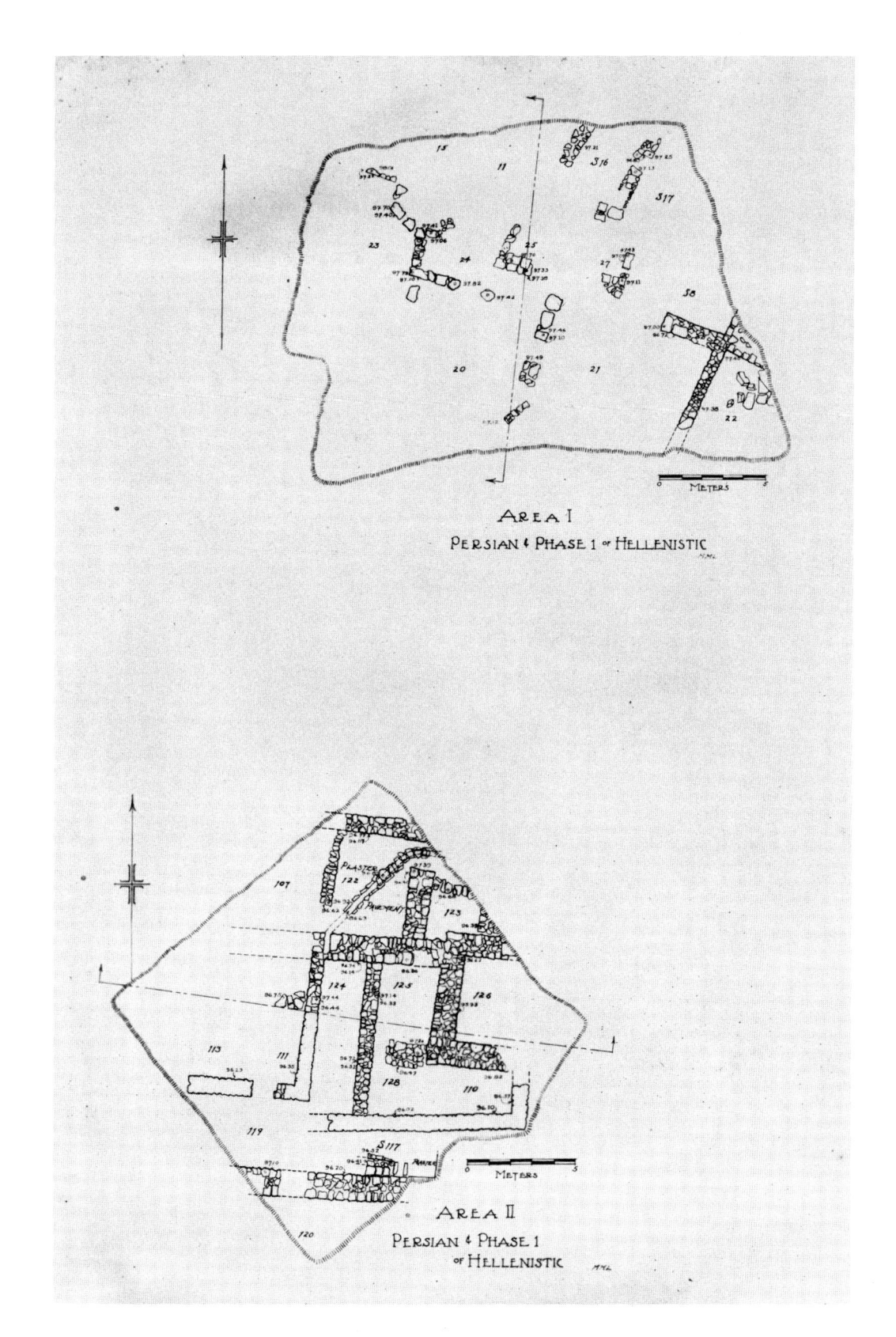

AREA II
PERSIAN & PHASE 1
OF HELLENISTIC

PLATE 7

AREA I
PHASES 2 & 3 OF HELLENISTIC

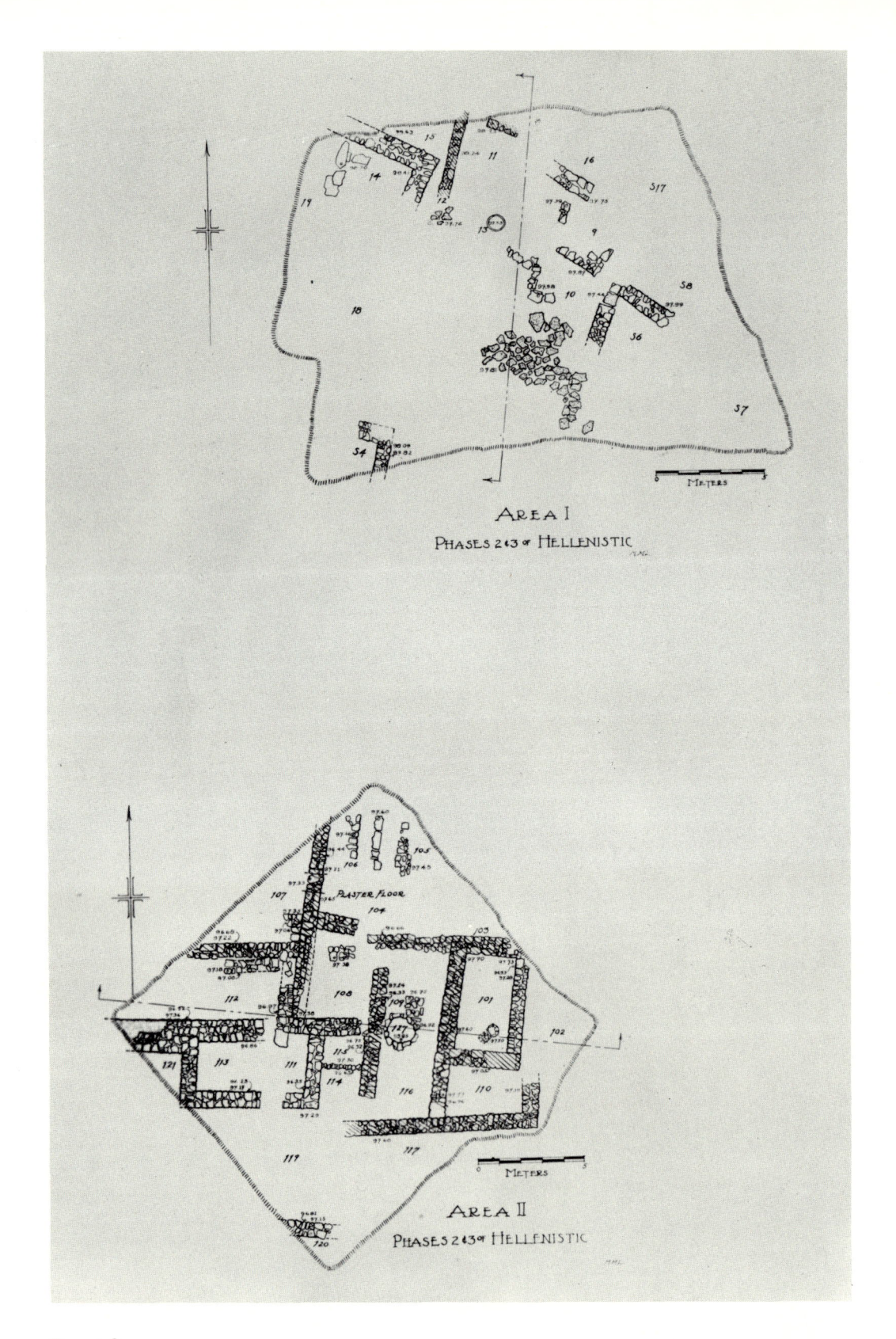

AREA II
PHASES 2 & 3 OF HELLENISTIC

PLATE 8

AREA I
ROMAN & BYZANTINE

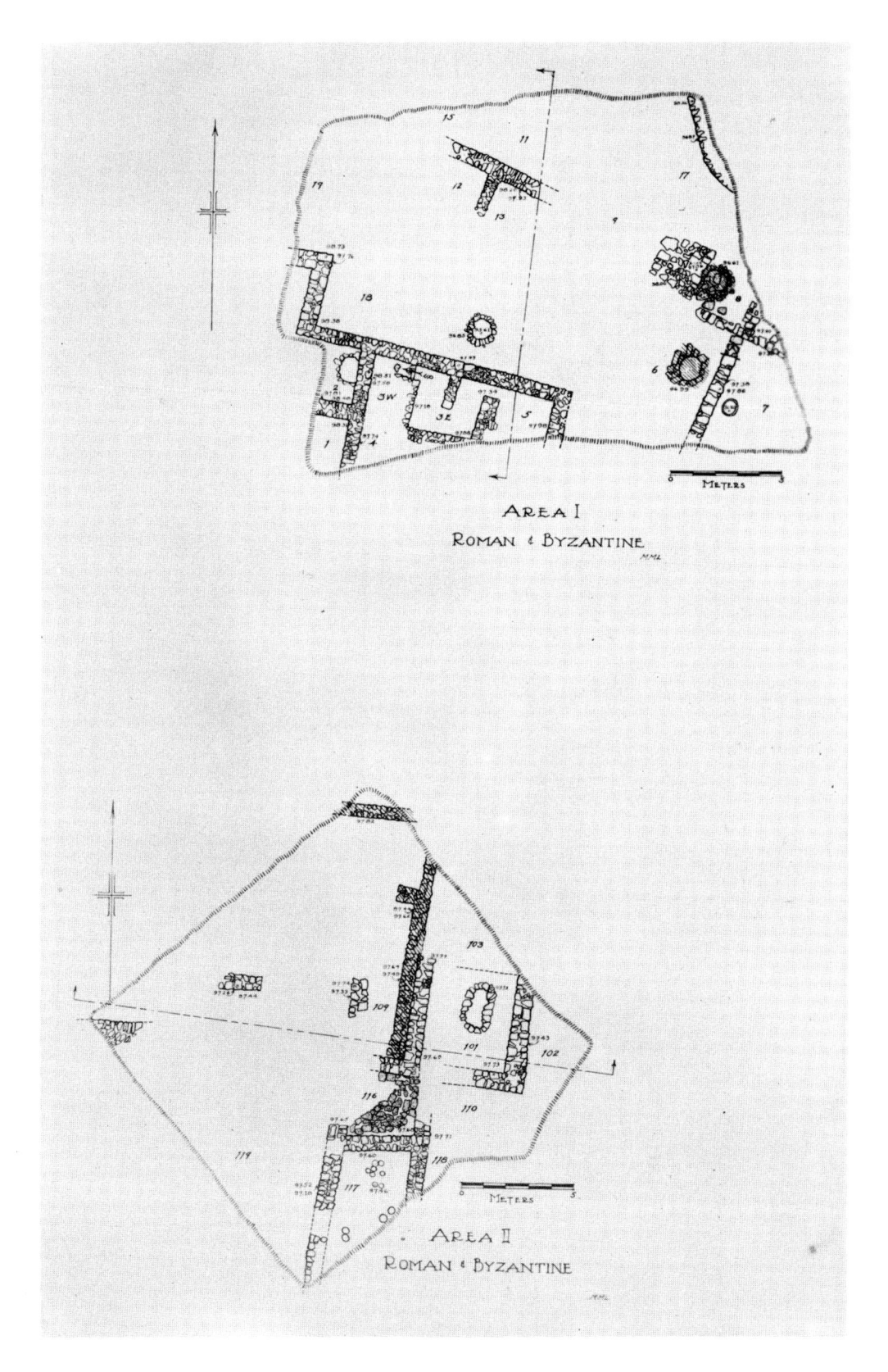

AREA II
ROMAN & BYZANTINE

PLATE 10

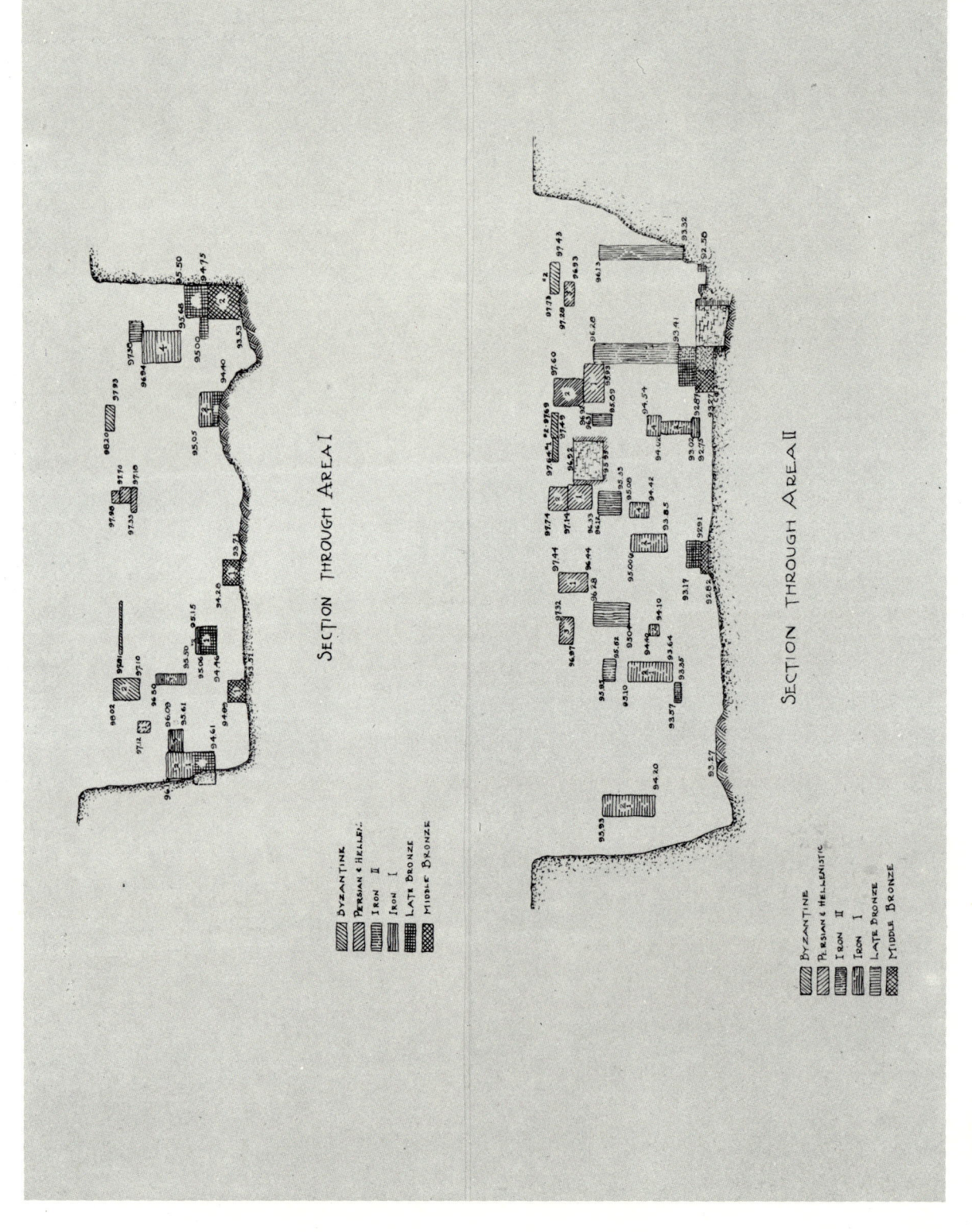

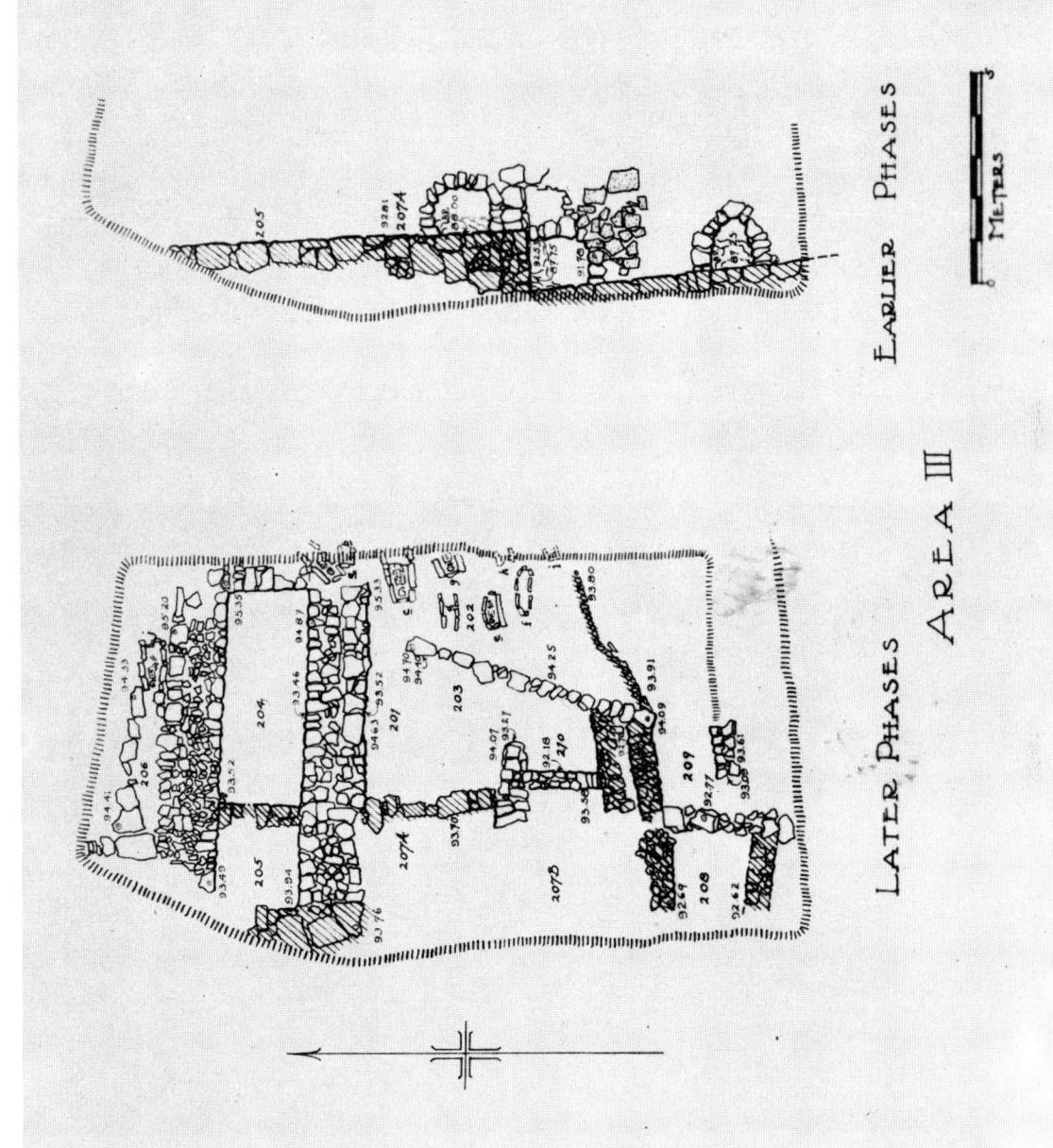

EARLIER PHASES

LATER PHASES   AREA III

PLATE 11

PLATE 12   a View of Beitîn village from the east.
b Iron II dye vat in a field east of area I.

PLATE 13
a Interior face of MB II B west city wall with Iron I silo in foreground. See plate 11 (earlier phase), 207A.
b Interior face of MB II B west city wall showing Iron I repairs, where stones stand on edge (to the left).

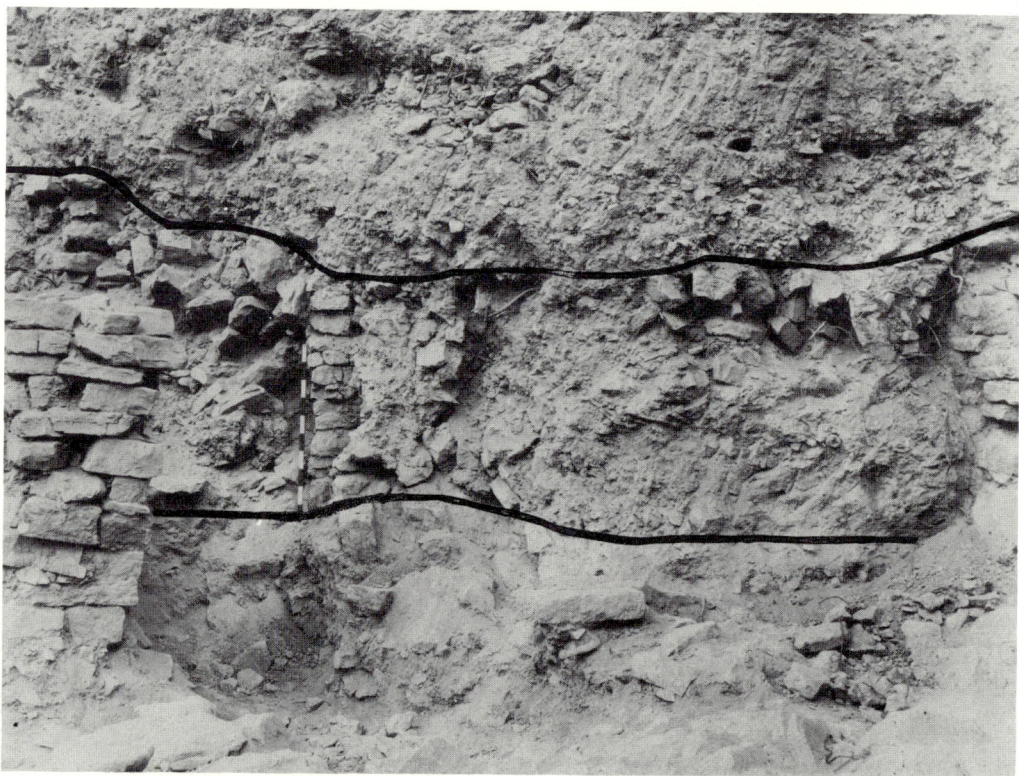

a Wall of LB II phase I destroyed by earthquake and left as it fell.
b Over a meter of ashes in destruction of LB II city (area II), shown between the wavy black lines.

a LB II walls of thin flat stones characteristic of that period. Under them with larger well-shaped stones are MB II walls. Note a drain in upper left.
b General view of area II. Higher walls are Iron I. Note pillar construction at extreme left. Lower walls are LB over MB II. Dark areas are bedrock or virgin soil.

PLATE 15

a General view of area II. LB II walls in foreground. Iron I and Iron II in background.
b LB II, area II. Stone pavements in left center. Stone table near the center of right edge. Walls in background are Iron I, Iron II, and Hellenistic.

PLATE 16

PLATE 17   Superimposed LB II flag stone pavements in L 165.

PLATE 18   a Excellent LB II dressed stone drain in L 169.
          b Blocked doorway in north wall of L 161, phase 2 of LB II.

a   Ḥúwar floor (upper right) above two stone drains crossing one another in X pattern.
b   Double stone drain under ḥúwar floor in L 160.

a LB II stone pavement, phase I, and house walls L 52.
b To the right is an Iron II tower with quoin construction cutting through earlier levels and resting on bedrock. To the left is an excellent LB II house wall and doorsill. (Upper course of outer face missing.)

a Iron I, area I, general view looking west. Pier constructions of large irregular-shaped stones at the left are 3rd phase of Iron I.

b Enlargement of lower left corner of 21 a. Lowest wall is LB II, phase 1. Other walls are Iron I, phase 1.

a Large massive walls in center belong to a patrician house in LB II. Meter stick is above doorway leading from central courtyard to L 56 (Plate 3, area 1). Iron I, phase 3, pier construction is seen above LB II house wall.

b Shows various types of piers used in Iron I walls. At upper left note pier technique used for a door jamb. The normal Palestine walls in photo are Iron I, phases 1 and 2.

a General view of area I looking northeast with typical variety of Iron I house walls.
b Best type of Iron I wall, L 146.

a   Clearing away phase 1 of Iron I before digging up LB II level.
b   LB II burning at bottom of photo.   Phase I of Iron I burning at top of meter stick.   Phase 2 burning near center of right edge.

PLATE 24

a All four phases of Iron I are represented in this photo, see 1 & 2, 3, 4. Walls of tallest house in background were begun in Iron I and remained in use until the destruction of the city in sixth century B.C.

b Various types of Iron I construction, including collapsed wall, are phases 1 and 2.

a Wall to the left with quoin construction is Iron II laid on three courses of LB II. This
   LB II masonry continues in the center. Wall to the right is Iron I.
b Two LB II walls abut on one another just left of the meter stick. L 165 with pavement was
   used in phases 1 and 2. L 171 is probably phase 2. Upper walls above L 165 are Iron II.

a   Iron II walls in area II looking north.
b   Iron II south wall of L 145. Wall behind meter stick is ninth century B.C. The wall above that was still used in sixth century B.C.

a Broken store jars and pottery loom weights found *in situ* in Iron II house L 29.
b Area I looking south. These structures made with stones taken from the old city wall may be sheep folds from the Persian period.

PLATE 28

PLATE 29 a Area II looking southeast. Hellenistic walls (all three phases). A perfectly preserved coin of Alexander the Great was found under the drain in the foreground.
b Area II looking north. Hellenistic walls are phases 2 and 3.

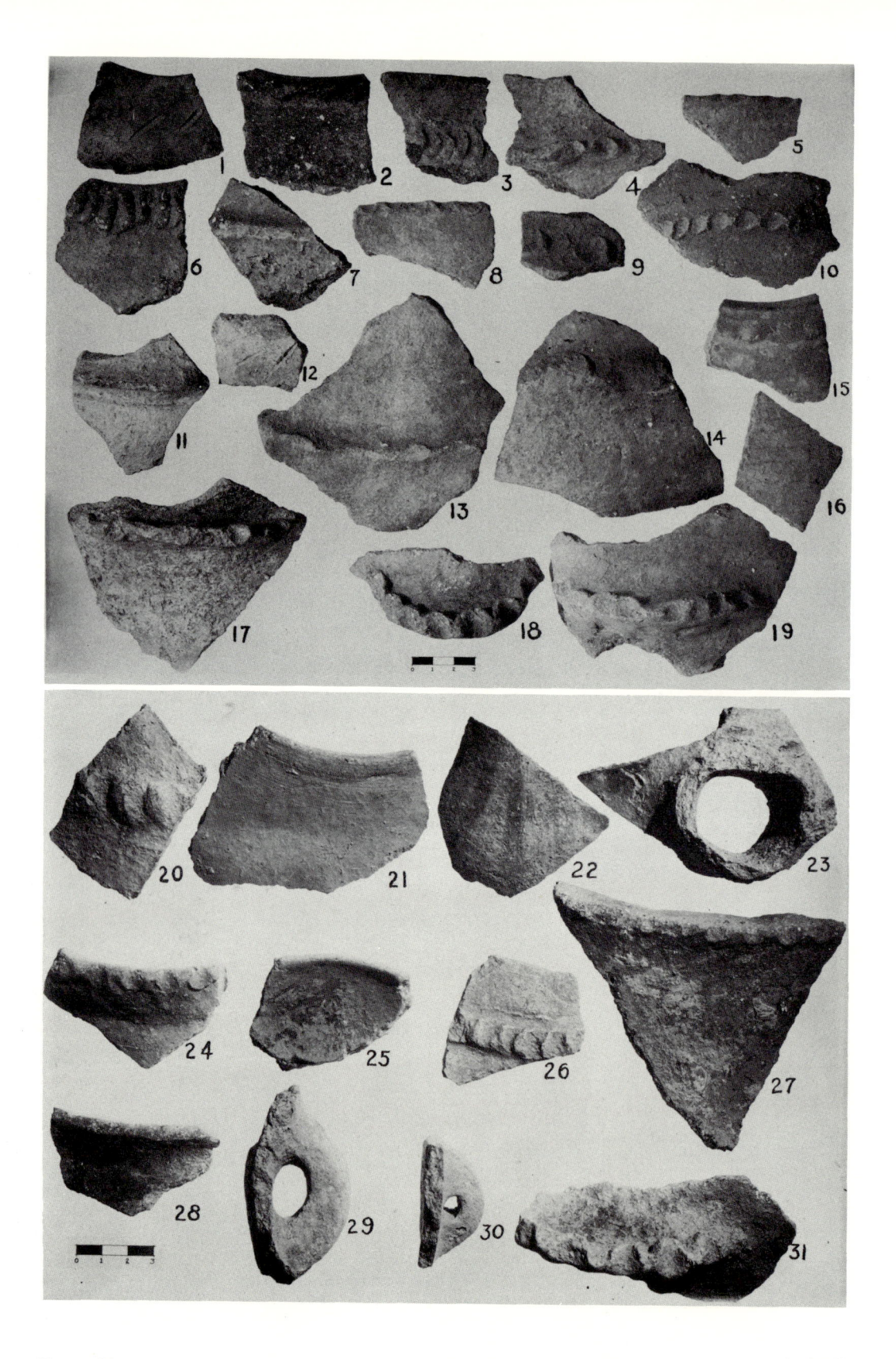

PLATE 30   Late Chalcolithic sherds.

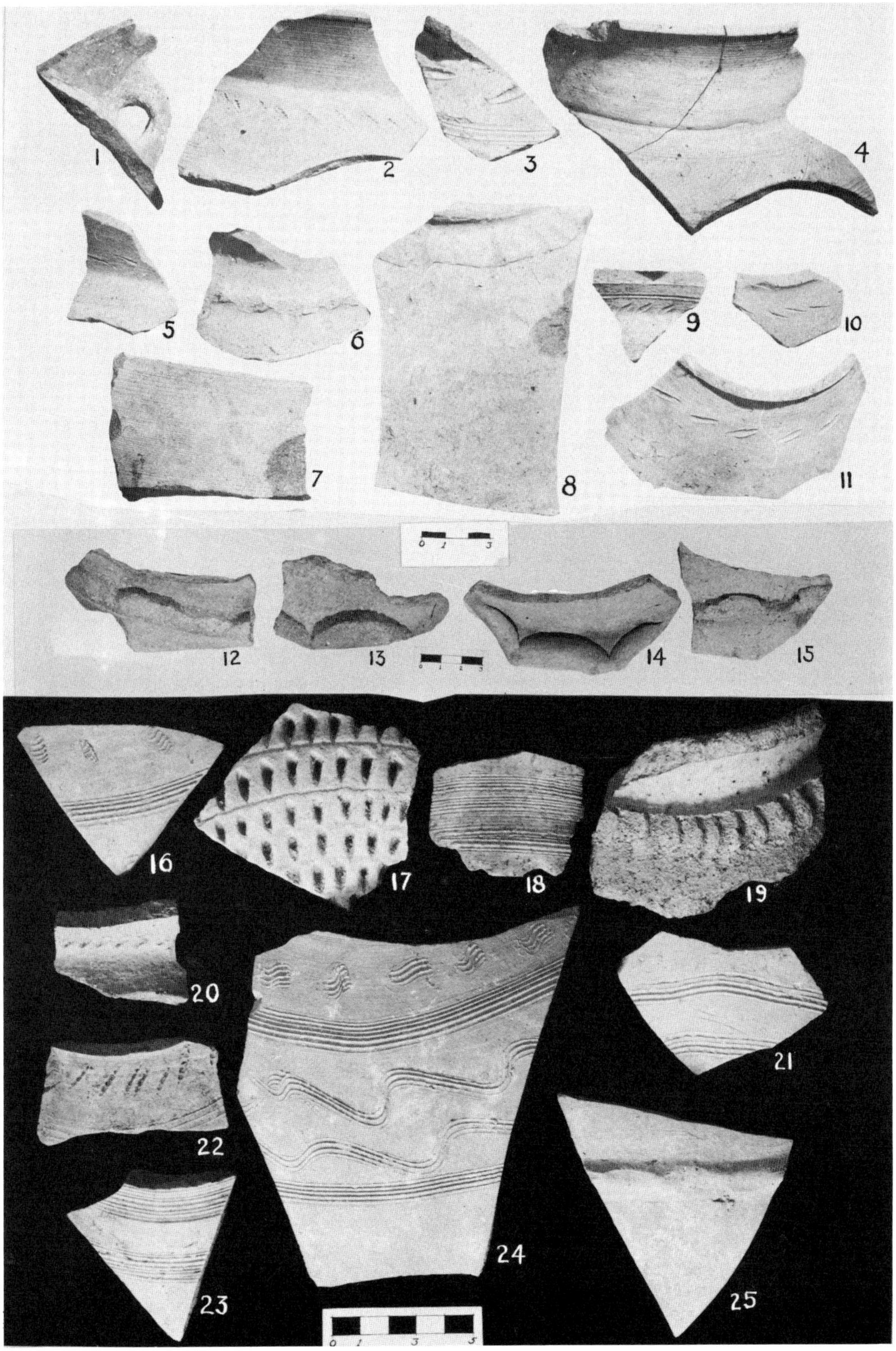

PLATE 31   Middle Bronze I sherds.

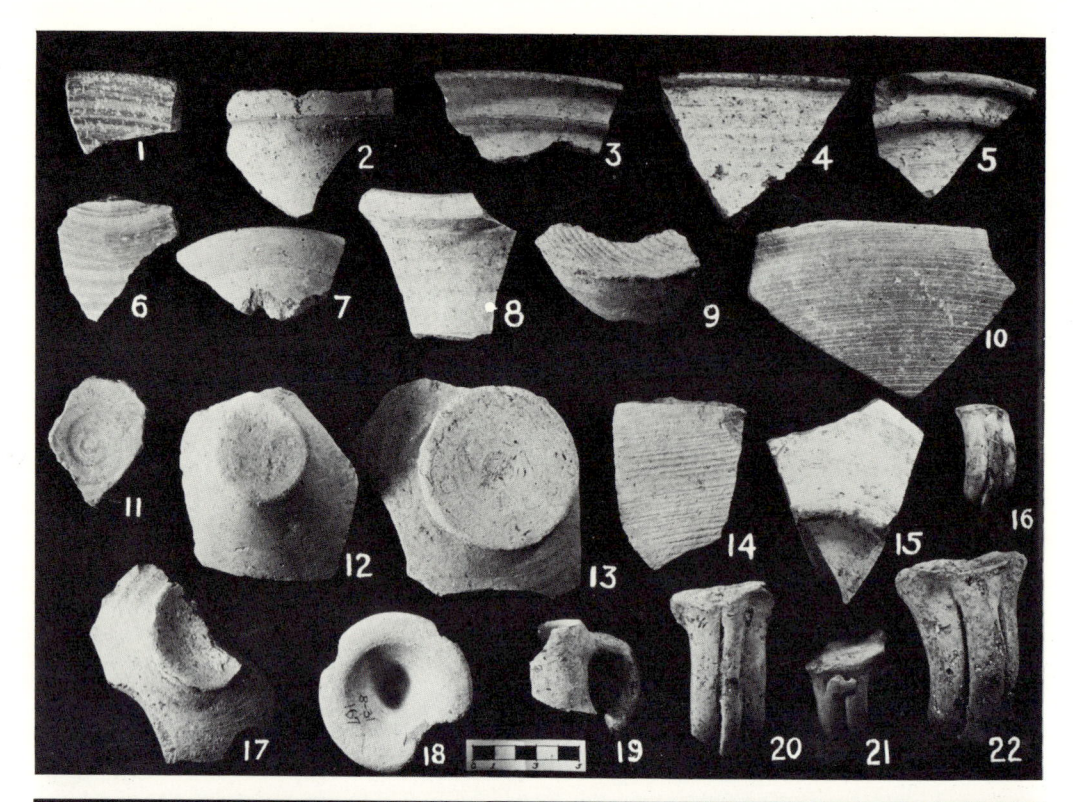

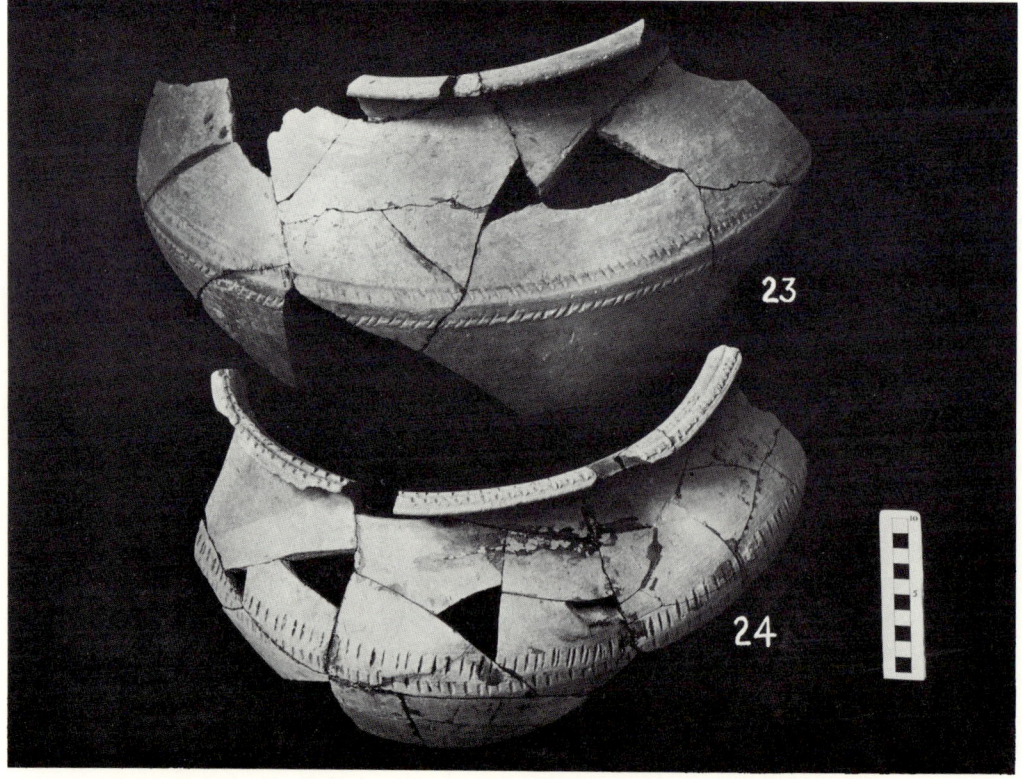

PLATE 32 Middle Bronze II sherds and vessels.

PLATE 33   Middle Bronze II sherds.

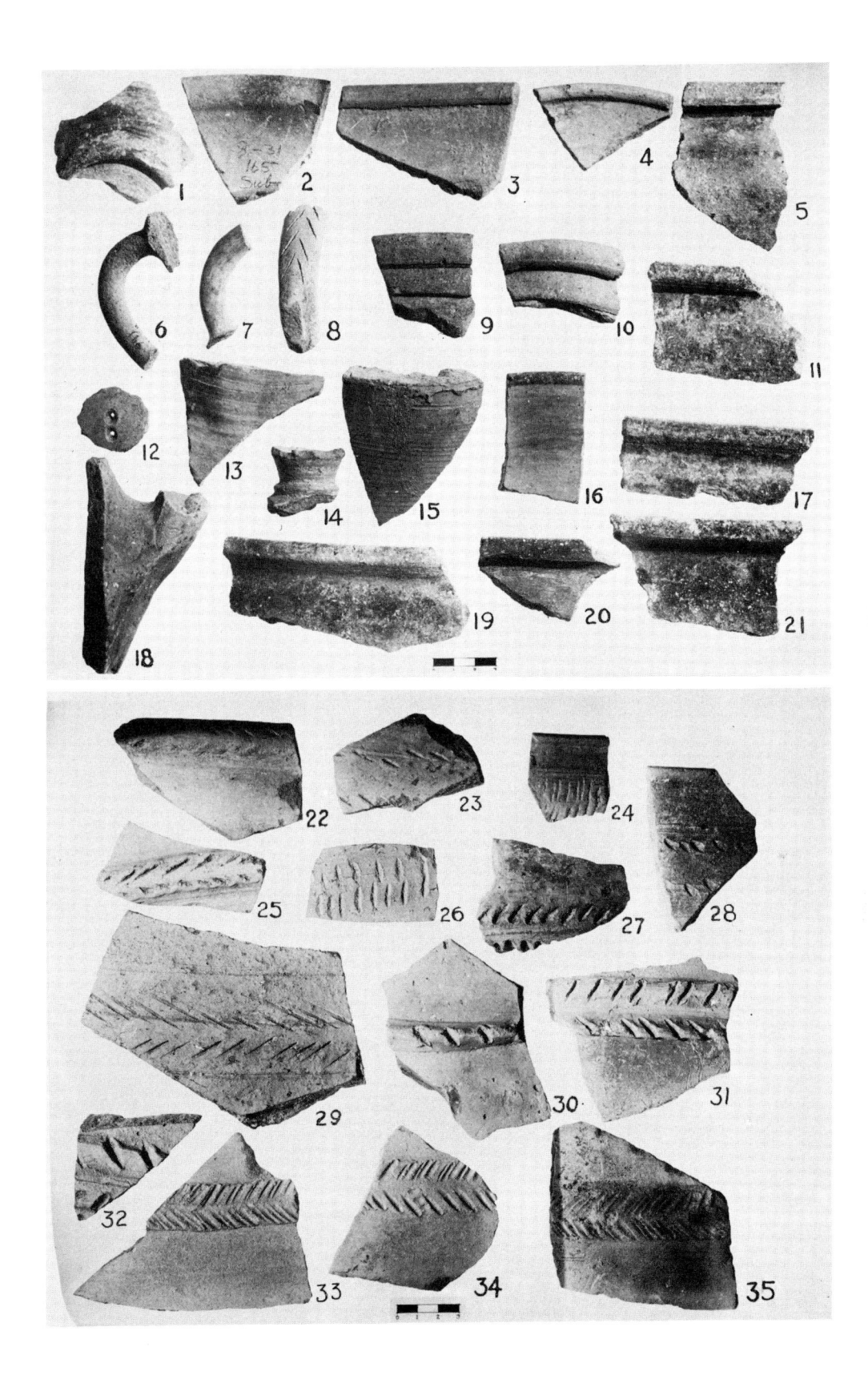

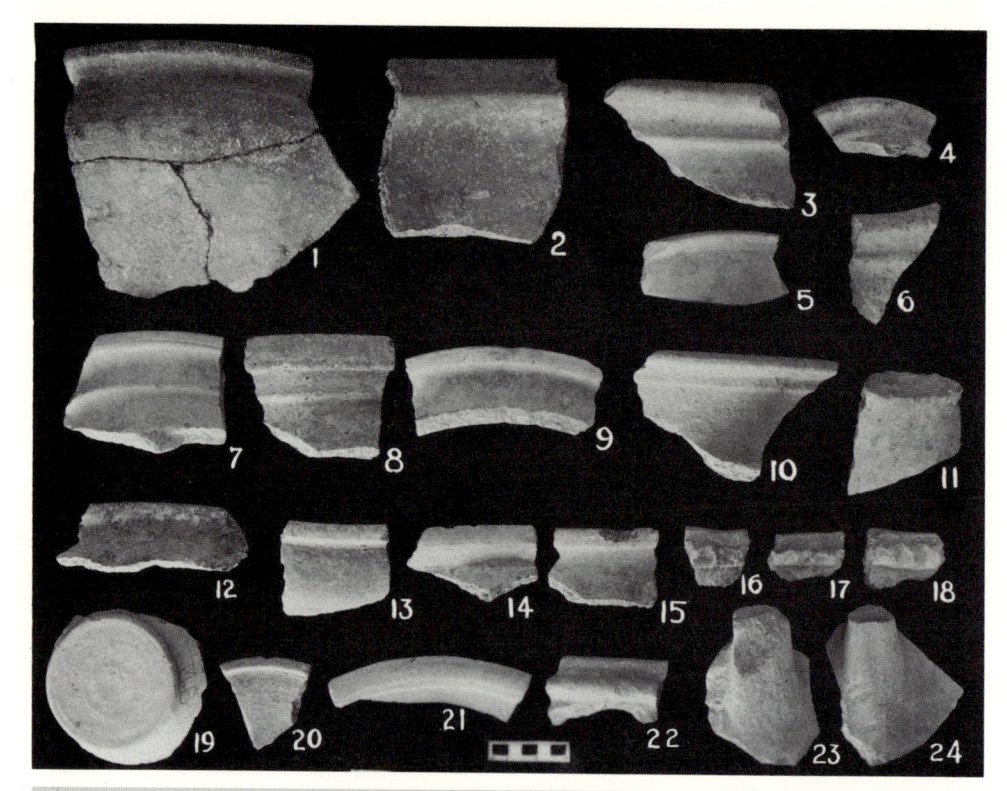

PLATE 34   Middle Bronze II sherds.

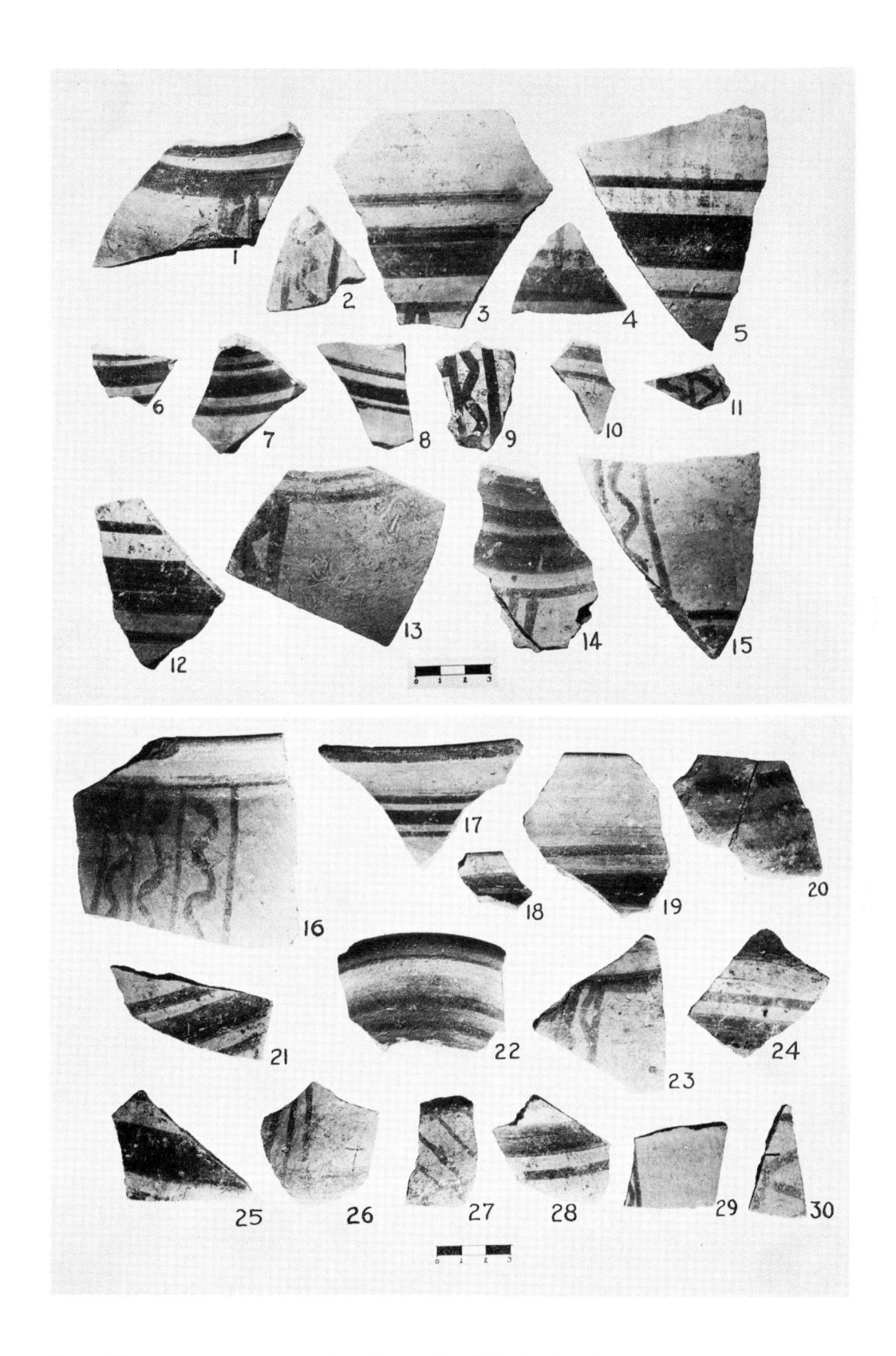

PLATE 35   Late Bronze painted sherds, phase 1.

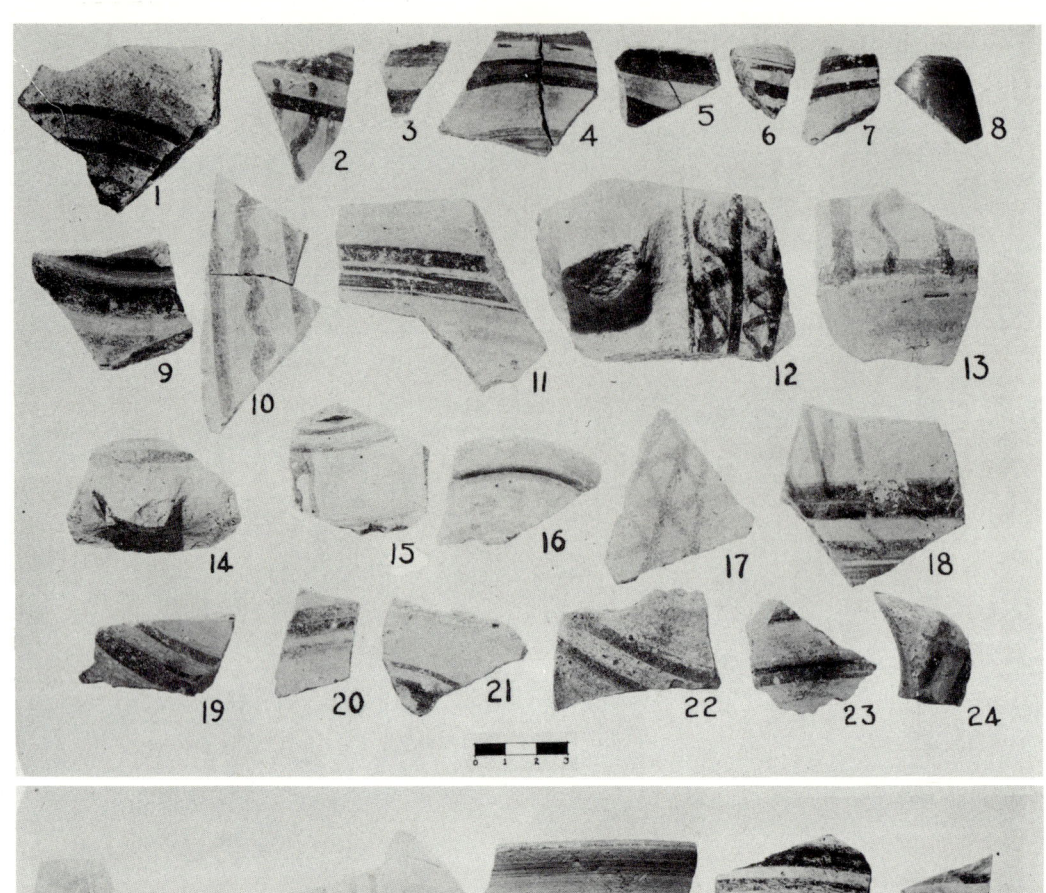

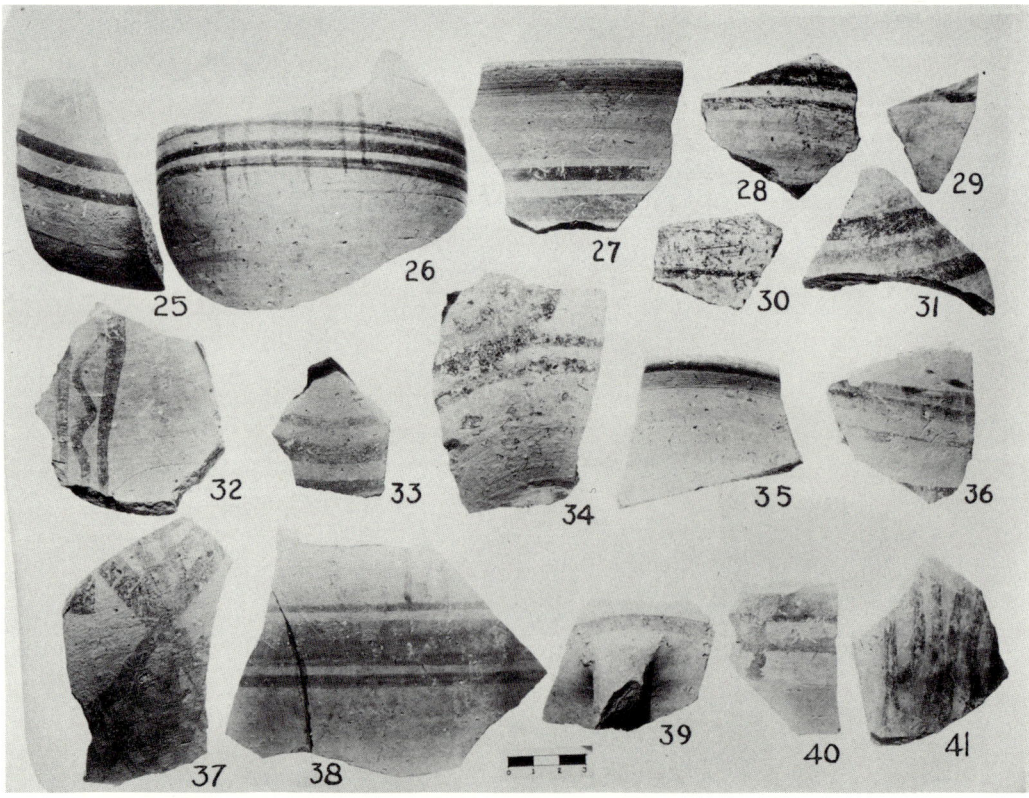

PLATE 36   Late Bronze painted sherds.

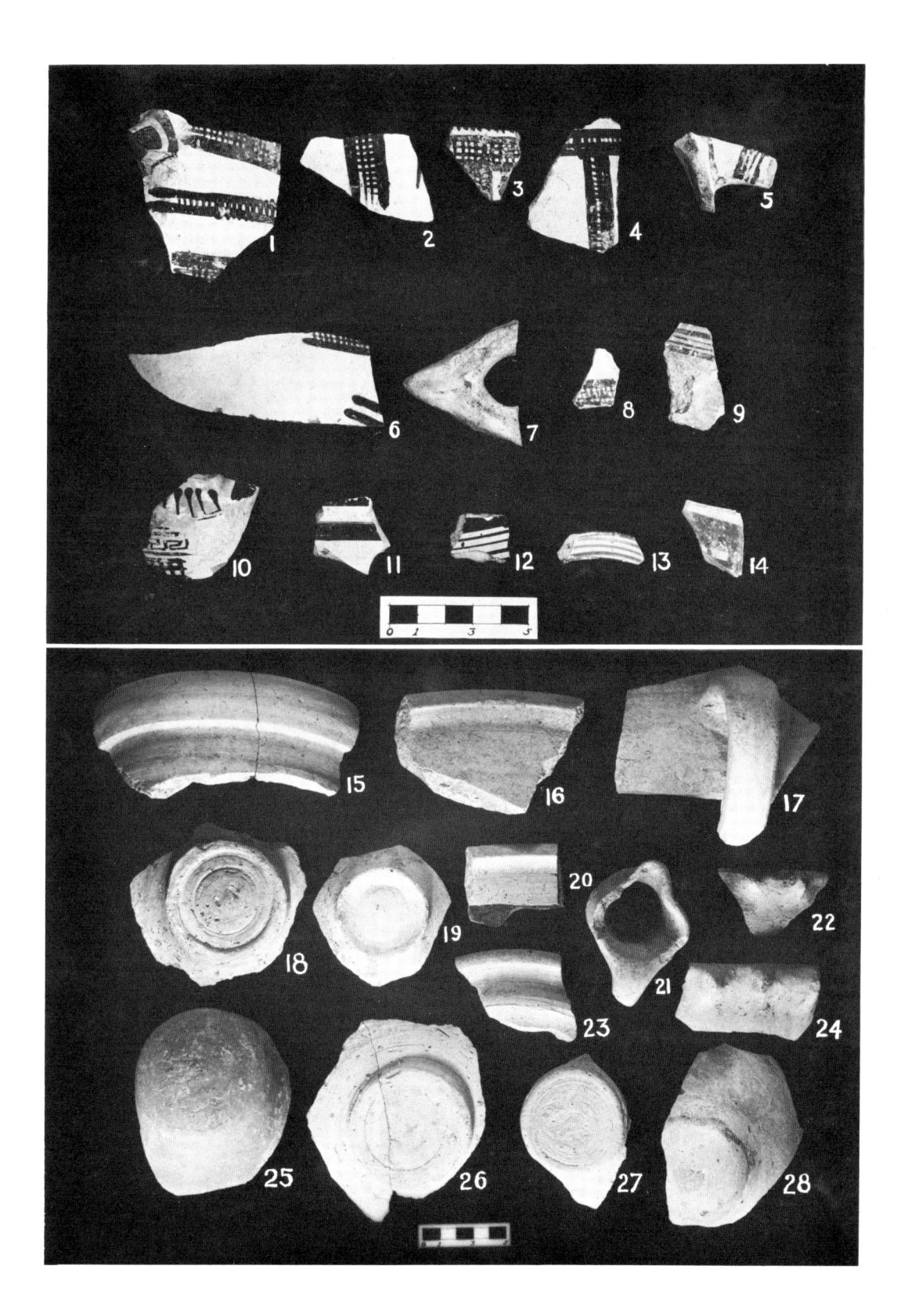

PLATE 37   a Late Bronze sherds of imported ware.
                b Late Bronze sherds.

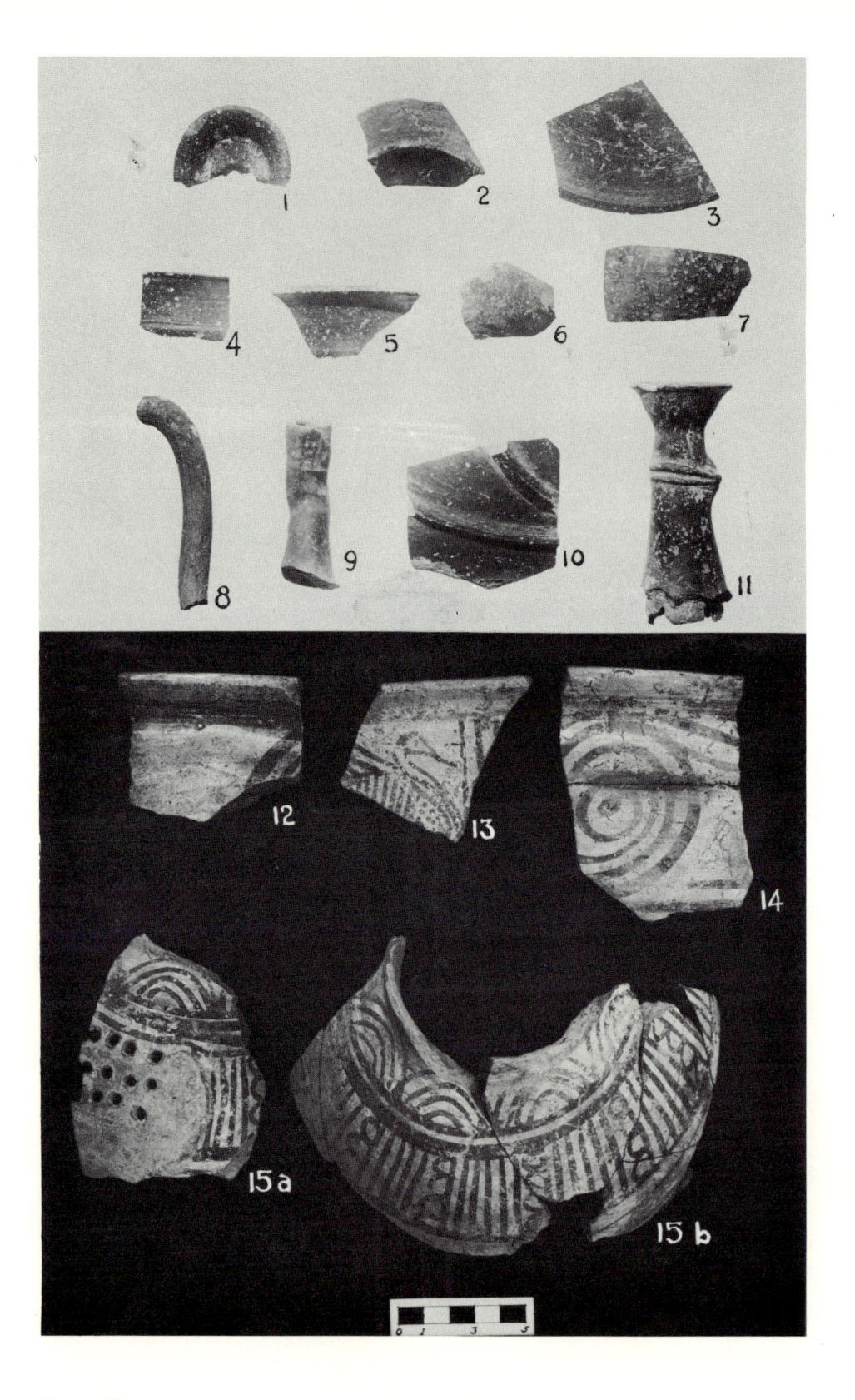

PLATE 38   a   Base-ring sherds.
          b   Philistine sherds.

PLATE 39   Iron I painted sherds.

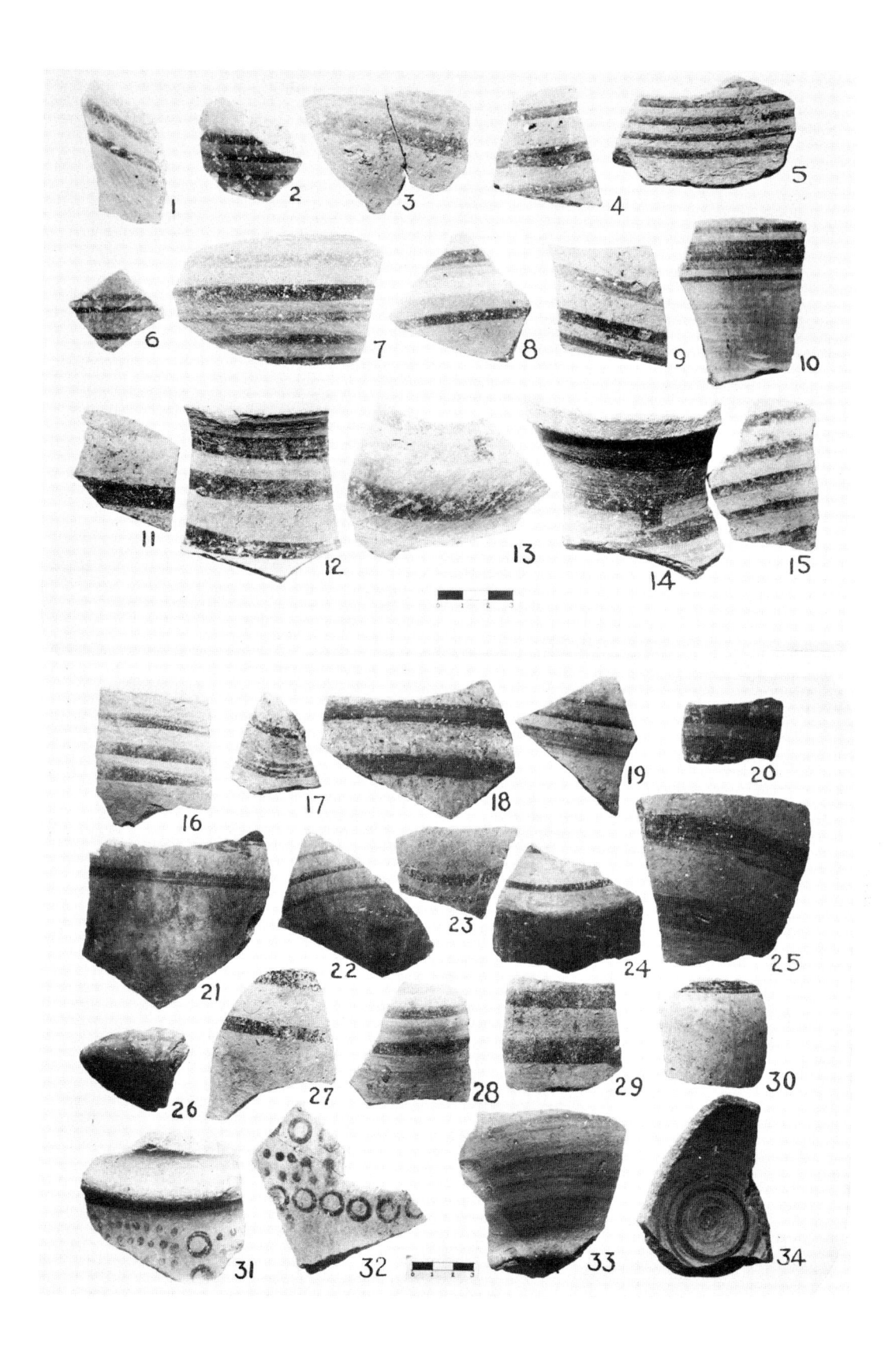

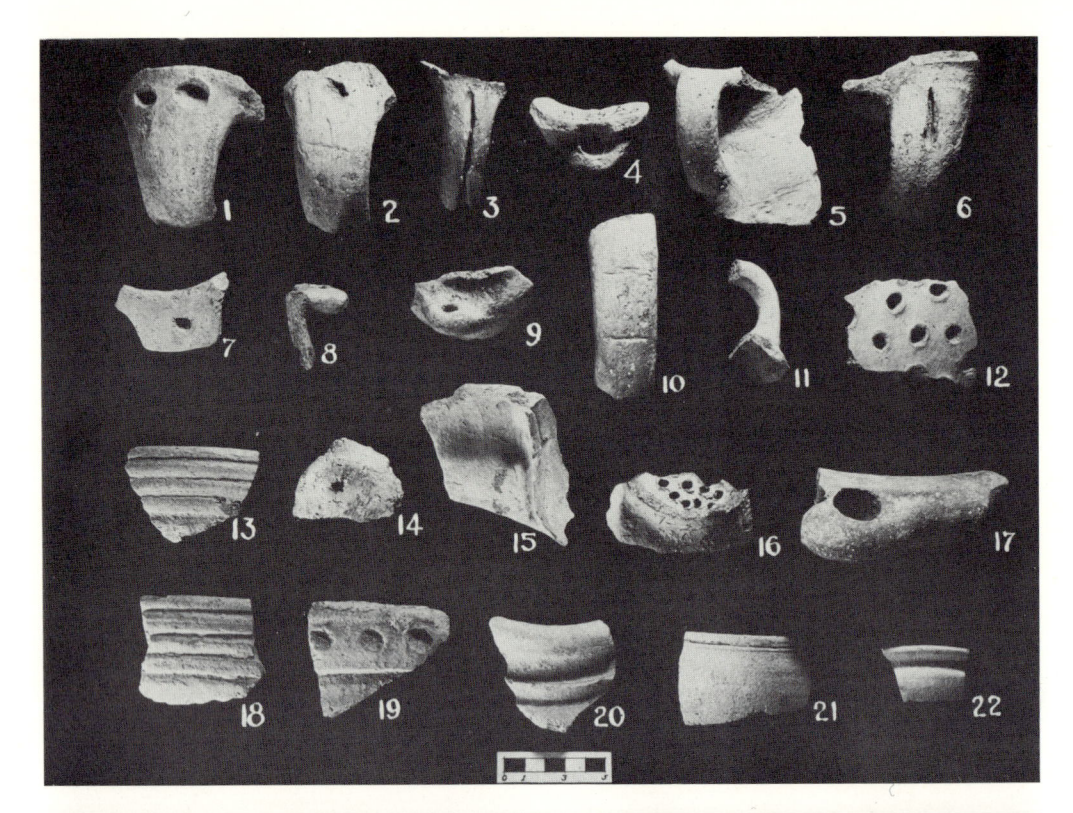

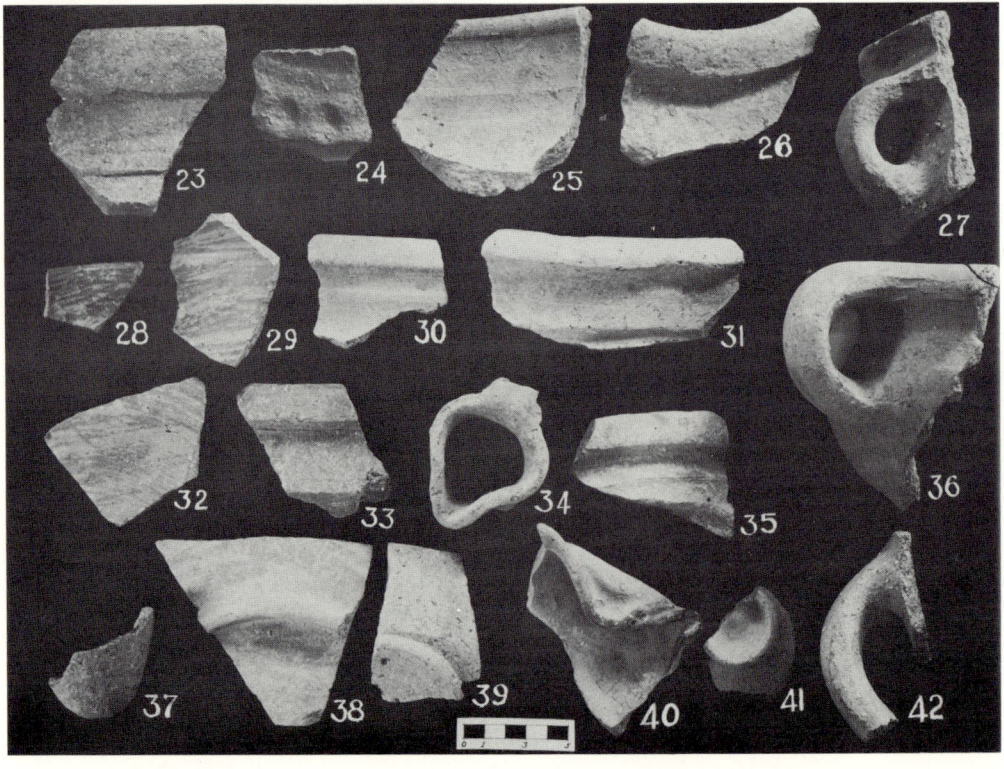

PLATE 40   Iron I sherds.

PLATE 41   Iron II sherds.

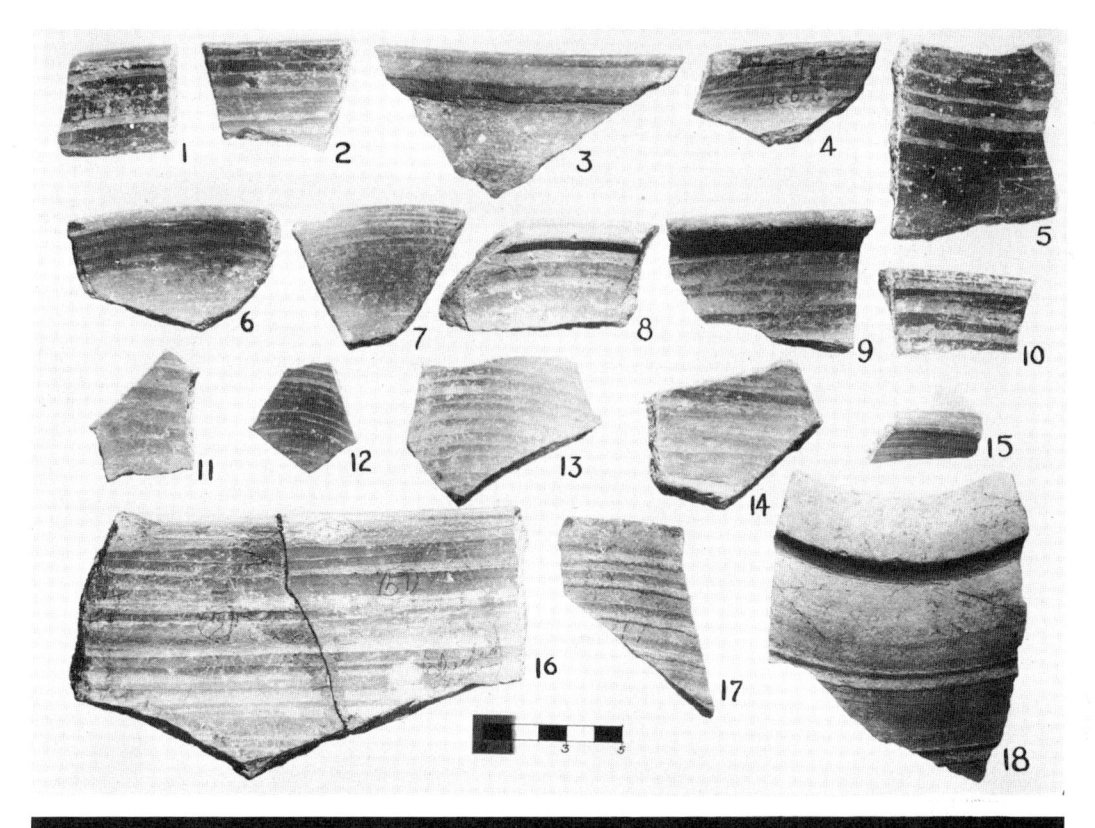

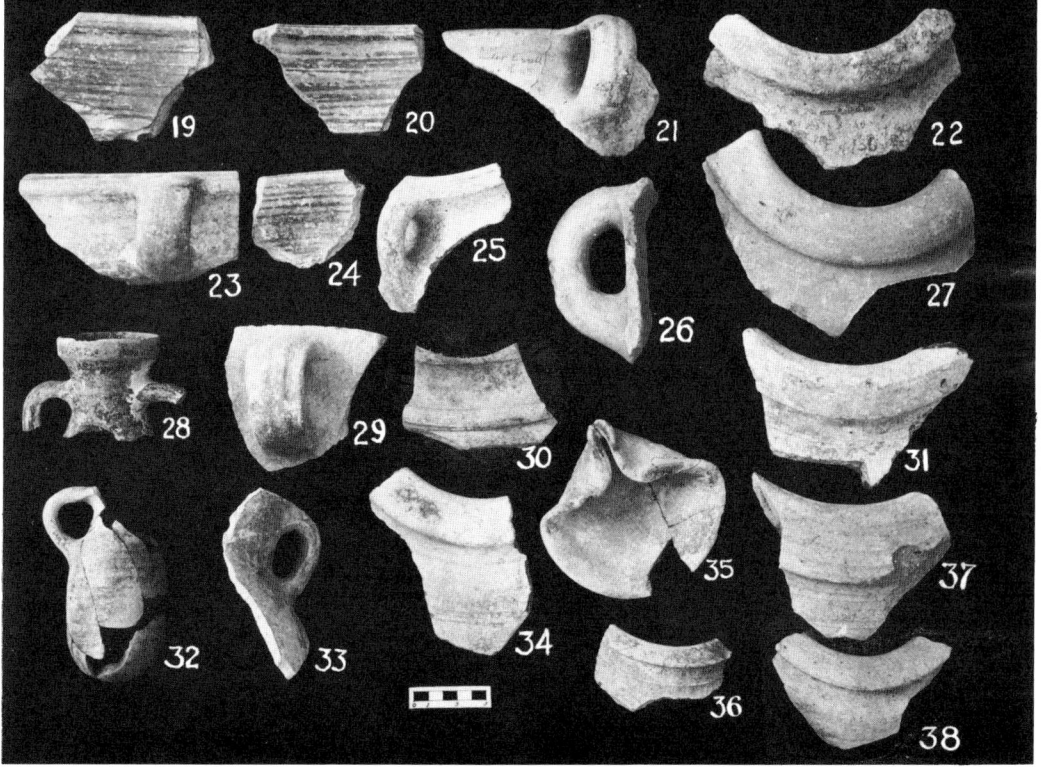

PLATE 42   Hathor sistrum handle.

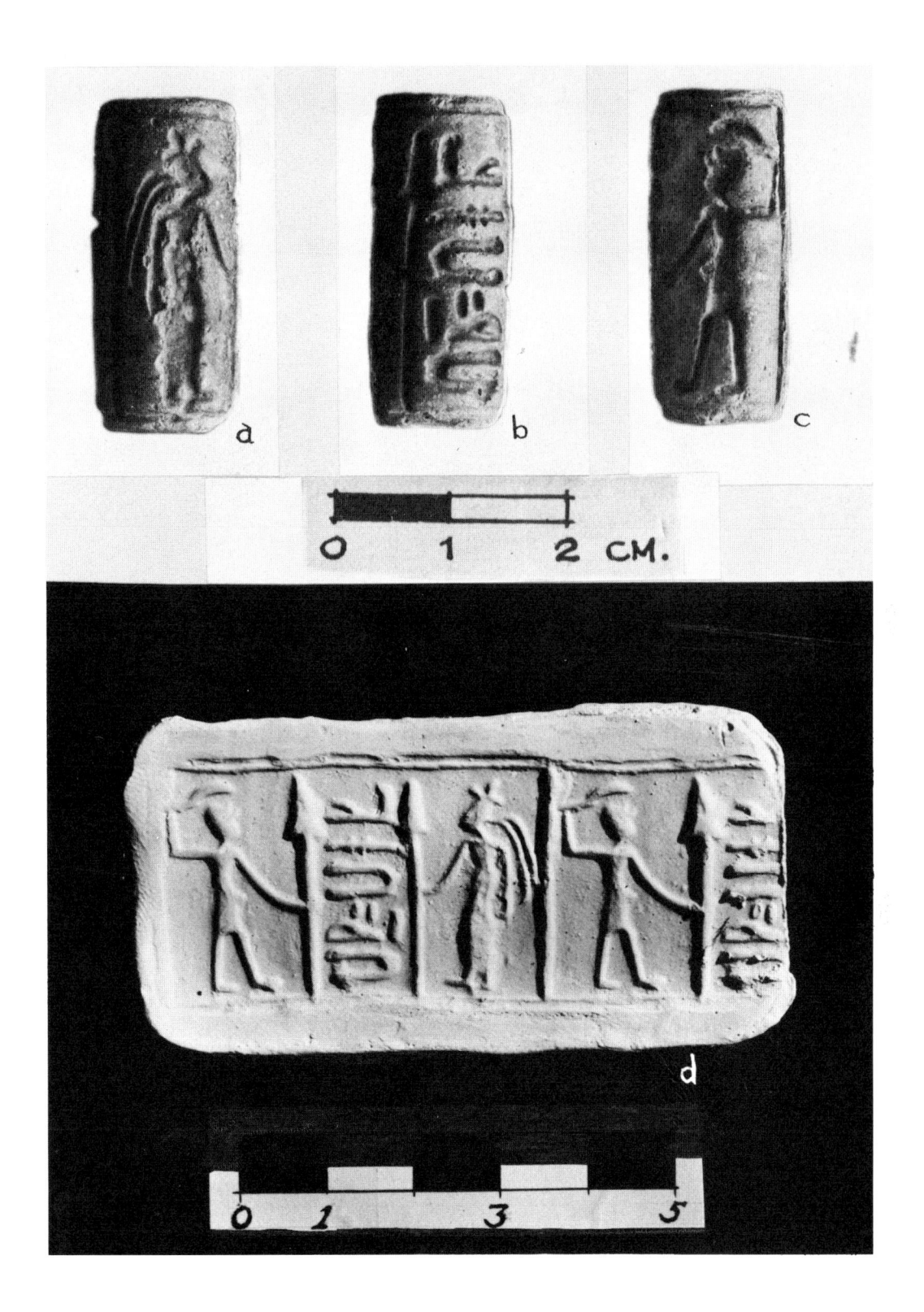

PLATE 43   Astarte seal cylinder.

PLATE 44   a Scarabs, scaraboid, seal, and weight.
          b Jar handle, human head.

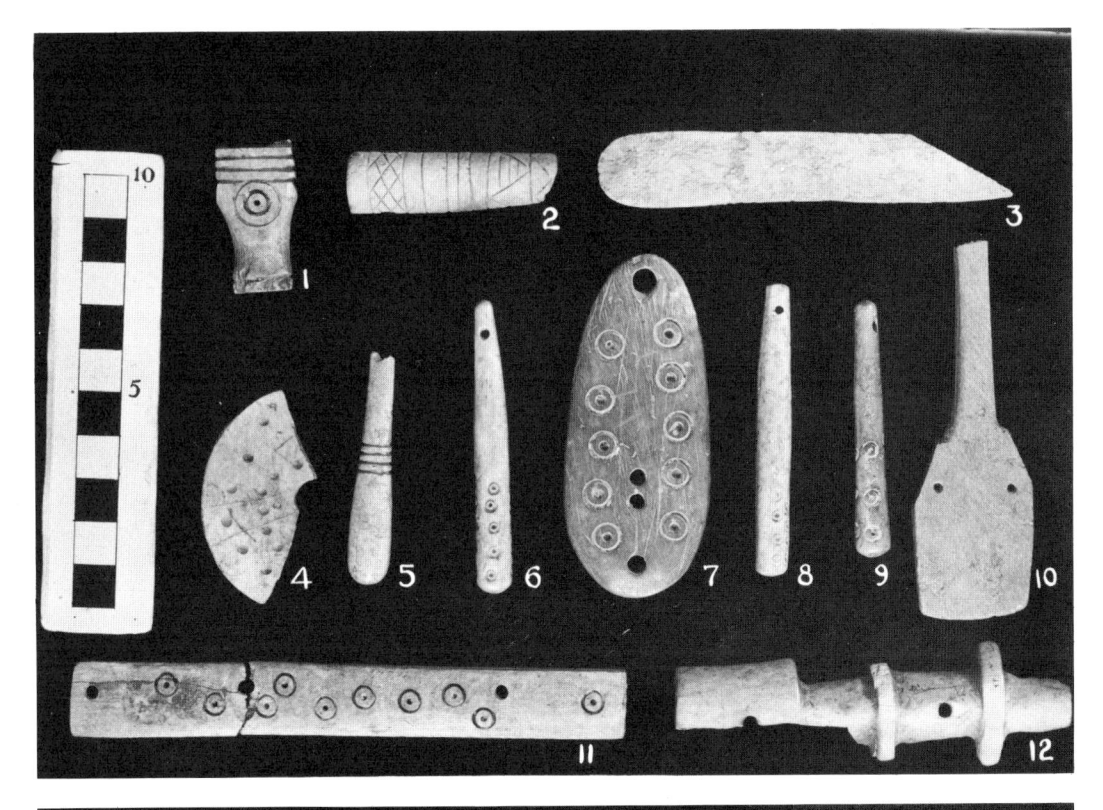

PLATE 45   Miscellaneous objects, bone, pottery, and stone.

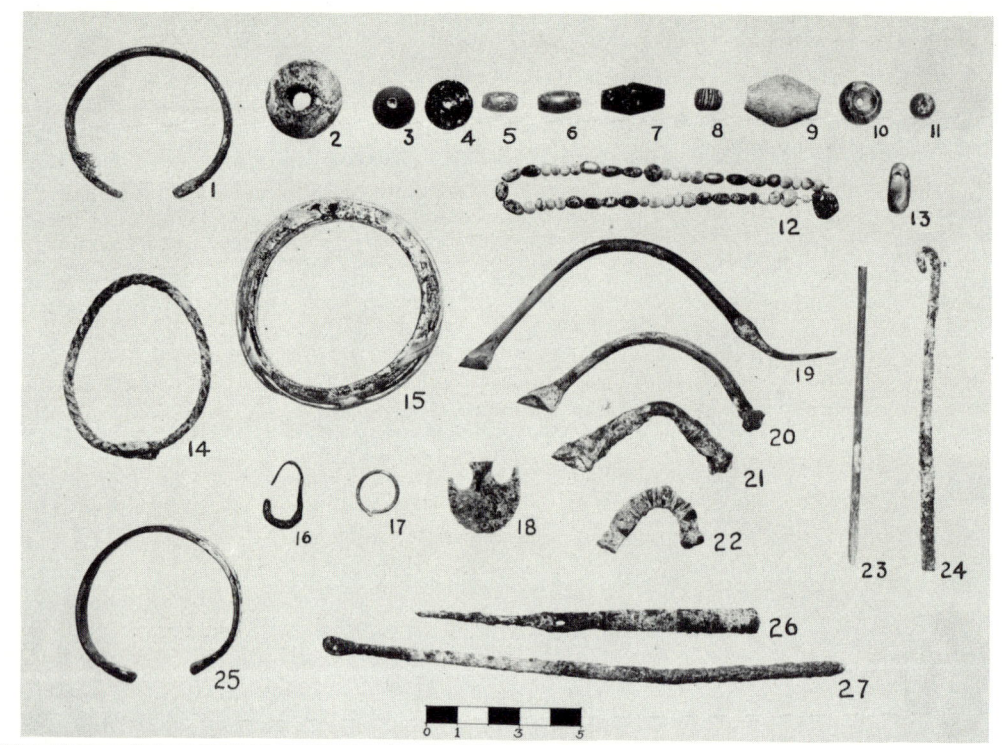

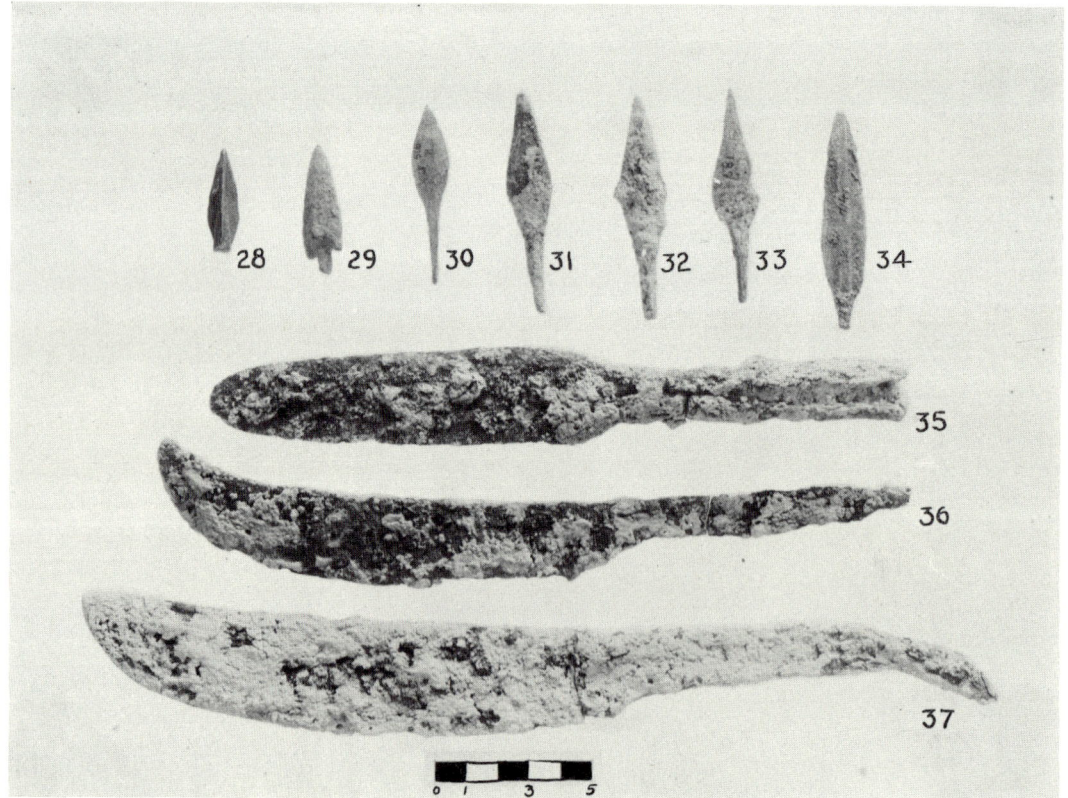

PLATE 46   Miscellaneous objects, beads, and metals.

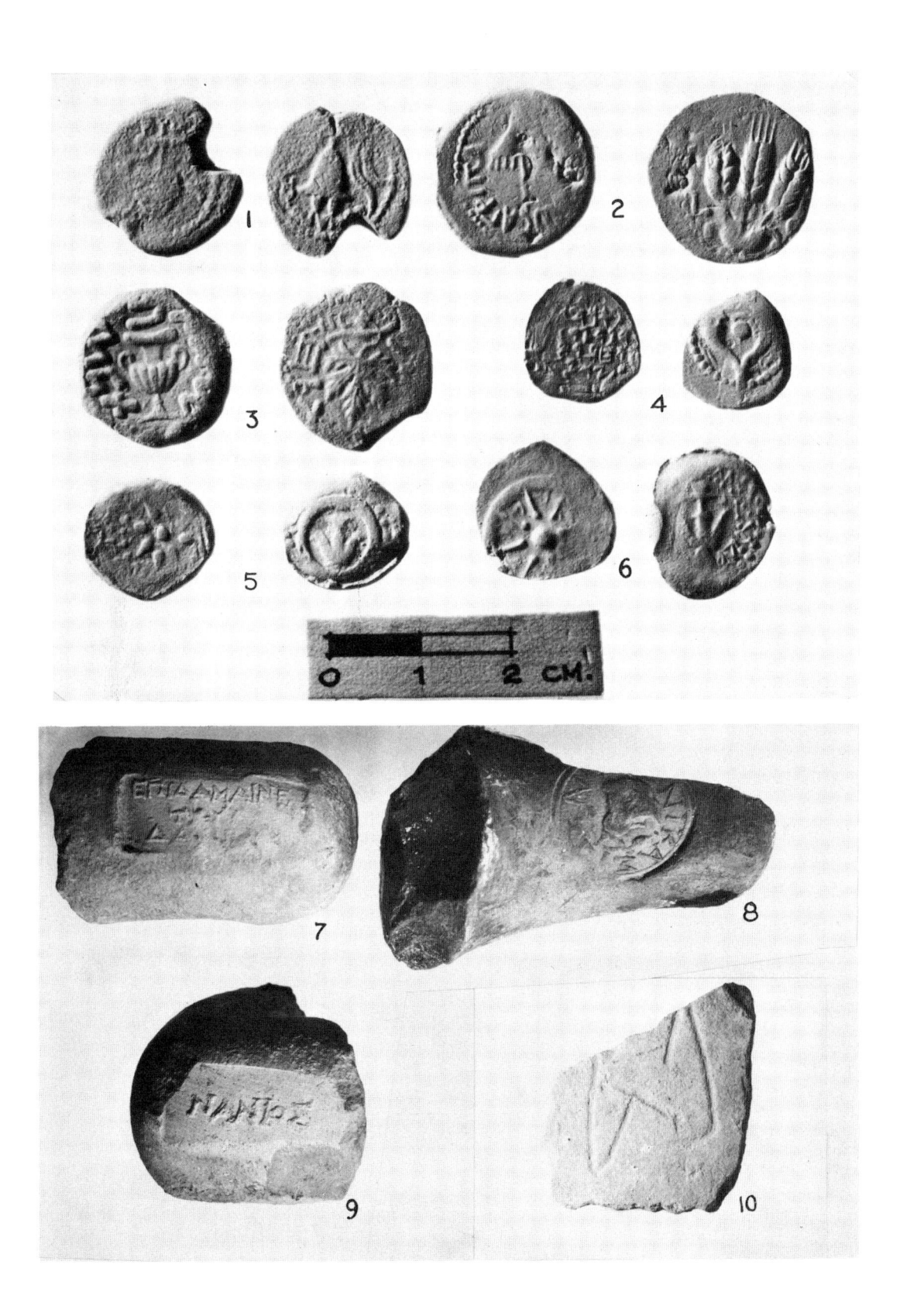

PLATE 47   a   Coins, obverses, and reverses.
            b   Rhodian jar handles and ostracon.

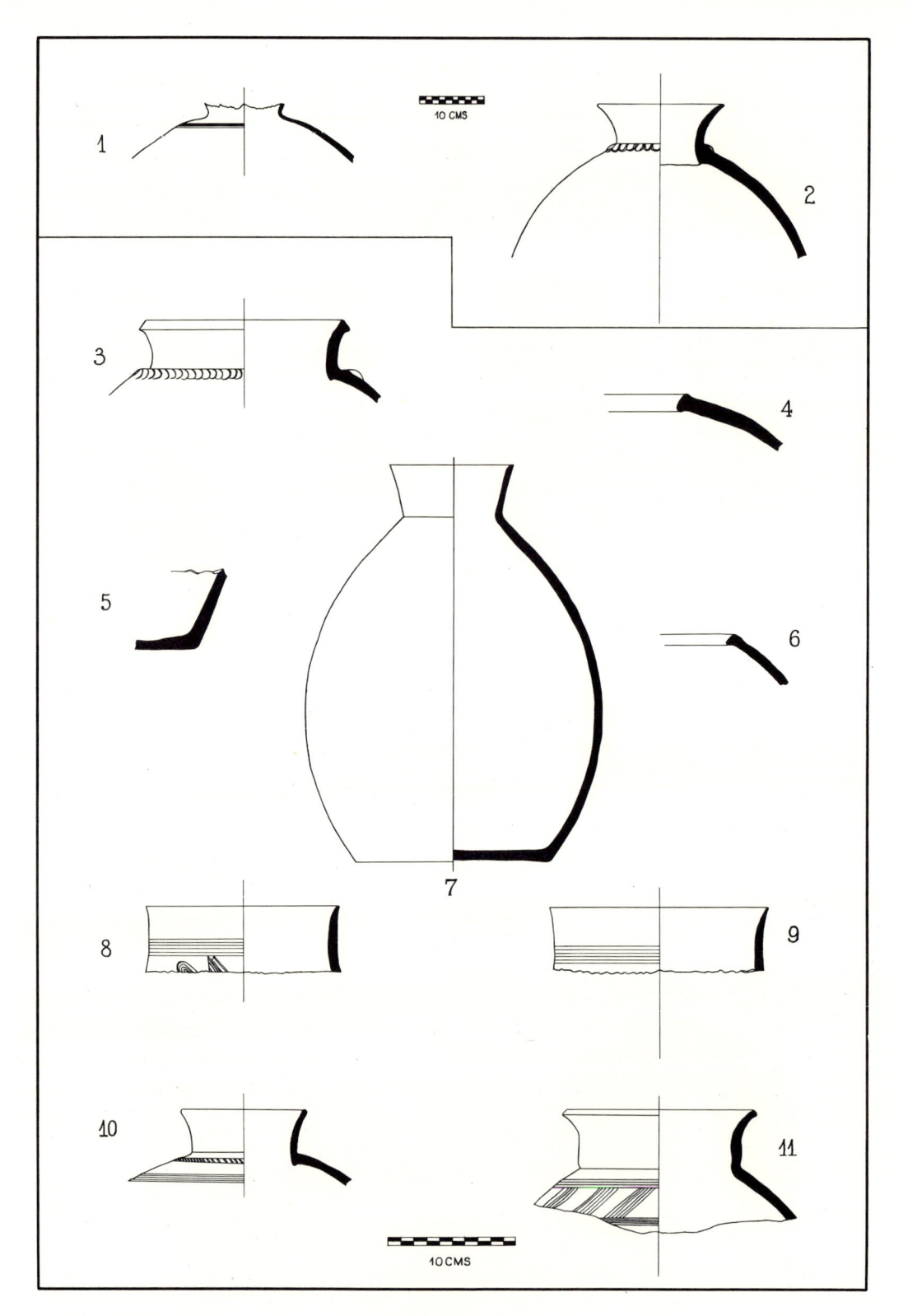

PLATE 48 Middle Bronze I pottery.

PLATE 49 Middle Bronze II pottery.

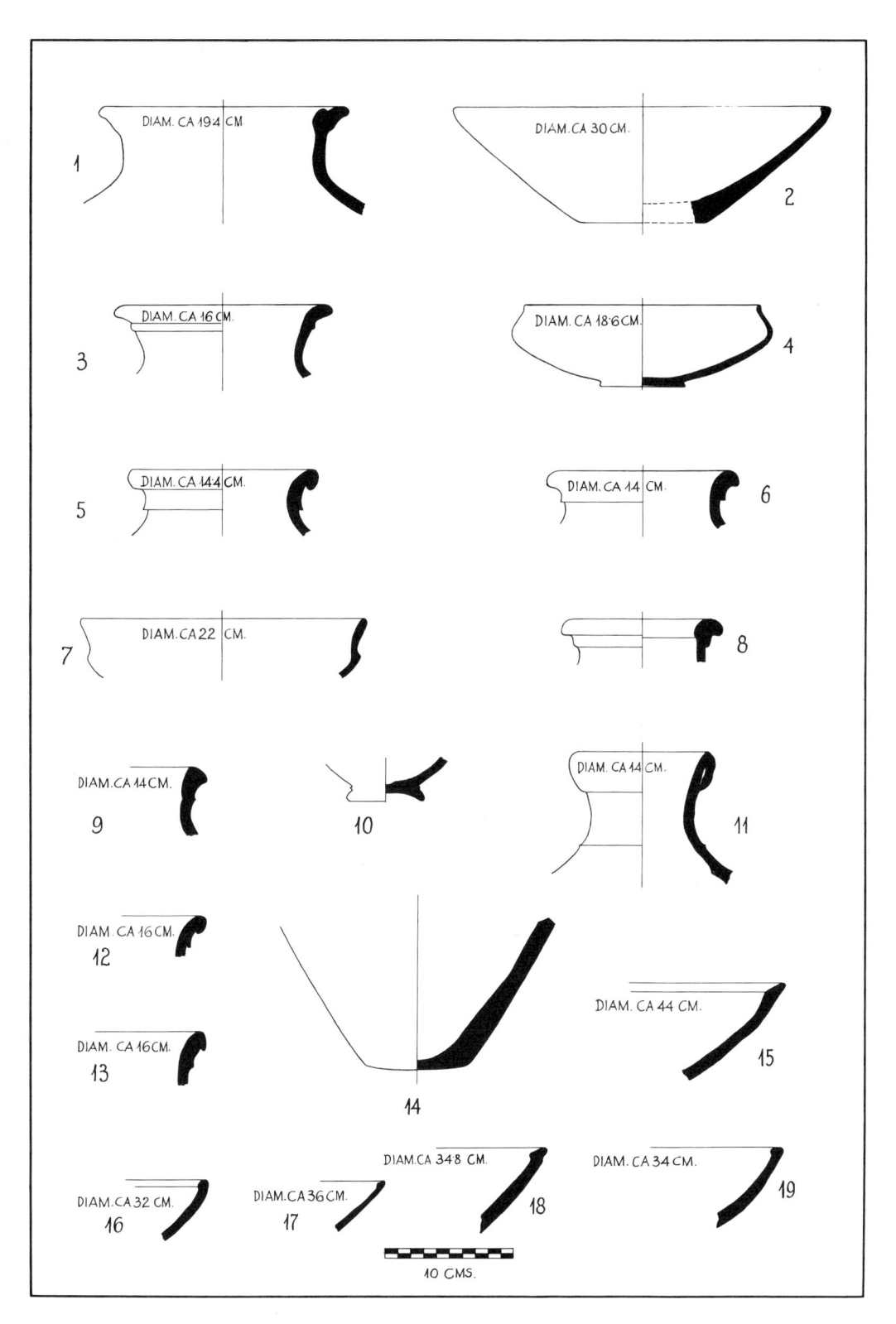

PLATE 50   Middle Bronze II pottery.

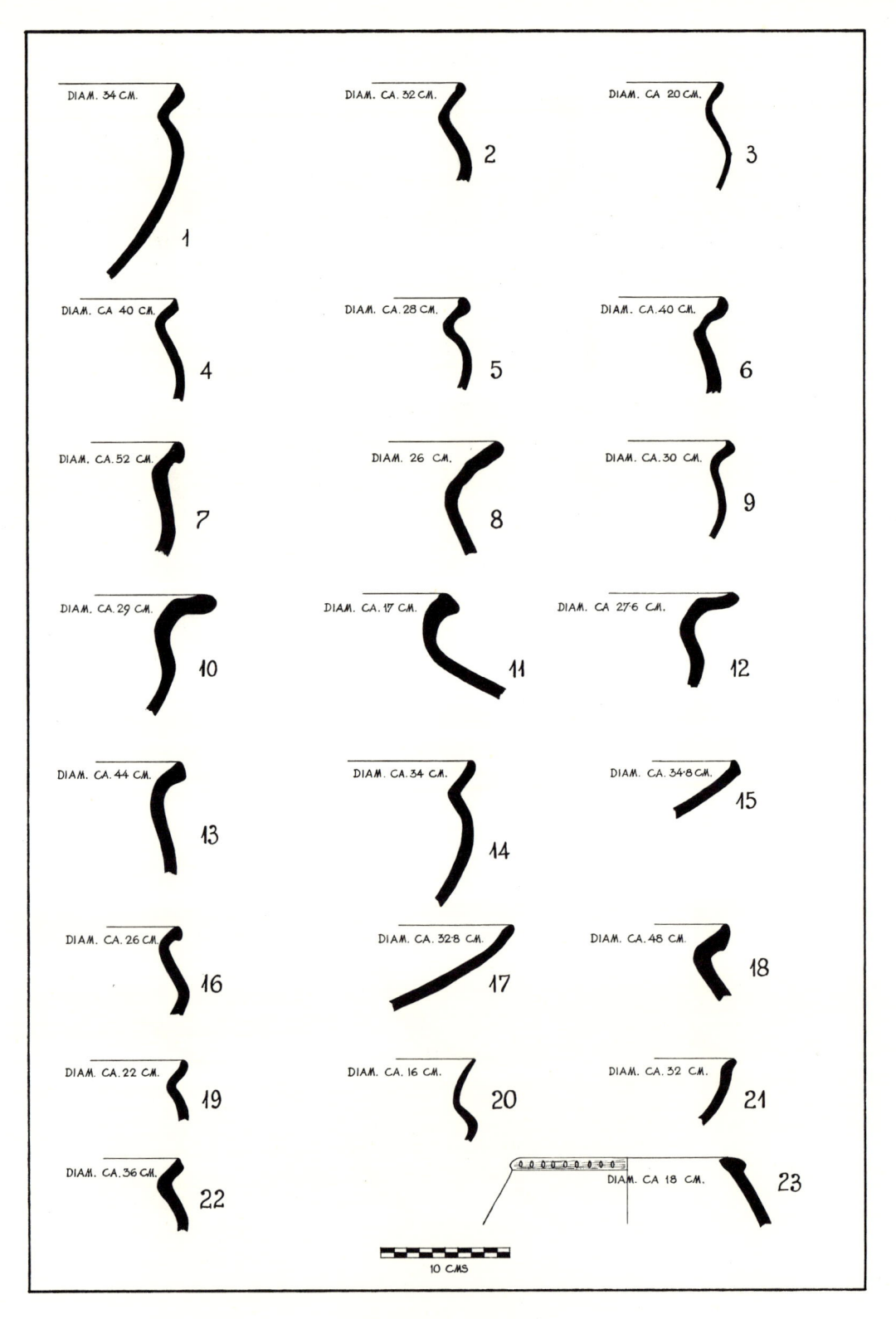

PLATE 51 Middle Bronze II pottery.

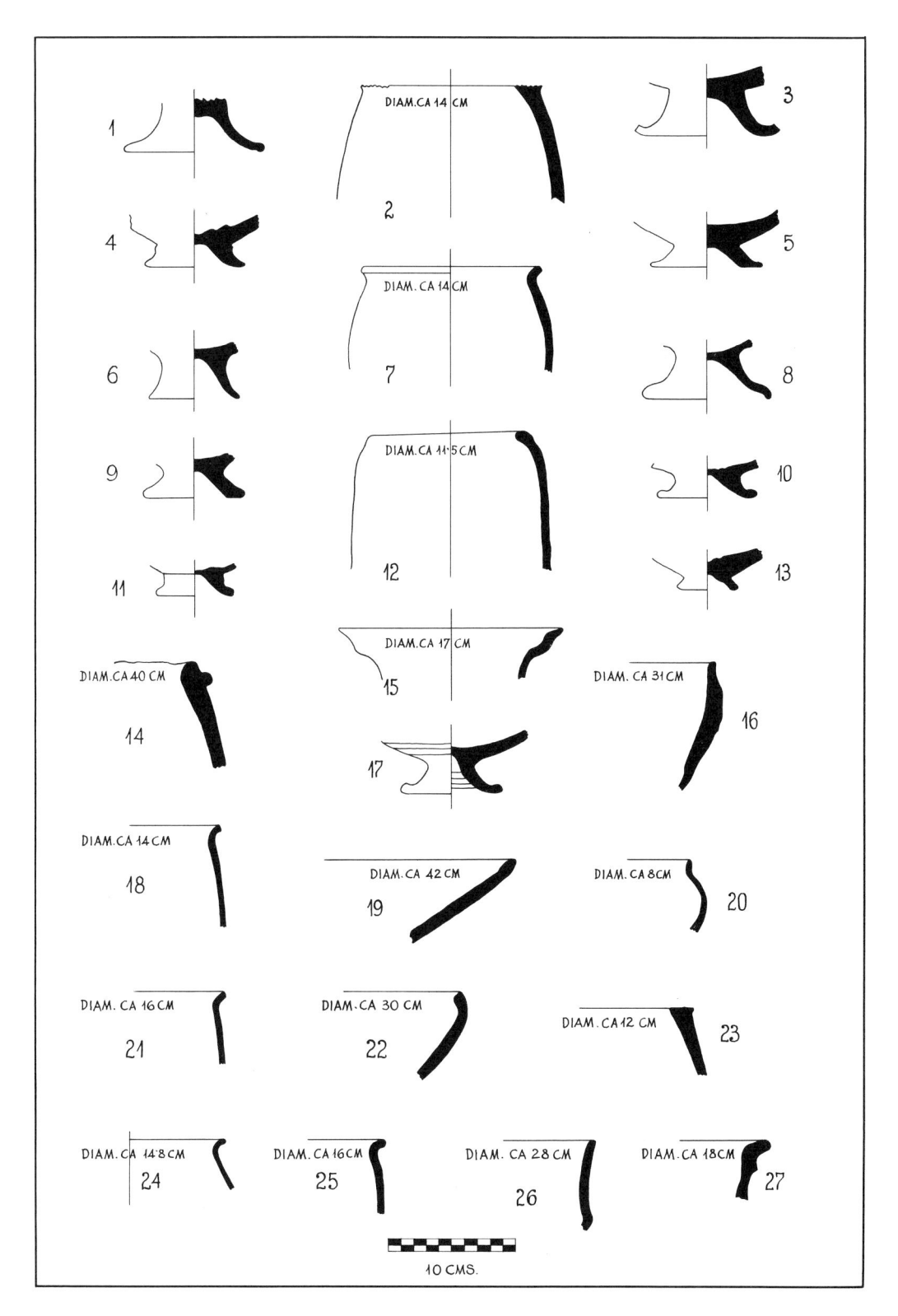

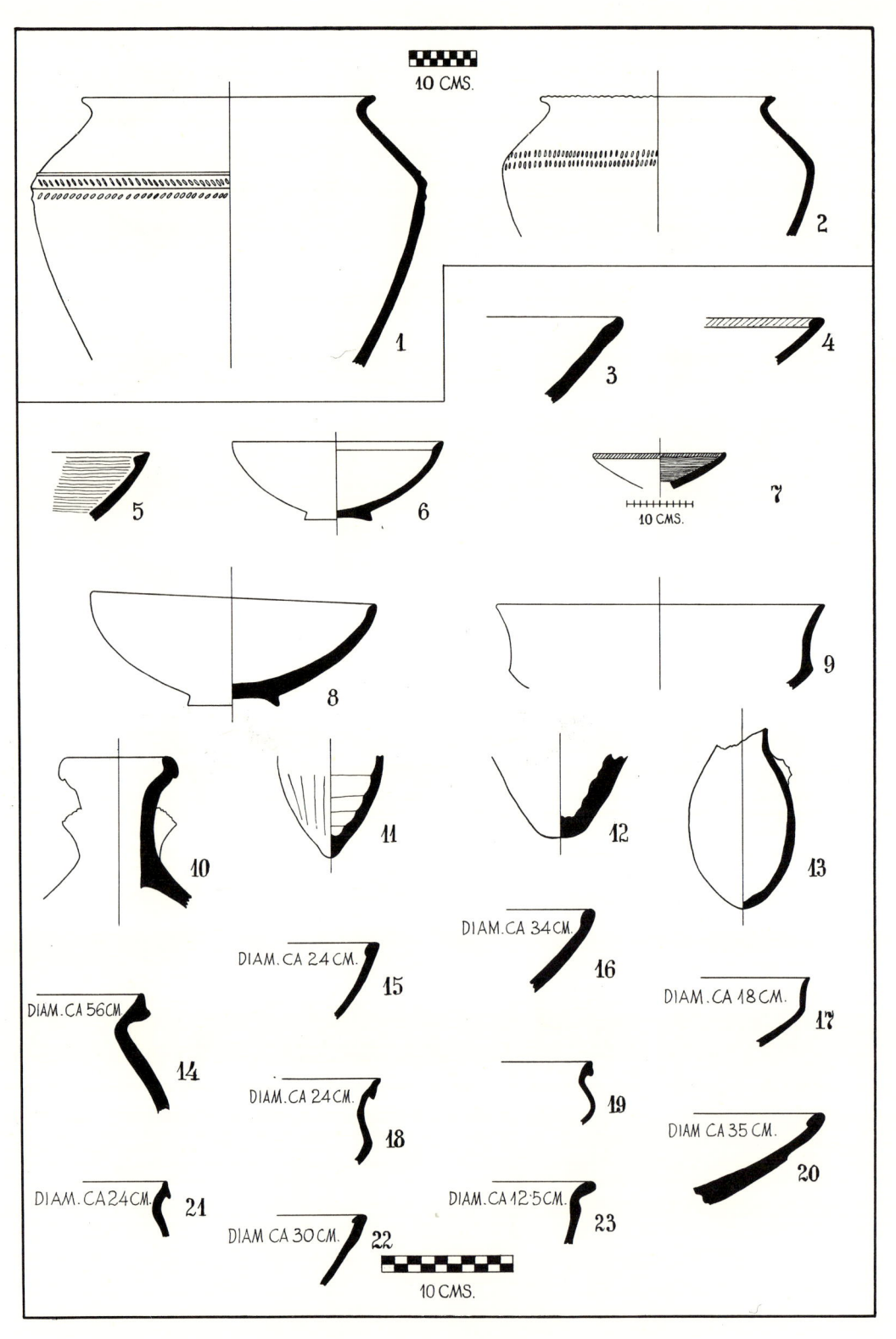

PLATE 52 Middle Bronze II (Nos. 1–5, 7) and Late Bronze, phase 1 (Nos. 6, 8–23) pottery.

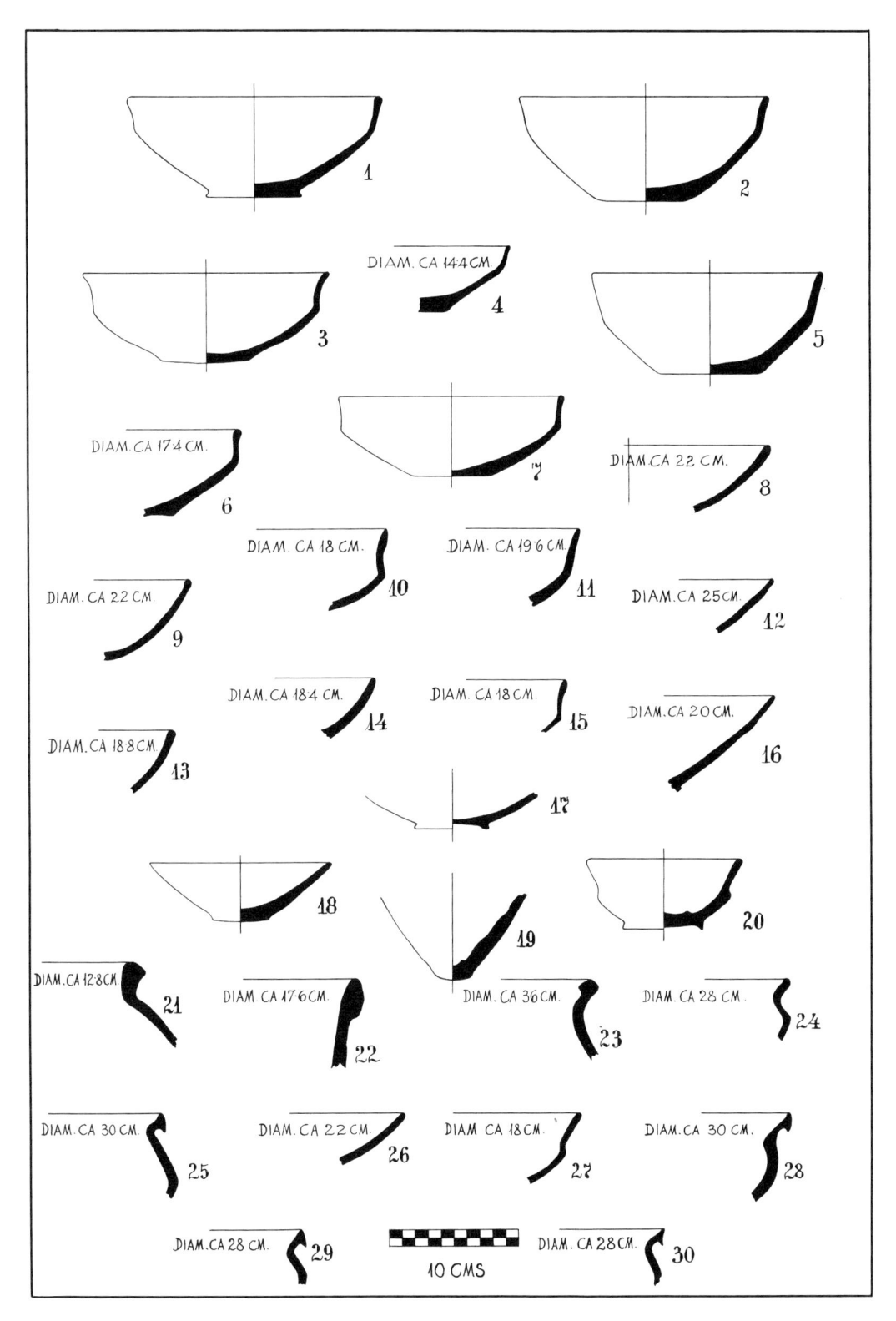

PLATE 53   Late Bronze, phase 2 (Nos. 1–15); phase uncertain (Nos. 16–30) pottery.

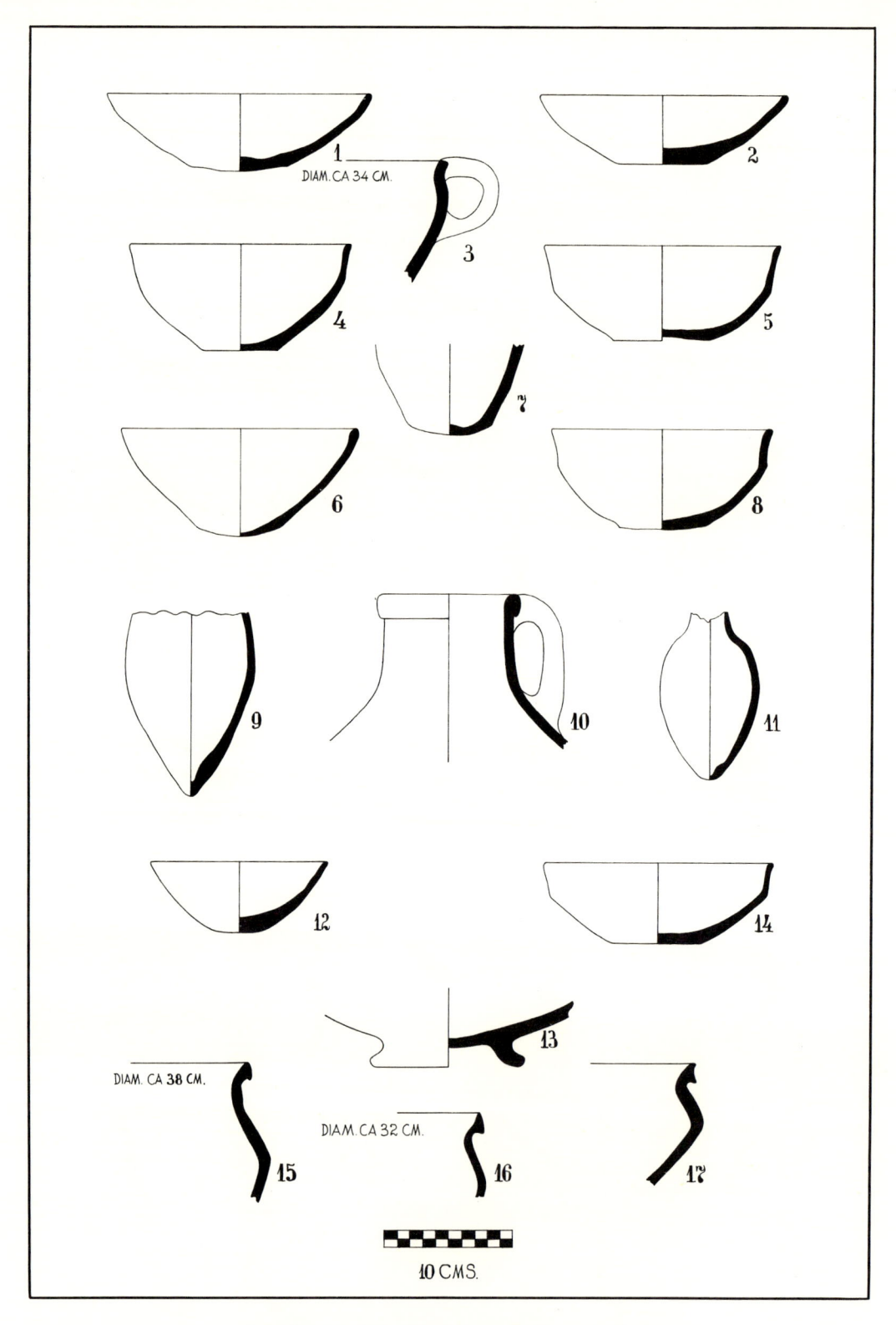

PLATE 54   Late Bronze, phase 2 (Nos. 1–14); phase uncertain (Nos. 16–17) pottery.

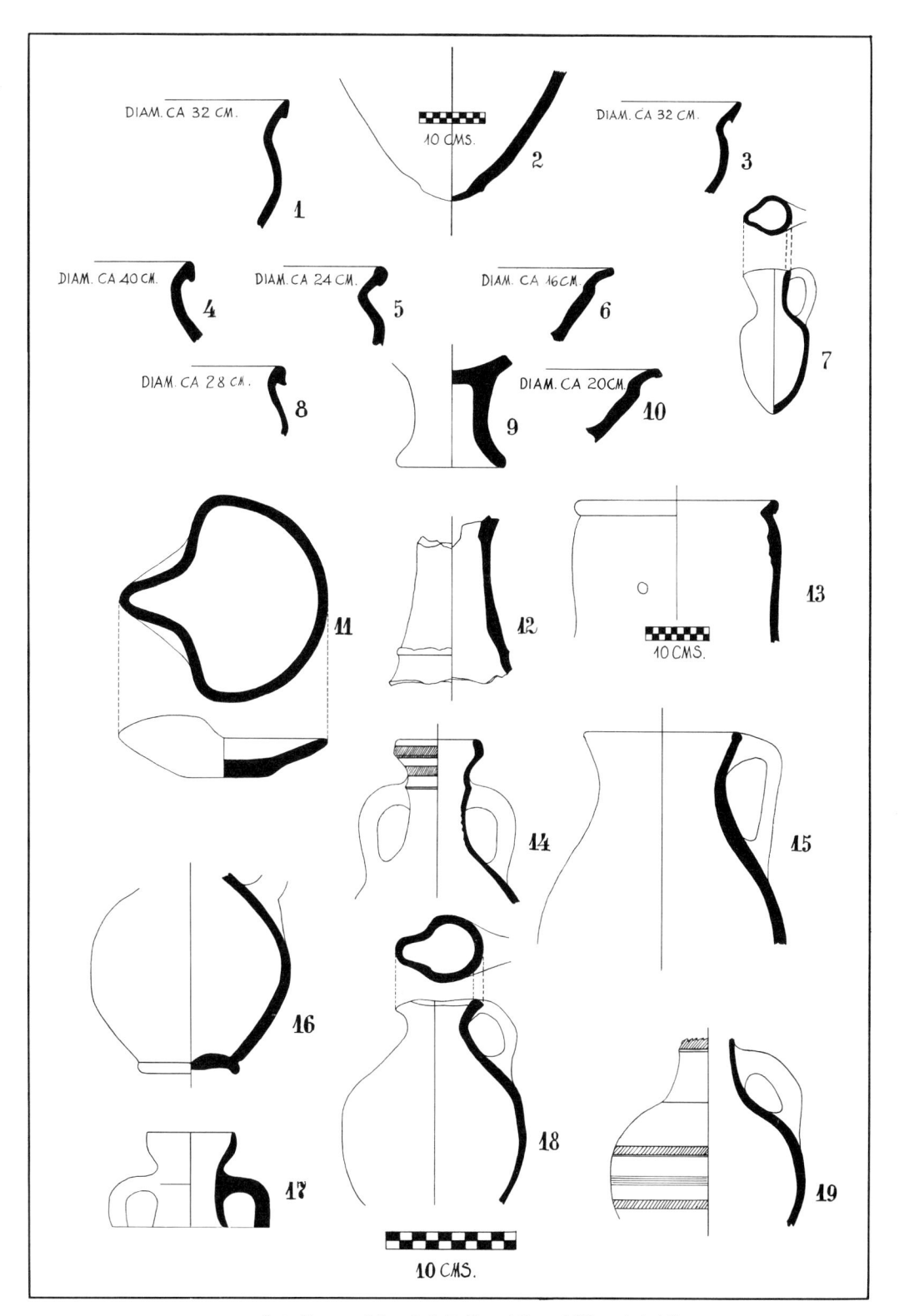

PLATE 55 Late Bronze (Nos. 1–5, 7–8) and Iron I (Nos. 6, 9–19) pottery.

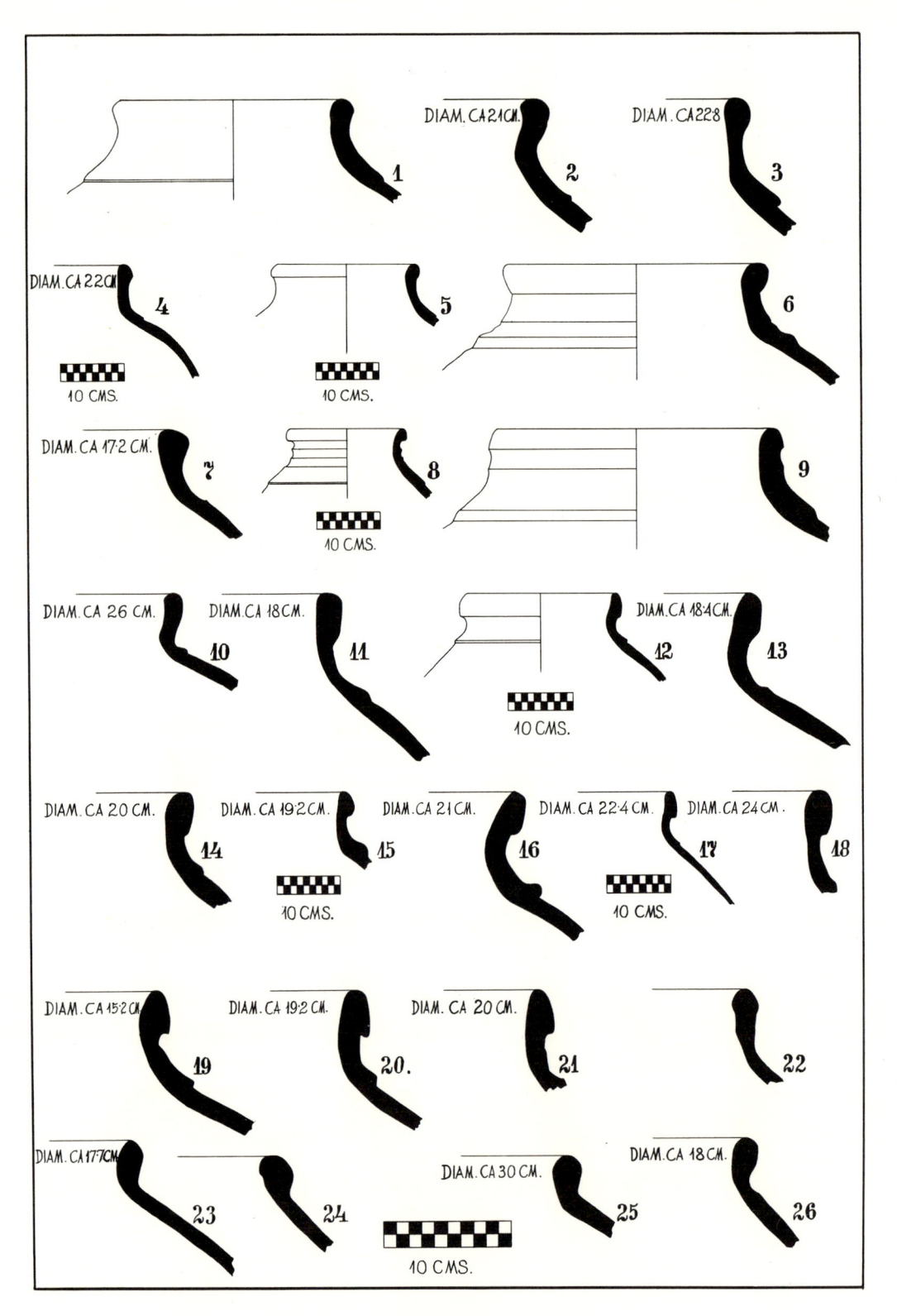

PLATE 56   Iron I pottery.

PLATE 57   Iron I pottery.

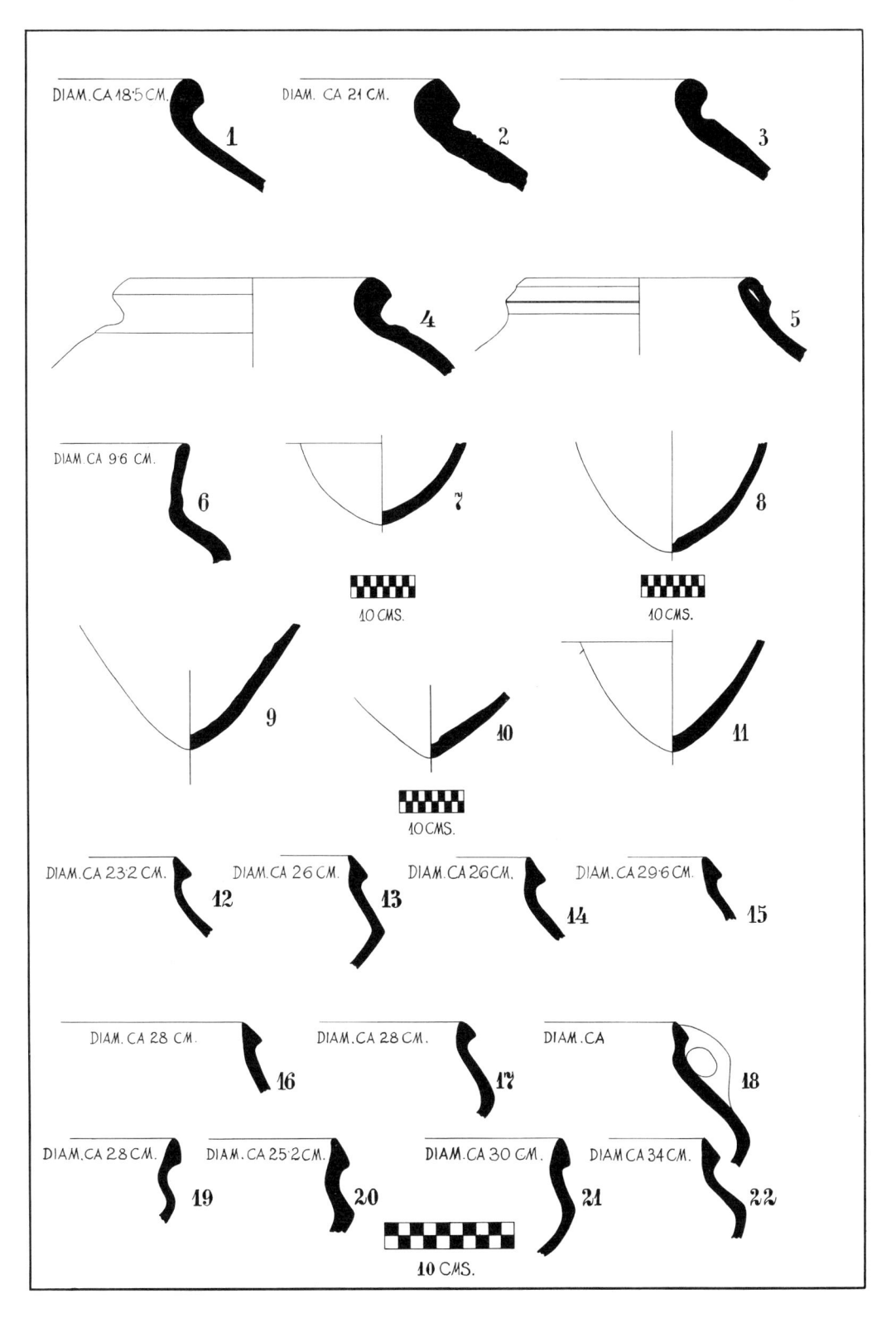

PLATE 58   Iron I pottery.

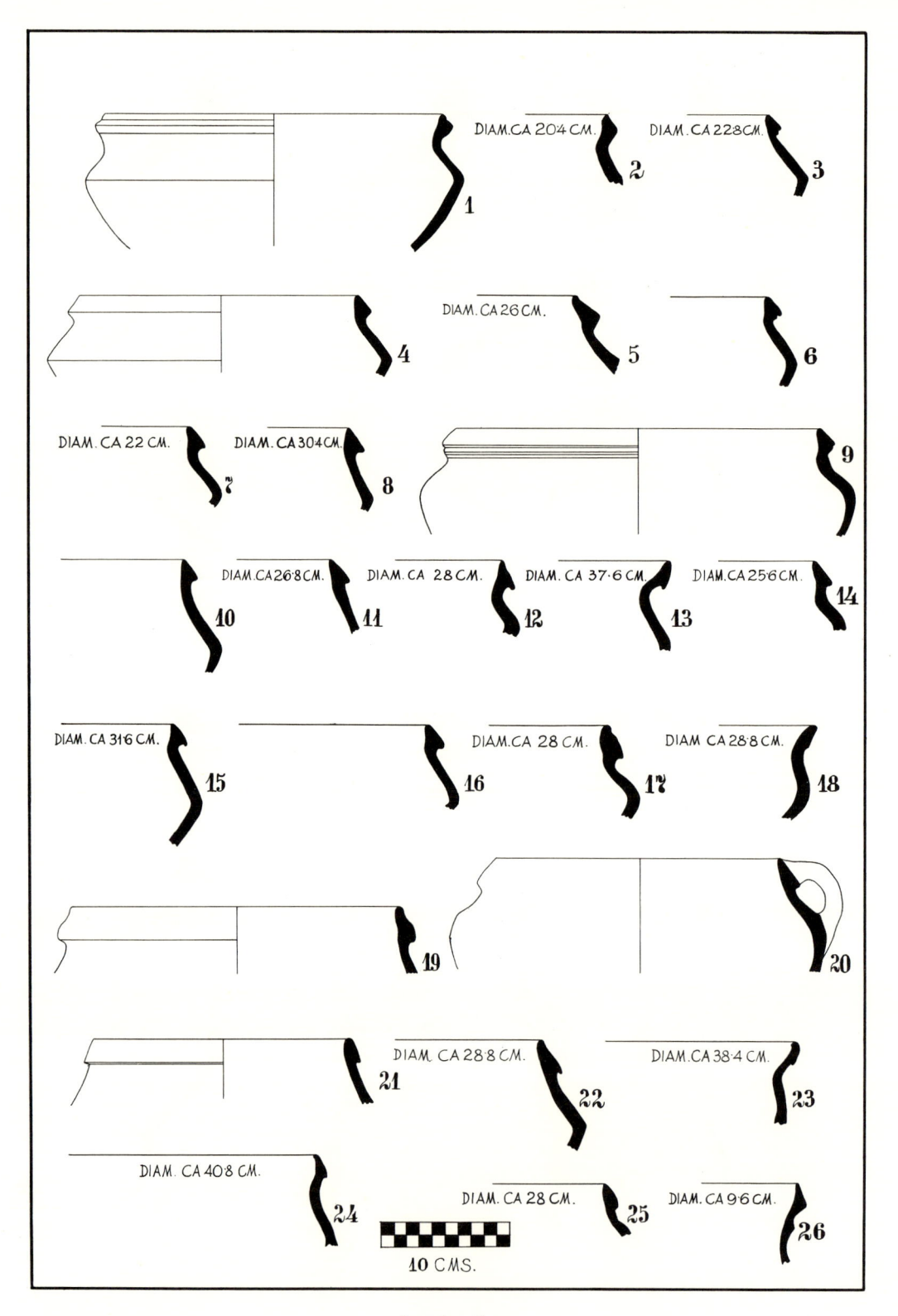

PLATE 59   Iron I pottery.

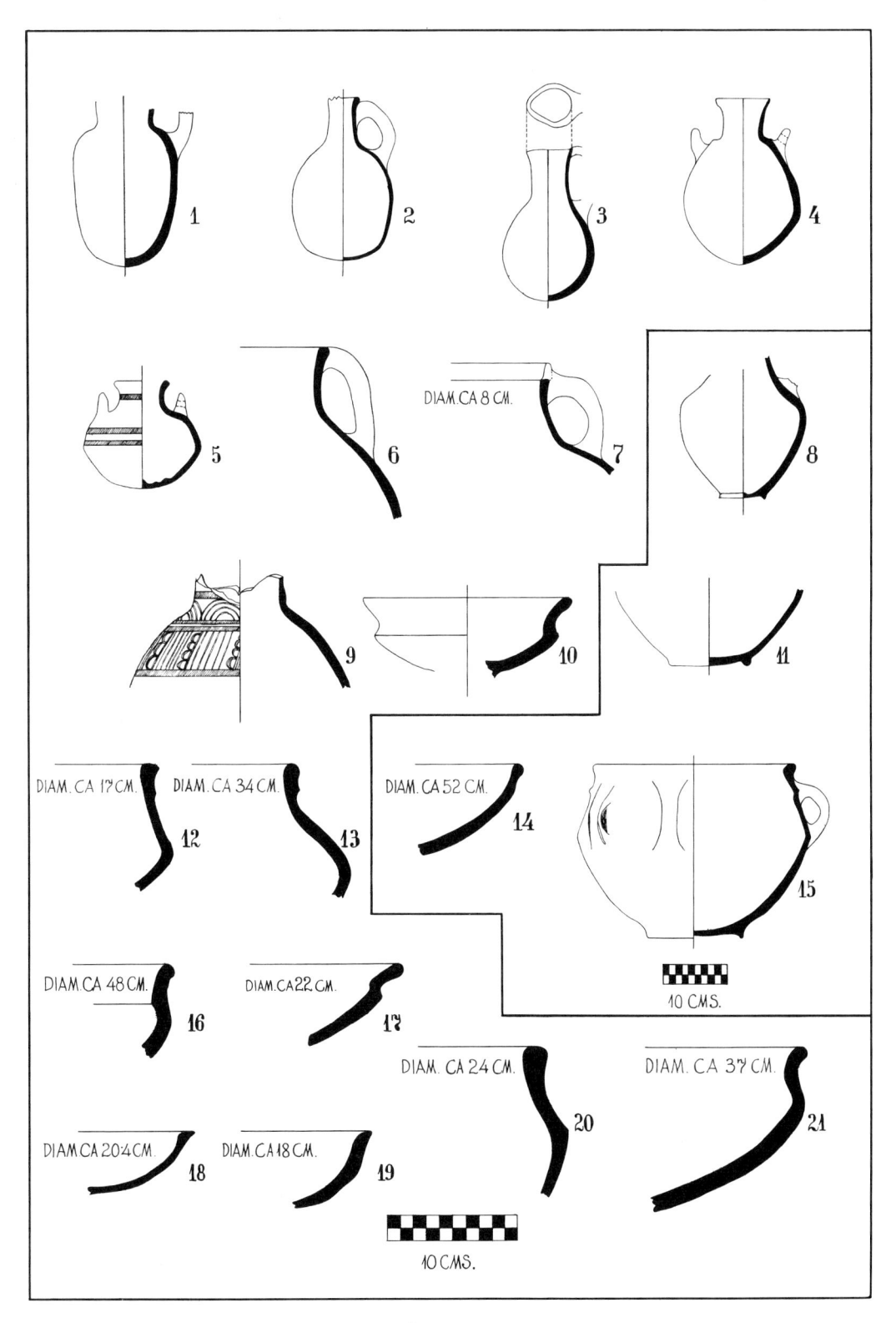

PLATE 60 Iron I pottery.

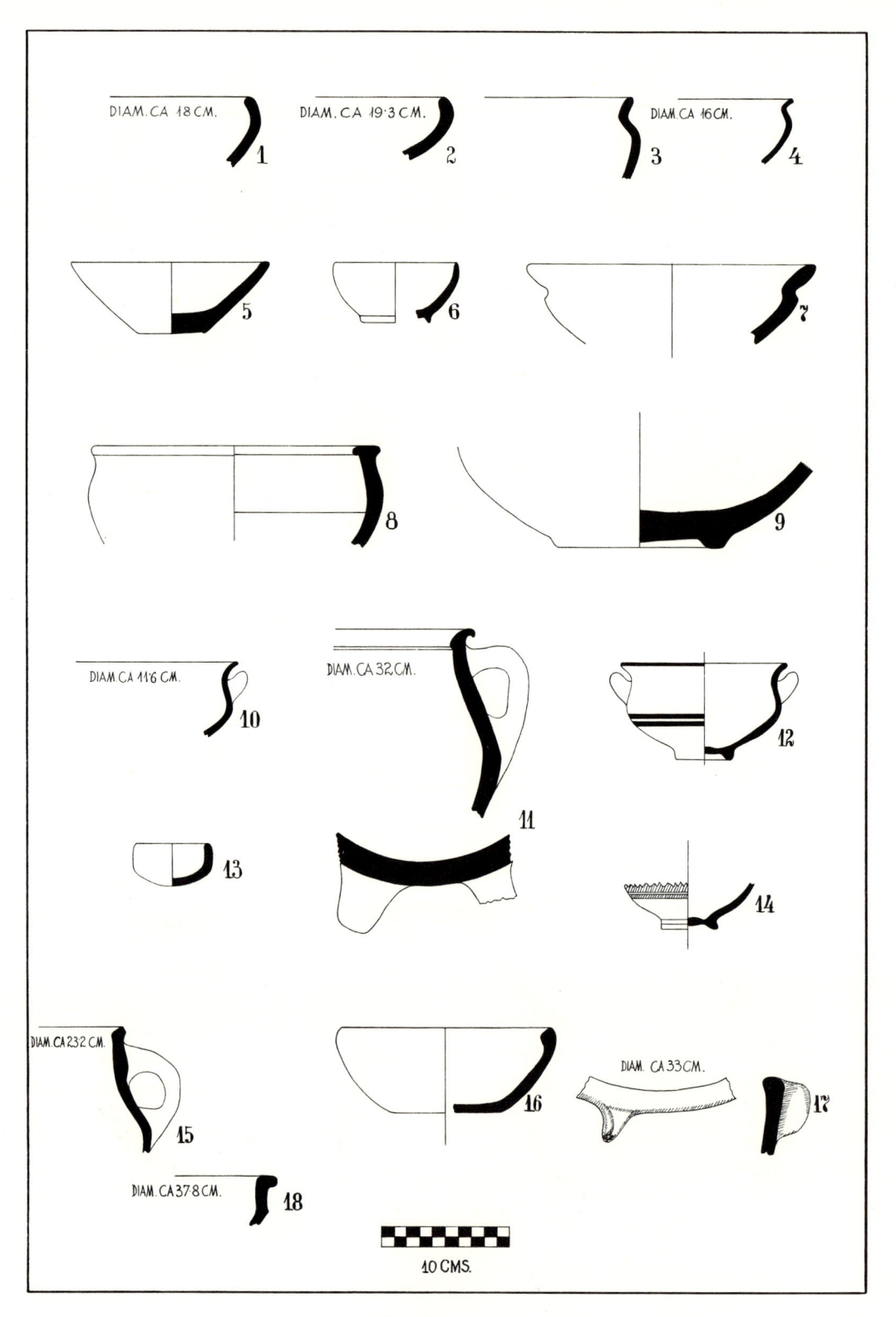

PLATE 61   Iron I pottery.

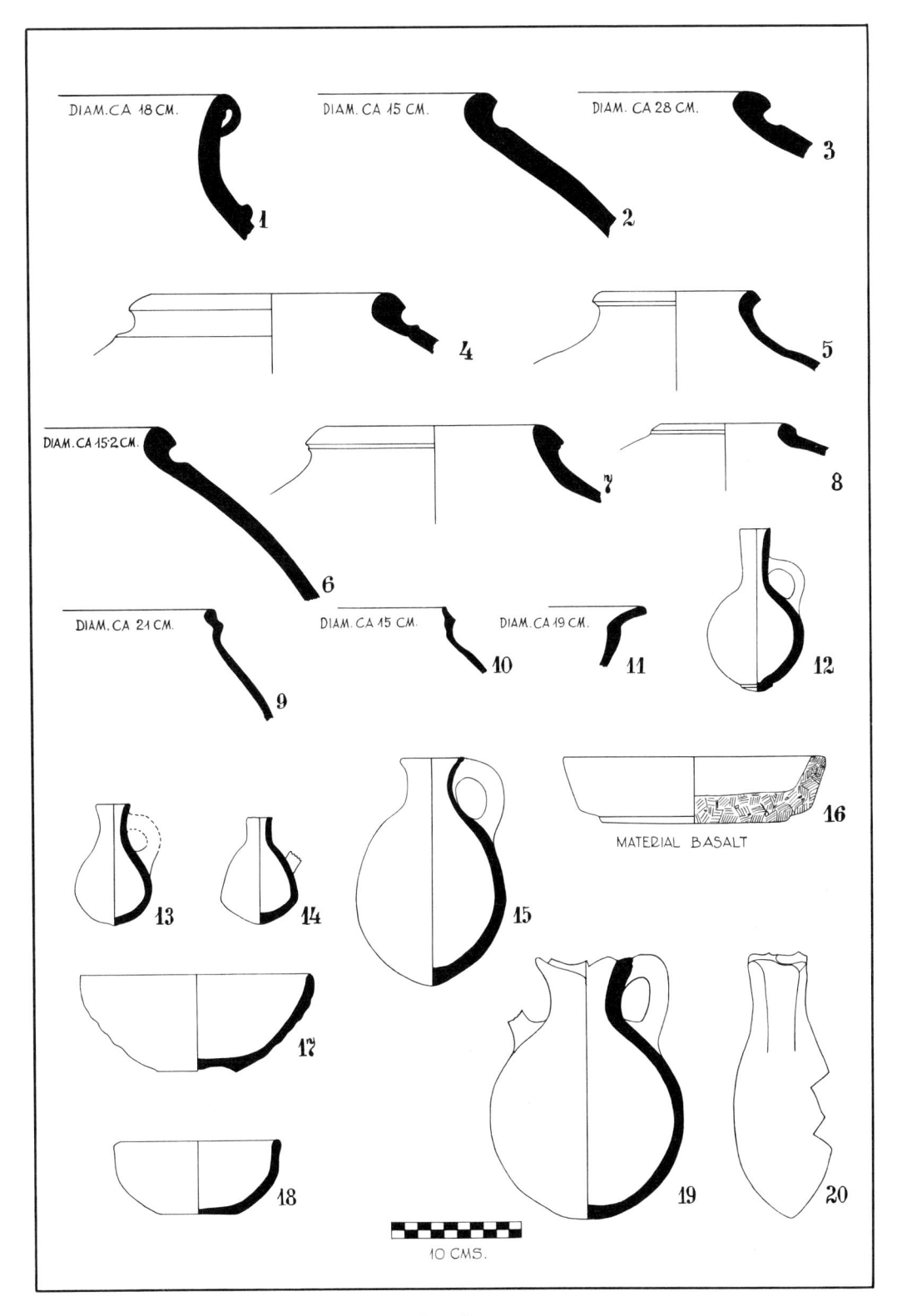

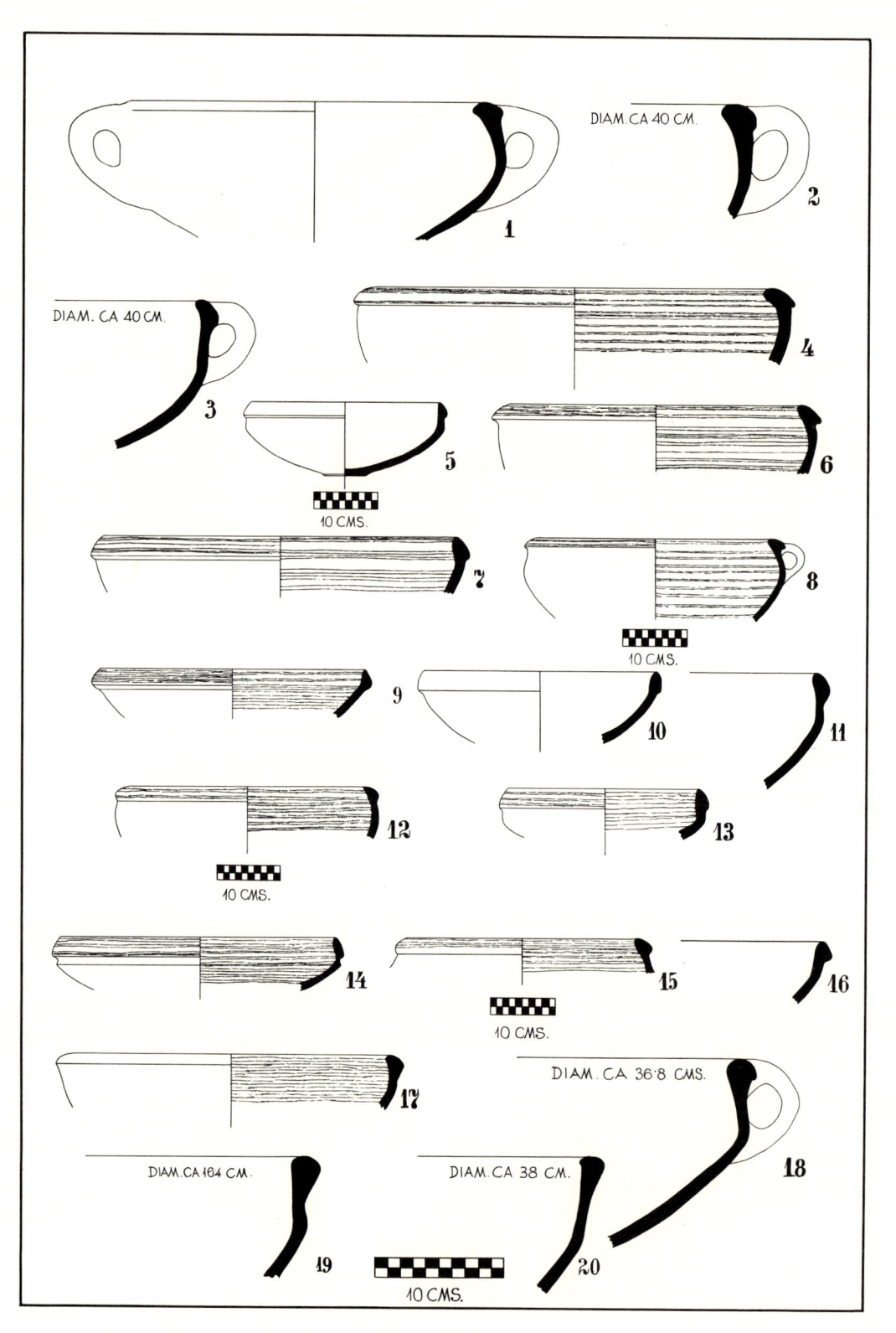

PLATE 62   Iron II pottery.

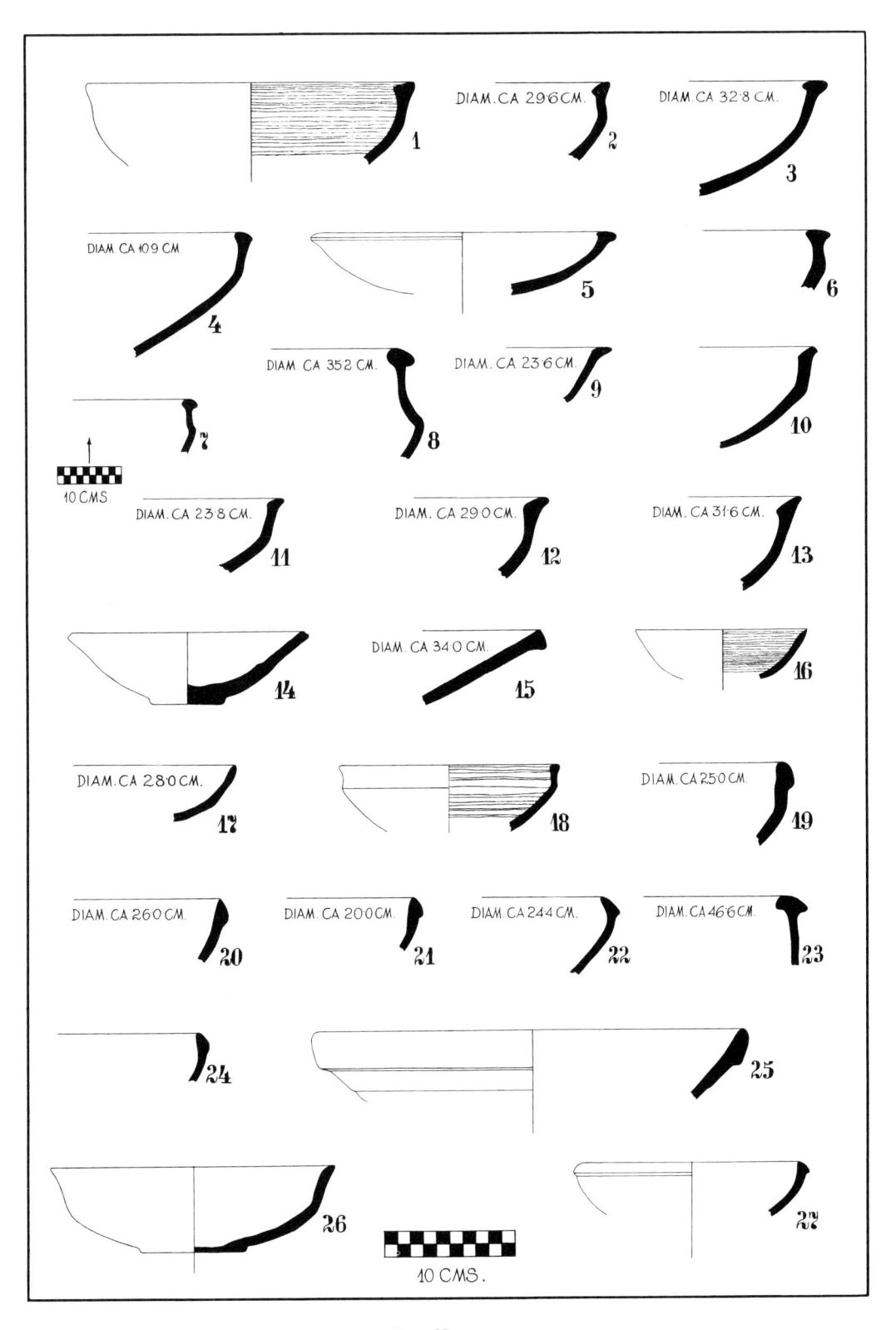

PLATE 63   Iron II pottery.

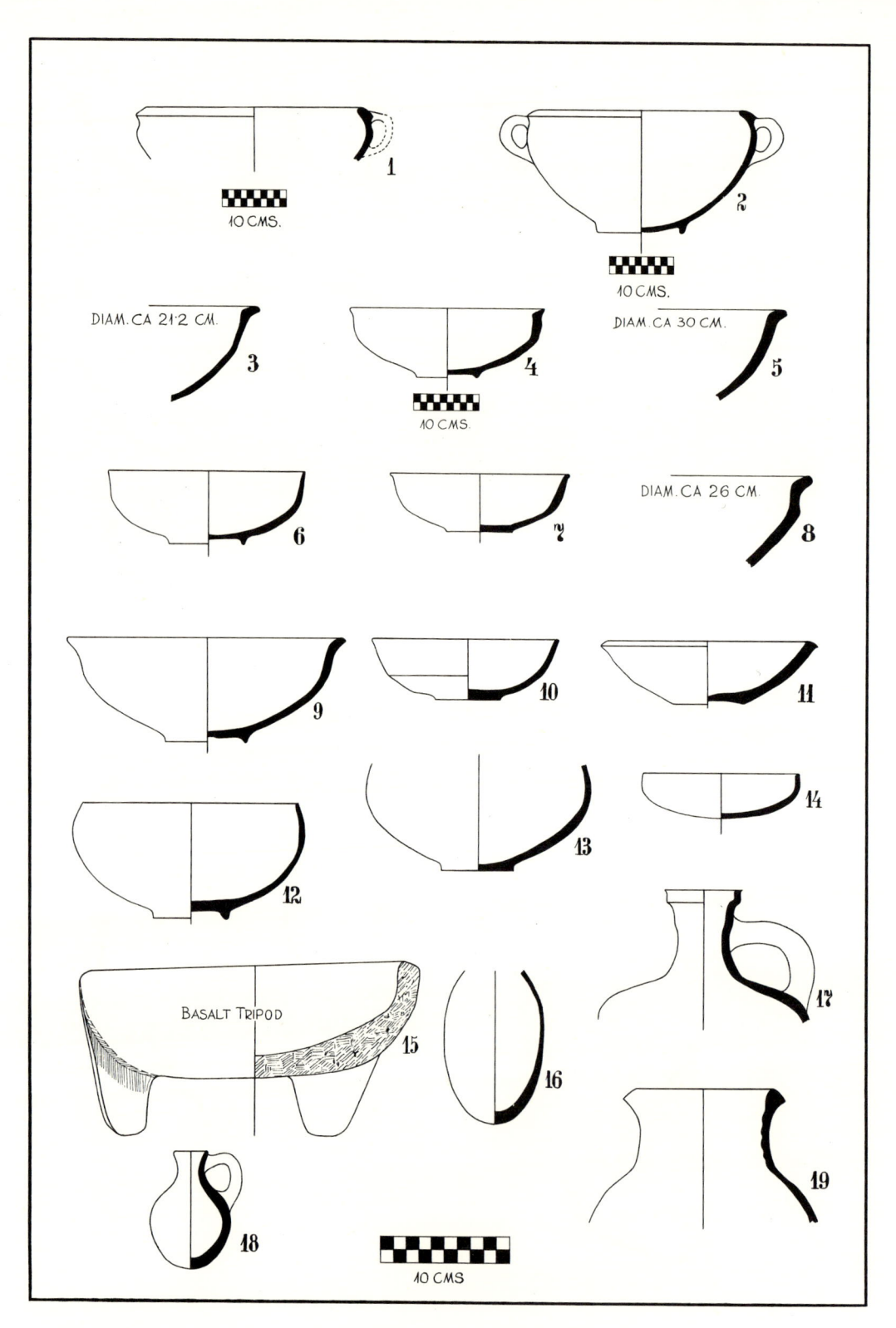

PLATE 64   Sixth century B.C. pottery.

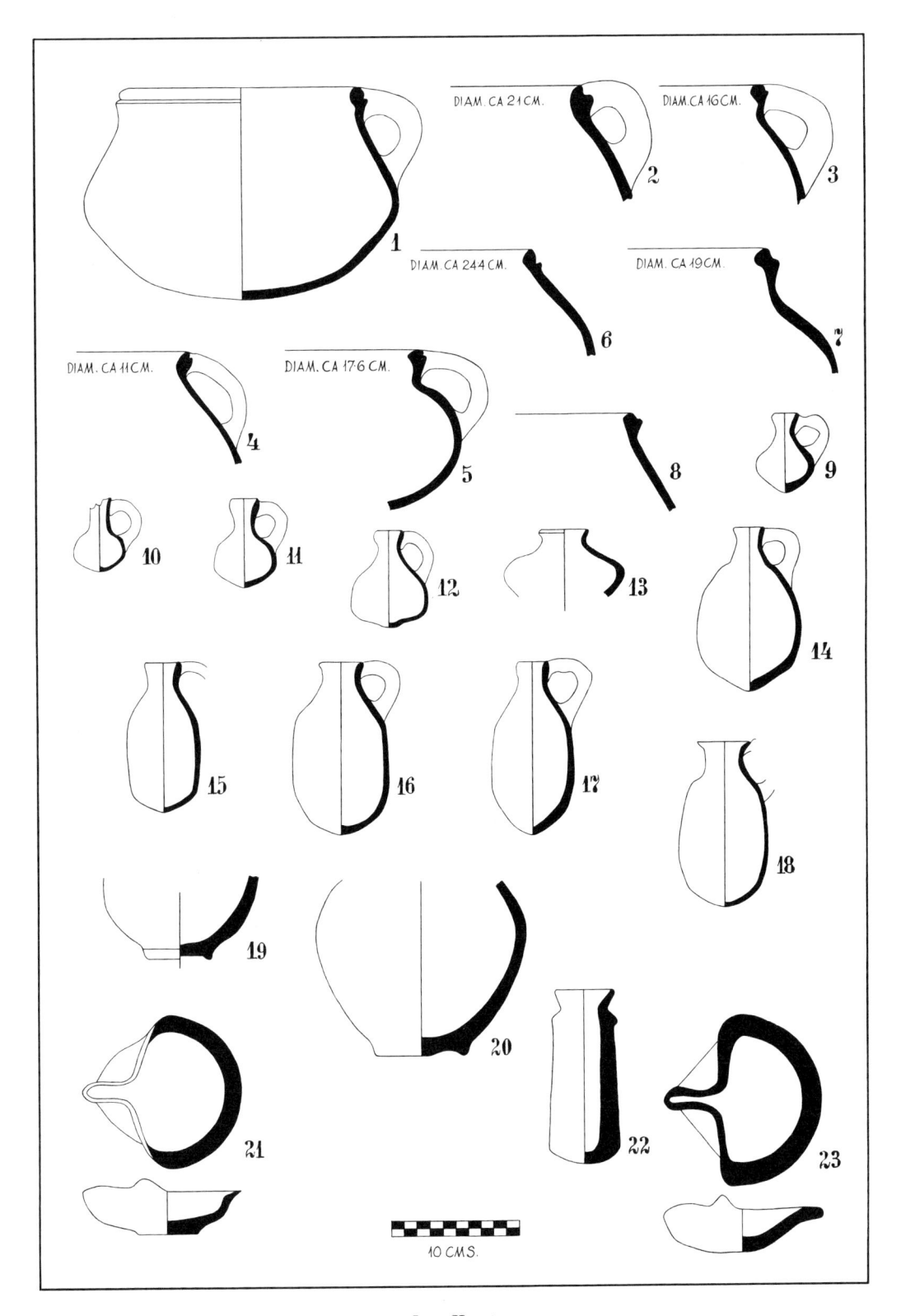

PLATE 65   Iron II pottery.

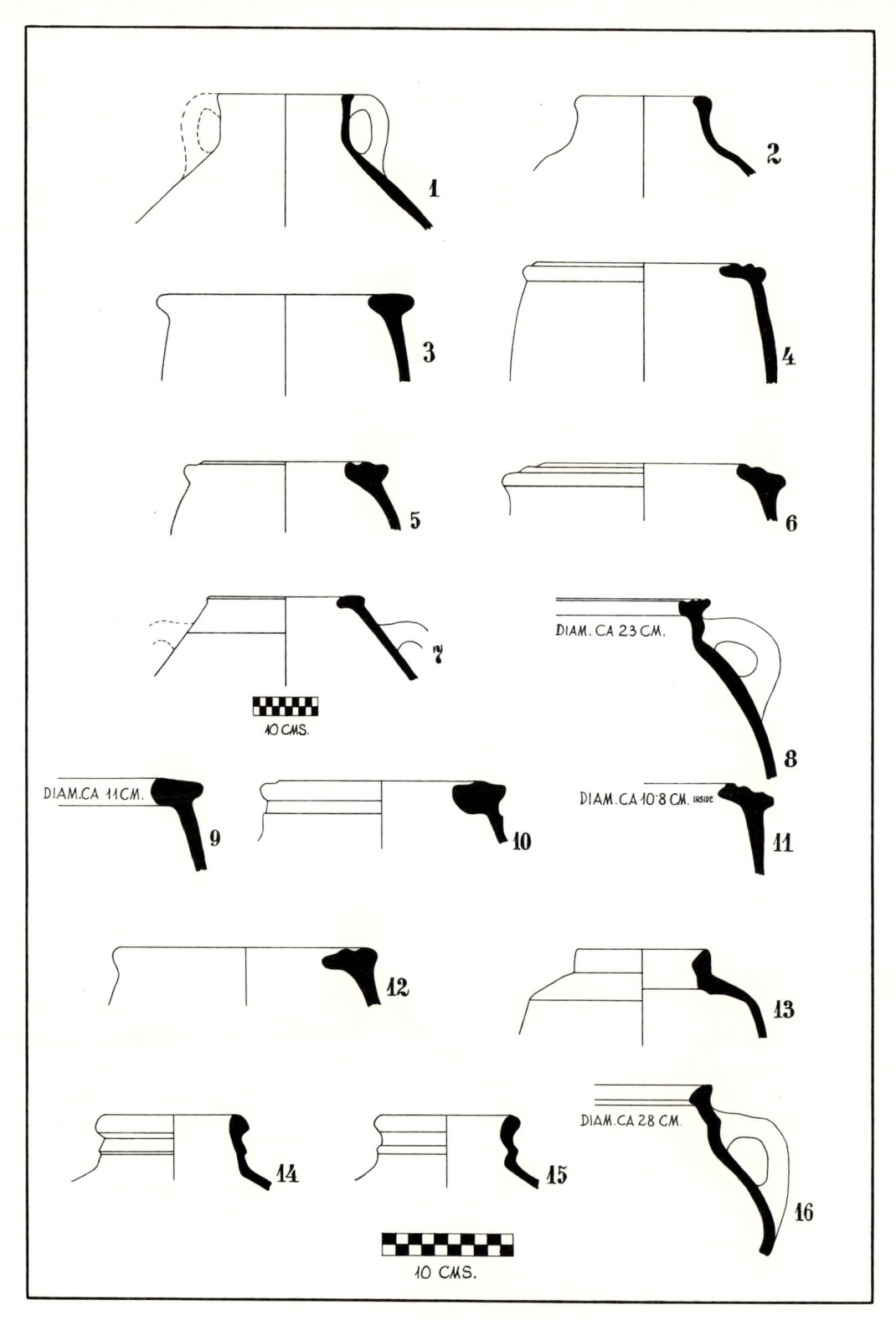

PLATE 66   Sixth century B.C. pottery.

PLATE 67   Sixth century B.C. pottery.

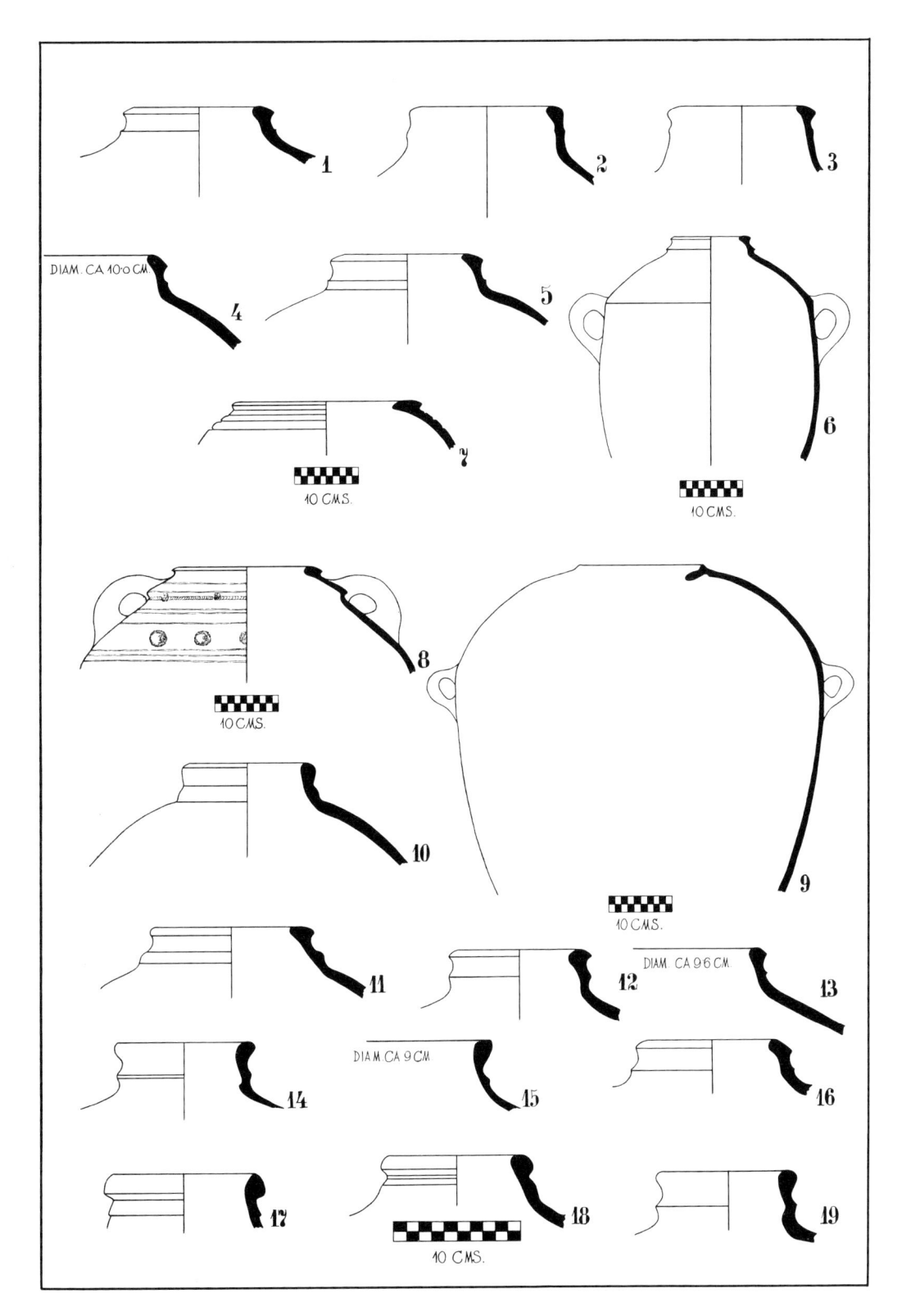

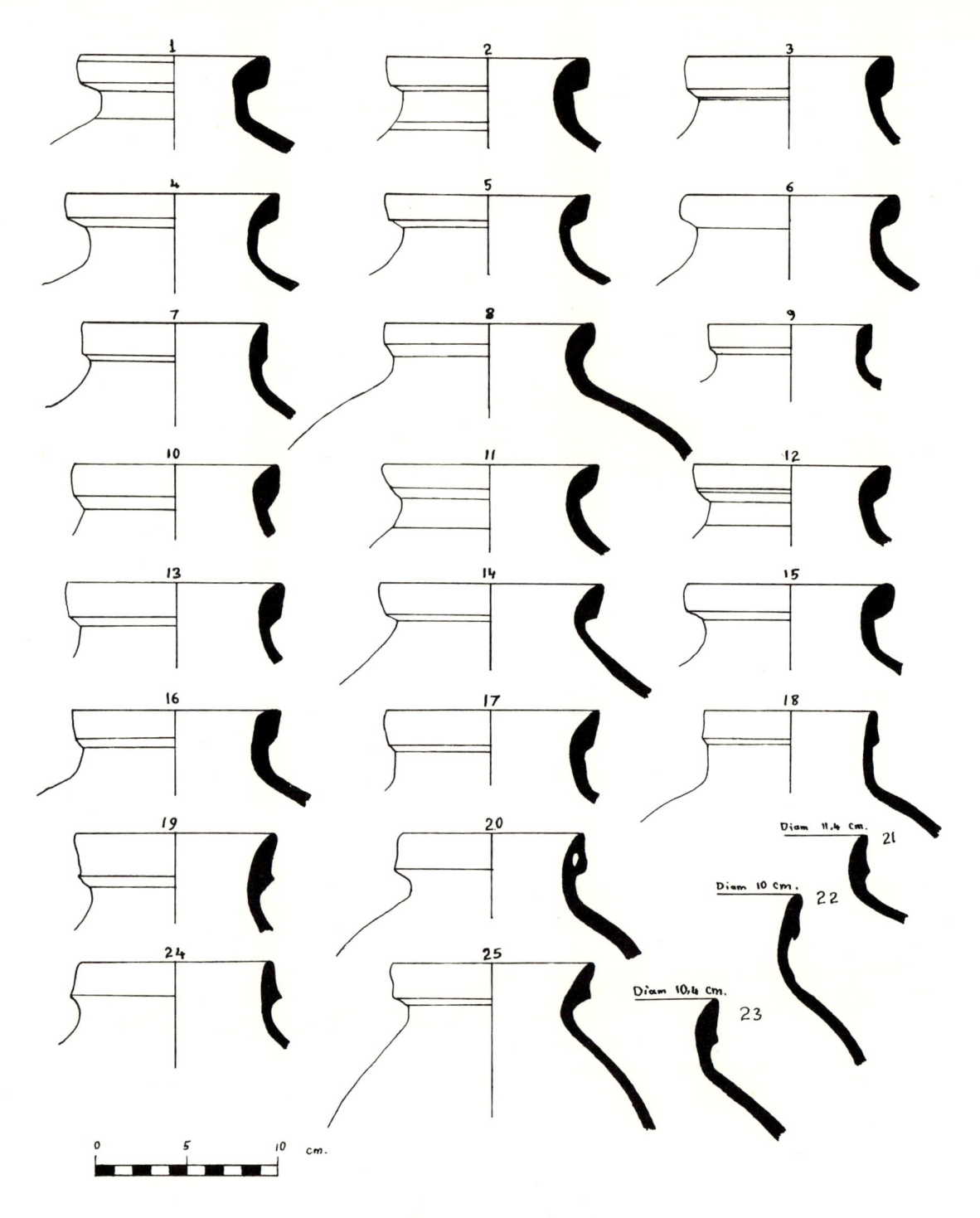

PLATE 68   Hellenistic pottery, phase 1.

Hellenistic pottery, phase 1 (1–9), phase 2 (10–23).

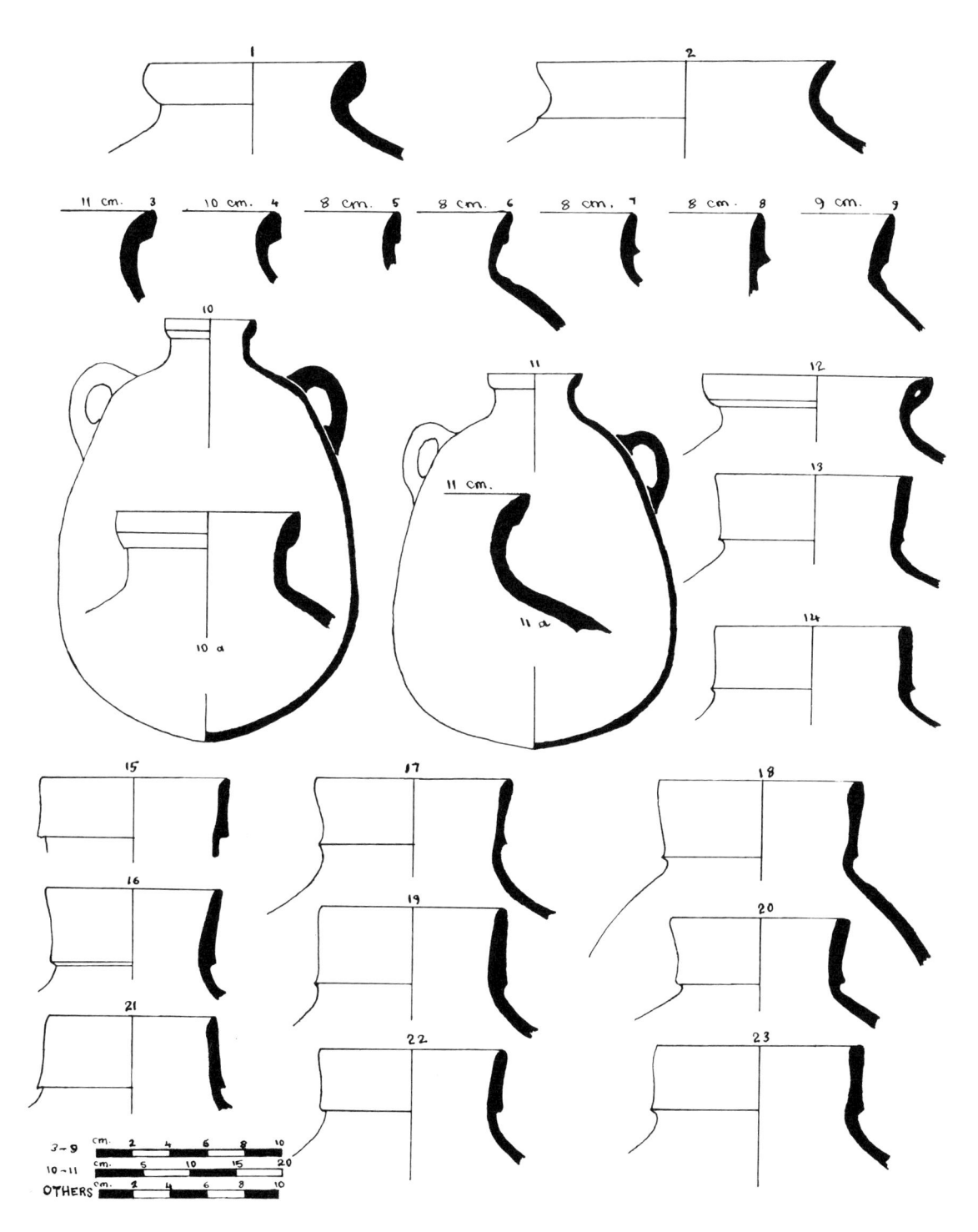

PLATE 69

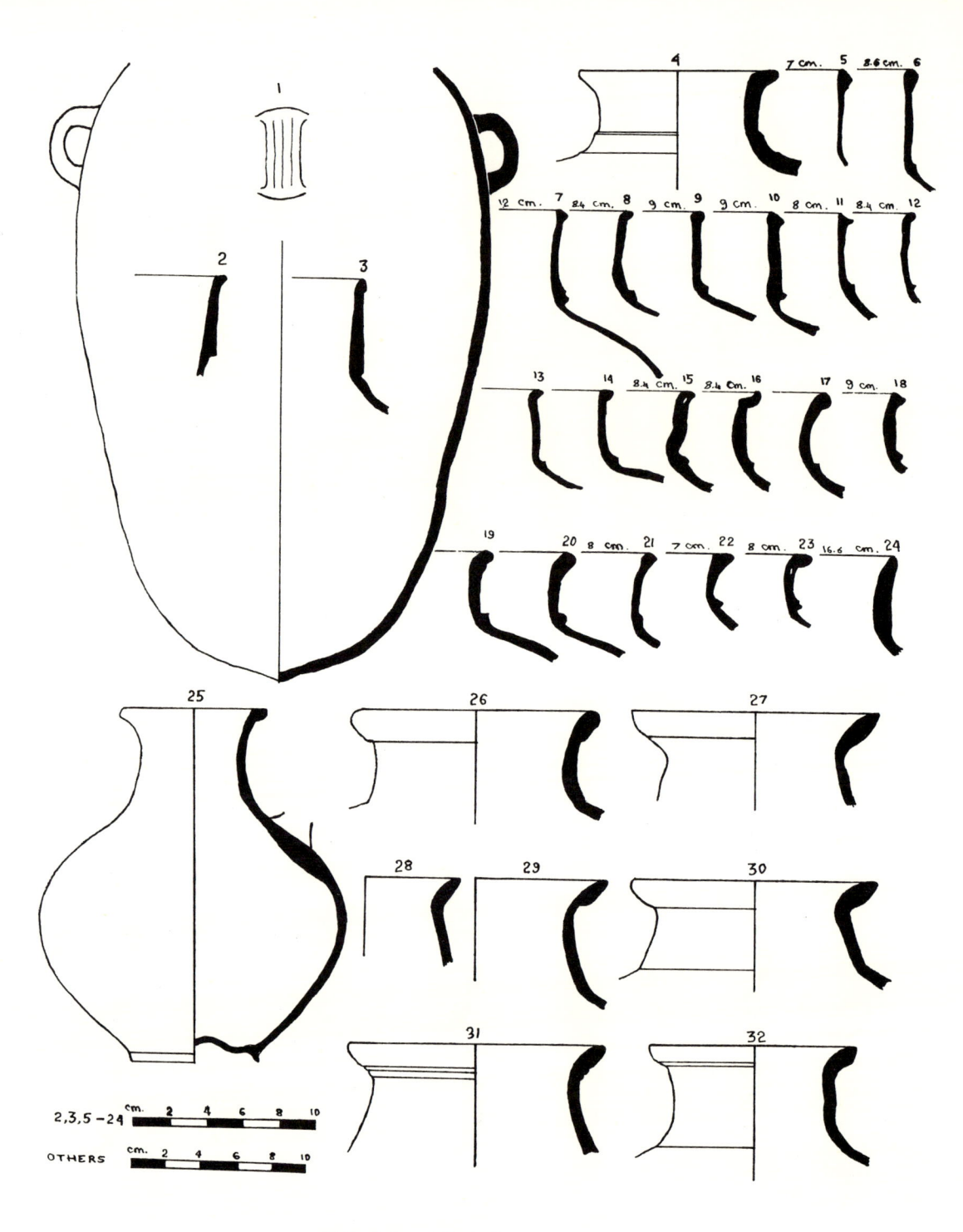

PLATE 70   Hellenistic and Early Roman pottery. Roman (1–24); Hellenistic (25–32).

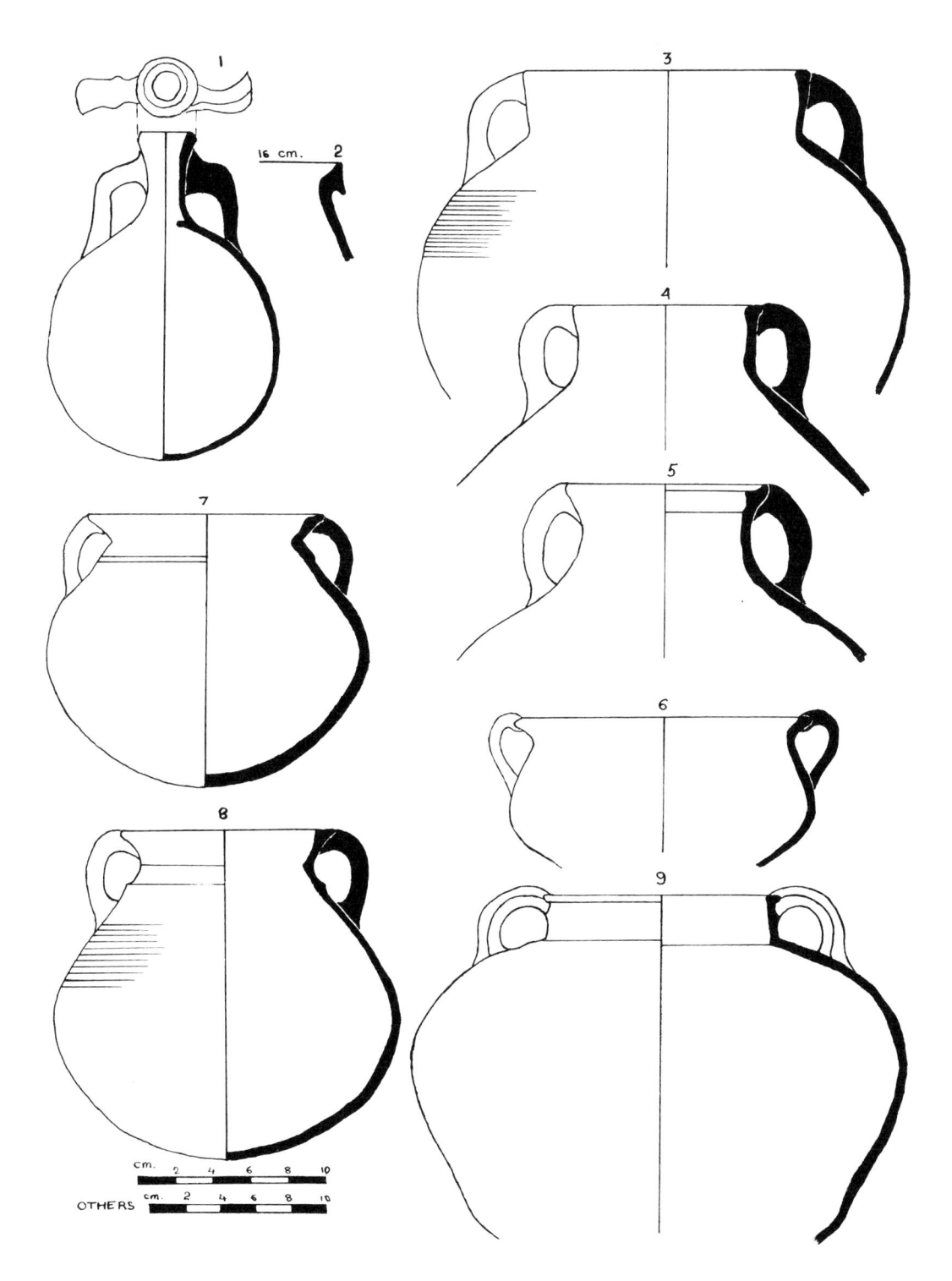

PLATE 71 Hellenistic and Early Roman pottery.

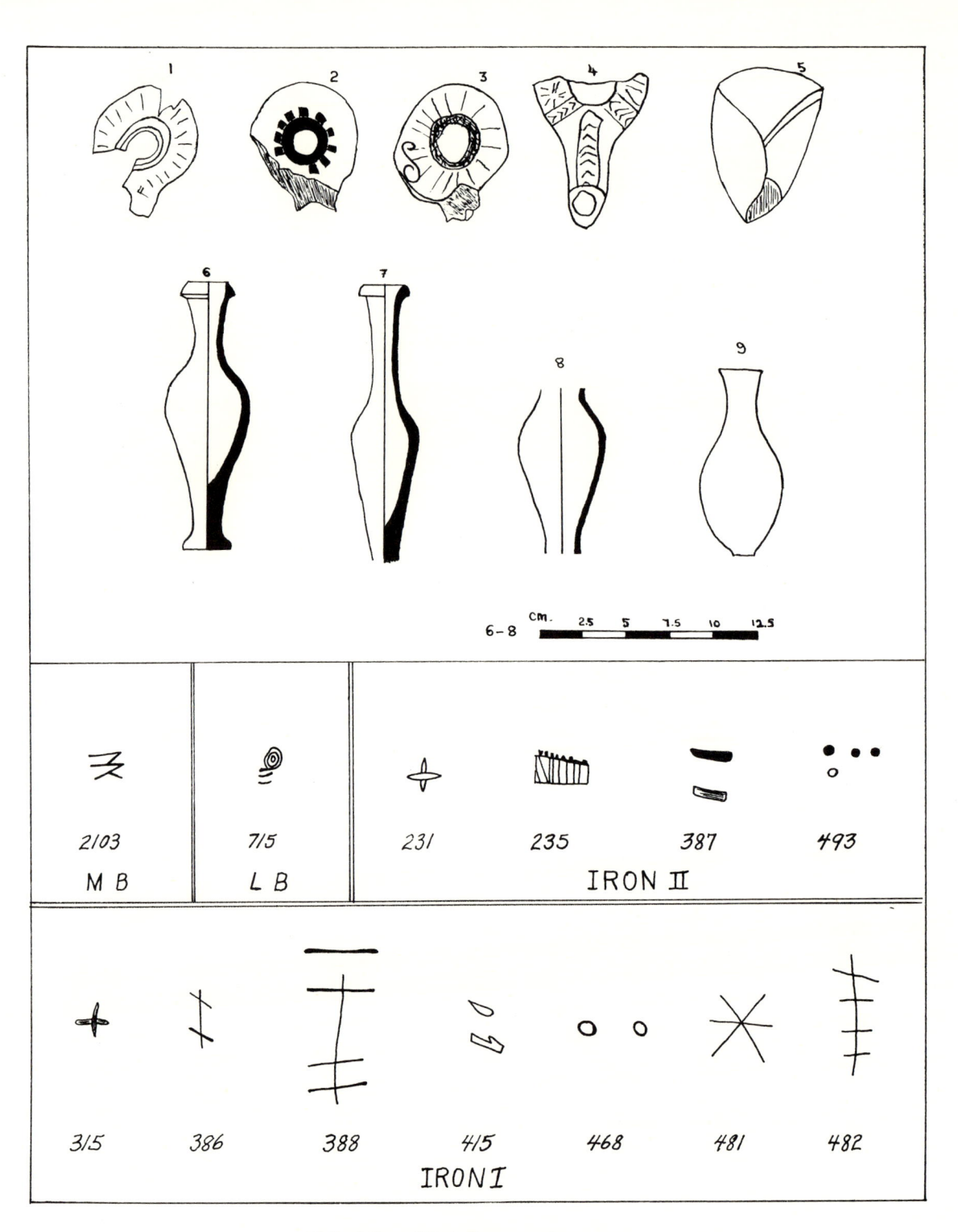

PLATE 72

a Hellenistic and Early Roman pottery.
b Stamped jar handles, Middle Bronze II–Iron II.

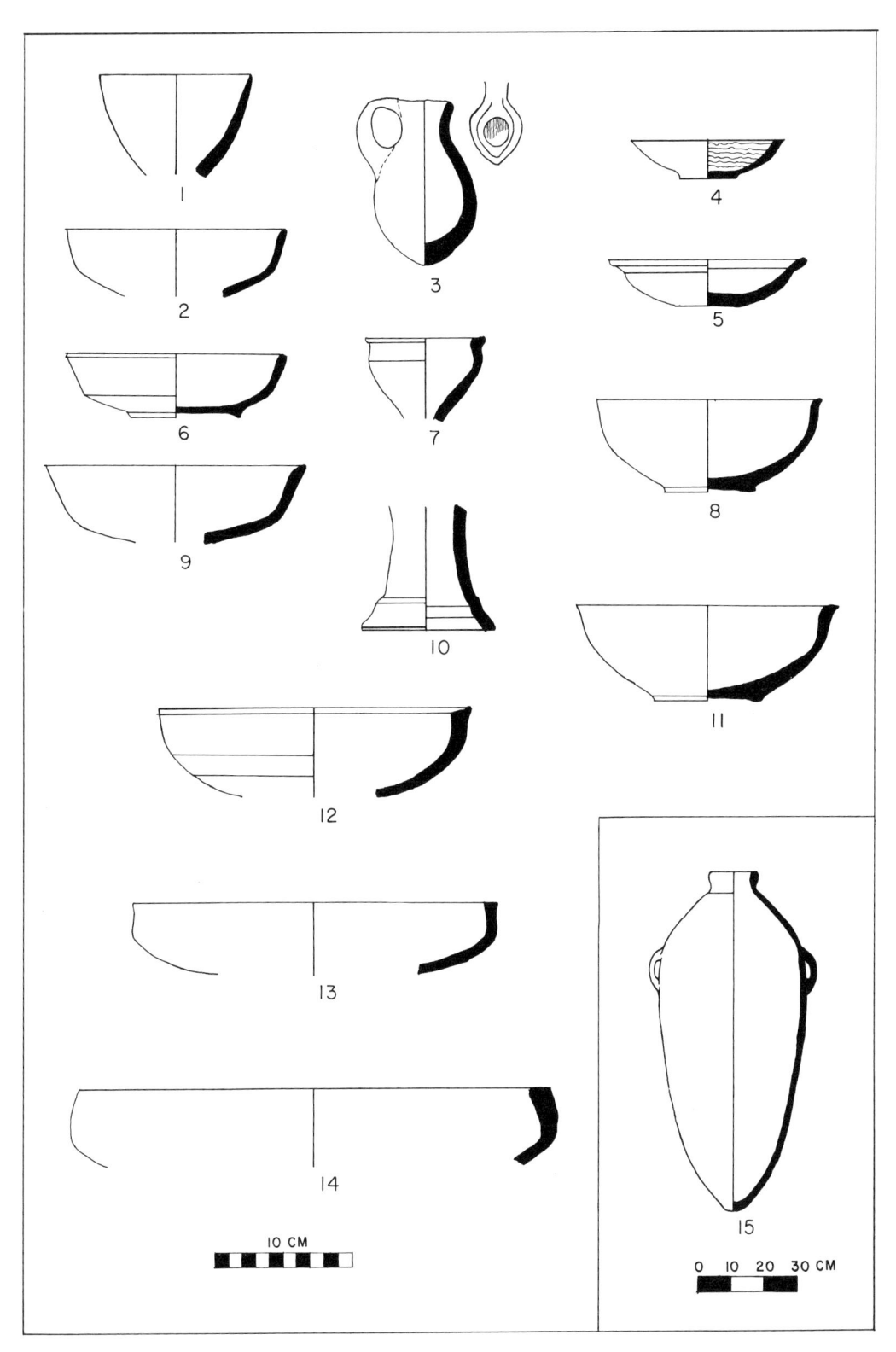

PLATE 73   Late Bronze (No. 1) and Iron I (Nos. 2–15) pottery, 1954.

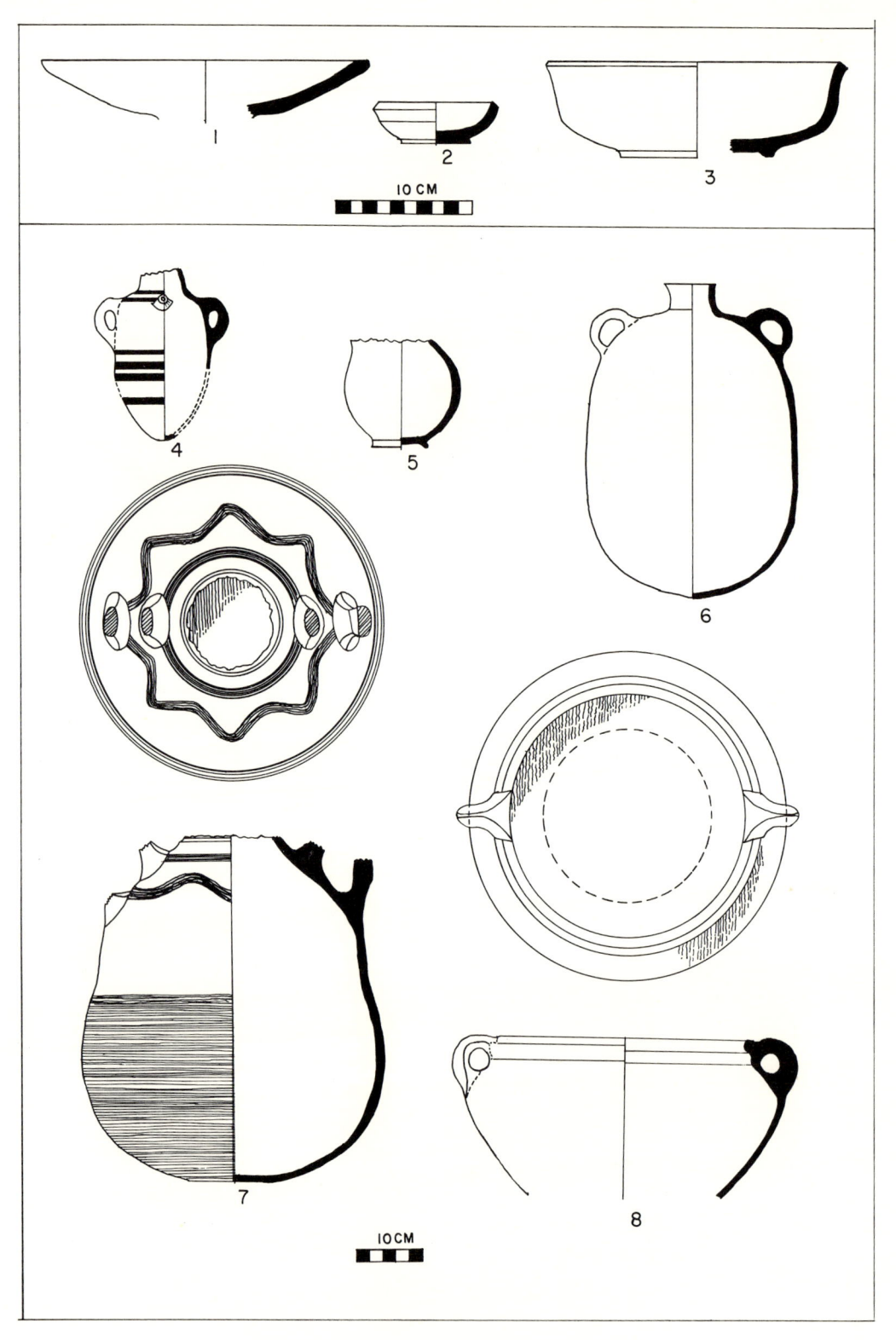

PLATE 74   Iron I (No. 4), Iron II (Nos. 1–3, 5, 8), Roman (No. 6) and Byzantine (No. 7) pottery, 1954.

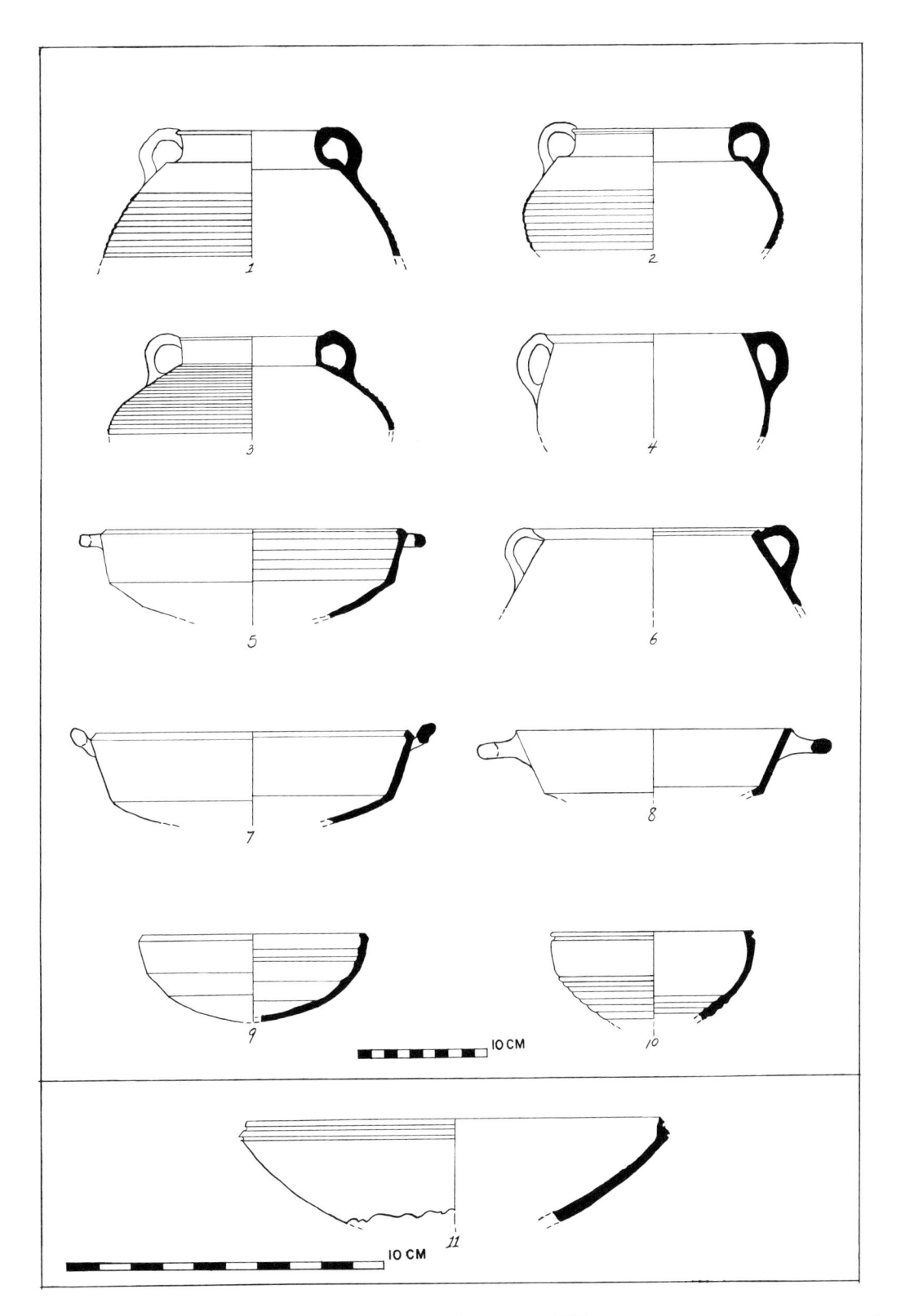

PLATE 75 Roman and Byzantine pottery, 1954.

PLATE 76   Roman and Byzantine pottery, 1954.

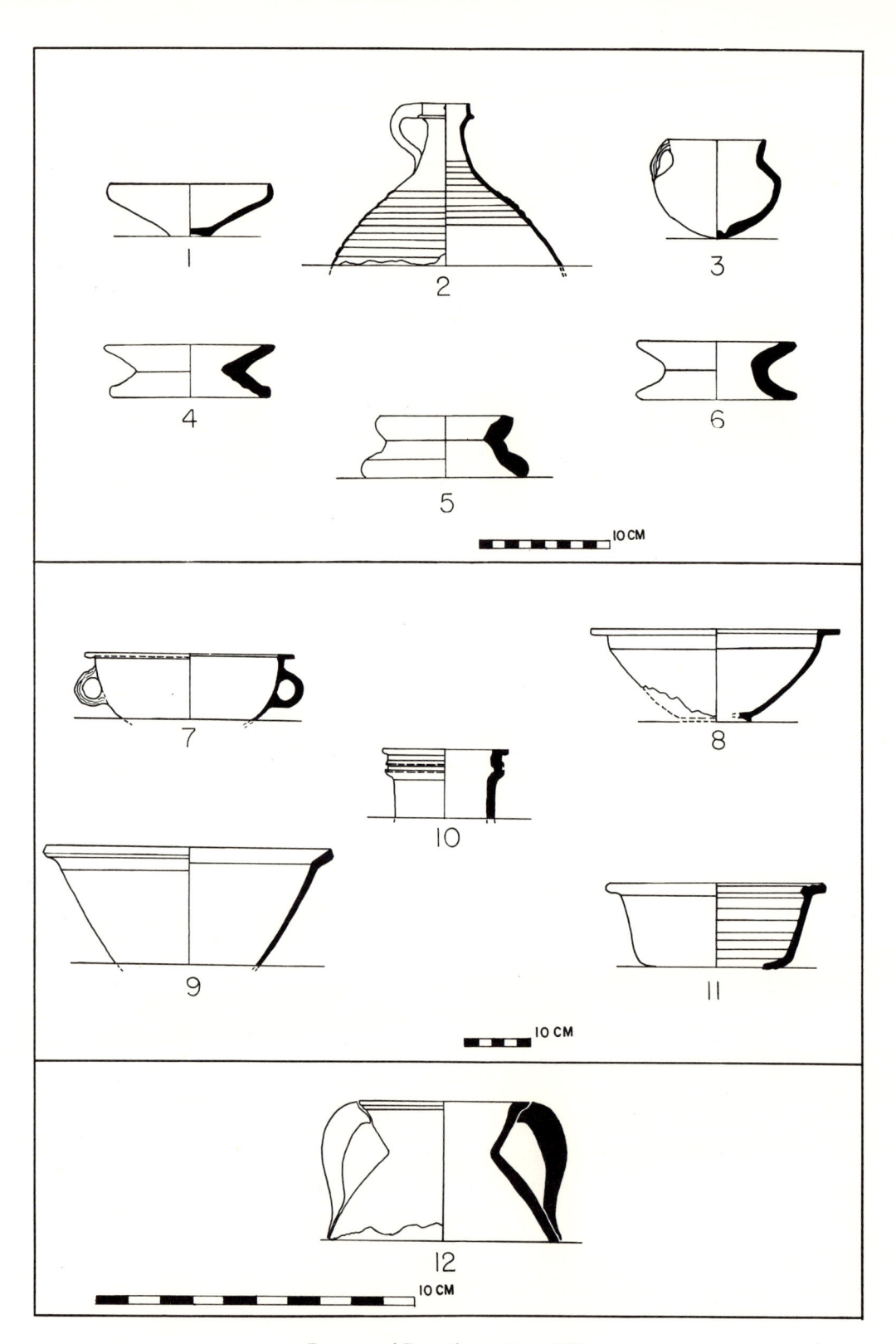

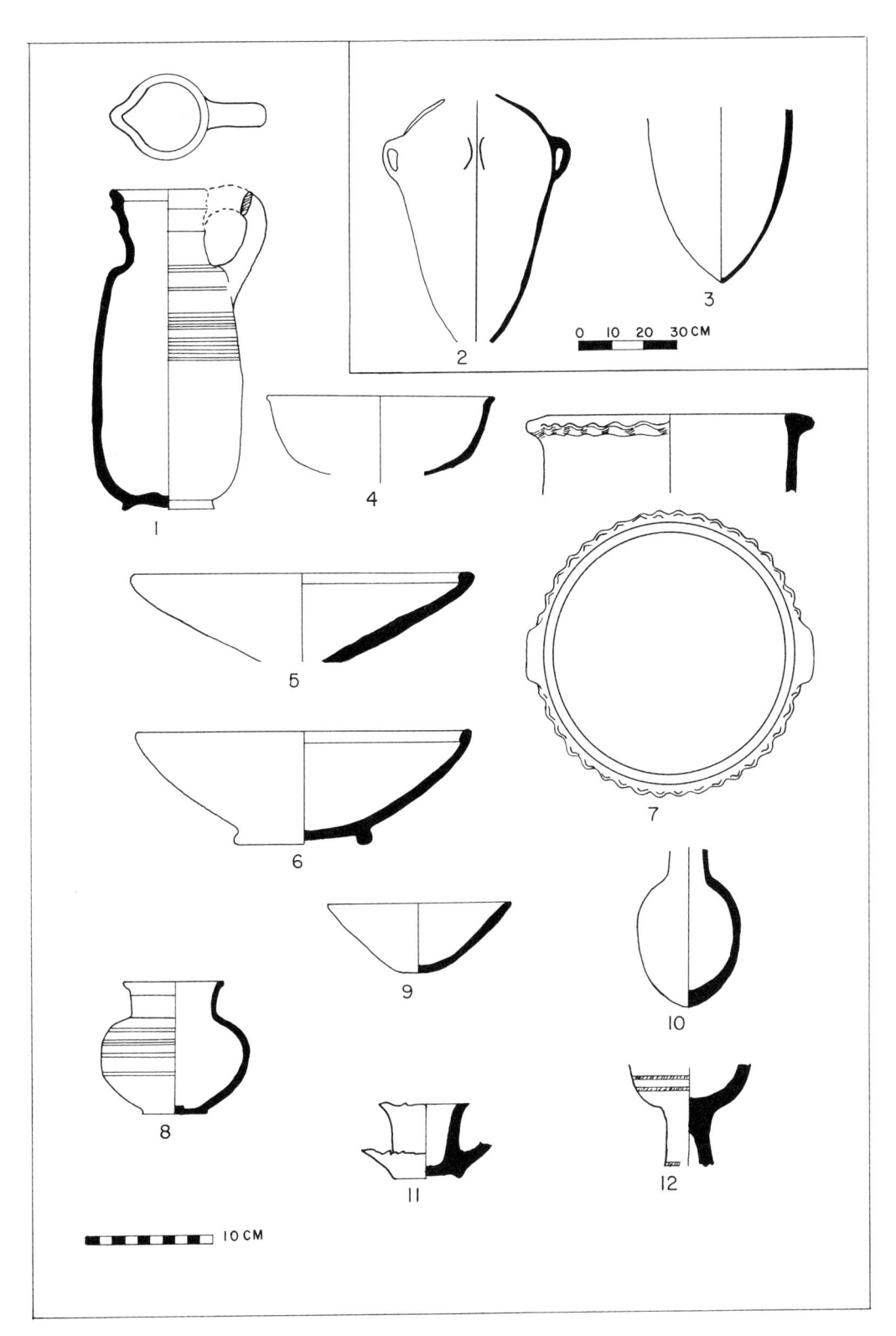

PLATE 77 Middle Bronze II (Nos. 1–7) and Late Bronze (Nos. 8–12) pottery, 1957.

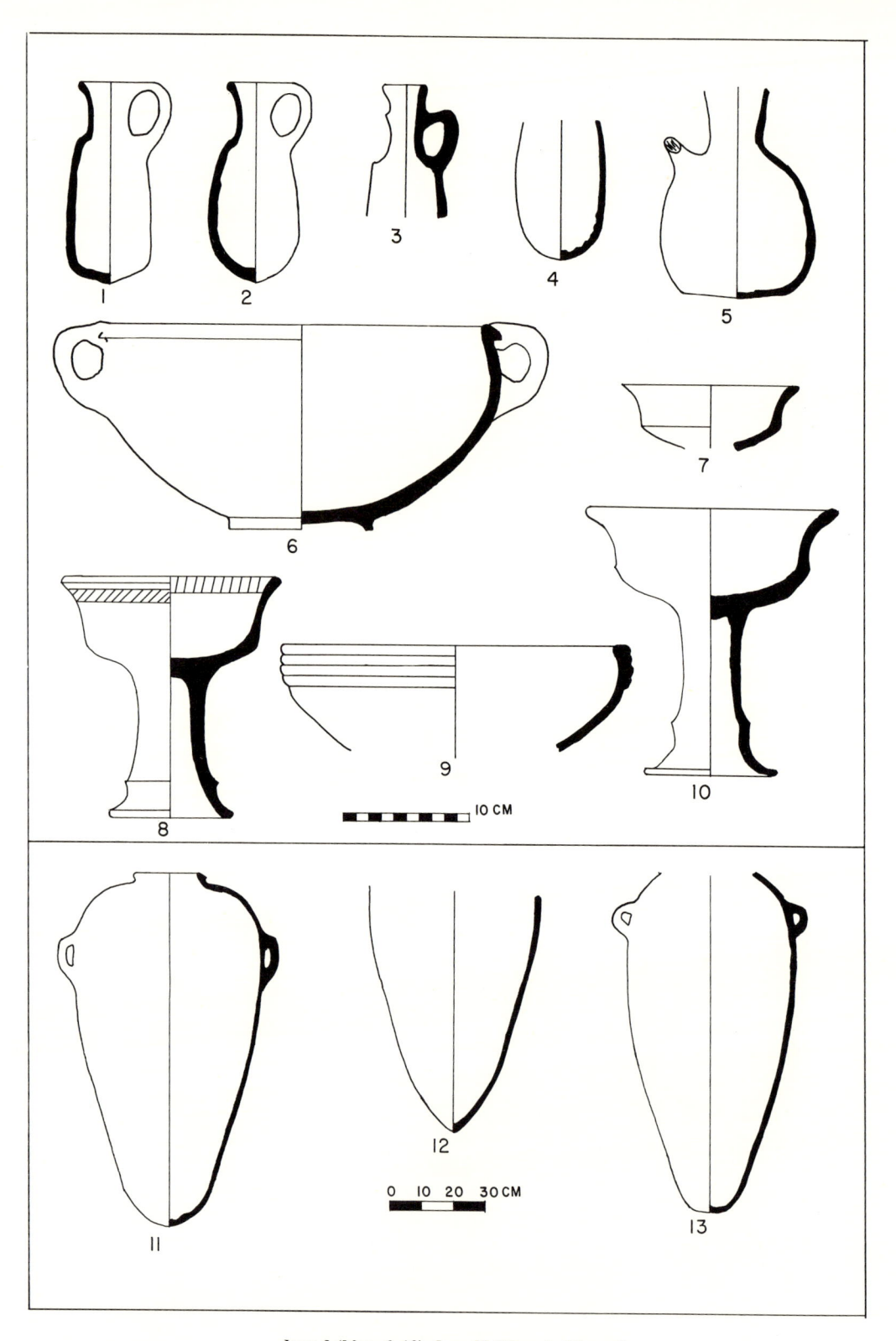

PLATE 78   Iron I (Nos. 6–12), Iron II (Nos. 4, 13), and sixth century B.C. (Nos. 1–3, 5) pottery, 1957.

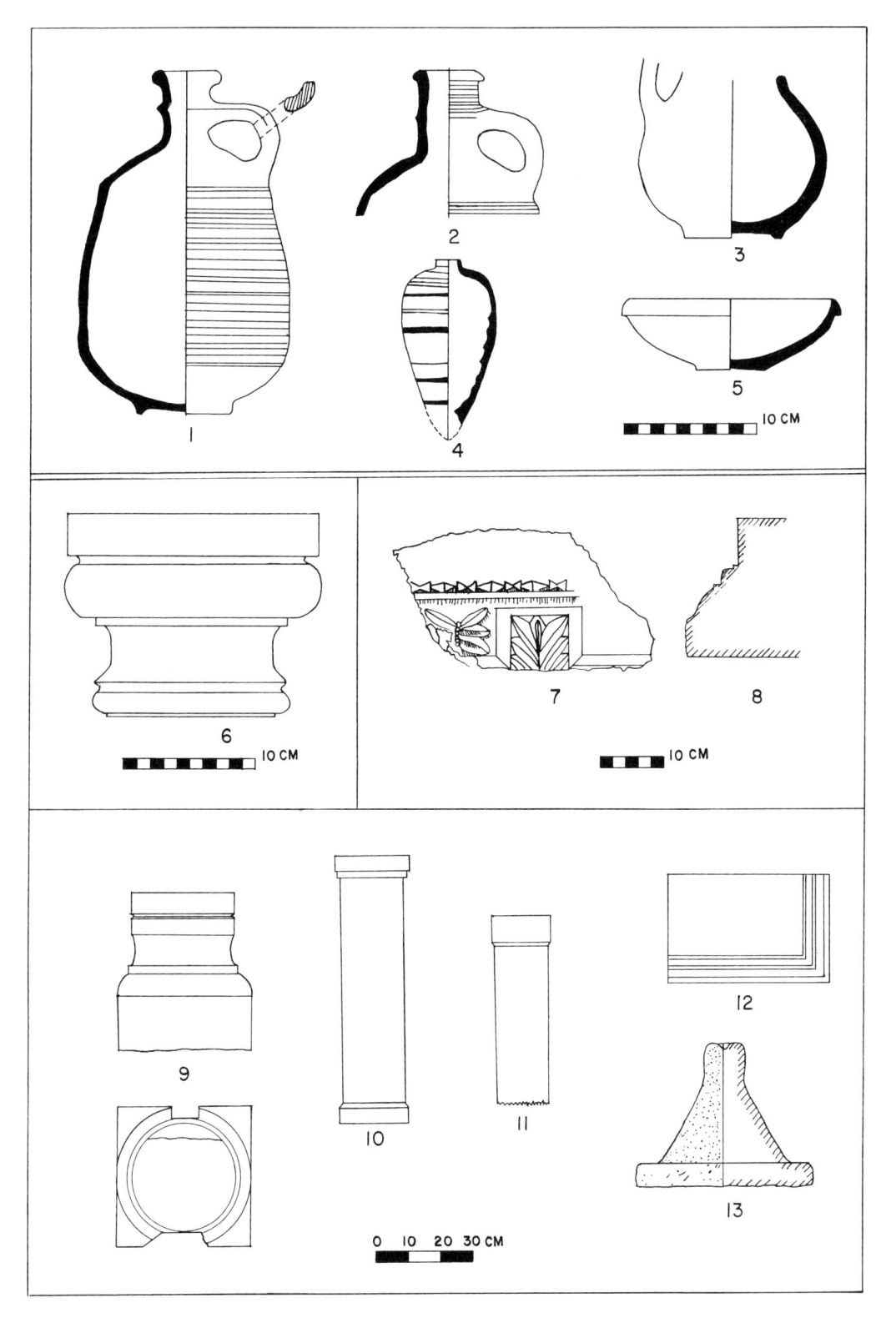

PLATE 79   Iron II (Nos. 1–5) pottery, 1957; Byzantine limestone architectural units (Nos. 7–12), 1954 and (No. 6), 1957; Roman millstone (No. 13), 1954.

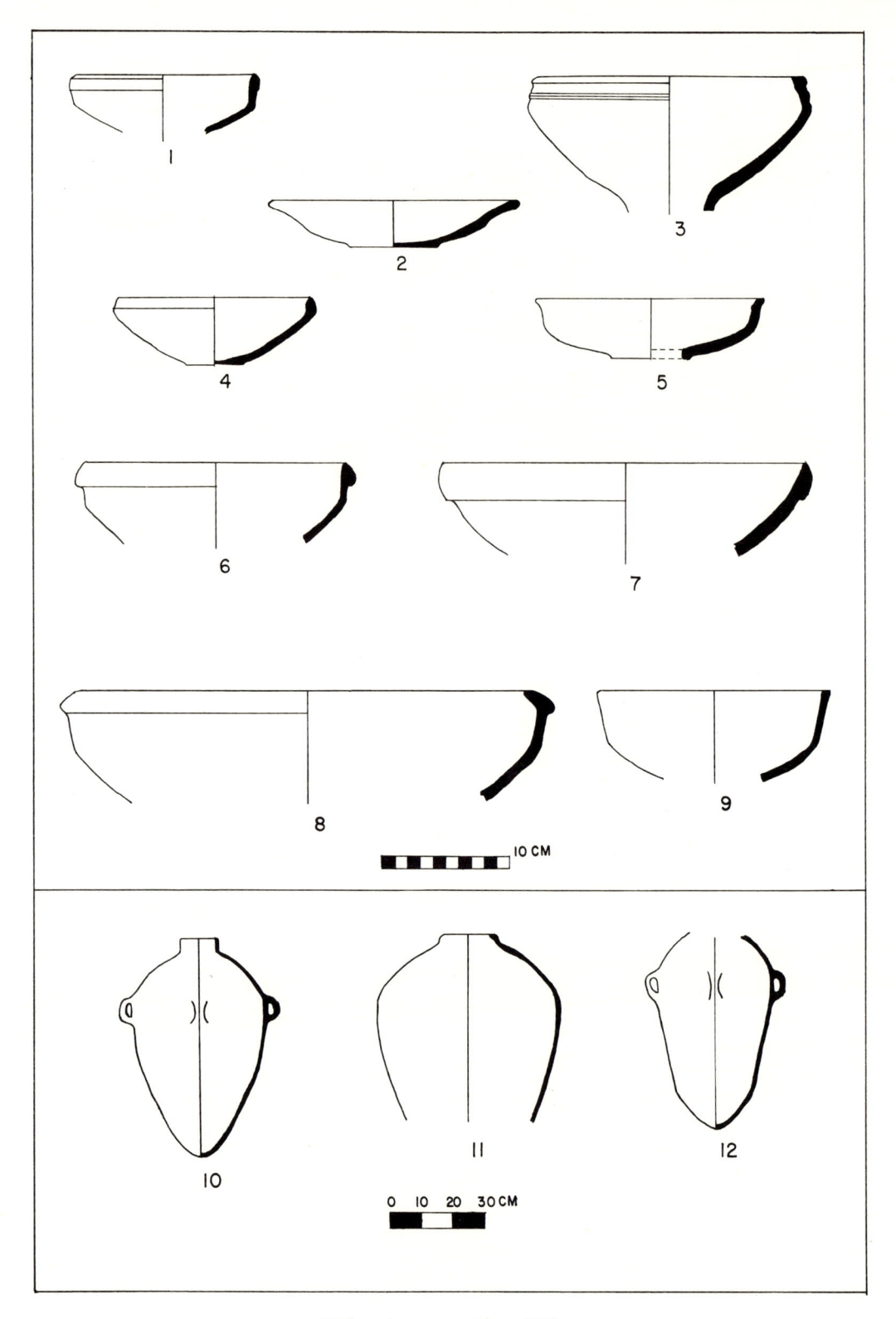

PLATE 80   Sixth century B.C. pottery, 1957.

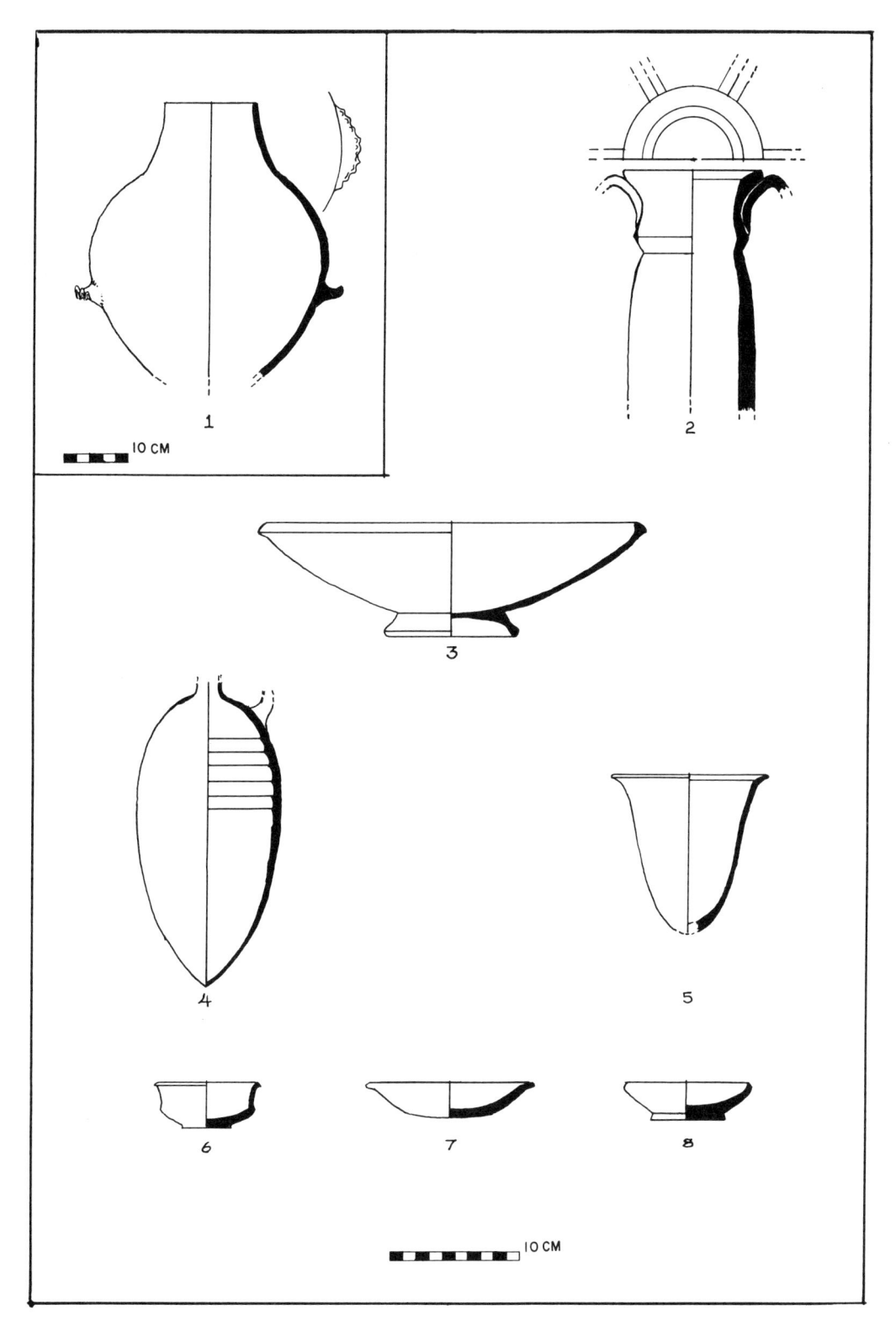

PLATE 81   Chalcolithic (No. 1), Middle Bronze II (Nos. 2–6, 8) and Iron II (No. 7) pottery, 1960.

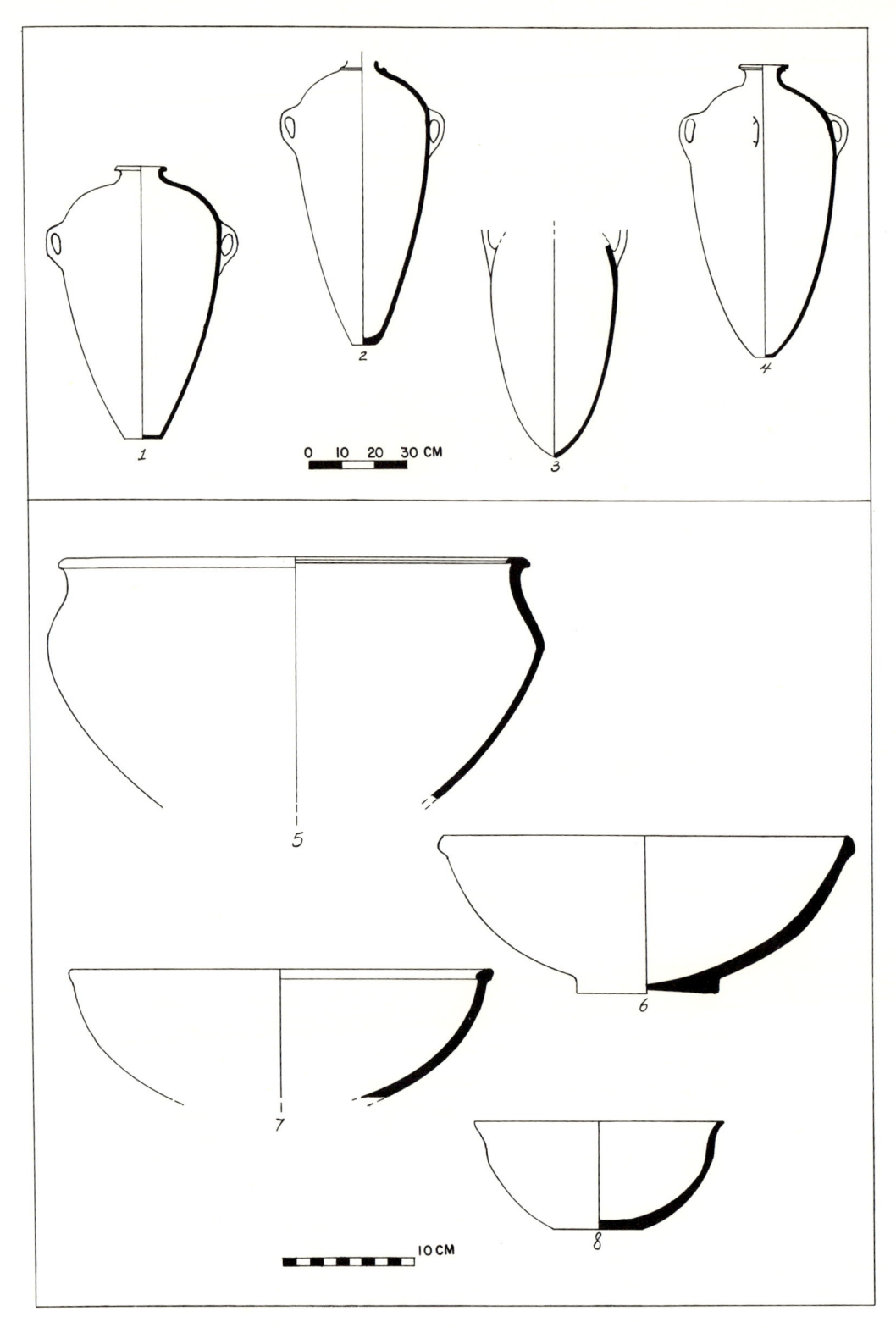

PLATE 82   Middle Bronze II (Nos. 1–2, 4) and Late Bronze (Nos. 3, 5–8) pottery, 1960.

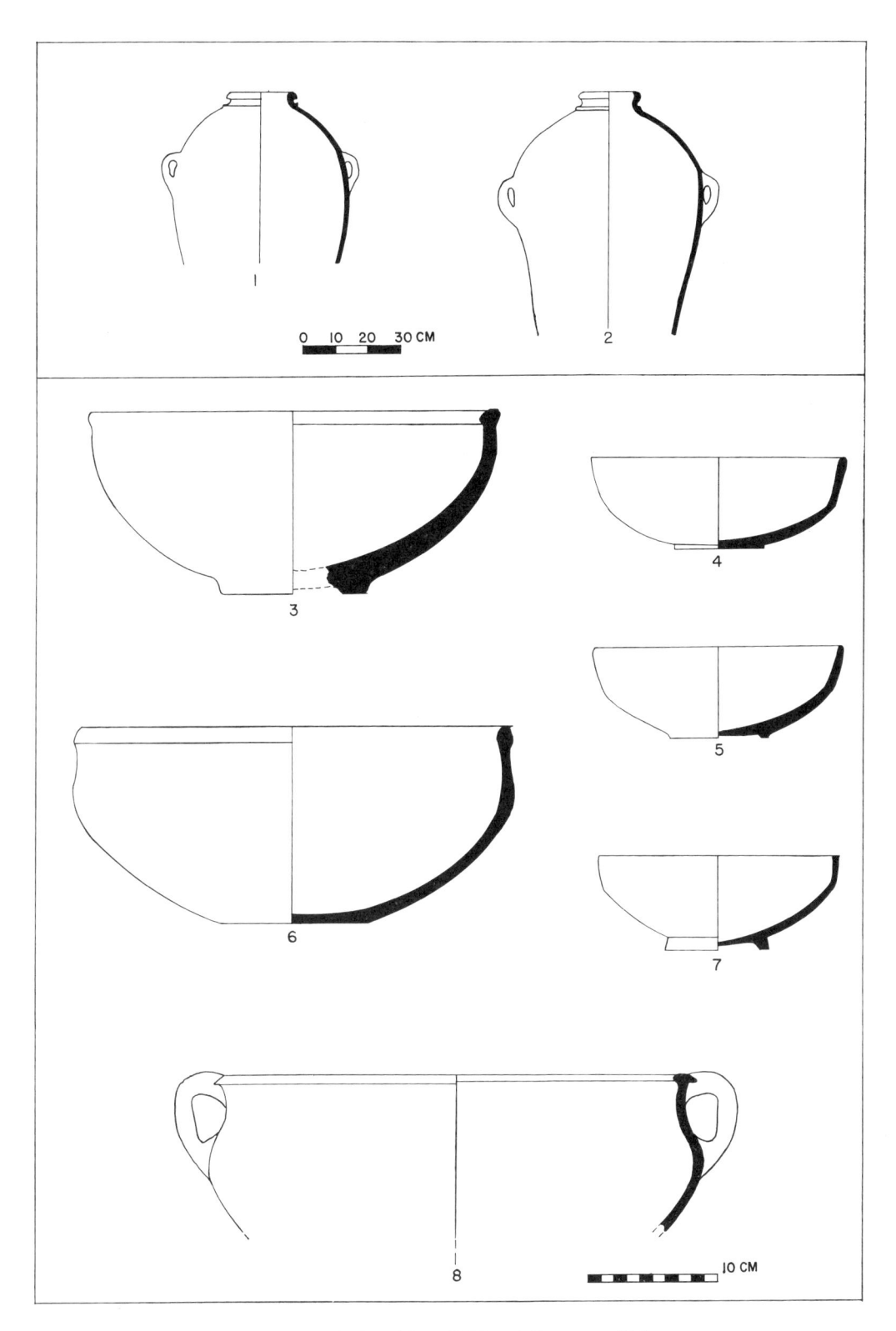

PLATE 83   Iron I (Nos. 3–8) and Iron II (Nos. 1–2) pottery, 1960.

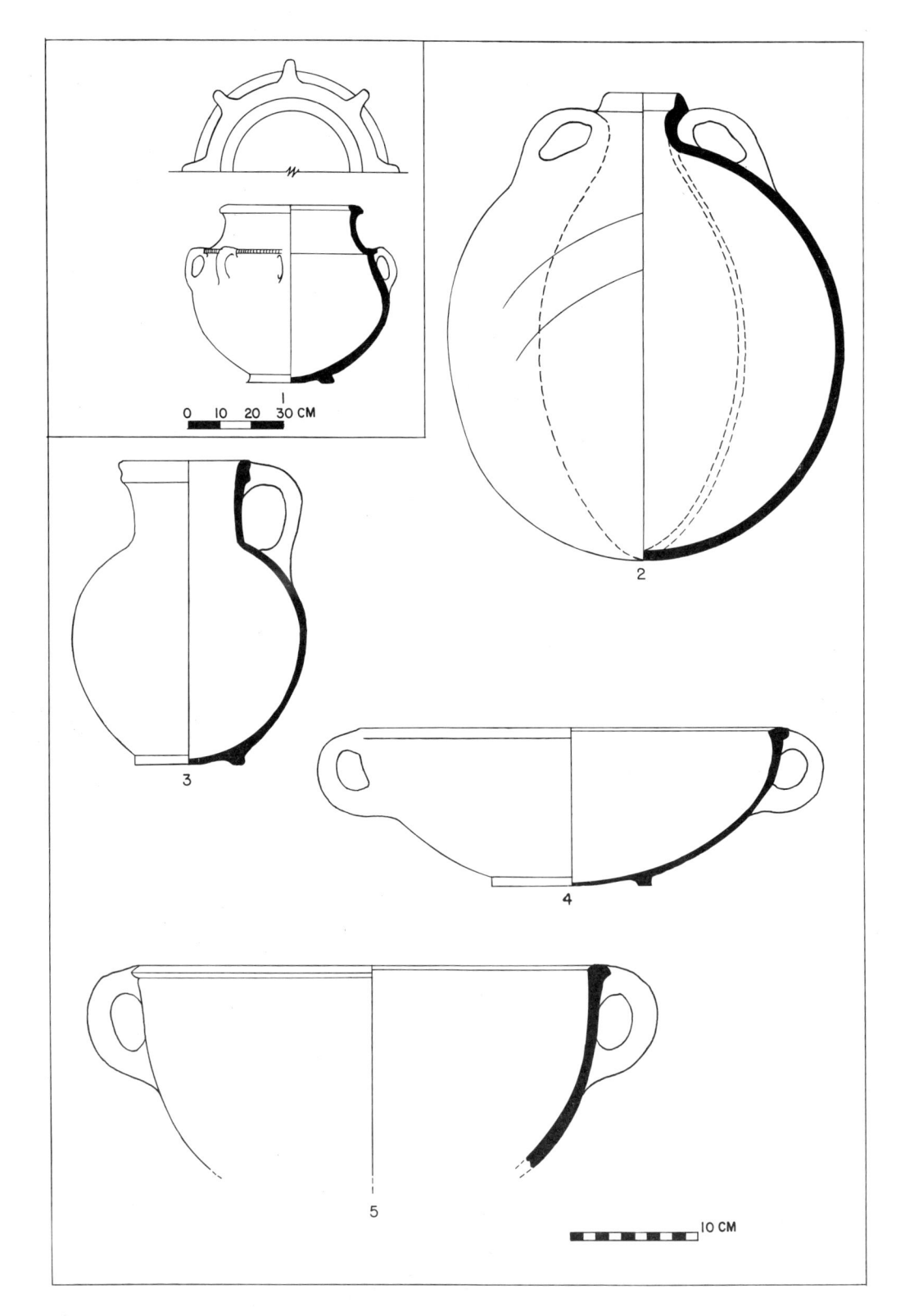

PLATE 84   Iron II pottery, 1960.

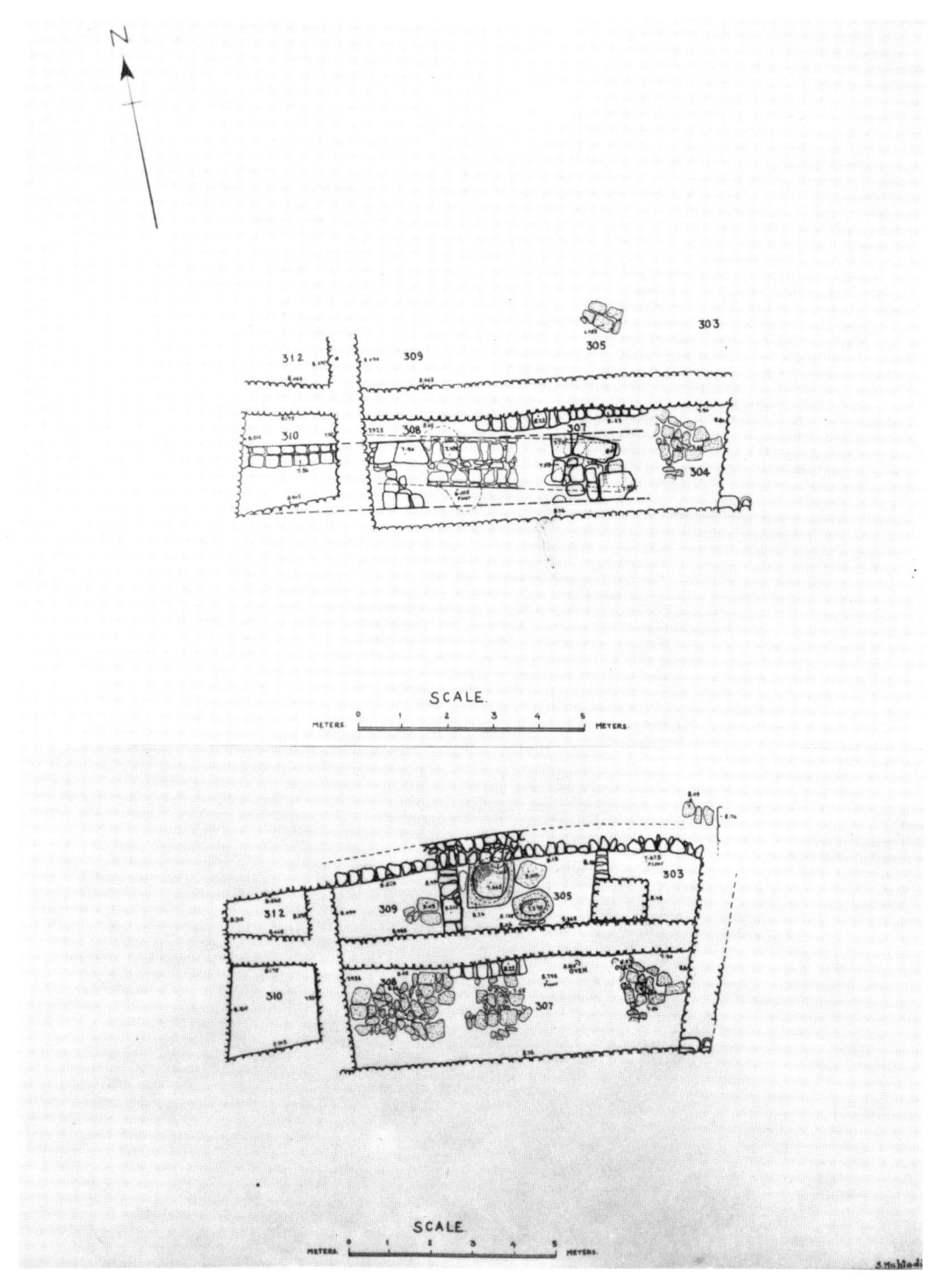

PLATE 85 a Middle Bronze II plans.
b Late Bronze plans.   Olive oil factory in L 305.

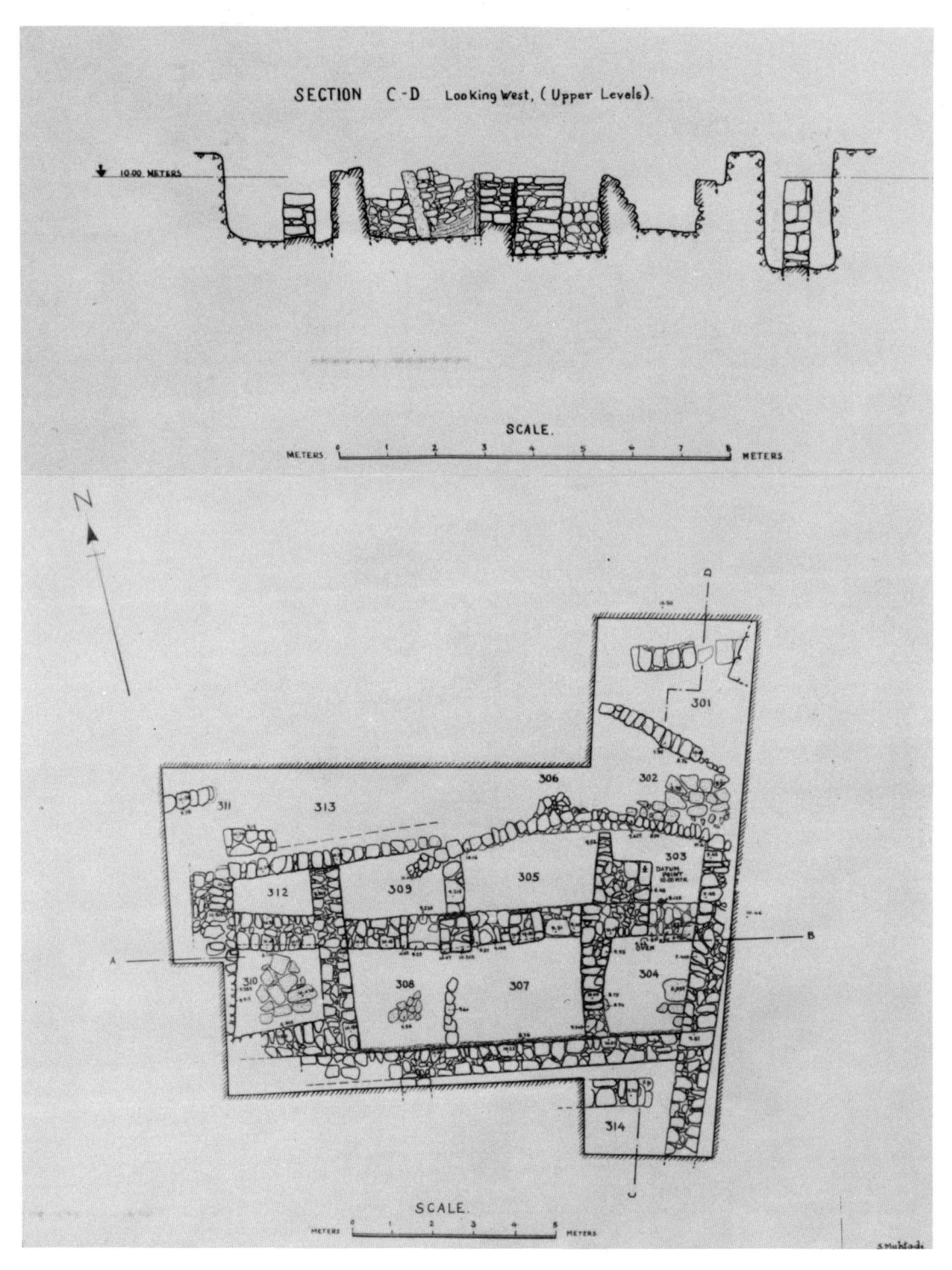

PLATE 86   a Iron I and II cross sections C-D.
          b Iron I and II plans. (Most Iron II houses follow Iron I plans.)

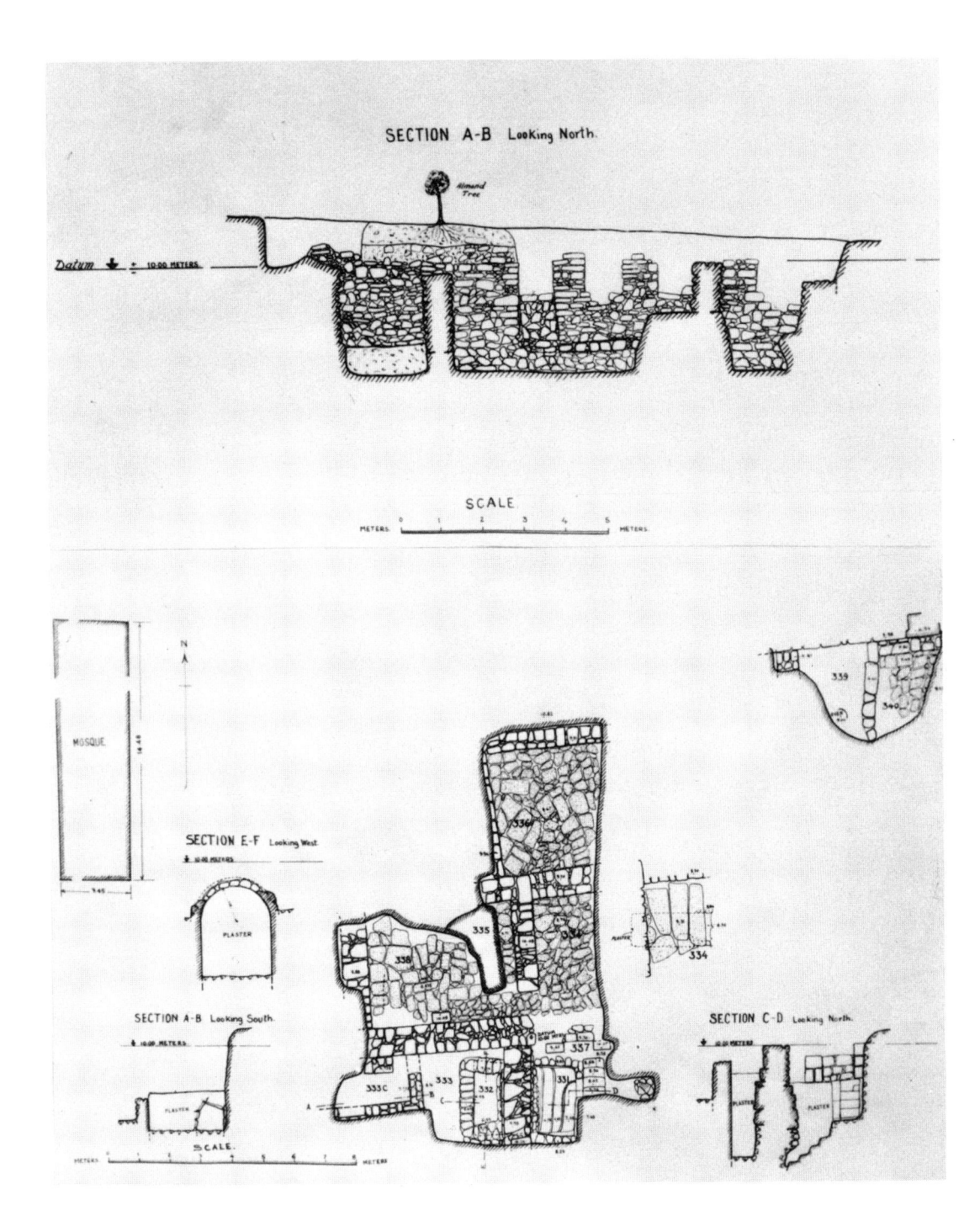

PLATE 87
a Iron I and II cross sections A-B.
b Mosque area plan.

PLATE 88
a Digging through floor of an Iron I house immediately above Late Bronze olive oil factory.
b Iron I wall built upon a Late Bronze foundation course, which is laid upon a wide Middle Bronze II wall.
c Socle of a wide Middle Bronze II wall.

PLATE 89
a Section of south wall of 304, 307, 308, 310, Iron I, phase 2 through Iron II.
c Late Bronze olive oil factory below Iron I walls. Upper walls and doorway are Iron II.
b Canaanite *maṣṣebah* used as doorjamb in Iron I. Doorway to the right was blocked up late in Iron II.
d Late Bronze olive oil factory.

PLATE 90
a Roman cistern mosque area. Shadow at top of photo is cast by part of the vault still intact.
c Roman cistern below; Byzantine walls above, mosque area.
b Pavement of Byzantine building, mosque area.
d Architectural units from Byzantine church and lower half of Roman millstone.

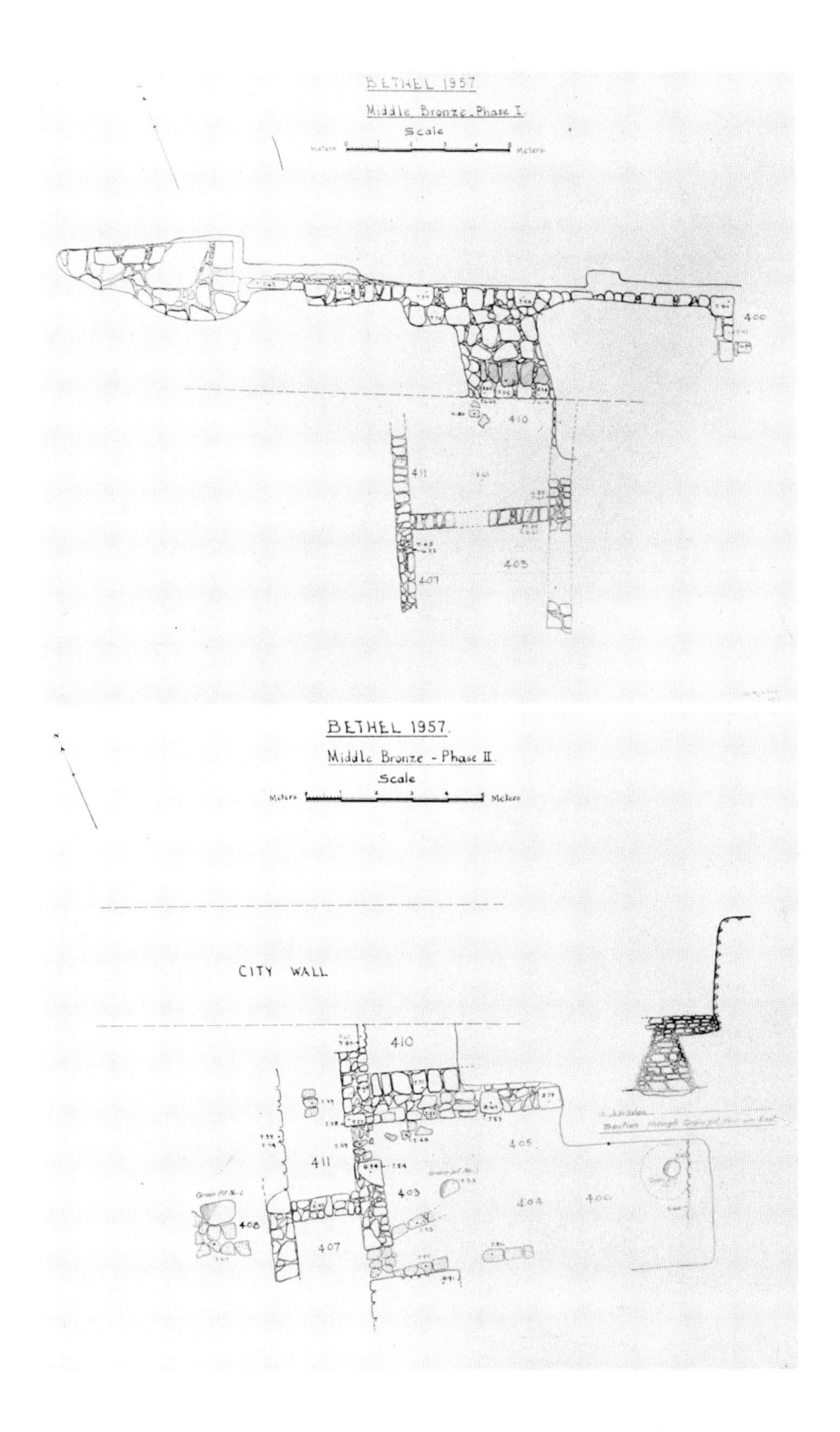

PLATE 91   a   Middle Bronze II plans, phase 1. North city wall and house walls.
           b   Middle Bronze II plans, phase 2. Patrician house with grain silos.

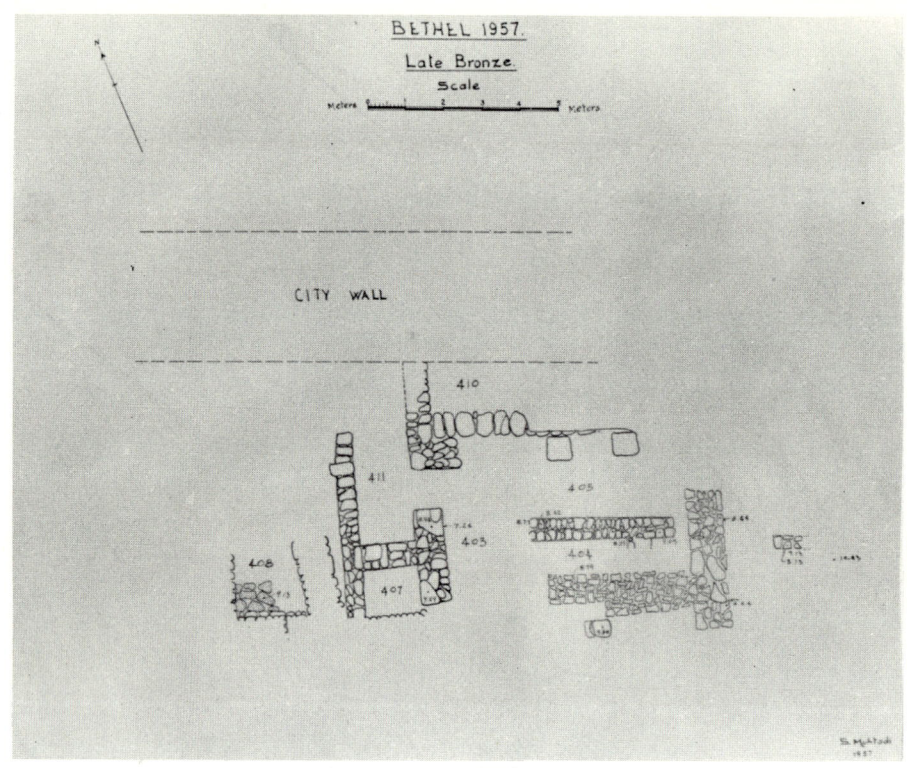

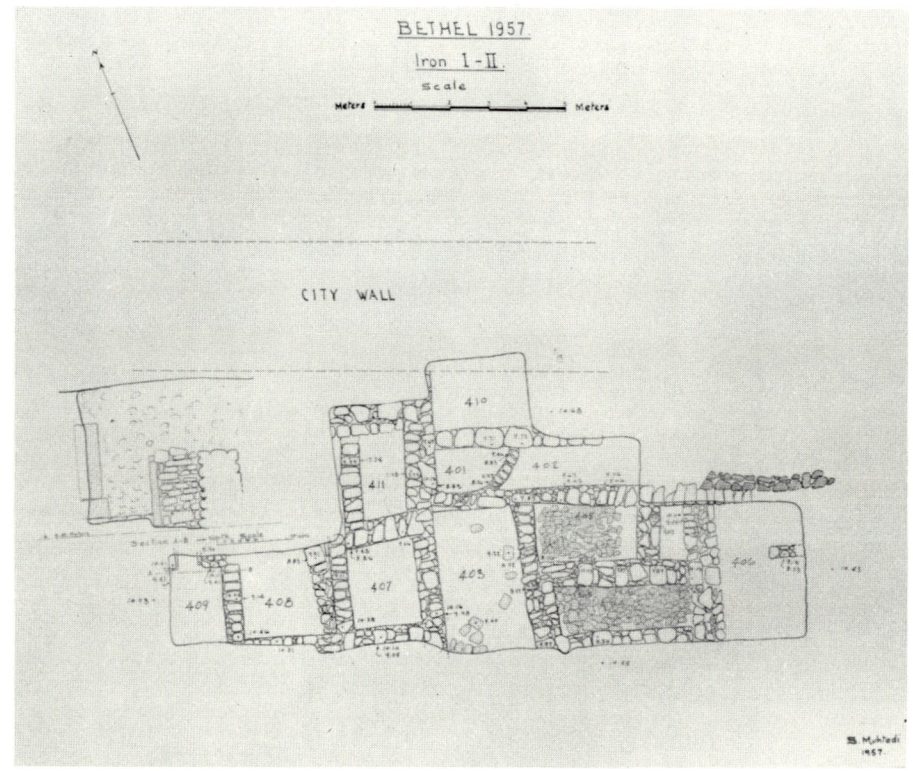

PLATE 92   a Late Bronze plans.
          b Iron I and II plans. (Most Iron II house walls follow Iron I plans.)

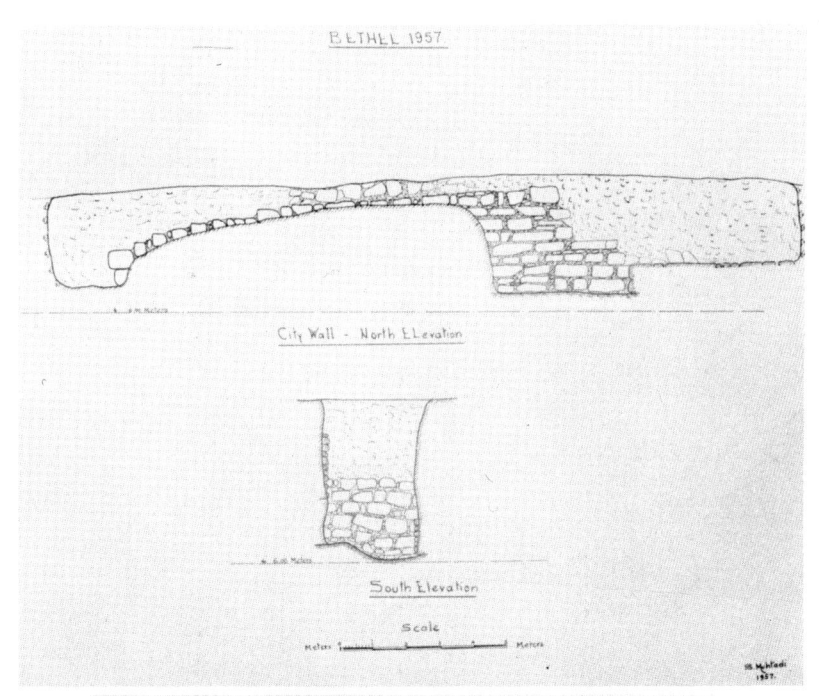

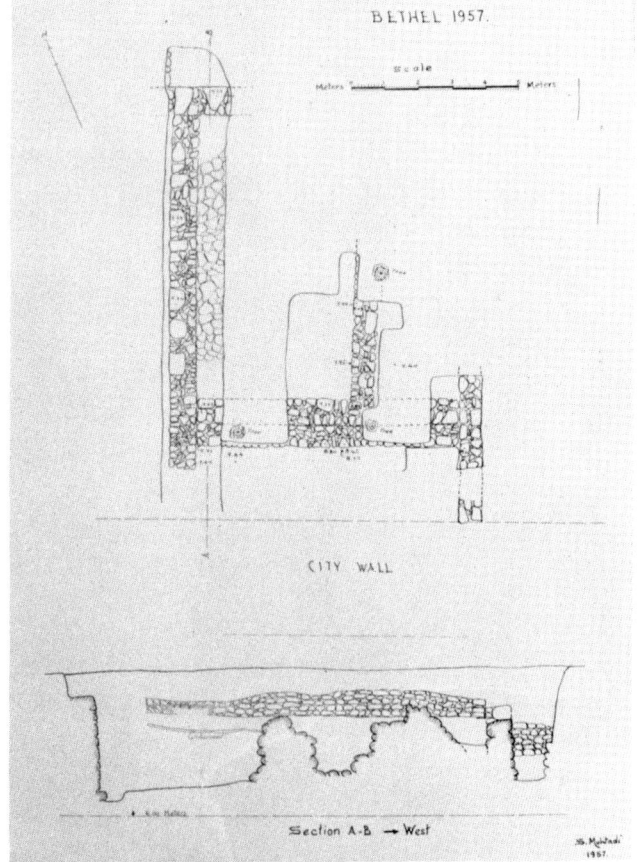

PLATE 93   a   North city wall, exterior view.
                 b   Hellenistic and Roman houses built across north city wall.
                 c   Cross section A-B of glacis of north city wall.

PLATE 94   a   West wall of city in Abu Tabar area.   b   *Maḍâfeh* area.

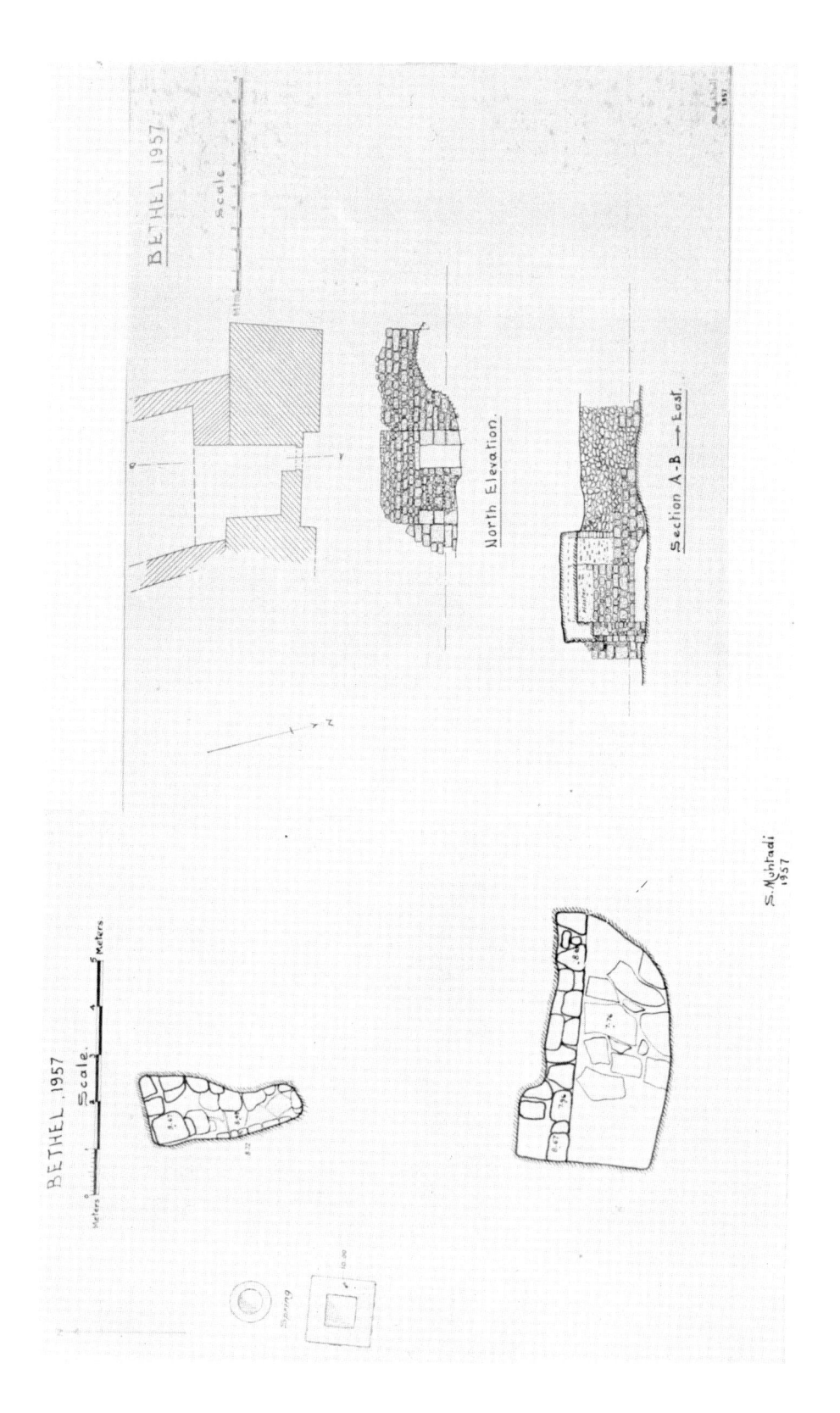

PLATE 95 a Foundations of south gate of Roman city   b Northeast city gate of Byzantine city.

PLATE 96   a   Outer face of north city wall; see also *BASOR*, No. 151, Fig. 2.

b   Revetment of Byzantine city wall forming rear wall of Arab house.

a Middle Bronze II room (with meter stick) abutting on north city wall (to the right).
b Inside view of north city wall with opposite house wall of the above room abutting on north city wall.

a   Exterior of west city wall (upper courses only).   See Plate 94a.
b   Courtyard of Middle Bronze II patrician house (403, 404, 405, 406) in foreground with 411 beyond the courtyard.   See Plate 91b.

PLATE 98

PLATE 99 a Doorway of an Iron I house with the right jamb made from a Late Bronze doorsill and the left one made from a stone taken from the Middle Bronze II city wall.

b Tower patch on west wall of city in Abu Tabar area probably blocking former city gate, see lower drawing in Plate 94a.

PLATE 100   a West wall of courtyard of a Middle Bronze II patrician house; upper center portion is a poor Late Bronze repair.
         b Two types of Iron I walls and a pavement.

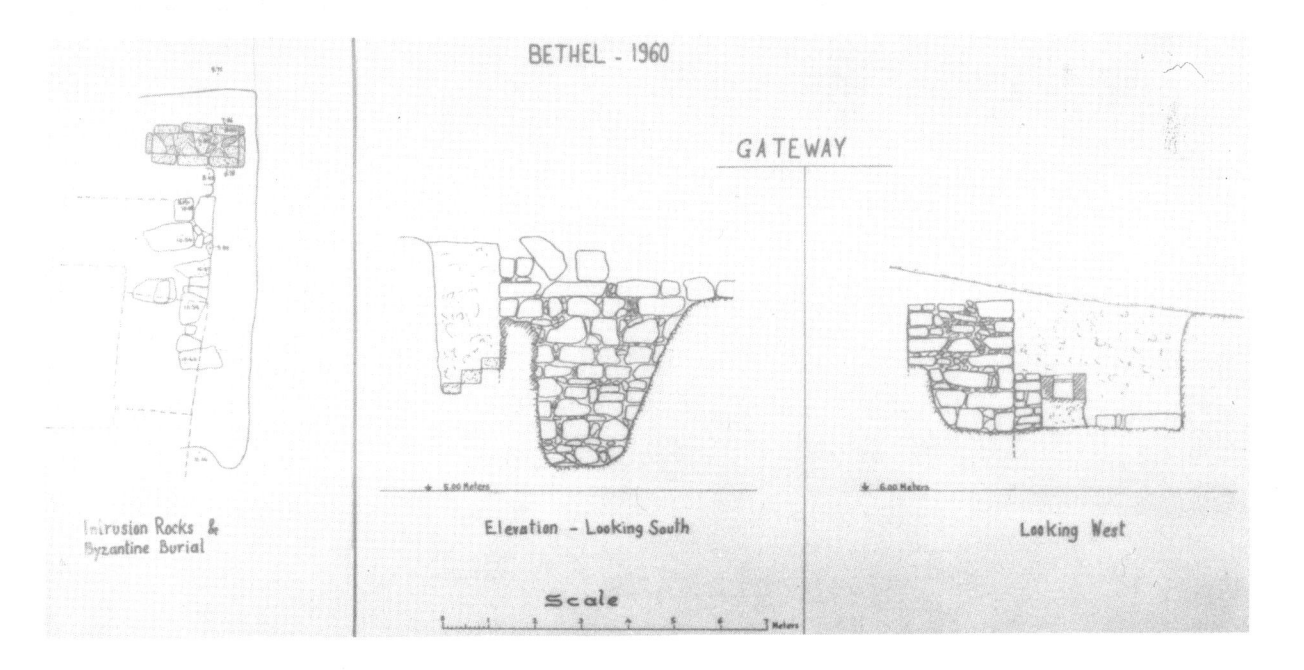

PLATE 101 Plan and elevation of Middle Bronze II gateway complex and Canaanite high place. The latter is shown in the right half of the long east-west passageway. The northwest city gate, with the three steps outside it, is at the east end of the passageway. Steps also lead up from the west end of the passageway toward the south. Then the gateway turns east. The *ḥáram* area lies north of the city gate.

PLATE 102 a West city wall where it abuts on the northwest city gate.

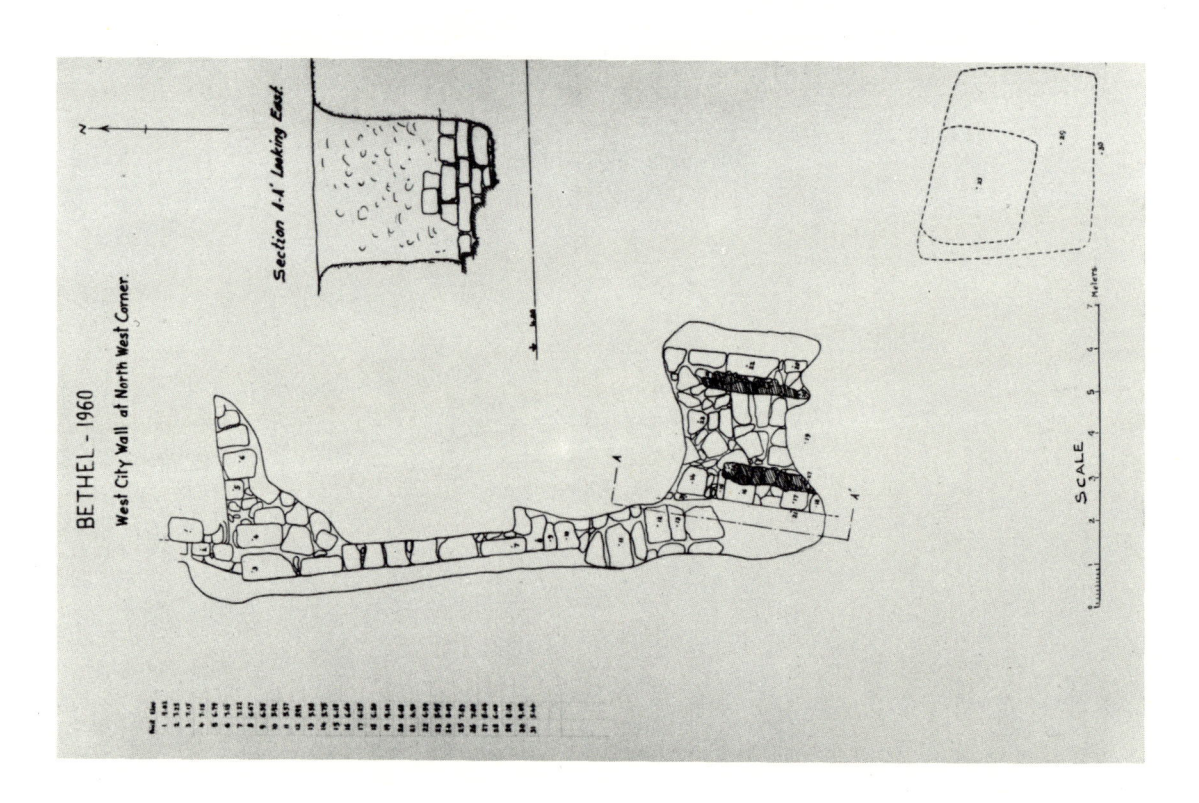

b West city wall running through a peasant's house.

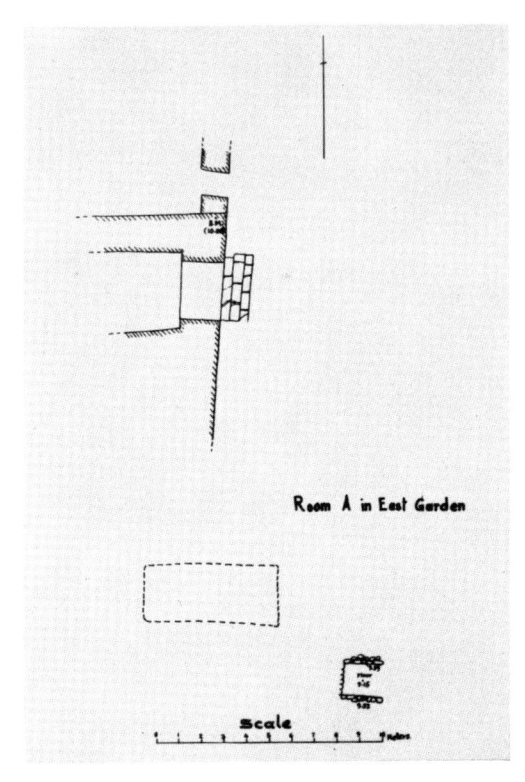

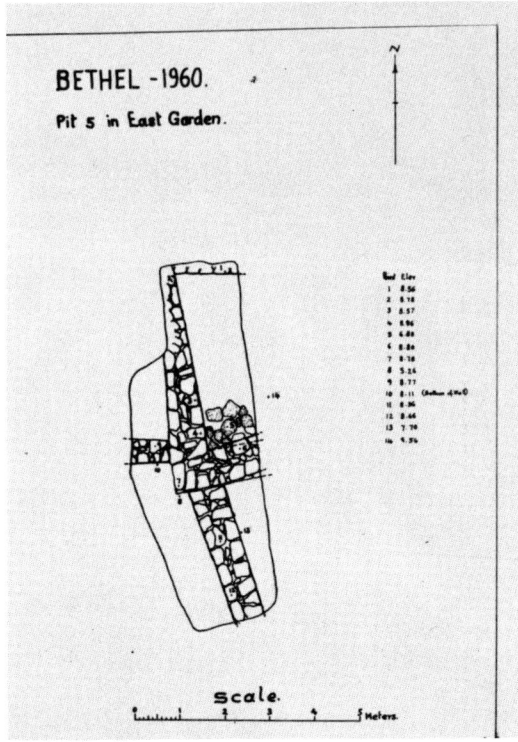

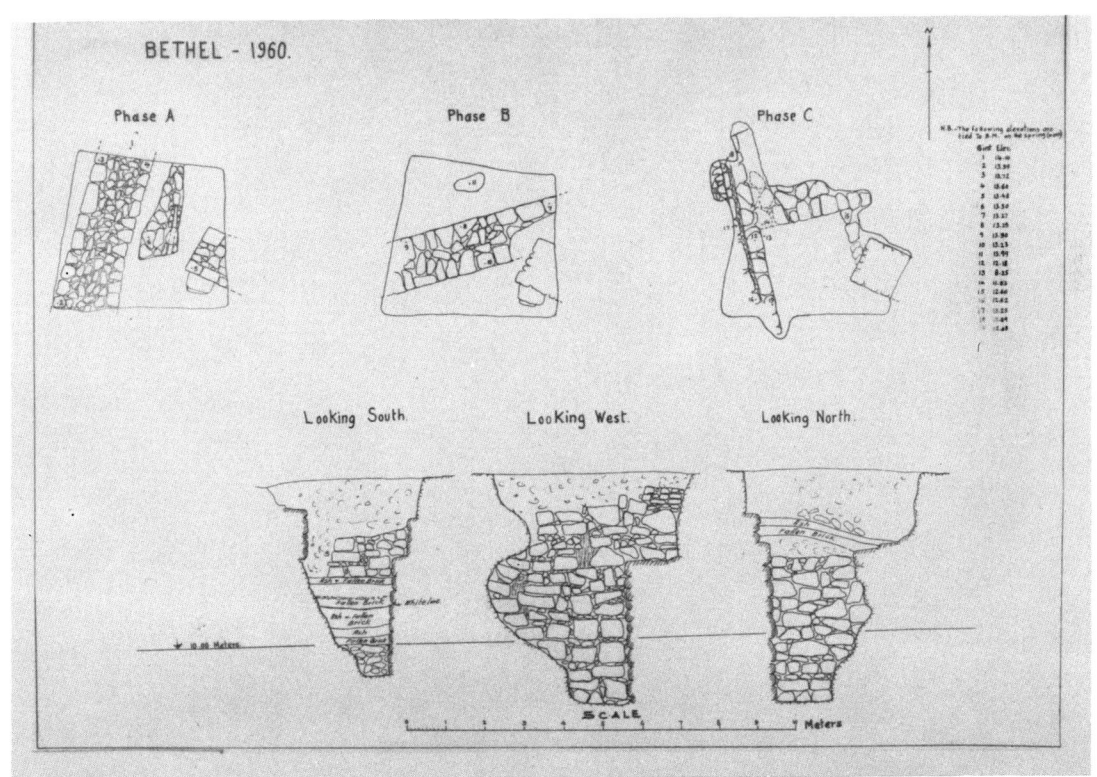

PLATE 103
    a Roman room (A) south of the northwest city gate.
    b Pit 5, southeast of the northwest city gate.
    c South city wall area, plans and elevations. For detailed description see § 70ff.

PLATE 104   a   Expedition staff: (standing left to right) Messrs. Abu Dayeh, Brownlee, Kelso, Jackson, R. Jones, Coughenour, McClellan, T. Taylor, (sitting left to right) Messrs. M. Taylor, Land-owner, Olsen, J. Jones, Mehl, Mrs. Wolfe, Bayyuk, Wolfe. For other members not in photo see § 31.

                    b   Northwest corner of U-shaped city gateway complex, looking almost due east early in the excavation. The gate itself is to the right and behind the meter stick. The *hâram* area was discovered under the debris to the left.

PLATE 105 a Steps leading southward from the west end of the north corridor of the northwest city gateway. A portion of the *ḥúwar* platform is visible behind the steps.
b Steps outside the same city gateway leading up to the gate proper.
c Middle Bronze II gateway, looking east from the passageway after the floor had been excavated. The east wall of the MB I temple with its blocked doorway lies immediately below the gateway.

PLATE 106 a Northwest city gate above; temple walls immediately below. *Húwar* floor of gateway in foreground.
 b Section of high place rock ledge with south wall of temple and some paving stones of temple floor above the ledge.

PLATE 107

a Doorway into ḥaram area. Top of meter stick leans against stones forming Byzantine grave.

c Dark areas are blood spots on the limestone at the east end of high place.

b East wall of northwest city gateway. In foreground is debris left by Byzantines who plundered the Middle Bronze II city wall for stone to build their new city wall.

d Bin of high place with temple walls above it.

PLATE 108

a Temple above the high place; south wall of temple below (with meter stick) and south wall of city gate above. The latter is laid directly on the former.

b High place ledge and north walls of temple and city gate. West end of the floor of the gate's north corridor is beyond the ledge.

PLATE 109

a Southwest corner of an MB II temple in pit 5.

b South jamb of northwest city gate (reconstruction).

PLATE 110

a West wall of city where it abuts on northwest city gate. Meter stick leans against the gateway complex.

b Interior face of west city wall (near northwest gate) with Middle Bronze II house wall abutting on it.

PLATE 111

a   Exterior face of west city wall showing junction of two units of that wall on slightly different alignments.

b   Exterior face of the west wall north of junction. Foundation courses in foreground.

PLATE 112

a At the top of photo is an Iron I wall. Below it a large triangular stone marks the preserved top of the Middle Bronze II B city wall. The main south wall is at the right. The one with the meter stick is the inner side of a south city gate or the outer side of a tower. The wall in foreground is Roman.

b Roman and Byzantine house walls above city's south wall. Roman city gate was under the house to the left and in front of it. Byzantine reservoir in background.

Middle Bronze I sherds with some earlier sherds from Canaanite high place area under the gateway complex.

PLATE 113

PLATE 114

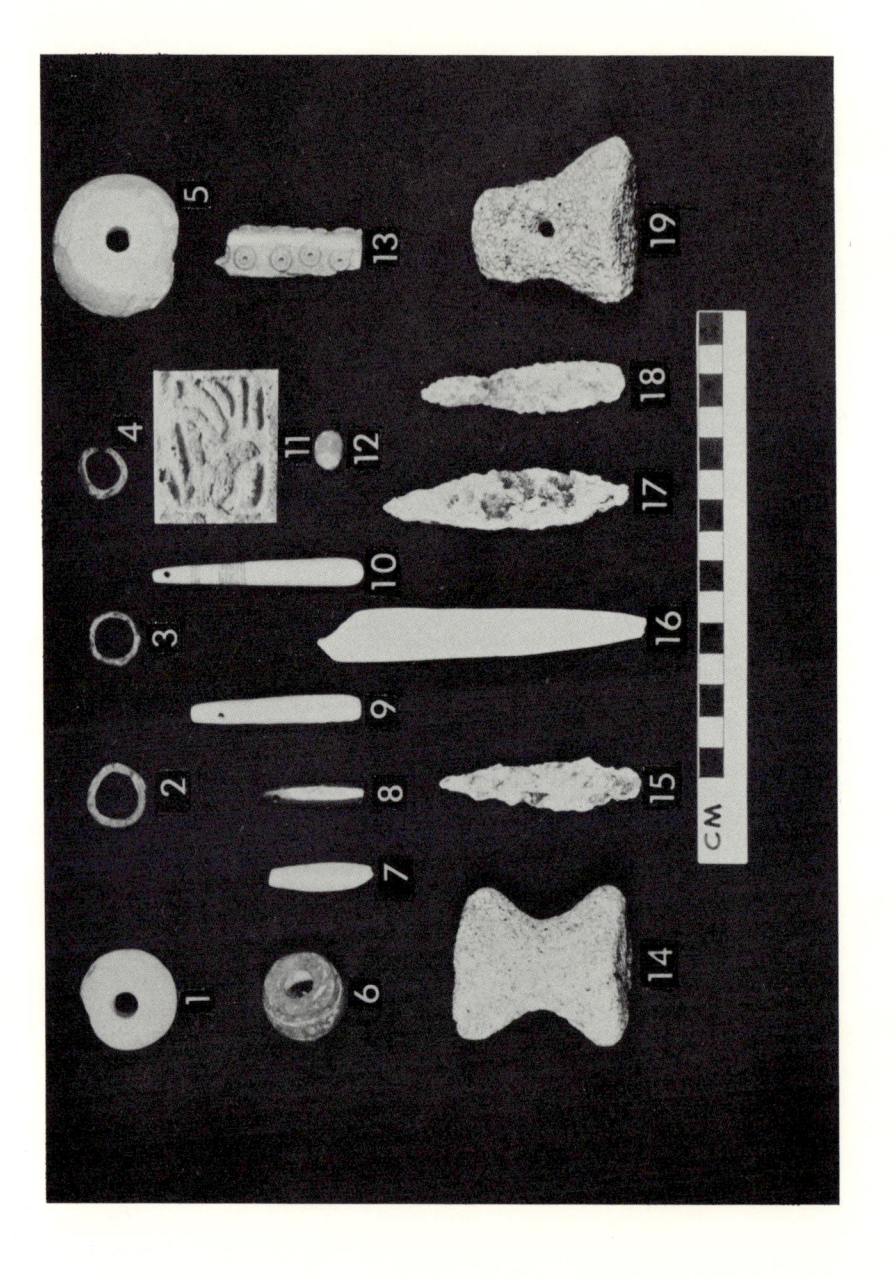

1954 artifacts.

PLATE 115

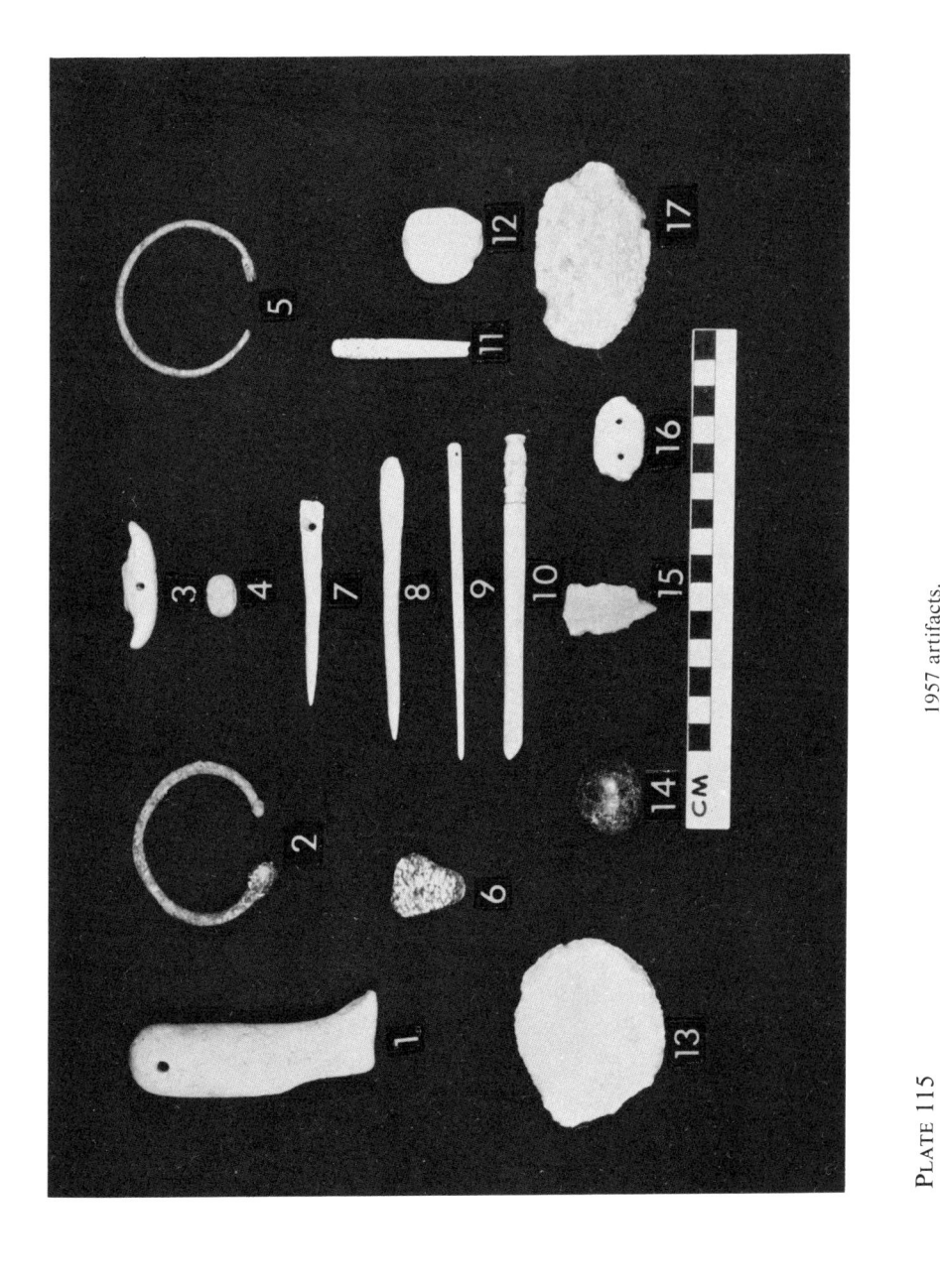

1957 artifacts.

PLATE 116   1960 artifacts.

PLATE 117   Iron I store-jars. Left to right, Nos. 2271, 1151, 2272.
The center jar is from the 1954 campaign, the others from 1957.

FIG. 1. Face of the South Arabian stamp from Bethel, showing the deeply gouged letters and line dividers.

FIG. 2. The upper surface of the stamp. The short random lines on the surface are impressions of straw temper.

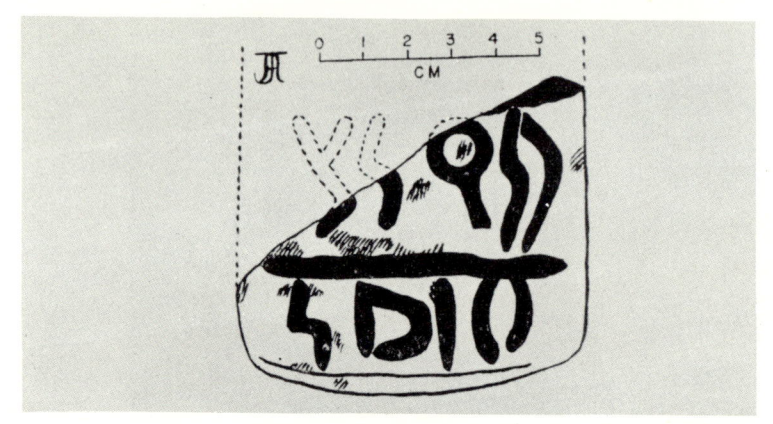

FIG. 3. Drawing of the inscription.

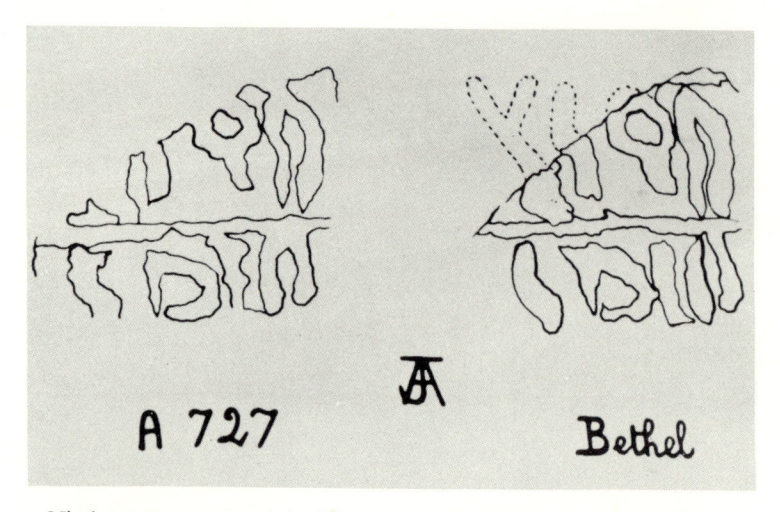

A 727

Bethel

Ninth century B.C. South Arabian stamp seal from Bethel. Bottom photo compares Bethel script with that from the Tübingen squeeze A 727.

PLATE 118

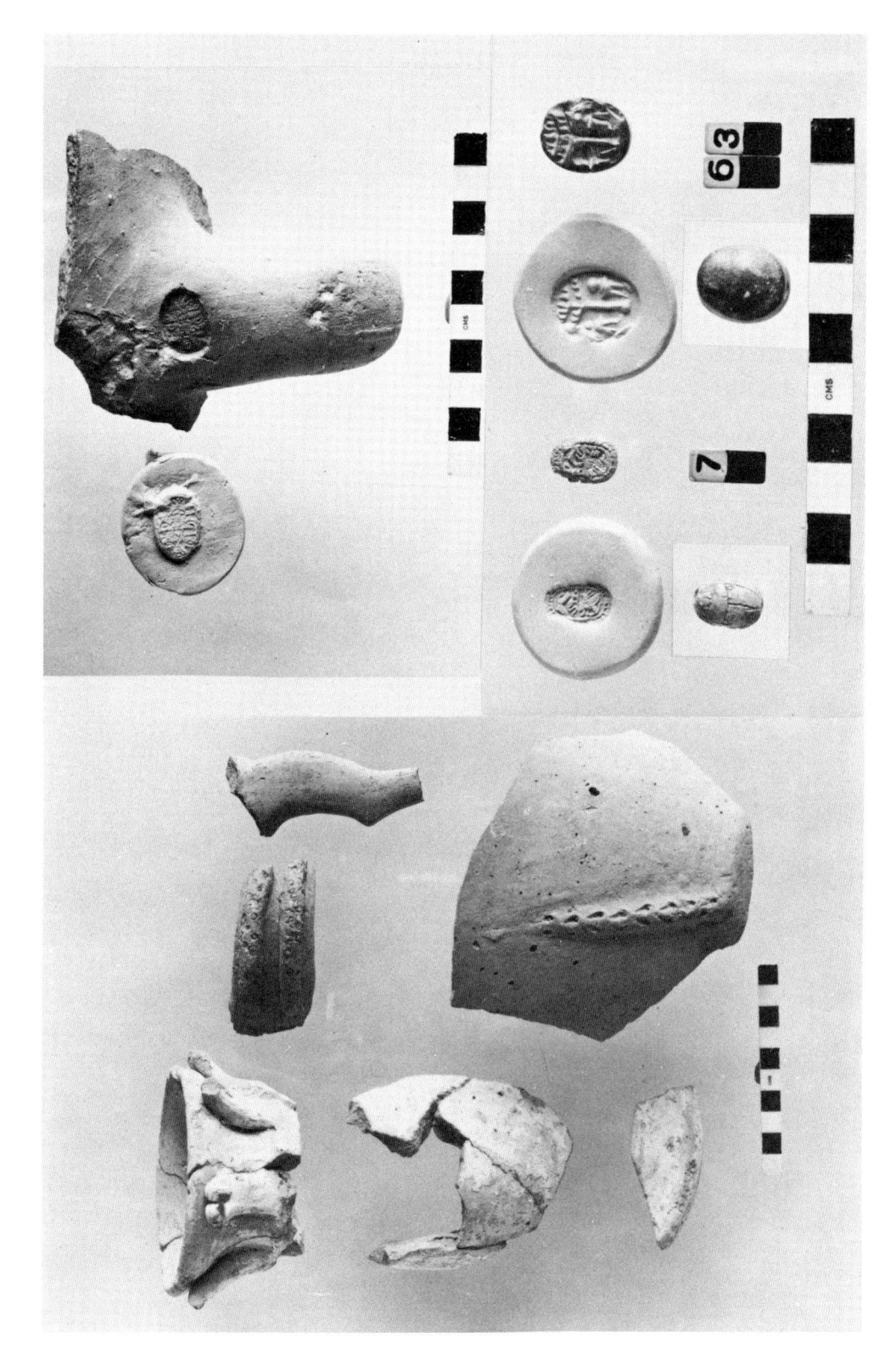

PLATE 119

a Ceramic pieces: Hathor pillar to left; handle with a serpent motif; serpent motif at bottom of store-jar and bull's leg to the right.
b Hyksos seal impression on jar handle.
c Scarabs 7 and 63 (Nos. 3007 and 3063). Plate 119 is from 1960 work.

BETHEL 1934-1960
SCALE 1:200

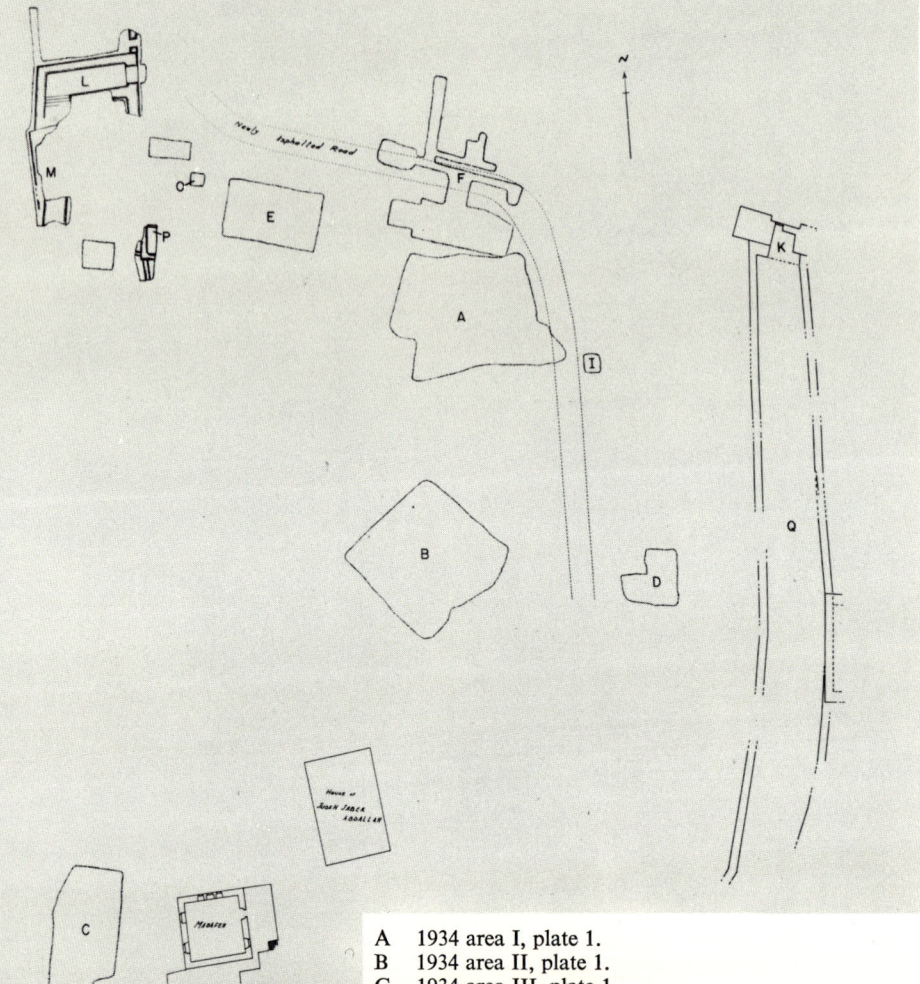

A   1934 area I, plate 1.
B   1934 area II, plate 1.
C   1934 area III, plate 1.
D   1934 area IV, plate 1.
E   1954 area of old 1934 campsite, plates 85 & 86.
    1954 mosque area, south of Beitîn, does not appear on this chart, plate 87.
F   1957 north wall of Bethel with house walls north and south of it, plates 91, 92, 93.
G   1957 Abu Tabor area with west wall of Bethel, plate 94.
H   1957 *Maḍáfeh* area, plate 94.
I   1957 test pit locating east wall of Bethel.
J   1957 south gate of Roman town does not appear on this plan, plate 95.
K   1957 Bethel's Byzantine gateway, plate 95.
L   1960 Bethel's northwest gate area, plate 101.
M   1960 west wall of Bethel where it joins northwest gate, plate 102.
N   1960 west wall and farmer's house, plate 102.
O   1960 Room A in east garden, plate 103.
P   1960 pit 5 in east garden, plate 103.
    1960 south wall of Bethel does not appear on this plan, plate 103.
Q   1960 main street of Byzantine Bethel.
    Areas not specified were test pits which yielded no valuable data.

PLATE 120

Plan of excavated areas 1934 through 1960.

FIG. 1

Conoid seal of agate, sixth to fifth century, B.C.

FIG. 2   Combing patterns on MB II pottery.